Shugo Chara!

1

PEACH-PIT

Translated by
June Kato

Adapted by
David Walsh

Lettered by
North Market Street Graphics

KODANSHA COMICS

Shugo Chara! volume 1 is a work of fiction. Names, characters, places, and incidents are the products of the author's imagination or are used fictitiously. Any resemblance to actual events, locales, or persons, living or dead, is entirely coincidental.

A Kodansha Comics Trade Paperback Original.

Published in the United States by Kodansha Comics, an imprint of Kodansha USA Publishing, LLC., New York.

Publication rights for this English edition arranged through Kodansha Ltd., Tokyo.

First published in Japan in 2006 by Kodansha Ltd., Tokyo.

ISBN 978-1-61262-313-9

Original cover design by Akiko Omo.

Printed in the United States of America.

www.kodanshacomics.com

9 8 7 6 5 4 3 2

Translator: June Kato
Adapter: David Walsh
Lettering: North Market Street Graphics

Contents

Honorifics Explained

Throughout the Kodansha Comics books, you will find Japanese honorifics left intact in the translations. For those not familiar with how the Japanese use honorifics and, more important, how they differ from American honorifics, we present this brief overview.

Politeness has always been a critical facet of Japanese culture. Ever since the feudal era, when Japan was a highly stratified society, use of honorifics—which can be defined as polite speech that indicates relationship or status—has played an essential role in the Japanese language. When addressing someone in Japanese, an honorific usually takes the form of a suffix attached to one's name (example: "Asuna-san"), is used as a title at the end of one's name, or appears in place of the name itself (example: "Negi-sensei," or simply "Sensei!").

Honorifics can be expressions of respect or endearment. In the context of manga and anime, honorifics give insight into the nature of the relationship between characters. Many English translations leave out these important honorifics and therefore distort the feel of the original Japanese. Because Japanese honorifics contain nuances that English honorifics lack, it is our policy at Kodansha Comics not to translate them. Here, instead, is a guide to some of the honorifics you may encounter in Kodansha Comics books.

-san: This is the most common honorific and is equivalent to
        Mr., Miss, Ms., Mrs. It is the all-purpose honorific
        and can be used in any situation where politeness is
        required.

-sama: This is one level higher than "-san" and is used to confer
        great respect.

-dono: This comes from the word "tono," which means "lord."
        It is an even higher level than "-sama" and confers
        utmost respect.

-kun: This suffix is used at the end of boys' names to express
        familiarity or endearment. It is also sometimes used
        by men among friends, or when addressing someone
        younger or of a lower station.

-chan: This is used to express endearment, mostly toward girls. It is also used for little boys, pets, and even among lovers. It gives a sense of childish cuteness.

Bozu: This is an informal way to refer to a boy, similar to the English terms "kid" and "squirt."

Sempai/Senpai: This title suggests that the addressee is one's senior in a group or organization. It is most often used in a school setting, where underclassmen refer to their upperclassmen as "sempai." It can also be used in the workplace, such as when a newer employee addresses an employee who has seniority in the company.

Kohai: This is the opposite of "sempai" and is used toward underclassmen in school or newcomers in the workplace. It connotes that the addressee is of a lower station.

Sensei: Literally meaning "one who has come before," this title is used for teachers, doctors, or masters of any profession or art.

-[blank]: This is usually forgotten in these lists, but it is perhaps the most significant difference between Japanese and English. The lack of honorific means that the speaker has permission to address the person in a very intimate way. Usually, only family, spouses, or very close friends have this kind of permission. Known as *yobisute*, it can be gratifying when someone who has earned the intimacy starts to call one by one's name without an honorific. But when that intimacy hasn't been earned, it can be very insulting.

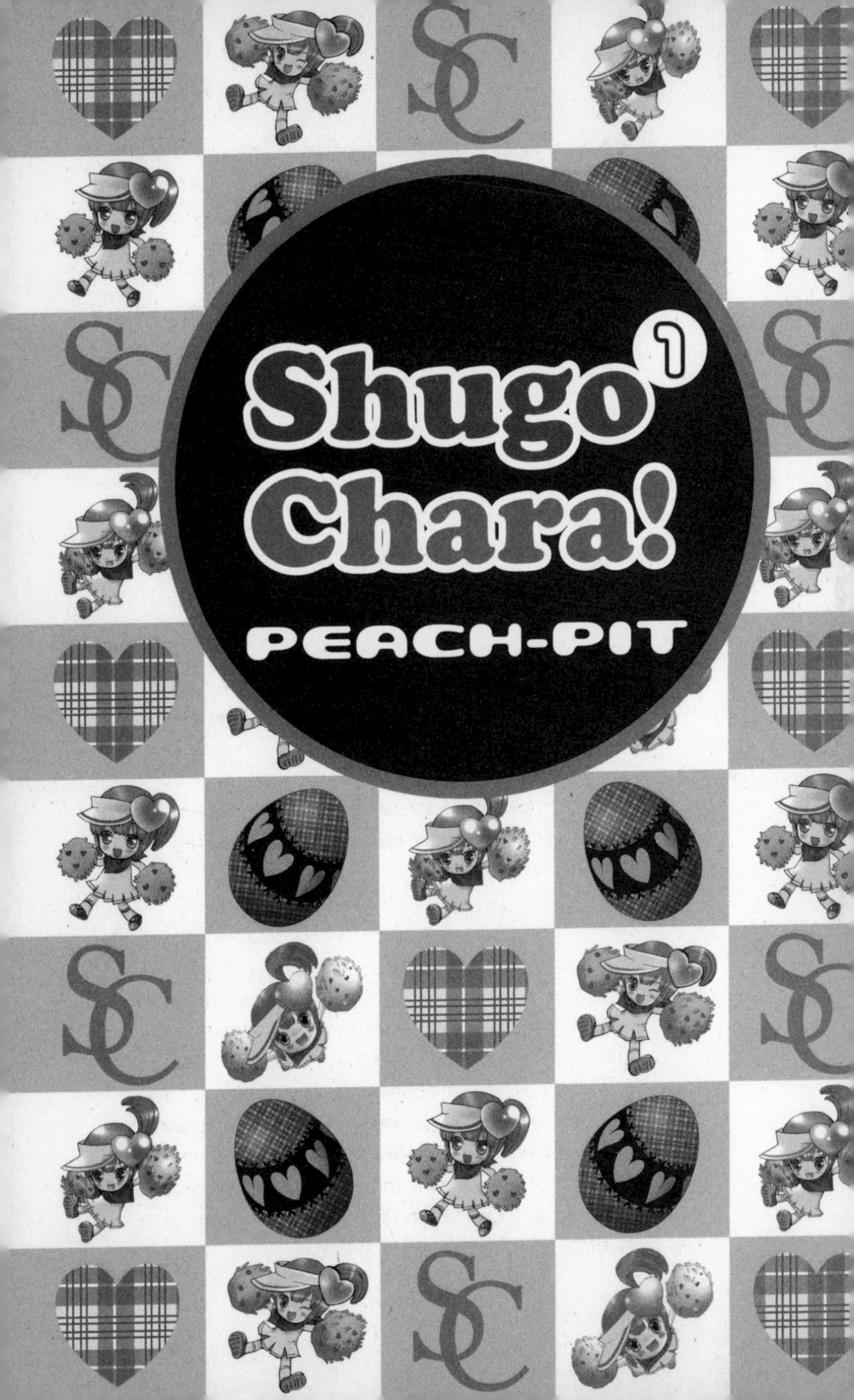
Shugo Chara! 1
PEACH-PIT

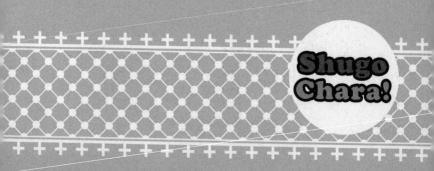

Shugo
Chara!

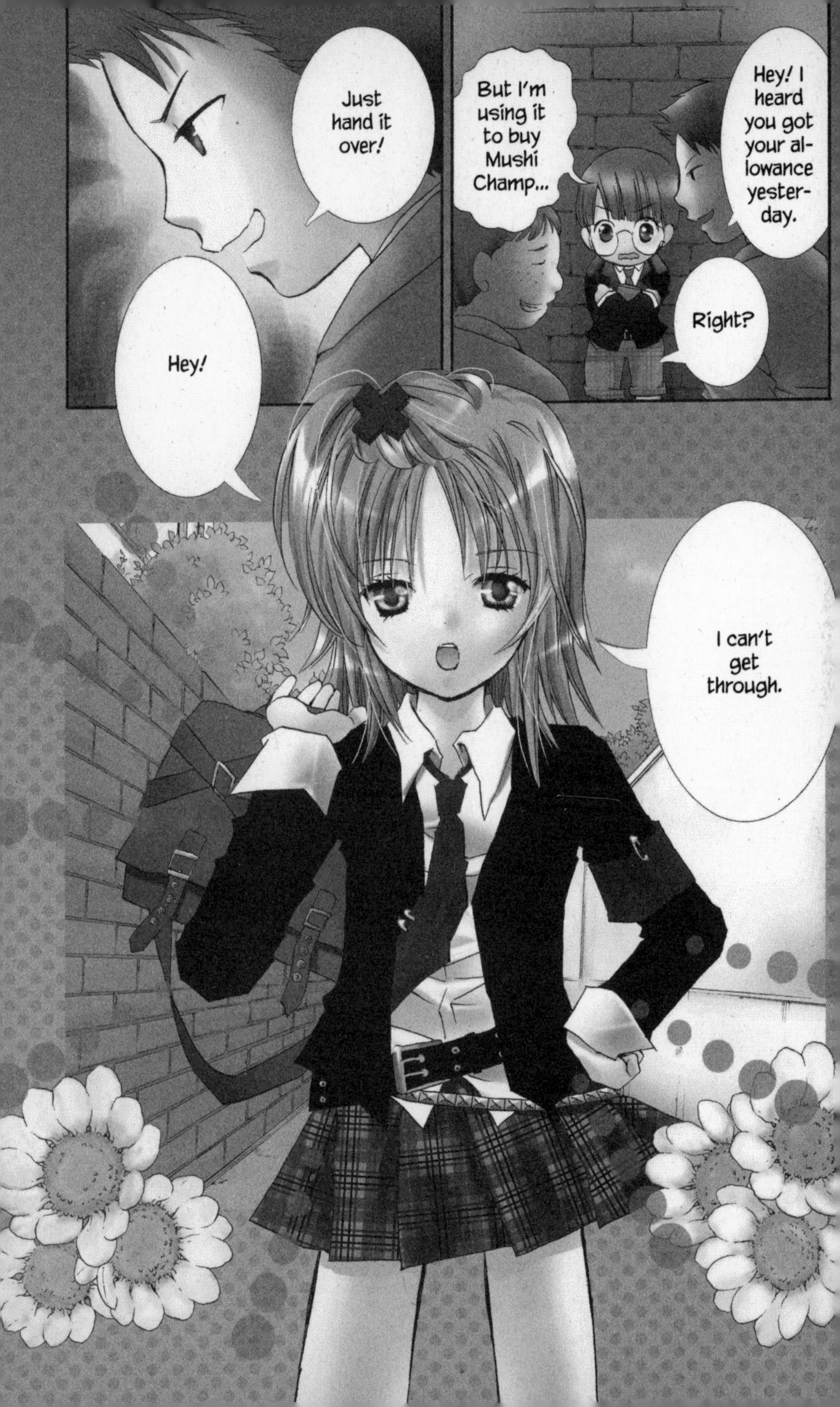
Hey! I heard you got your allowance yesterday.
Right?
But I'm using it to buy Mushi Champ...
Just hand it over!
Hey!
I can't get through.

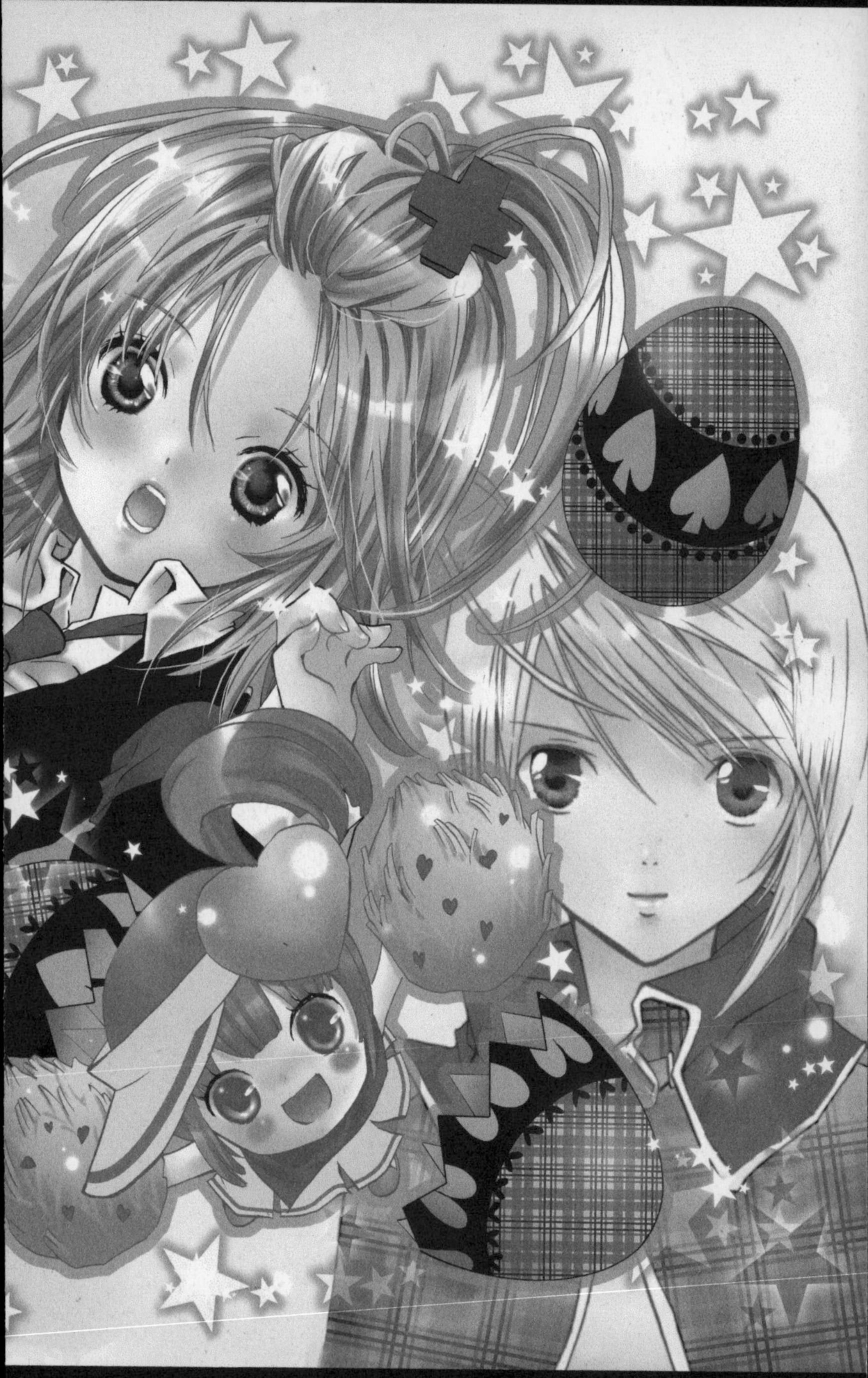

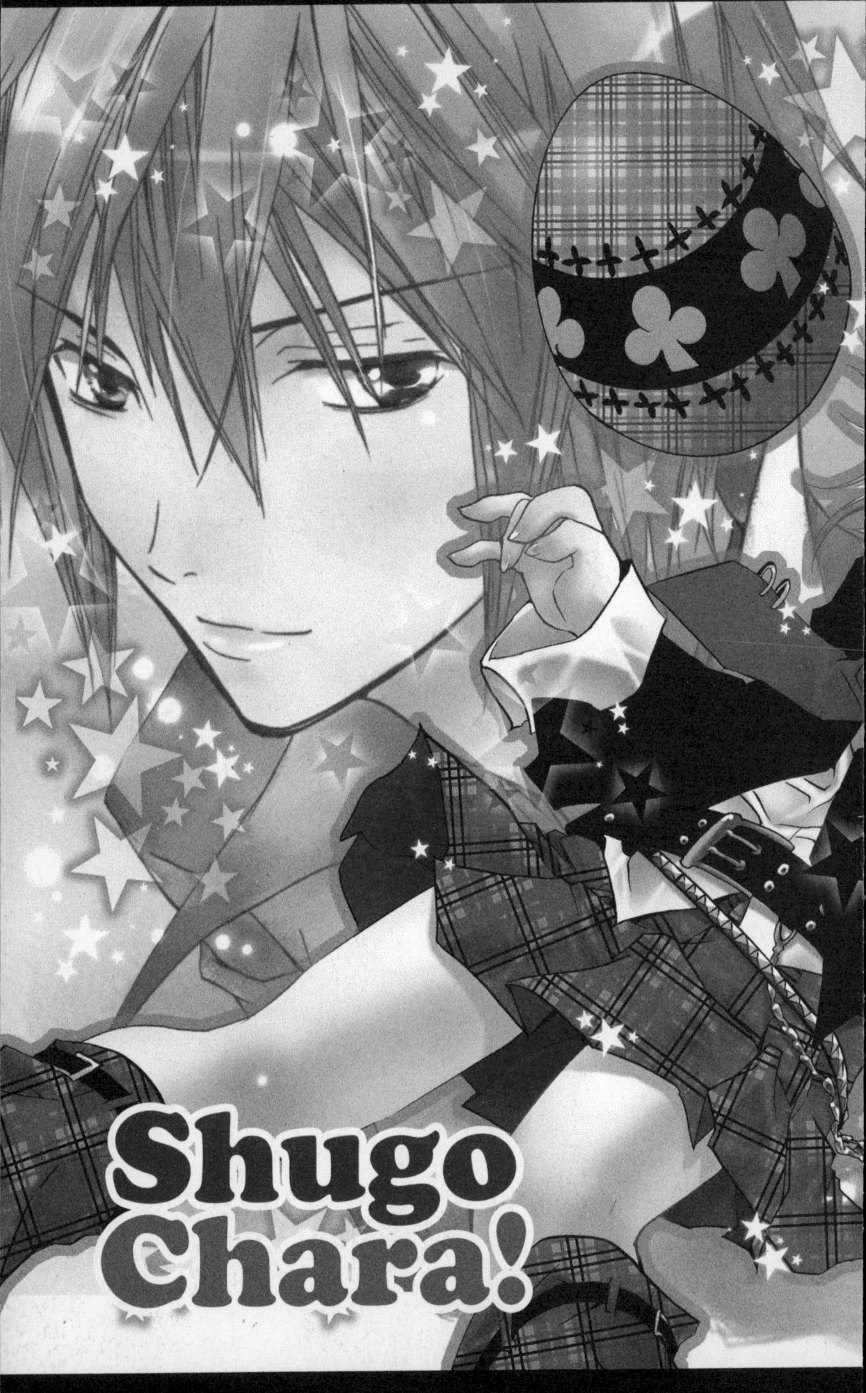
Shugo
Chara!

Shugo Chara!

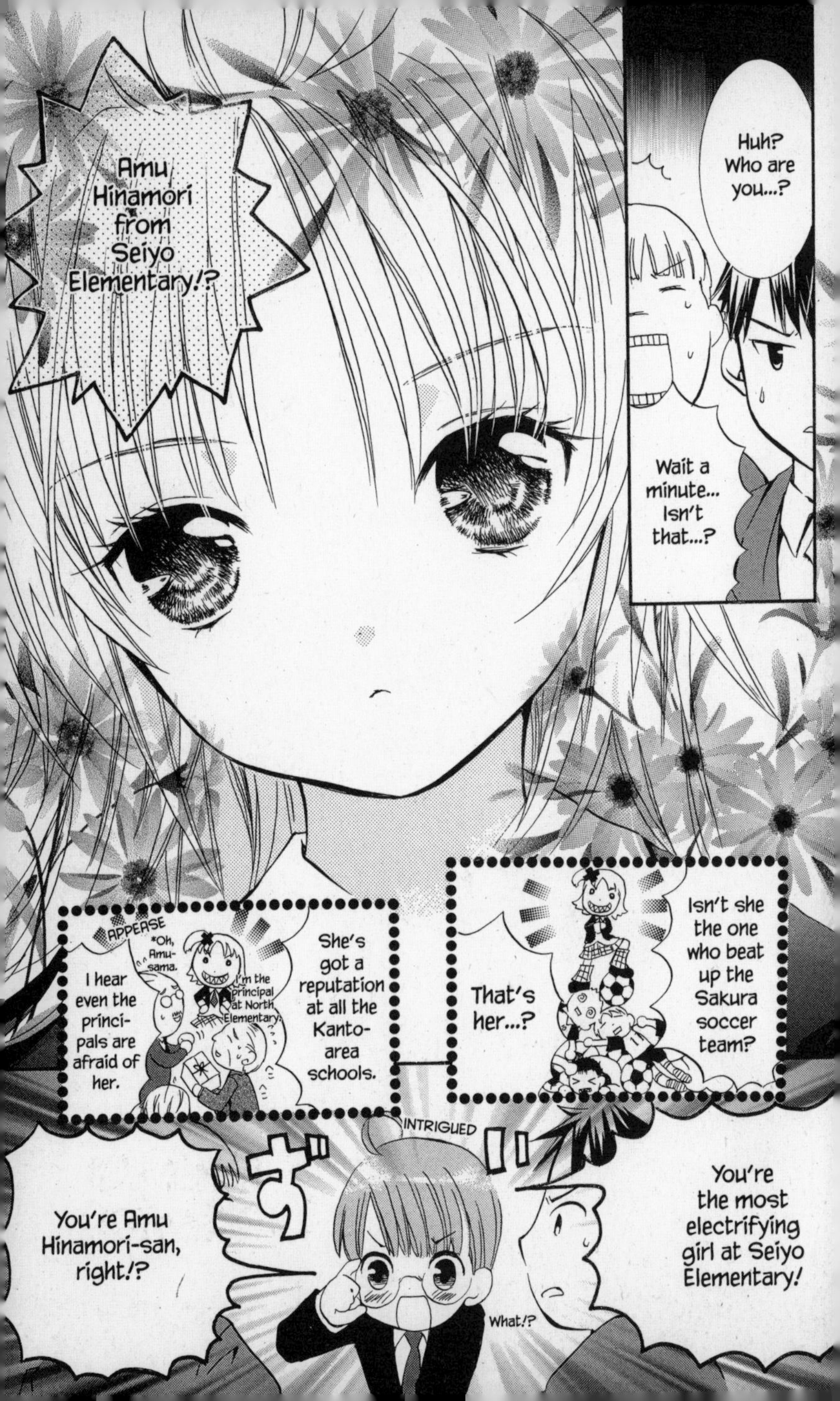

Huh? Who are you...?
Wait a minute... Isn't that...?
Amu Hinamori from Seiyo Elementary!?
Isn't she the one who beat up the Sakura soccer team?
That's her...?
She's got a reputation at all the Kanto-area schools.
APPEASE
*Oh, Amu-sama.
I'm the principal at North Elementary.
I hear even the principals are afraid of her.
INTRIGUED
You're the most electrifying girl at Seiyo Elementary!
What!?
You're Amu Hinamori-san, right!?

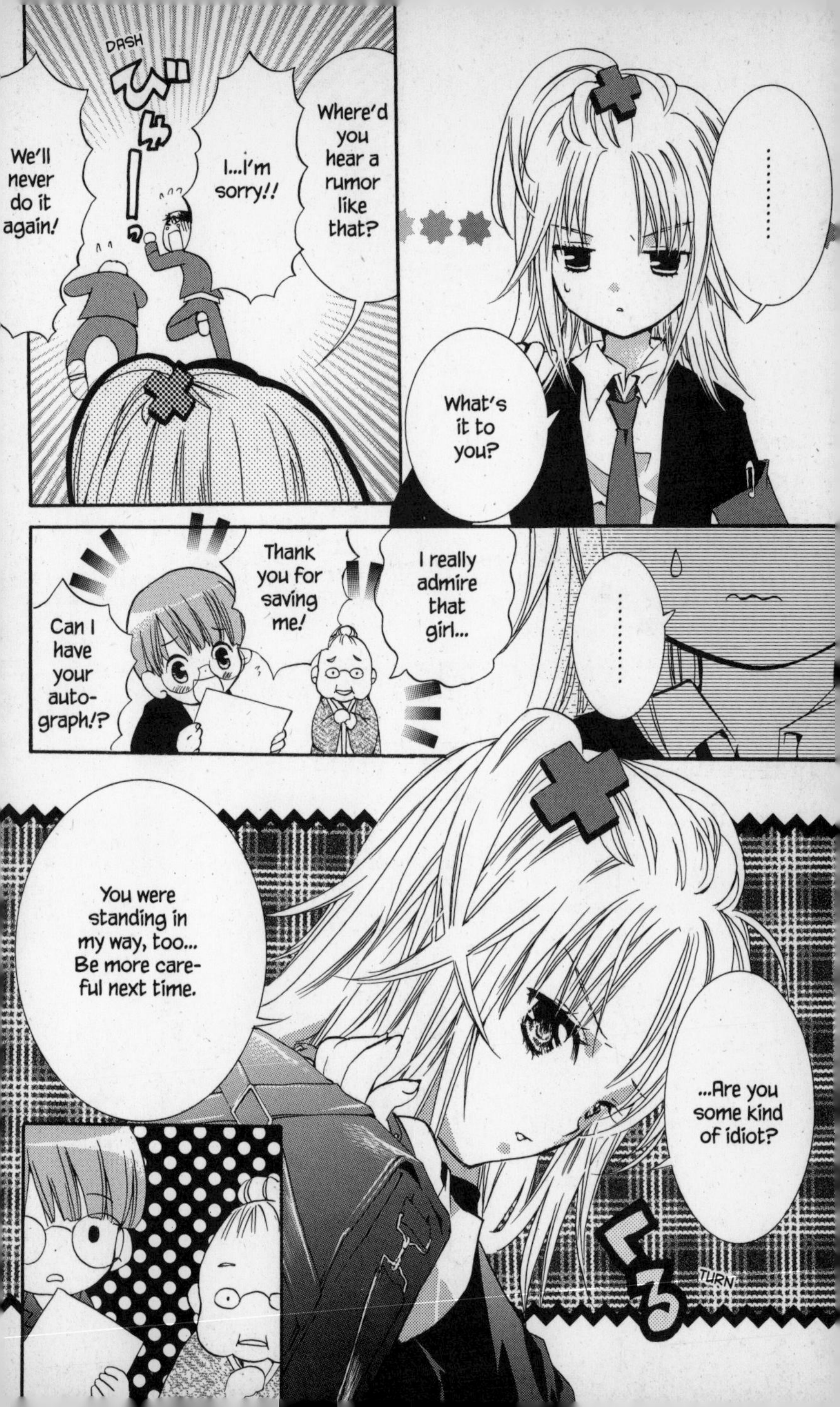
......
What's it to you?
Where'd you hear a rumor like that?
DASH
I...I'm sorry!!
We'll never do it again!
......
I really admire that girl...
Thank you for saving me!
Can I have your autograph!?
...Are you some kind of idiot?
TURN
You were standing in my way, too... Be more careful next time.

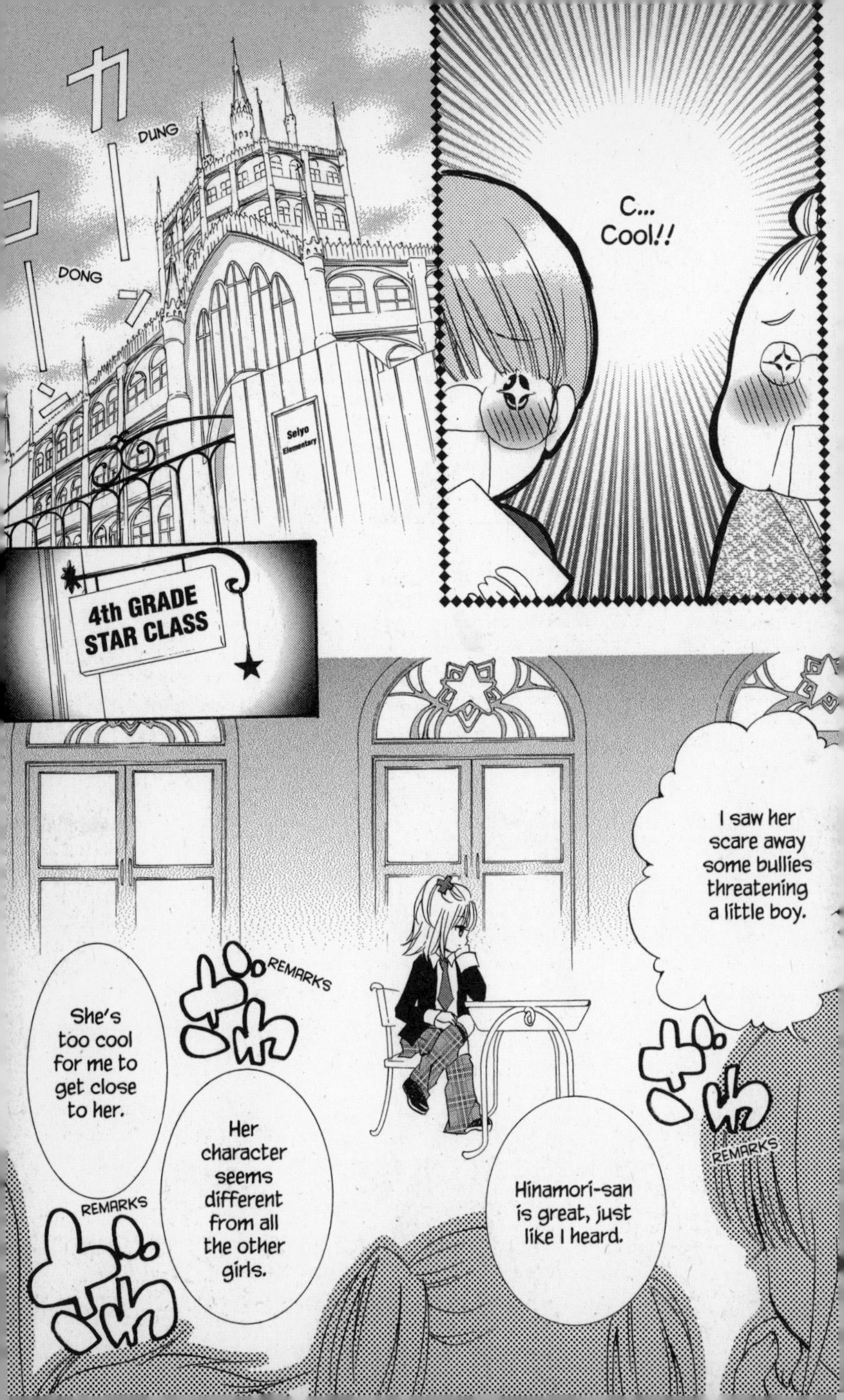
C... Cool!!
DUNG
DONG
Seiyo Elementary
4th GRADE STAR CLASS
I saw her scare away some bullies threatening a little boy.
REMARKS
Hinamori-san is great, just like I heard.
Her character seems different from all the other girls.
She's too cool for me to get close to her.
REMARKS
REMARKS

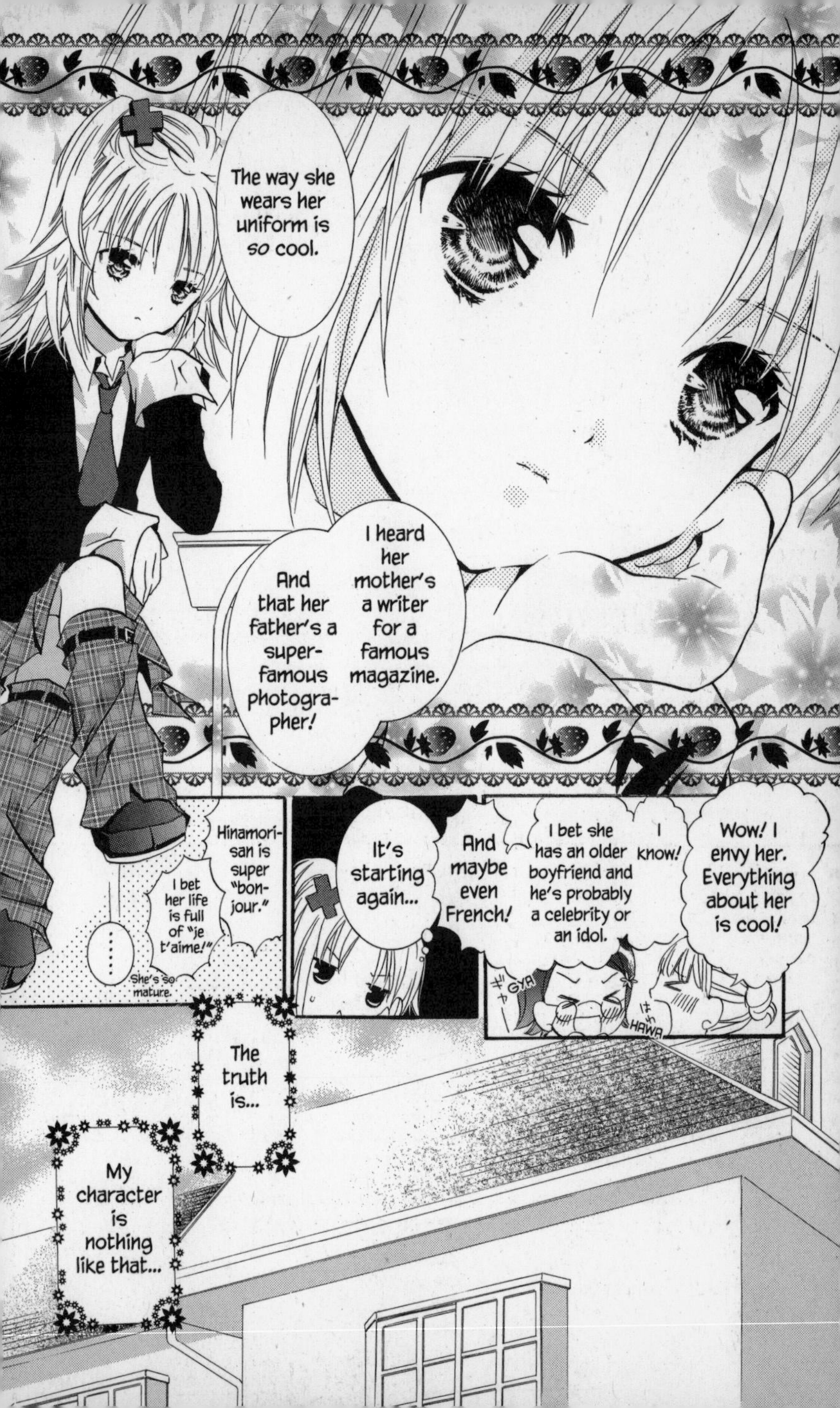

The way she wears her uniform is so cool.
I heard her mother's a writer for a famous magazine.
And that her father's a super-famous photographer!
Wow! I envy her. Everything about her is cool!
I know!
I bet she has an older boyfriend and he's probably a celebrity or an idol.
And maybe even French!
ギャー GYA
はわ HAWA
It's starting again...
Hinamori-san is super "bon-jour."
I bet her life is full of "je t'aime!"
She's so mature.
......
The truth is...
My character is nothing like that...

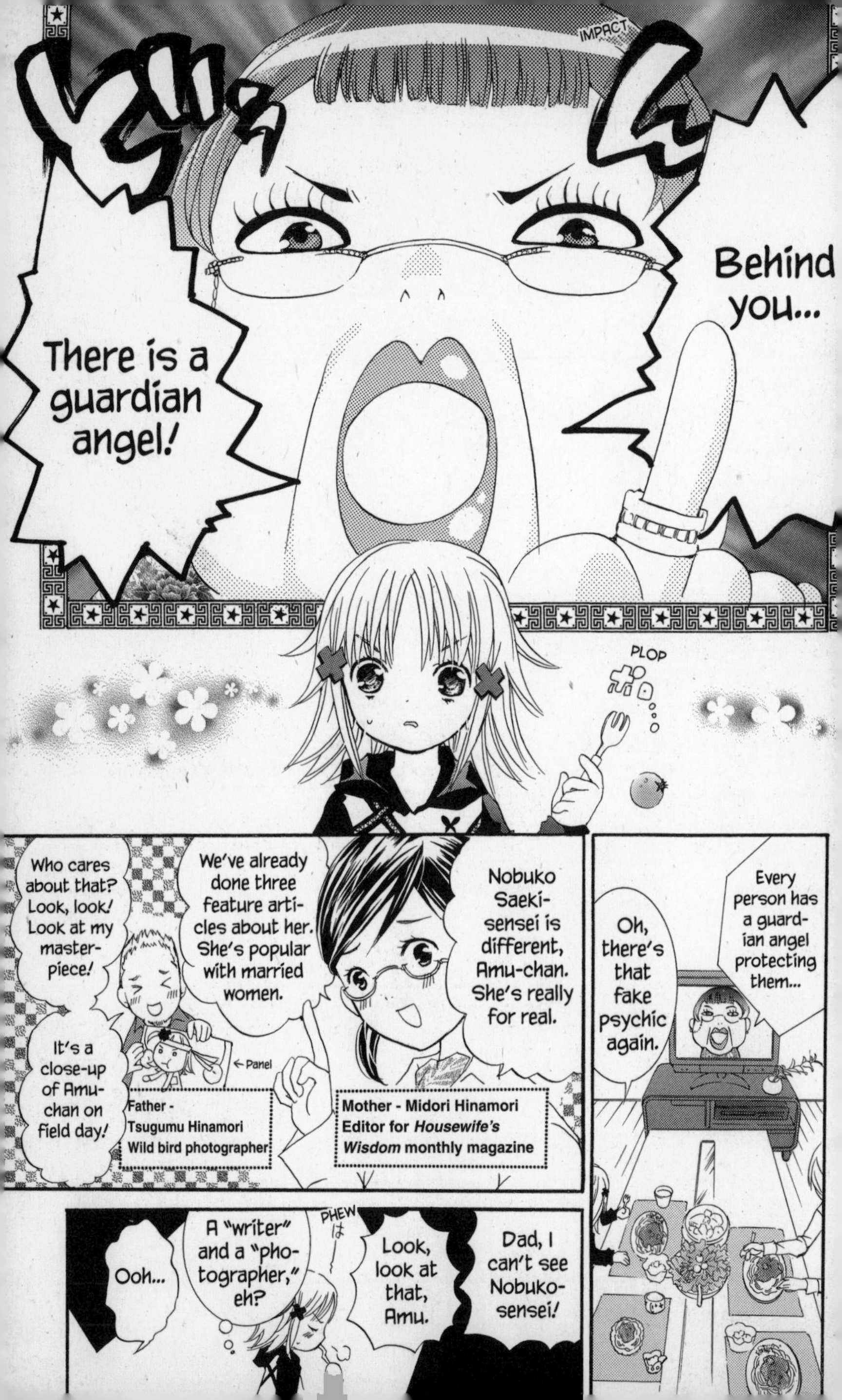
IMPACT
Behind you...
There is a guardian angel!
PLOP
Every person has a guardian angel protecting them...
Oh, there's that fake psychic again.
Nobuko Saeki-sensei is different, Amu-chan. She's really for real.
We've already done three feature articles about her. She's popular with married women.
Mother - Midori Hinamori Editor for *Housewife's Wisdom* monthly magazine
Who cares about that? Look, look! Look at my masterpiece!
It's a close-up of Amu-chan on field day!
← Panel
Father - Tsugumu Hinamori Wild bird photographer
Dad, I can't see Nobuko-sensei!
Look, look at that, Amu.
PHEW
A "writer" and a "photographer," eh?
Ooh...

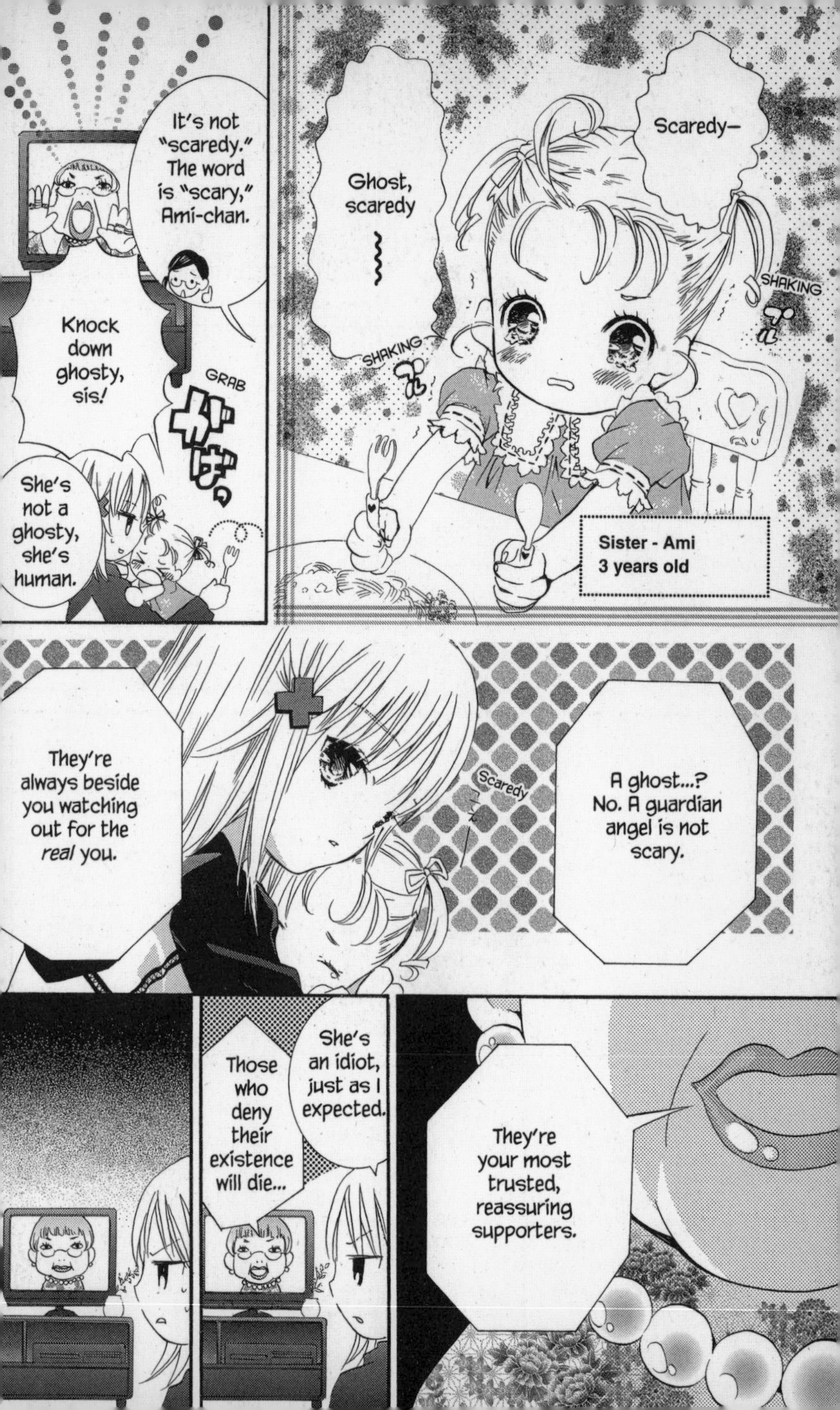

Scaredy—
SHAKING
Ghost, scaredy
~
SHAKING
Sister - Ami
3 years old
It's not "scaredy." The word is "scary," Ami-chan.
Knock down ghosty, sis!
GRAB
She's not a ghosty, she's human.
A ghost...? No. A guardian angel is not scary.
Scaredy
They're always beside you watching out for the *real* you.
They're your most trusted, reassuring supporters.
She's an idiot, just as I expected.
Those who deny their existence will die...

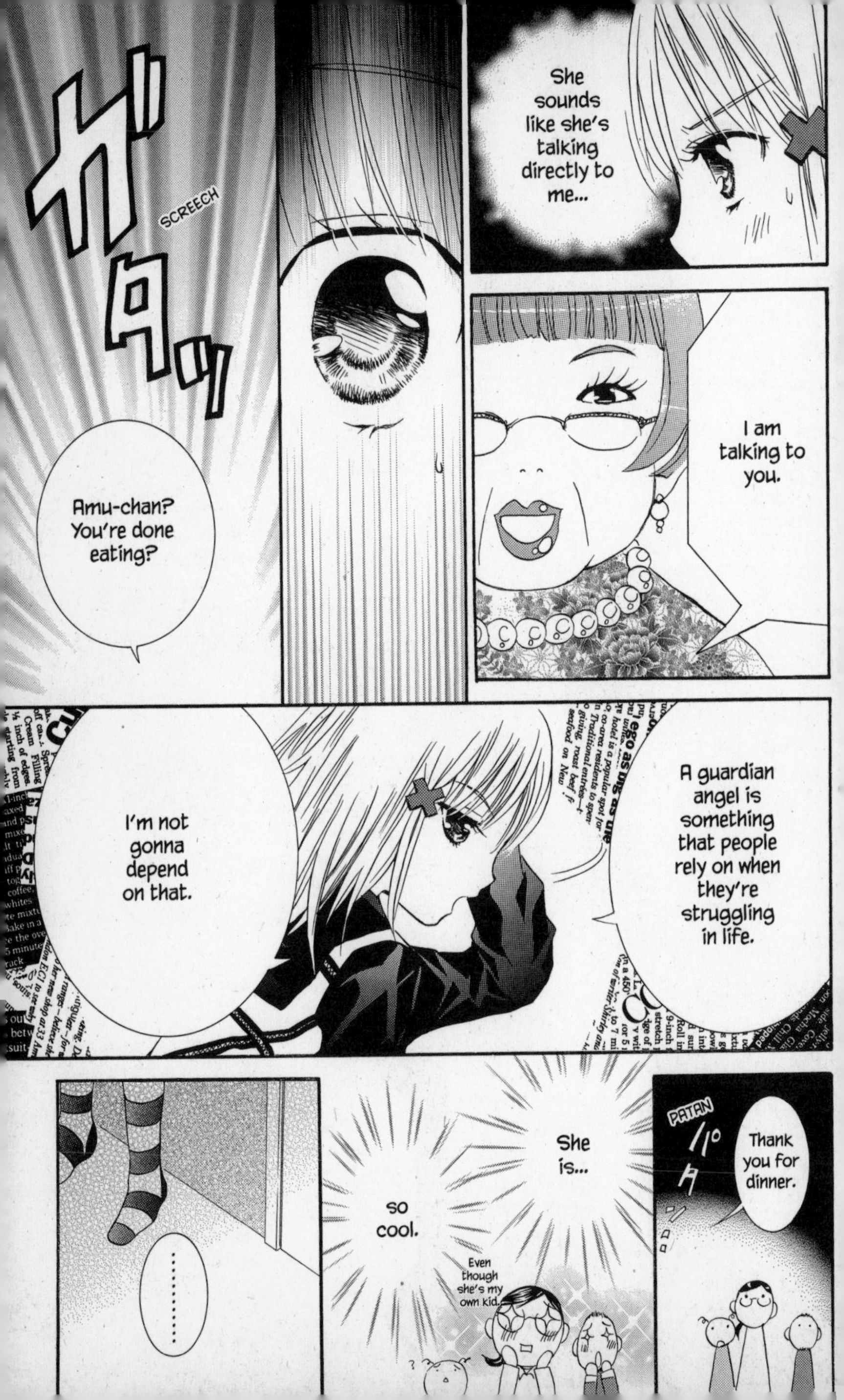
She sounds like she's talking directly to me...
I am talking to you.
ガタッ
SCREECH
Amu-chan? You're done eating?
A guardian angel is something that people rely on when they're struggling in life.
I'm not gonna depend on that.
PATAN
パタン
Thank you for dinner.
She is...
so cool.
Even though she's my own kid.
......

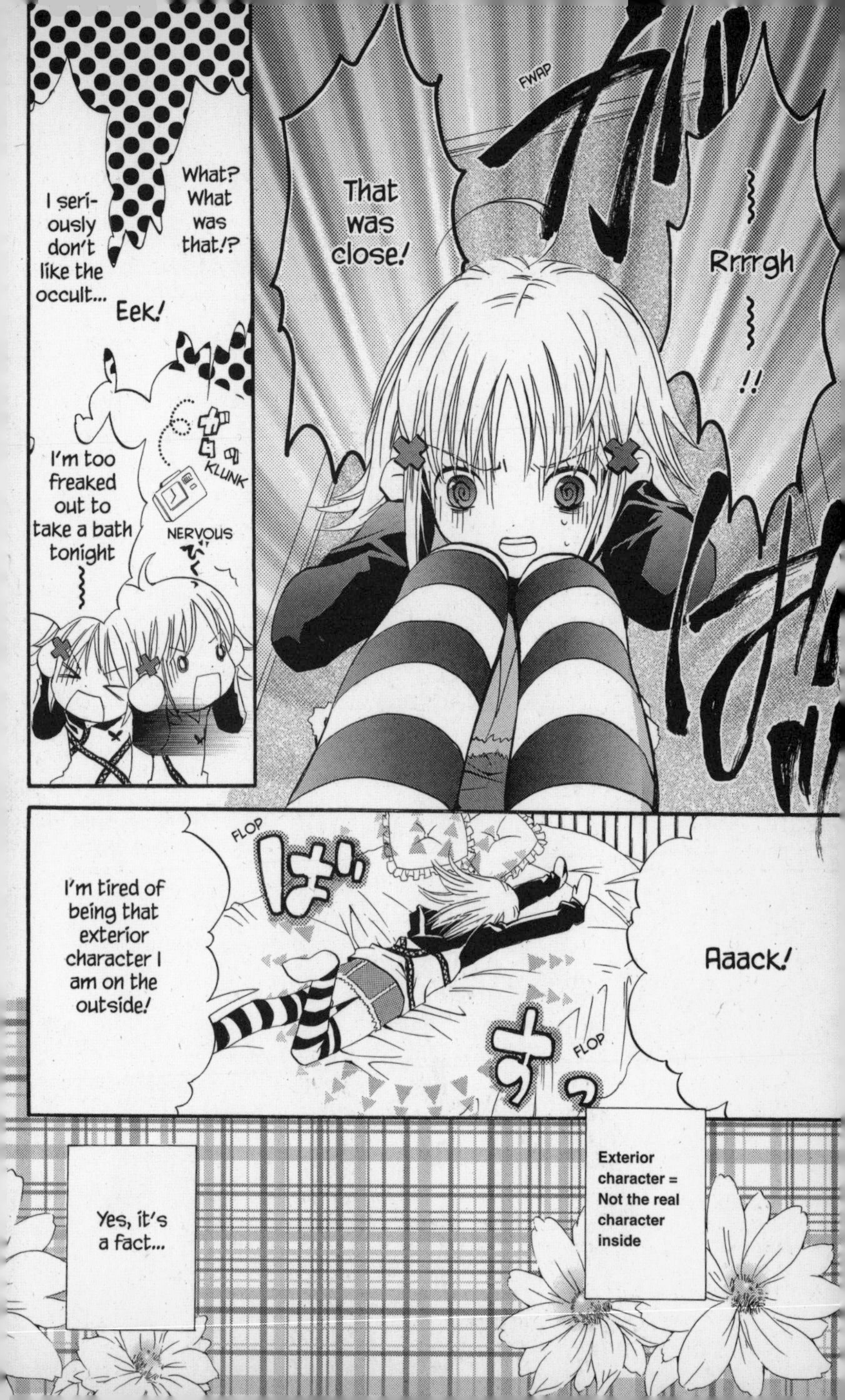
FWAP
That was close!
Rrrrgh ~~ !!
What? What was that!?
I seri-ously don't like the occult...
Eek!
KLUNK
NERVOUS
I'm too freaked out to take a bath tonight ~
Aaack!
FLOP
FLOP
I'm tired of being that exterior character I am on the outside!
Exterior character = Not the real character inside
Yes, it's a fact...

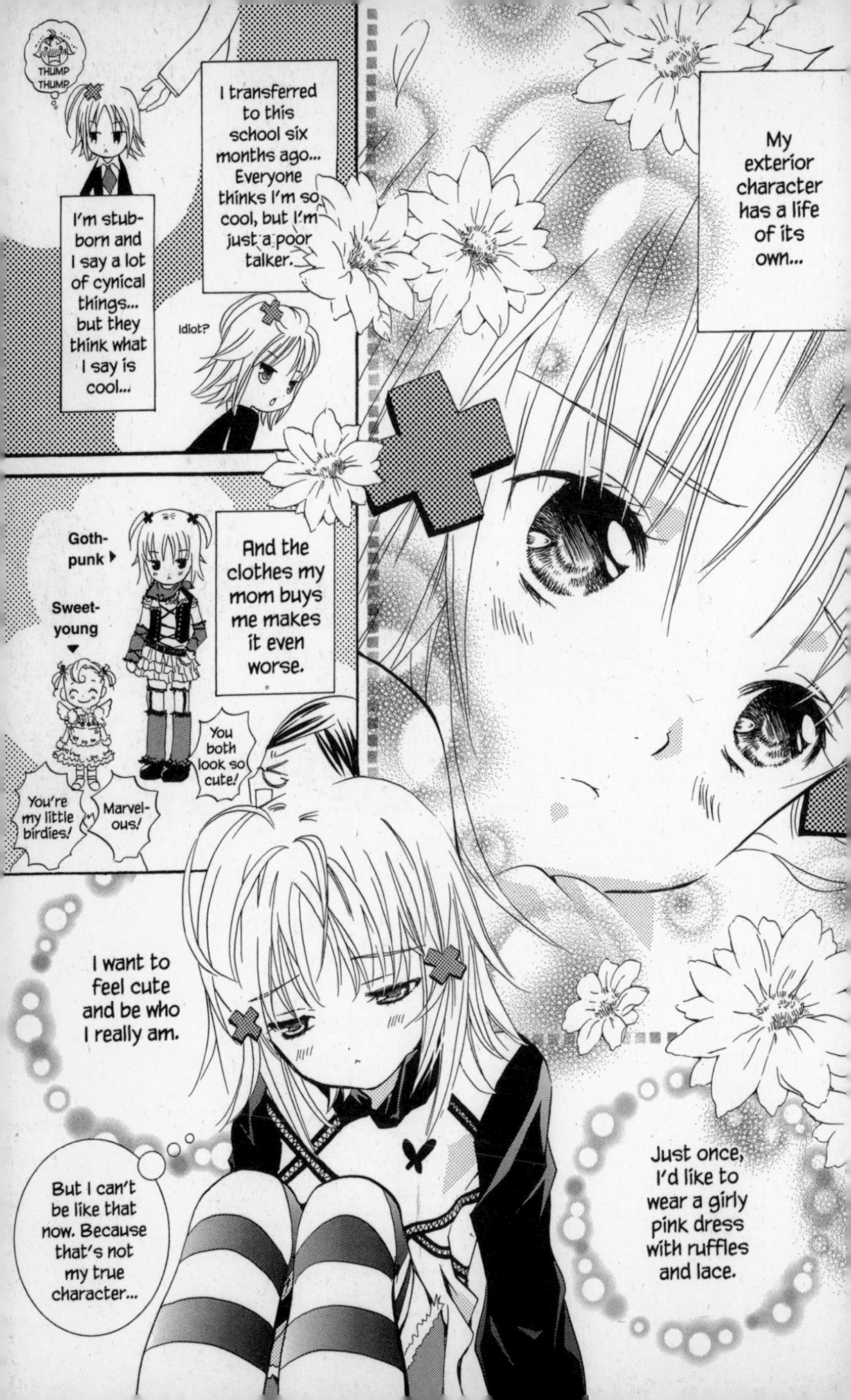
My exterior character has a life of its own...
I transferred to this school six months ago... Everyone thinks I'm so cool, but I'm just a poor talker.
I'm stubborn and I say a lot of cynical things... but they think what I say is cool...
Idiot?
THUMP THUMP
And the clothes my mom buys me makes it even worse.
Goth-punk
Sweet-young
You both look so cute!
Marvelous!
You're my little birdies!
Just once, I'd like to wear a girly pink dress with ruffles and lace.
I want to feel cute and be who I really am.
But I can't be like that now. Because that's not my true character...

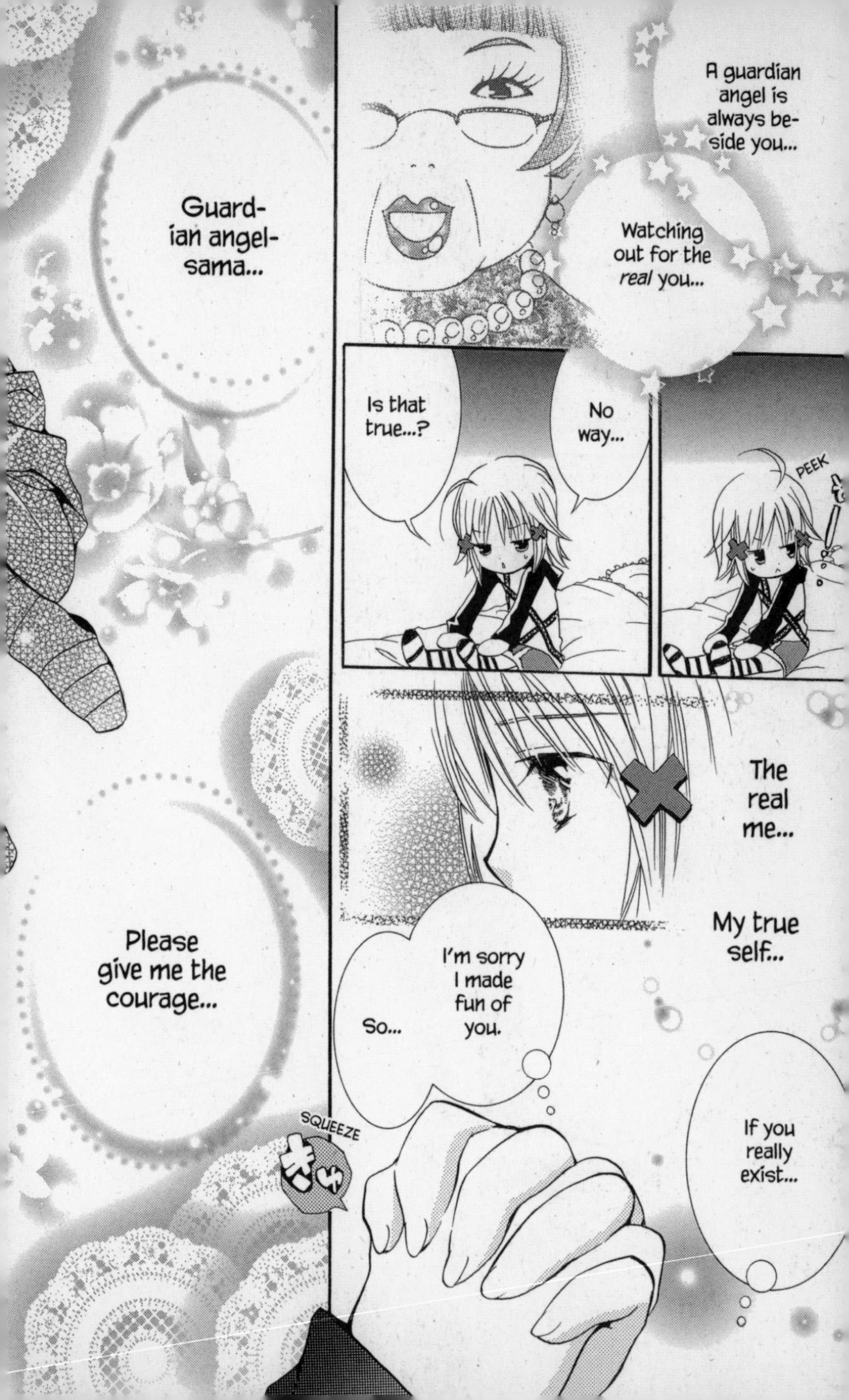
A guardian angel is always beside you...
Watching out for the *real* you...
PEEK
No way...
Is that true...?
The real me...
My true self...
If you really exist...
So... I'm sorry I made fun of you.
SQUEEZE
Guardian angel-sama...
Please give me the courage...

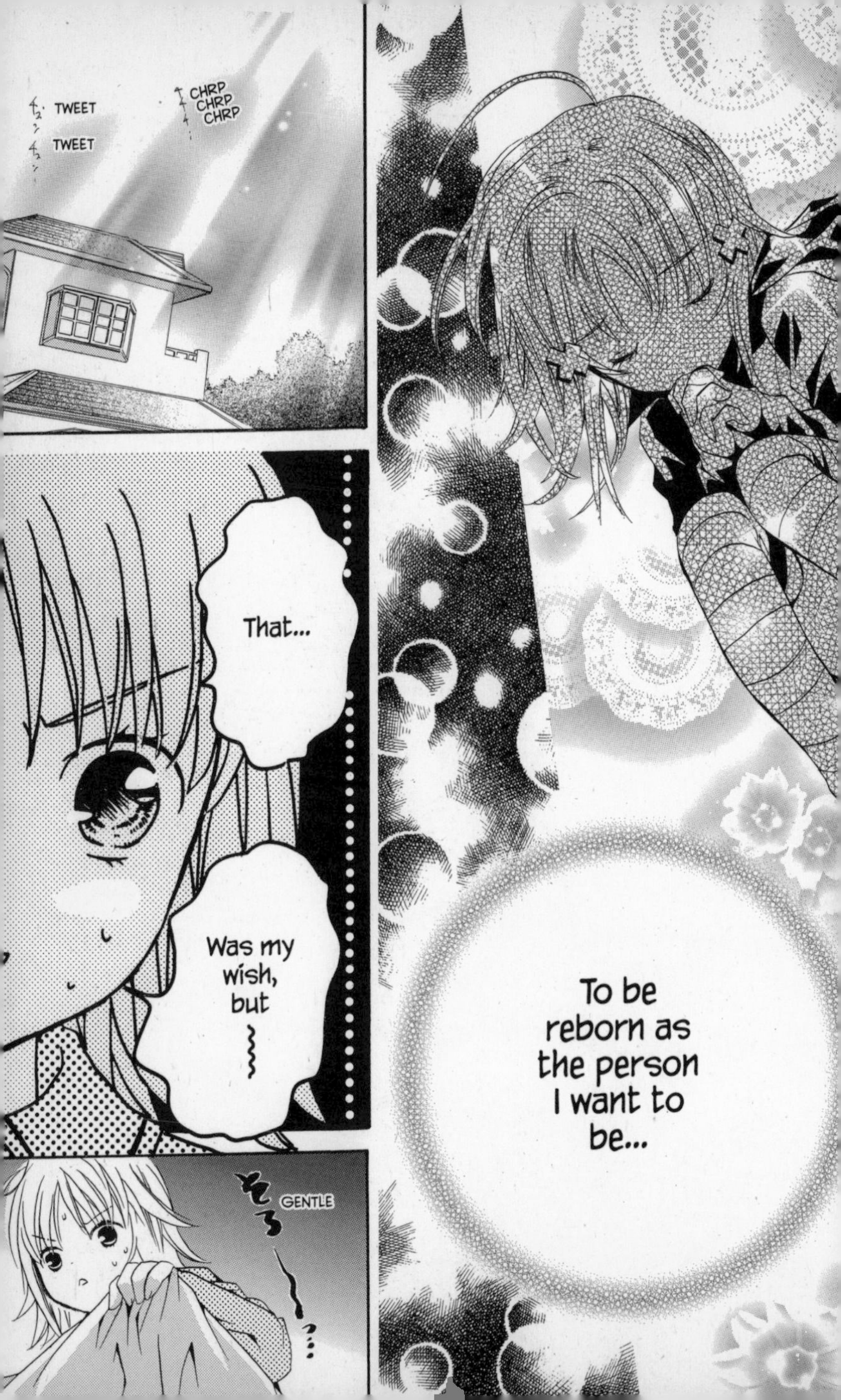

To be reborn as the person I want to be...
CHRP CHRP CHRP
TWEET
TWEET
That...
Was my wish, but
GENTLE

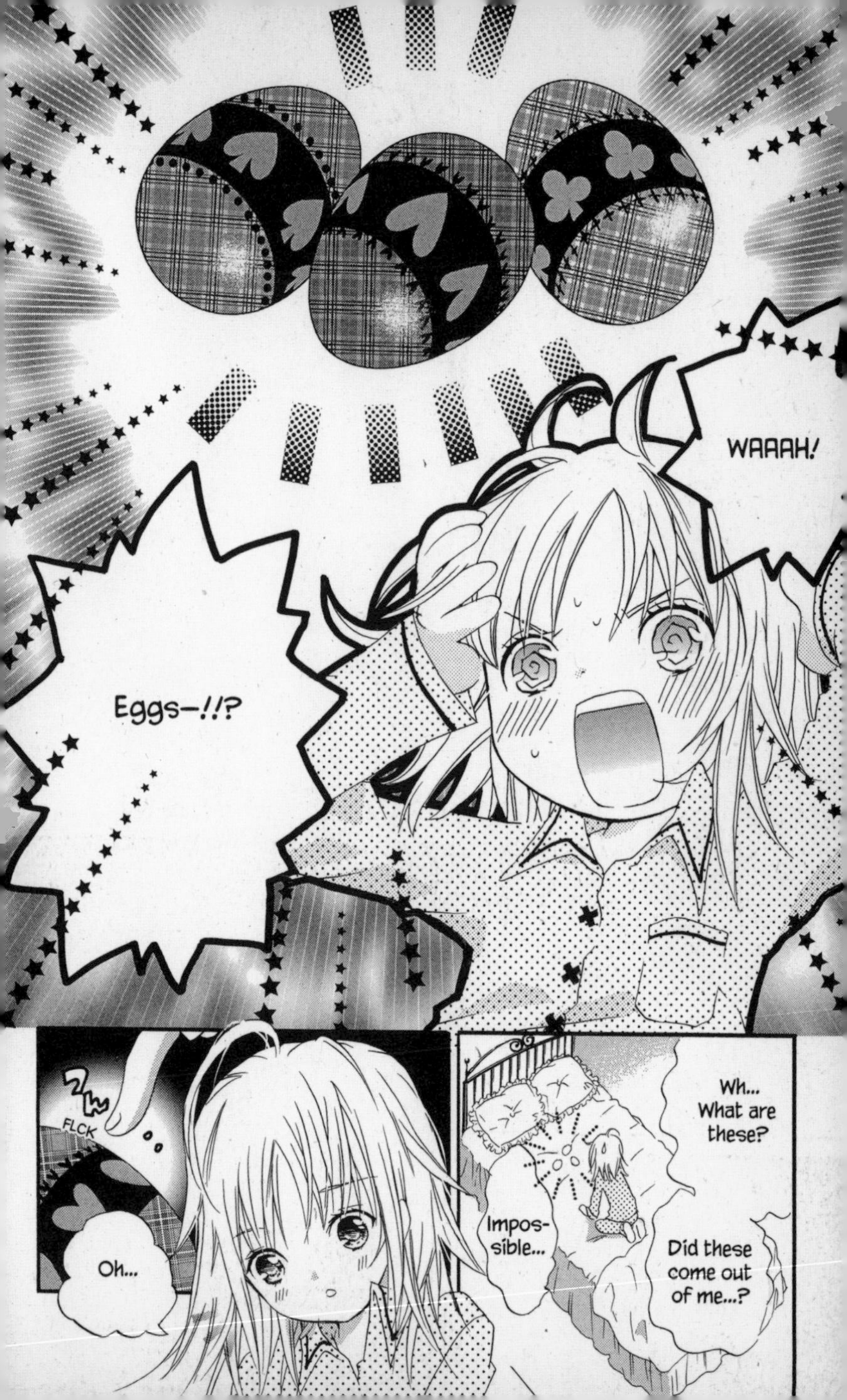
WAAAH!
Eggs—!!?
Wh... What are these?
Impos-sible...
Did these come out of me...?
FLCK
Oh...

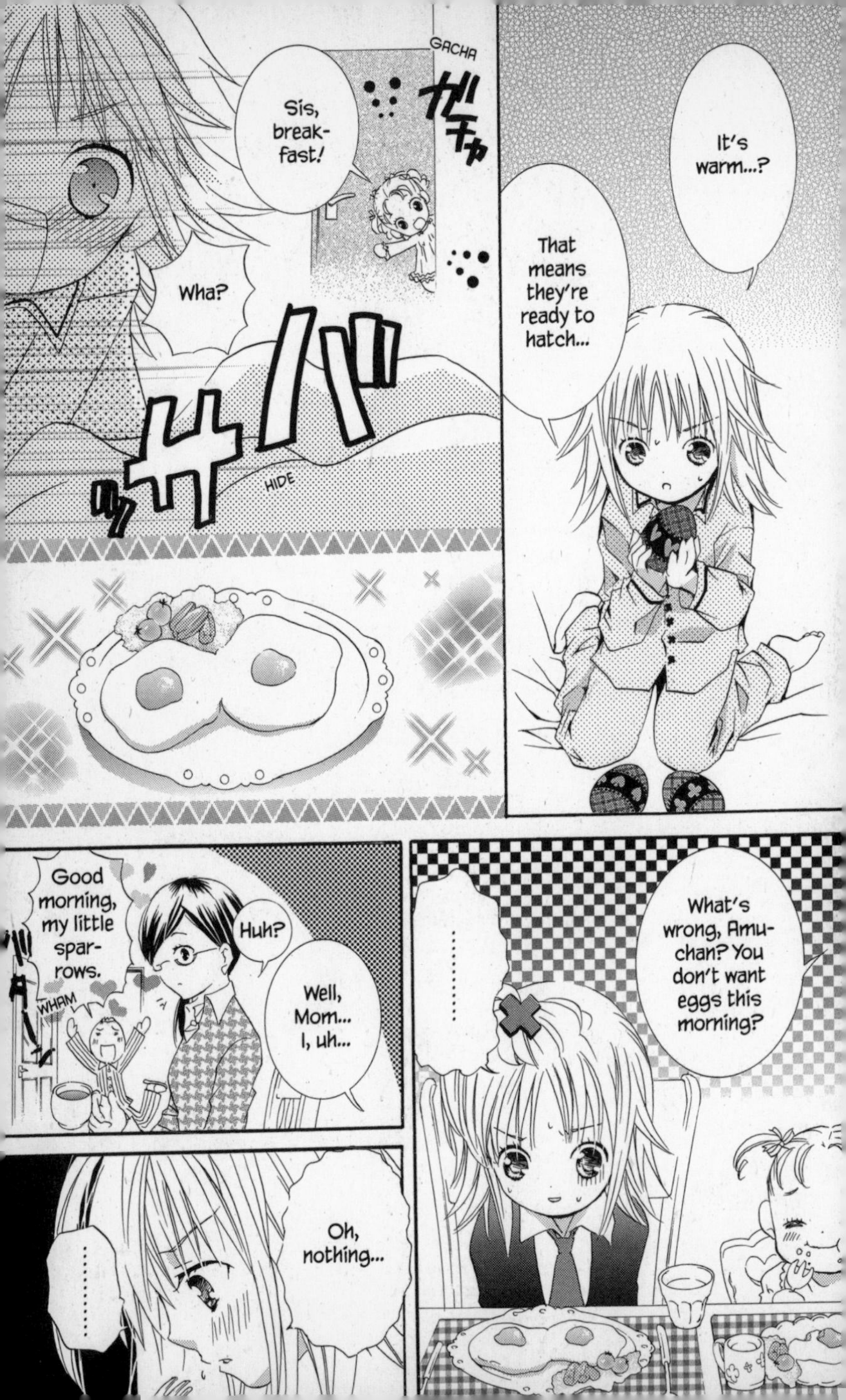

It's warm...?
That means they're ready to hatch...
GACHA
Sis, break-fast!
Wha?
HIDE
What's wrong, Amu-chan? You don't want eggs this morning?
......
Huh?
Well, Mom... I, uh...
Good morning, my little spar-rows.
WHAM
Oh, nothing...
......

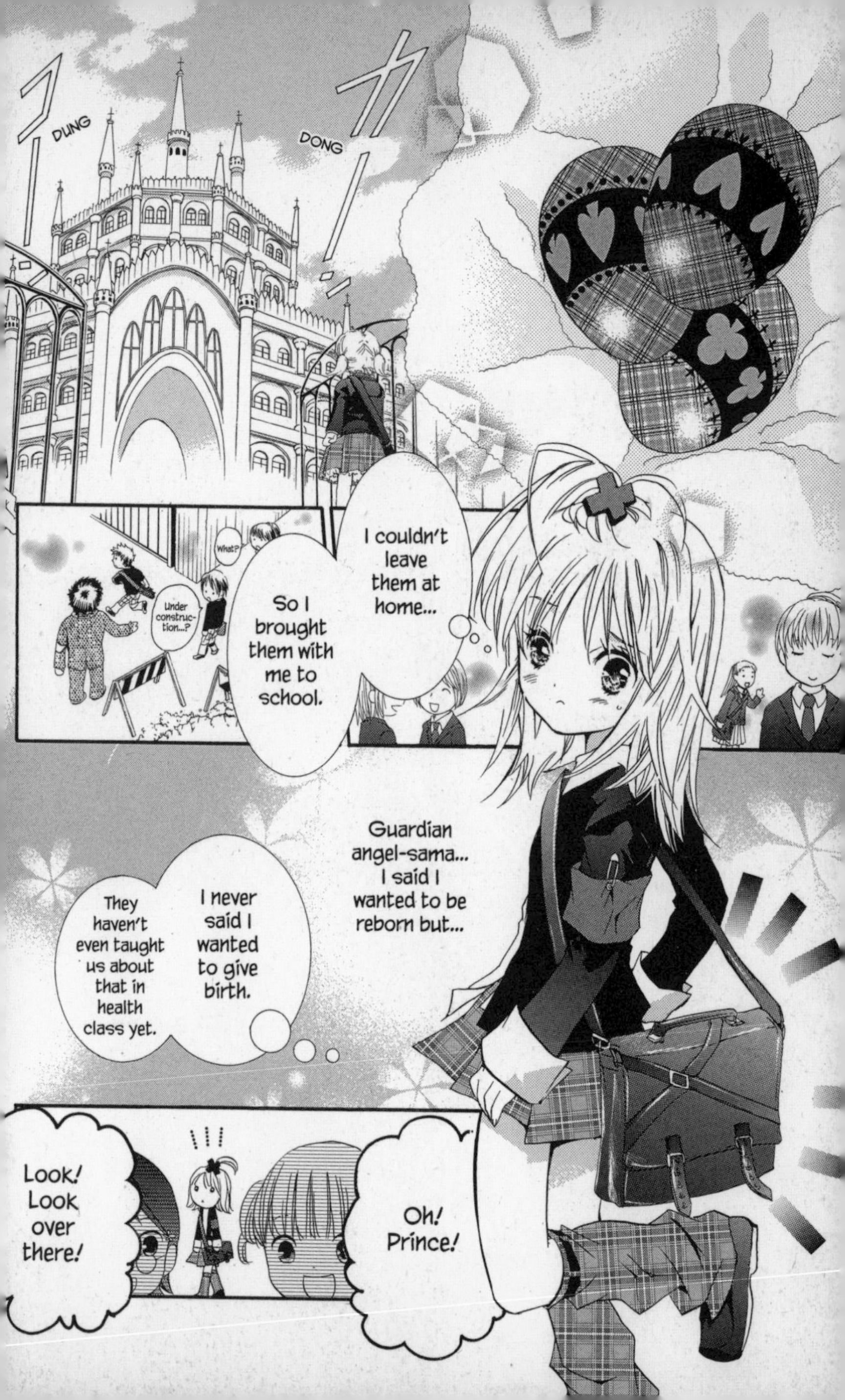

DONG
DUNG
I couldn't leave them at home...
So I brought them with me to school.
What?
Under construction...?
Guardian angel-sama... I said I wanted to be reborn but...
I never said I wanted to give birth.
They haven't even taught us about that in health class yet.
Oh! Prince!
!!!
Look! Look over there!

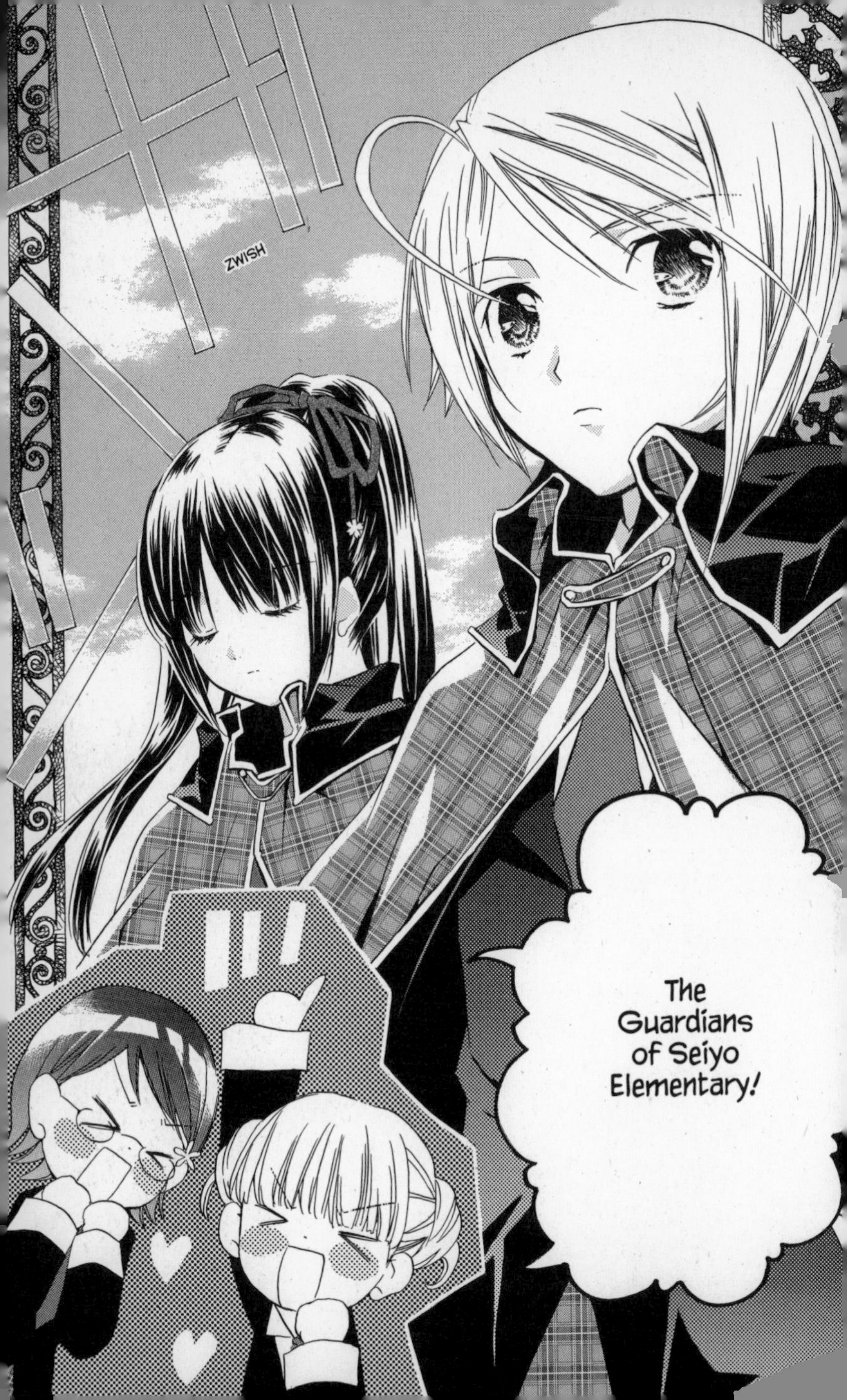
ZWISH
The Guardians of Seiyo Elementary!

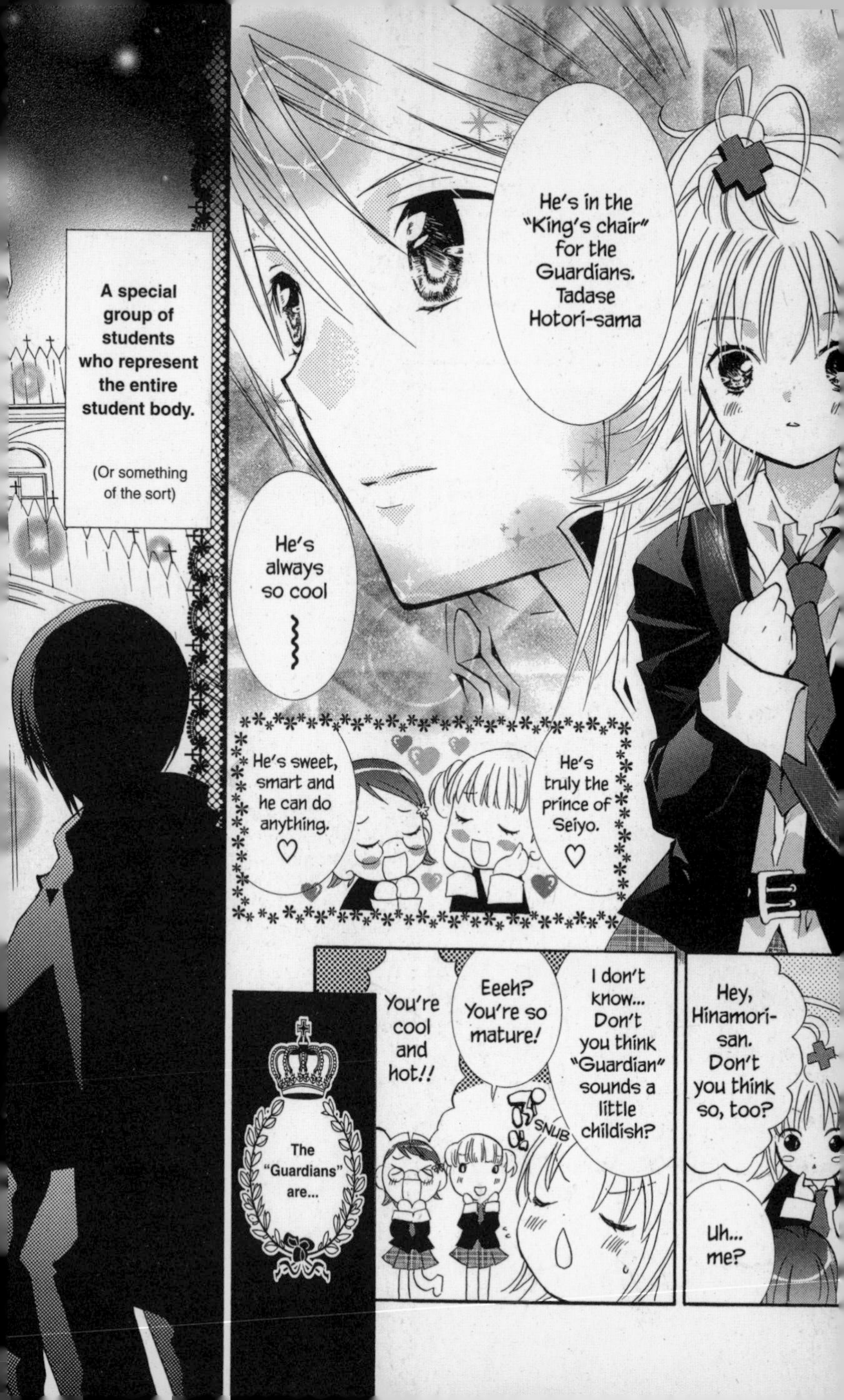

He's in the "King's chair" for the Guardians. Tadase Hotori-sama
He's always so cool
He's truly the prince of Seiyo. ♡
He's sweet, smart and he can do anything. ♡
Hey, Hinamori-san. Don't you think so, too?
Uh... me?
I don't know... Don't you think "Guardian" sounds a little childish?
SNUB
Eeeh? You're so mature!
You're cool and hot!!
The "Guardians" are...
A special group of students who represent the entire student body.
(Or something of the sort)

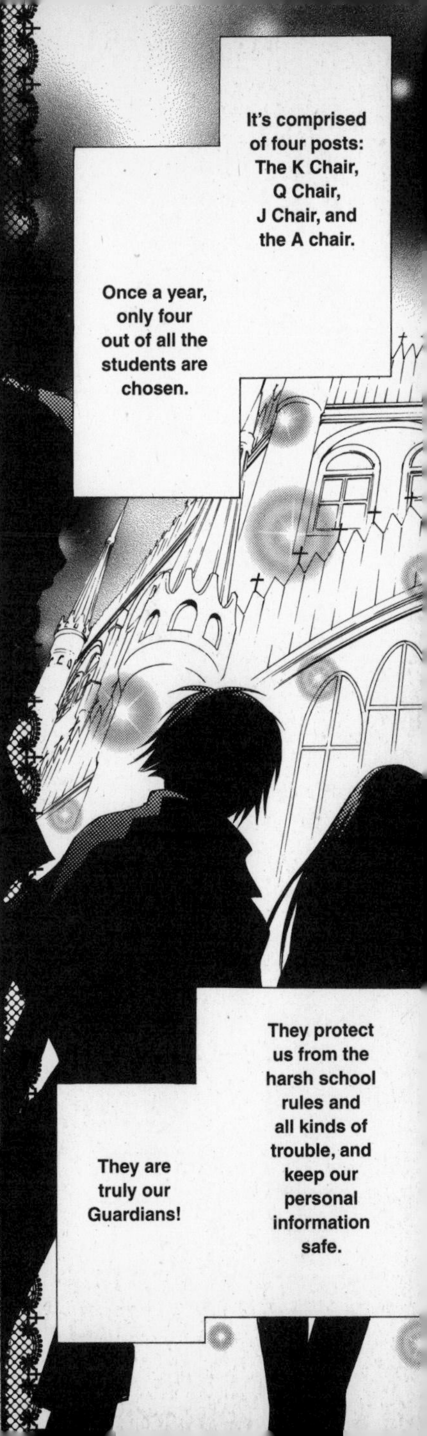
It's comprised of four posts: The K Chair, Q Chair, J Chair, and the A chair.
Once a year, only four out of all the students are chosen.
They protect us from the harsh school rules and all kinds of trouble, and keep our personal information safe.
They are truly our Guardians!

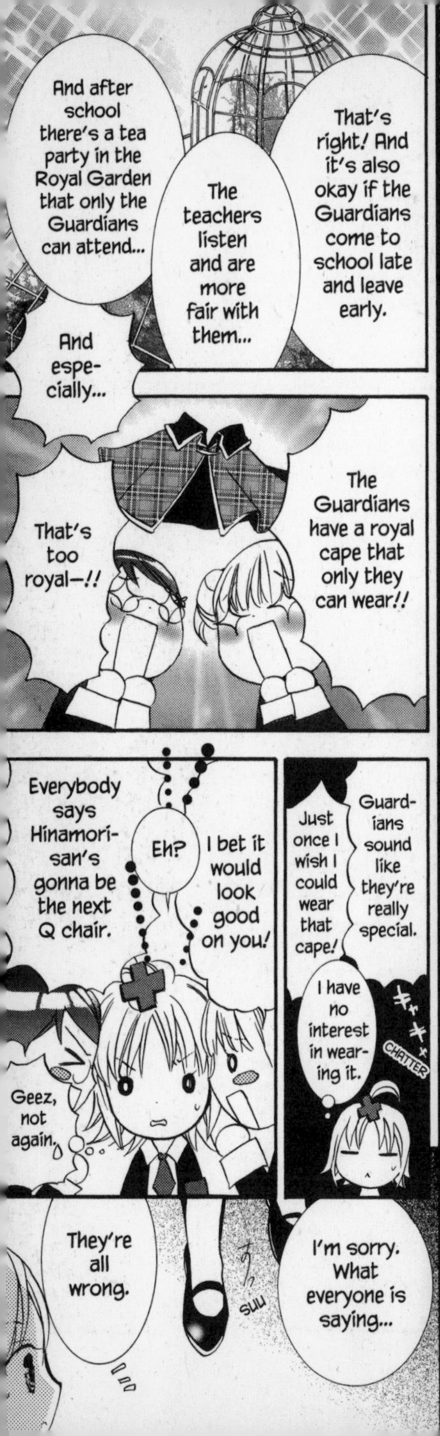
That's right! And it's also okay if the Guardians come to school late and leave early.
The teachers listen and are more fair with them...
And after school there's a tea party in the Royal Garden that only the Guardians can attend...
And espe-cially...
The Guardians have a royal cape that only they can wear!!
That's too royal—!!
Guard-ians sound like they're really special.
Just once I wish I could wear that cape!
I have no interest in wear-ing it.
CHATTER
I bet it would look good on you!
Eh?
Everybody says Hinamori-san's gonna be the next Q chair.
Geez, not again.
I'm sorry. What everyone is saying...
SUU
They're all wrong.

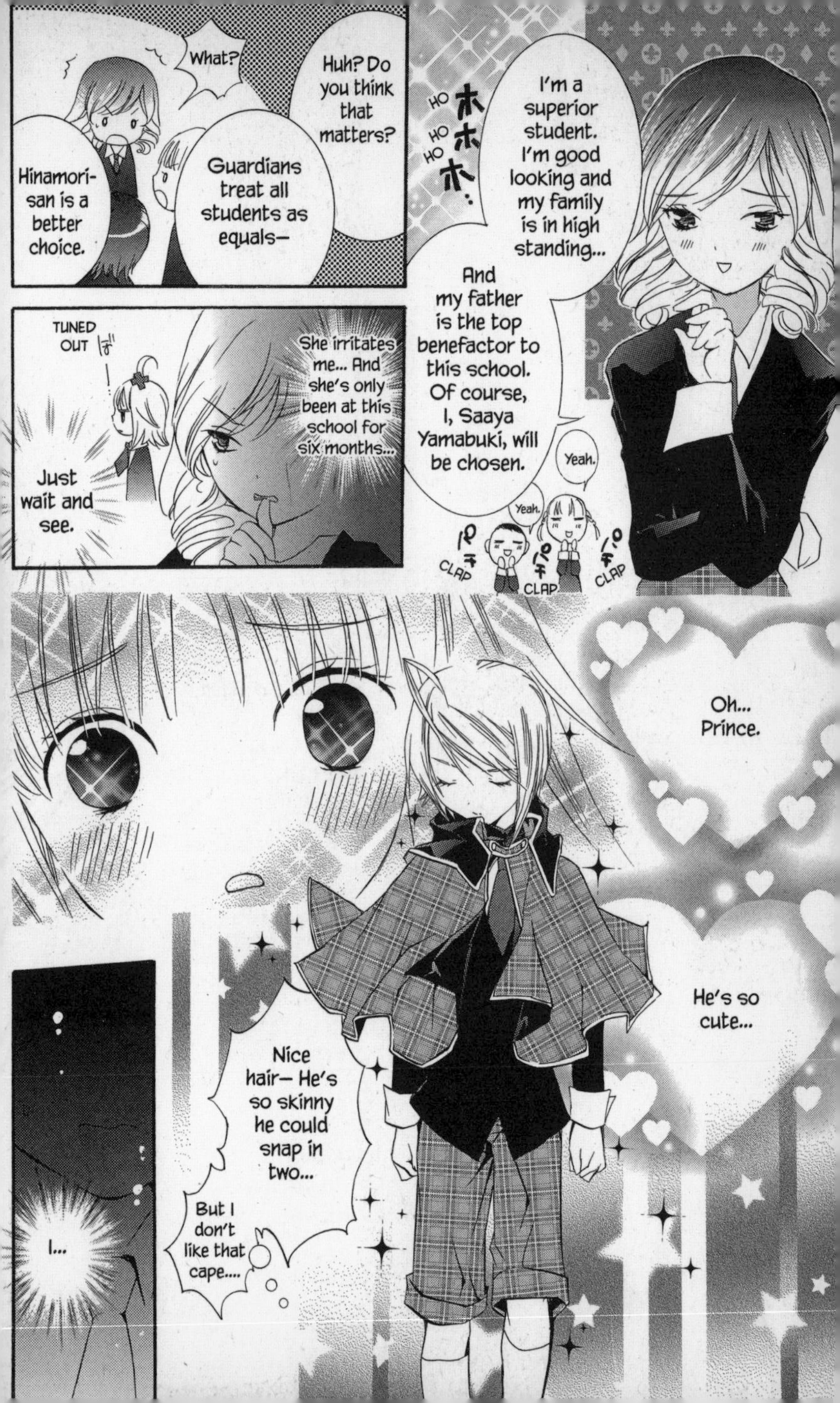
HO HO HO
I'm a superior student. I'm good looking and my family is in high standing...
And my father is the top benefactor to this school. Of course, I, Saaya Yamabuki, will be chosen.
Yeah.
Yeah.
CLAP CLAP CLAP
Huh? Do you think that matters?
What?
Guardians treat all students as equals—
Hinamori-san is a better choice.
She irritates me... And she's only been at this school for six months...
TUNED OUT
Just wait and see.
Oh... Prince.
He's so cute...
Nice hair— He's so skinny he could snap in two...
But I don't like that cape....
I...

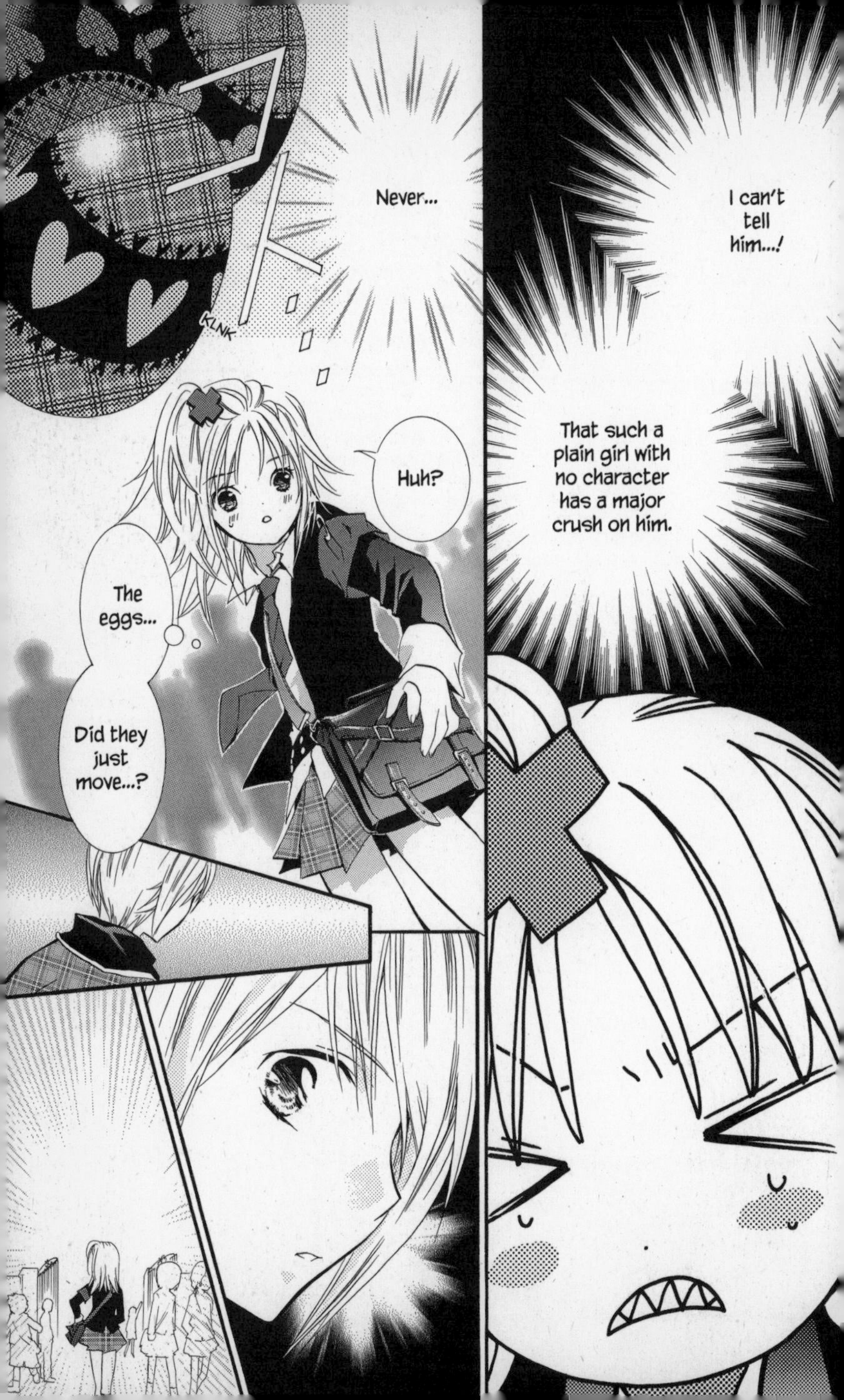
I can't tell him...!
That such a plain girl with no character has a major crush on him.
Never...
KLNK
Huh?
The eggs...
Did they just move...?

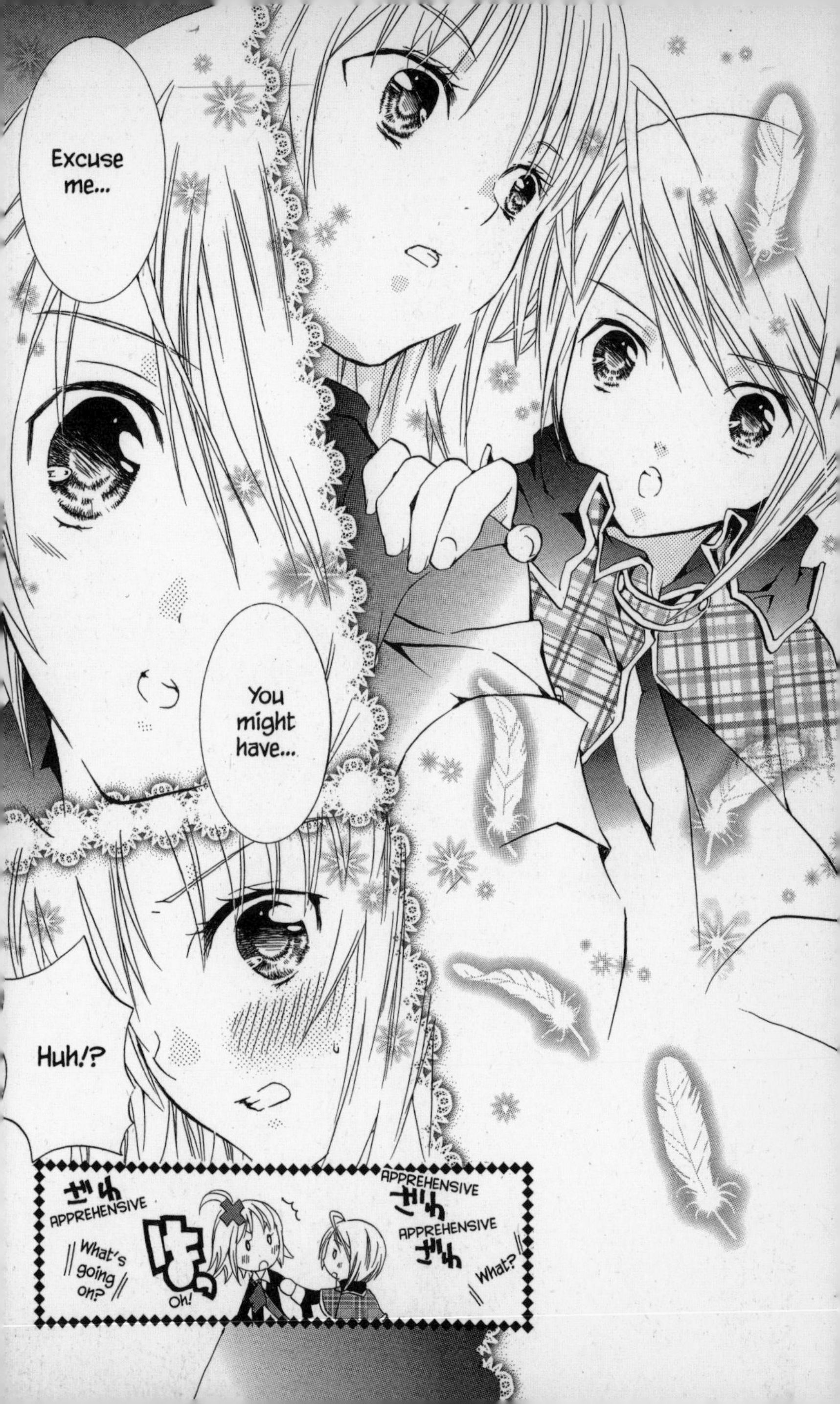

Excuse me...
You might have...
Huh!?
APPREHENSIVE
ざわ
APPREHENSIVE
ざわ
What?
はっ
Oh!
ざわ
APPREHENSIVE
What's going on?

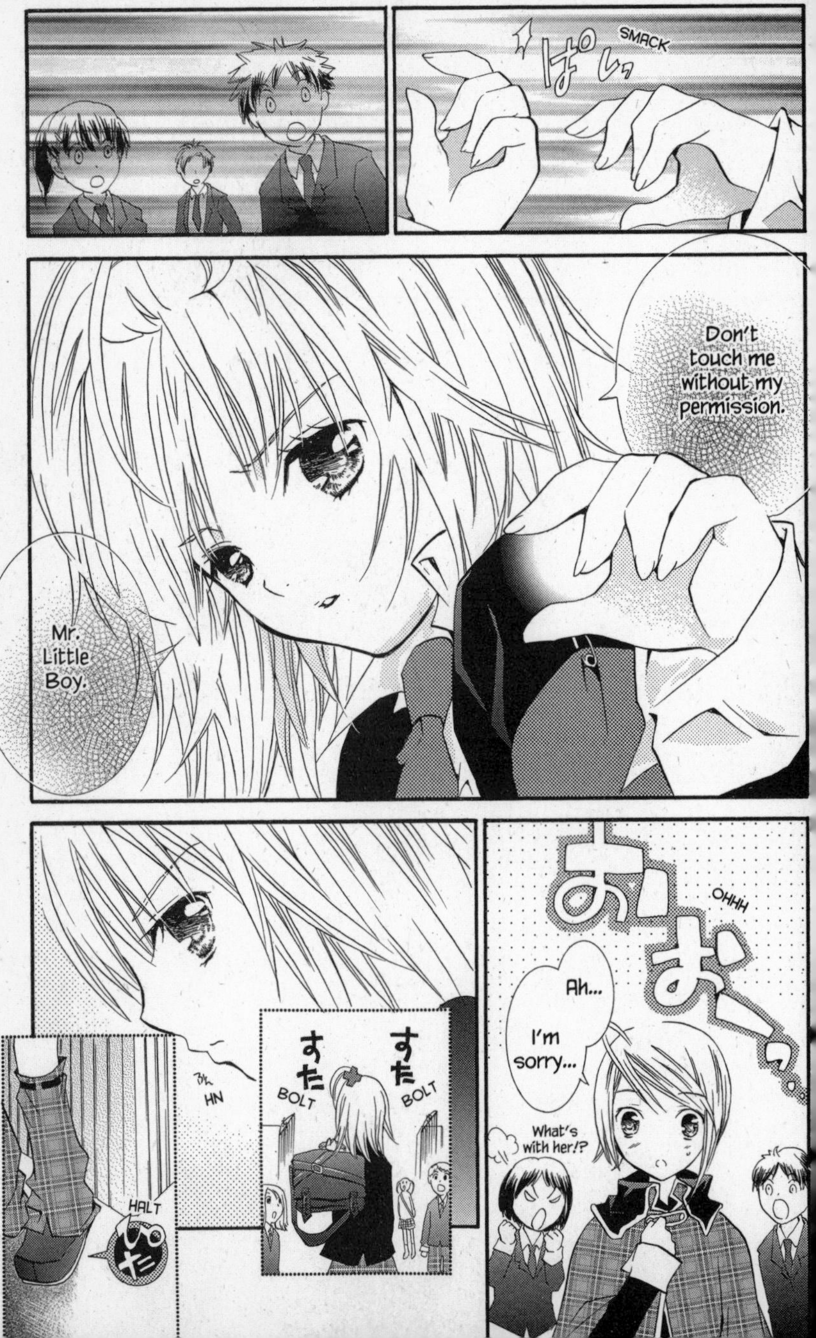
SMACK
Don't touch me without my permission.
Mr. Little Boy.
OHHH
Ah...
I'm sorry...
What's with her!?
HN
すた
BOLT
すた
BOLT
HALT

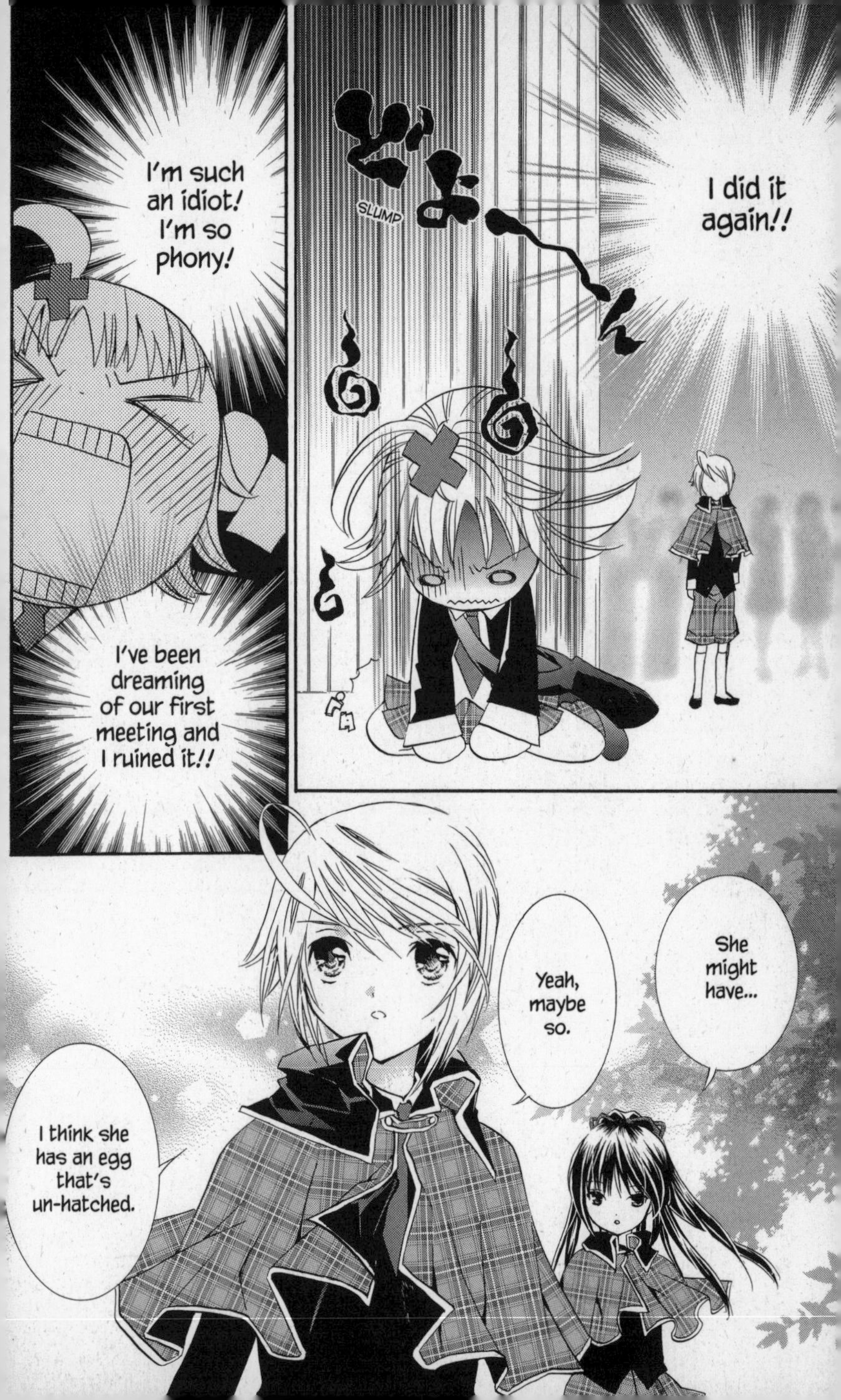
I did it again!!
SLUMP
I'm such an idiot! I'm so phony!
I've been dreaming of our first meeting and I ruined it!!
She might have...
Yeah, maybe so.
I think she has an egg that's un-hatched.

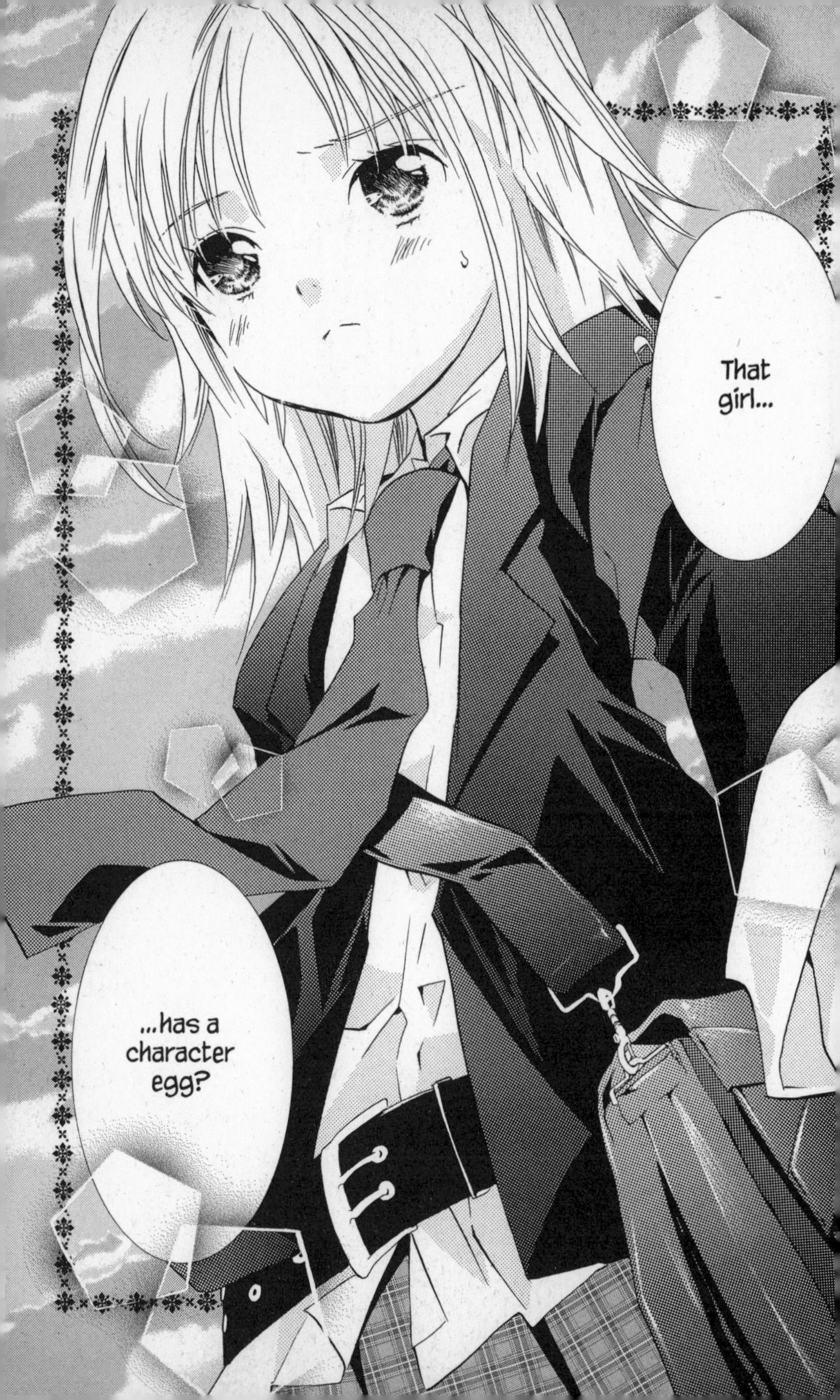
That girl...
...has a character egg?

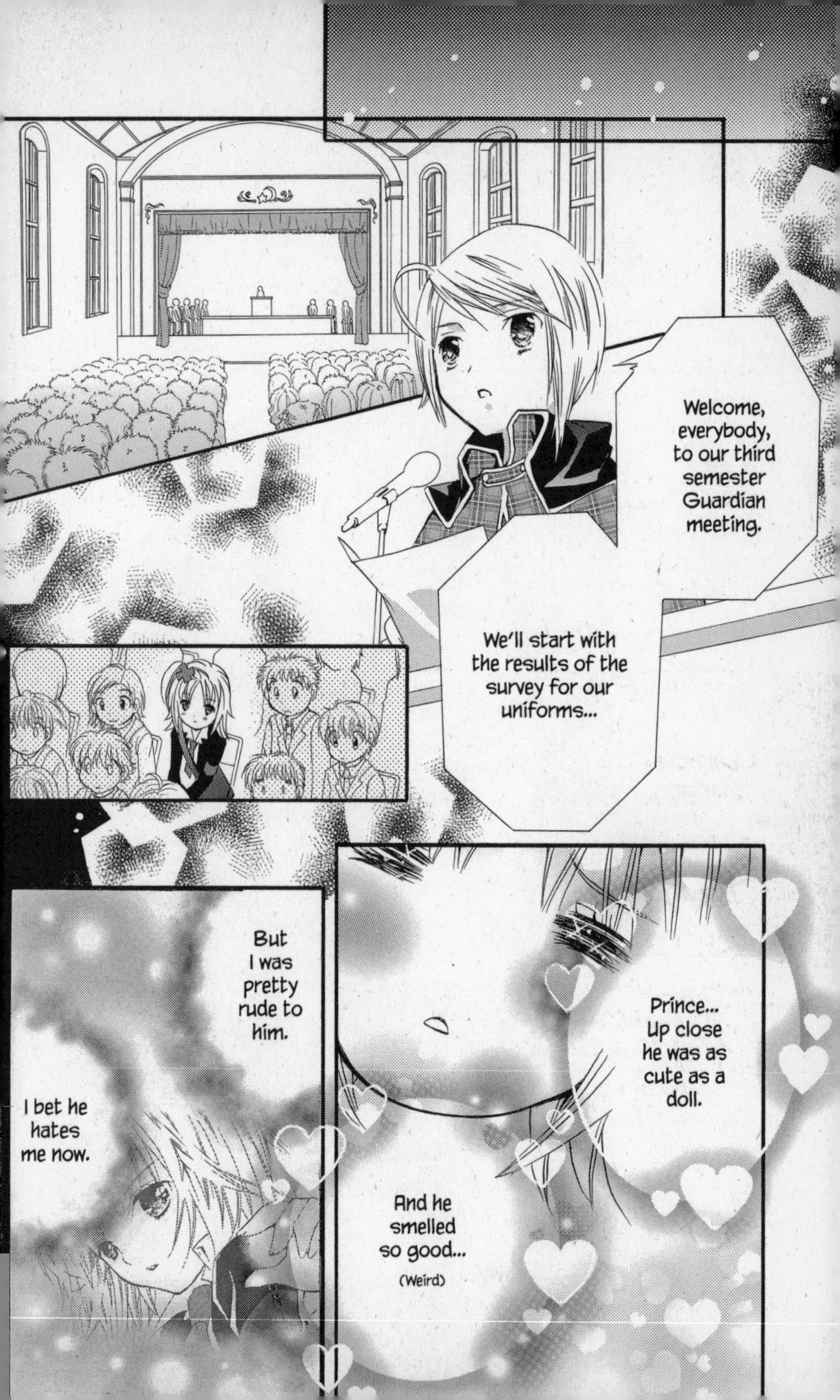
Welcome, everybody, to our third semester Guardian meeting.
We'll start with the results of the survey for our uniforms...
Prince... Up close he was as cute as a doll.
And he smelled so good...
(Weird)
But I was pretty rude to him.
I bet he hates me now.

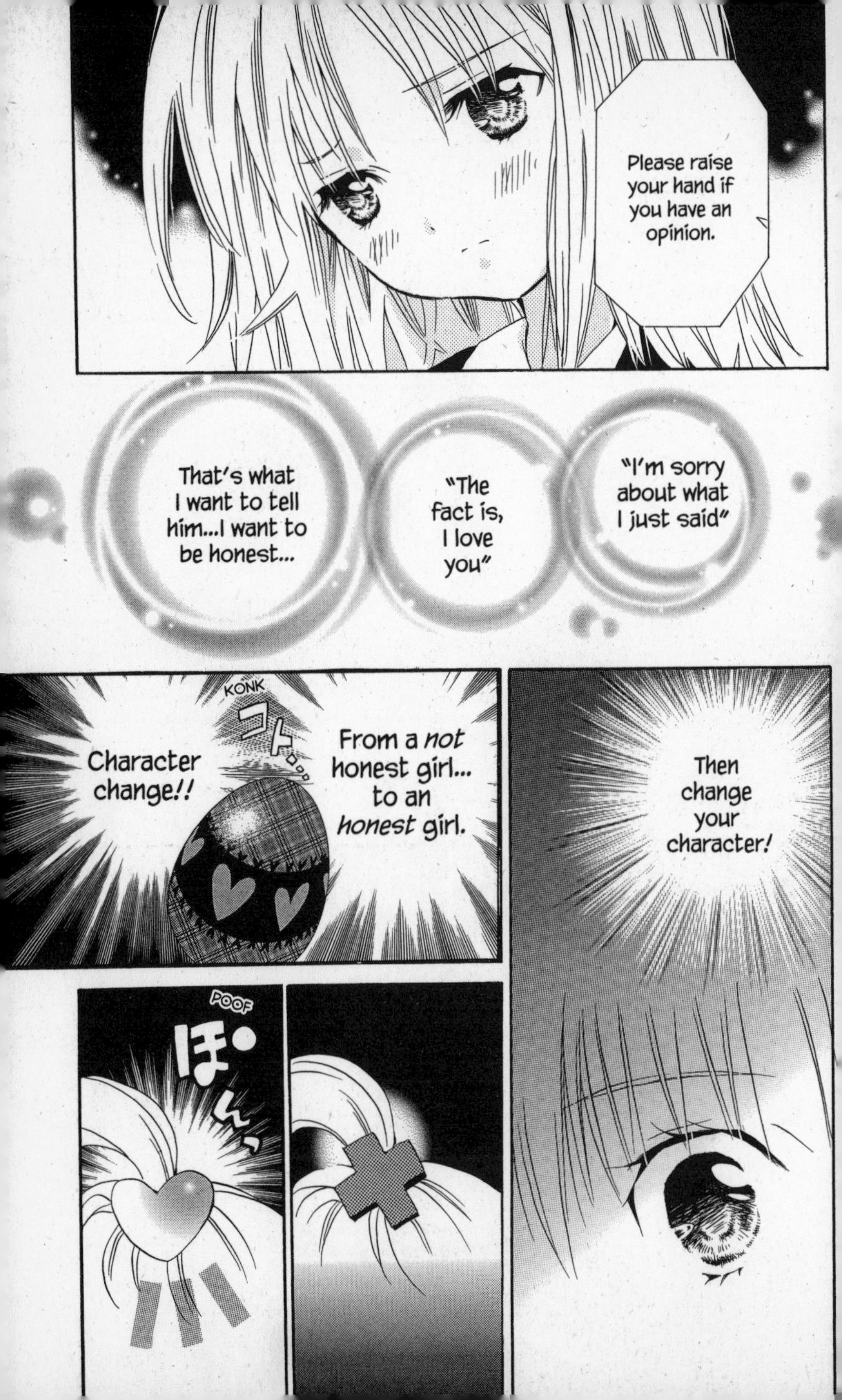
Please raise your hand if you have an opinion.
"I'm sorry about what I just said"
"The fact is, I love you"
That's what I want to tell him...I want to be honest...
Then change your character!
From a *not* honest girl... to an *honest* girl.
KONK
コト
Character change!!
POOF
ぽん

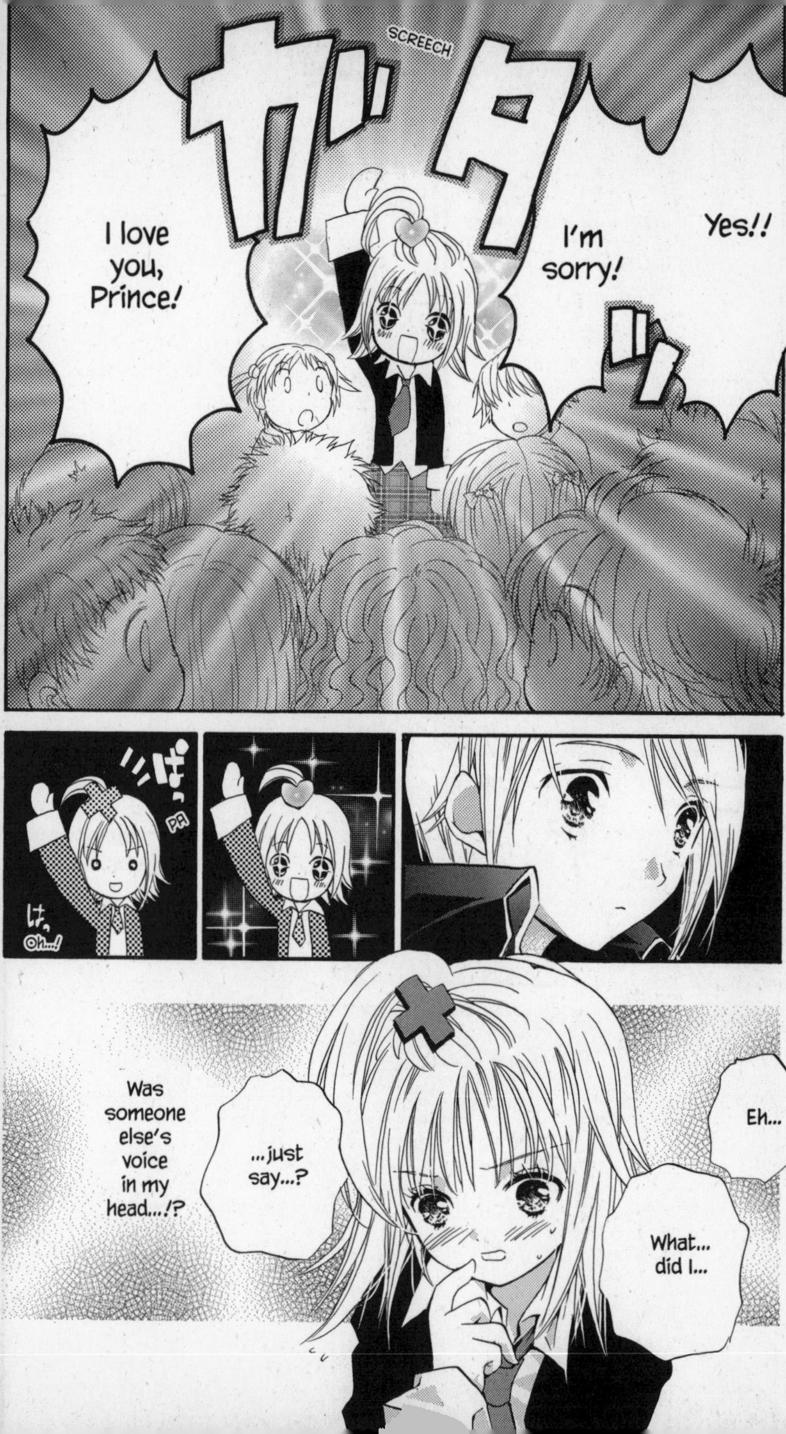
ガタッ
SCREECH
Yes!!
I'm sorry!
I love you, Prince!
ぱっ
PA
はっ
Oh...!
Eh...
What... did I...
...just say...?
Was someone else's voice in my head...!?

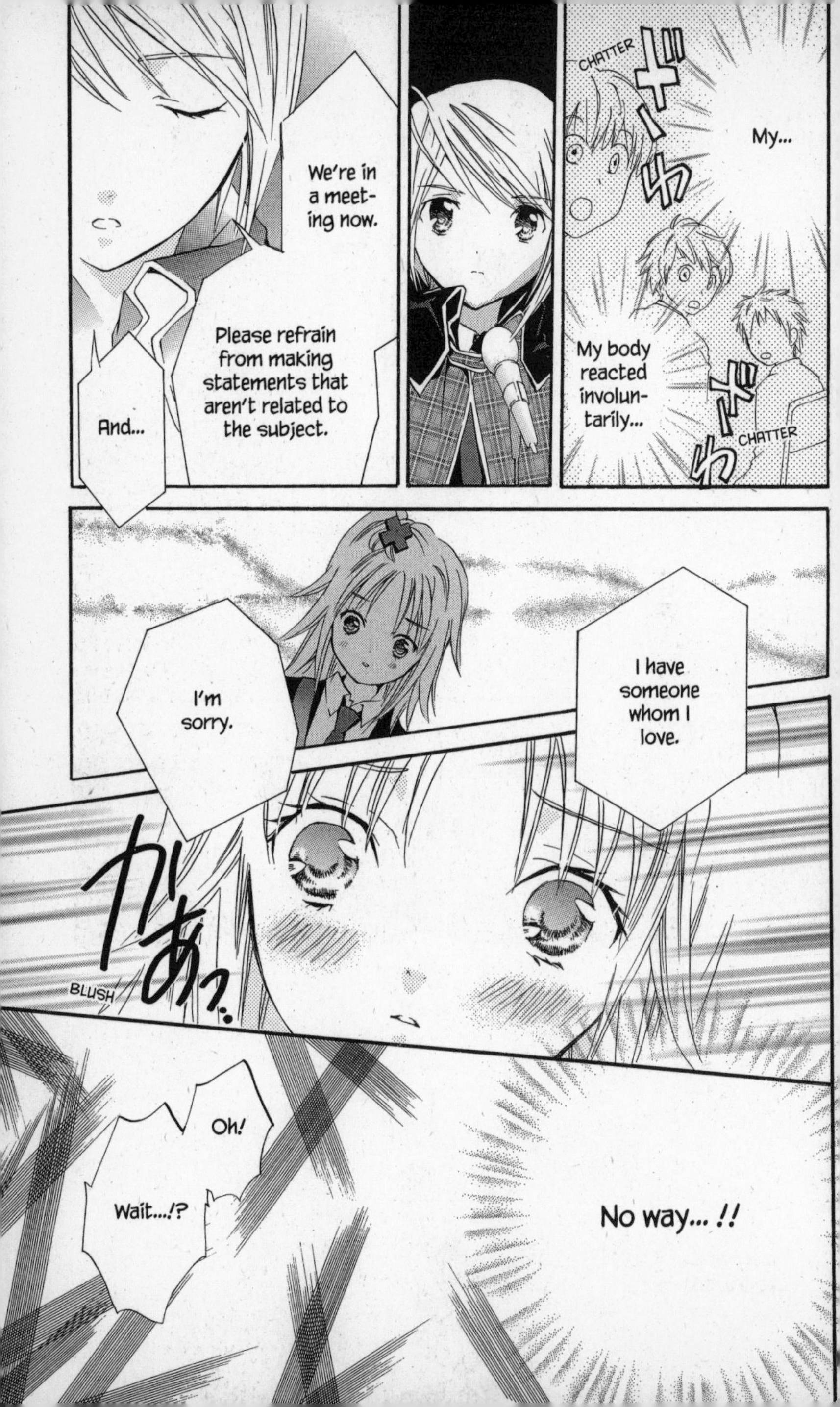
CHATTER
ザわ
My...
My body reacted involuntarily...
ザわ
CHATTER
We're in a meeting now.
Please refrain from making statements that aren't related to the subject.
And...
I have someone whom I love.
I'm sorry.
かあっ
BLUSH
No way... !!
Oh!
Wait...!?

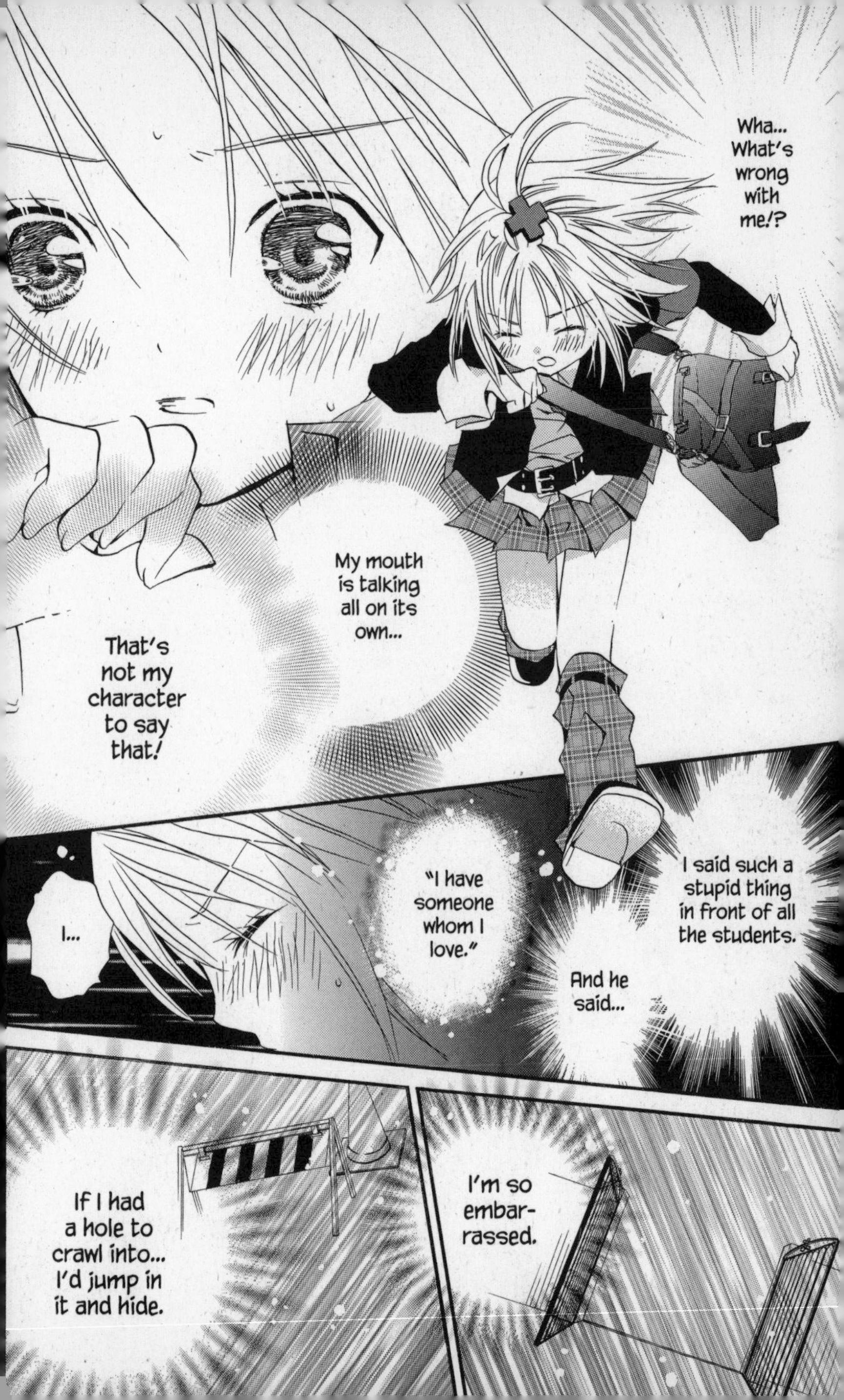
Wha... What's wrong with me!?
My mouth is talking all on its own...
That's not my character to say that!
I said such a stupid thing in front of all the students.
And he said...
"I have someone whom I love."
I...
I'm so embarrassed.
If I had a hole to crawl into... I'd jump in it and hide.

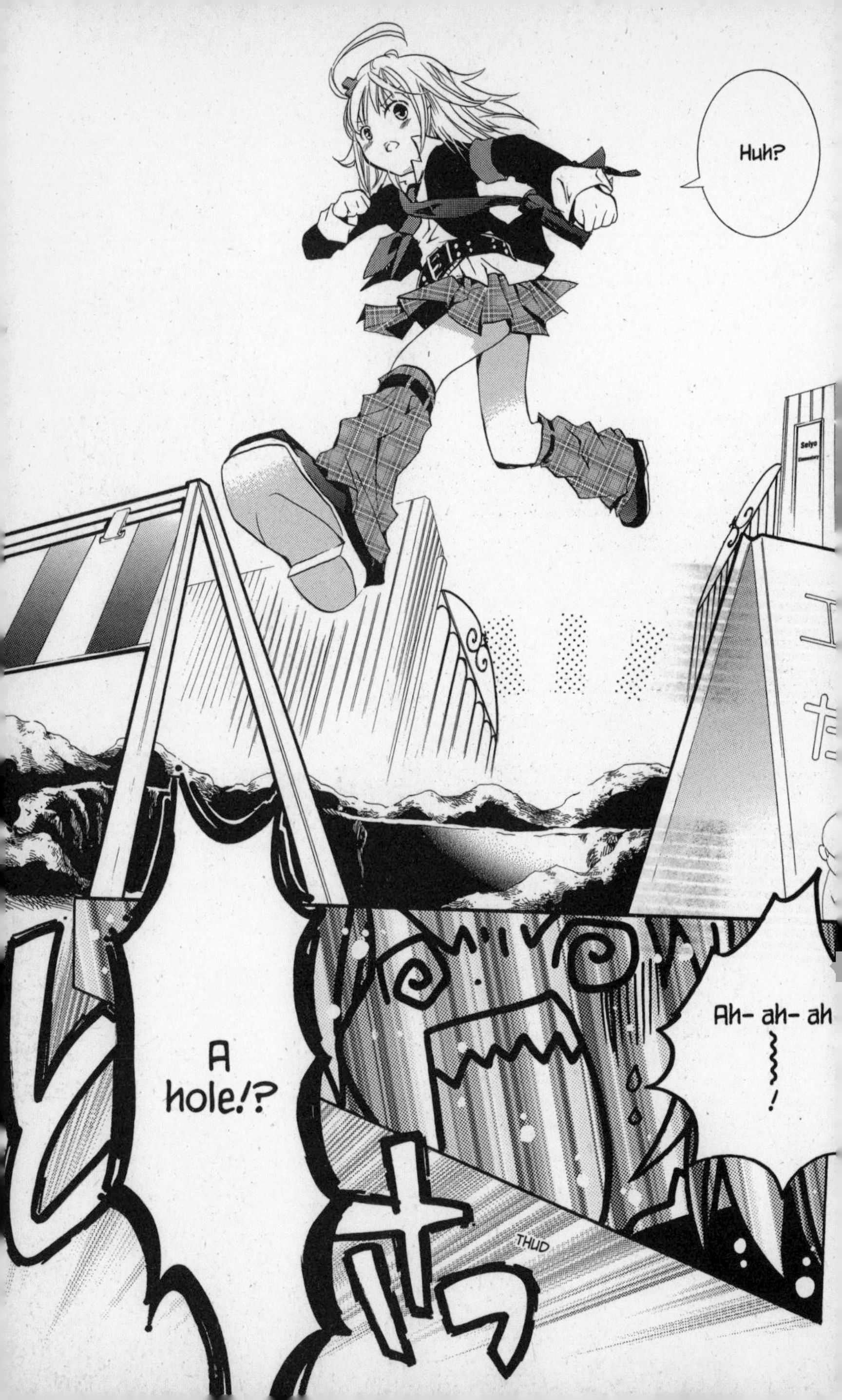
Huh?
Ah- ah- ah
~~~!
A hole!?
THUD
~~~

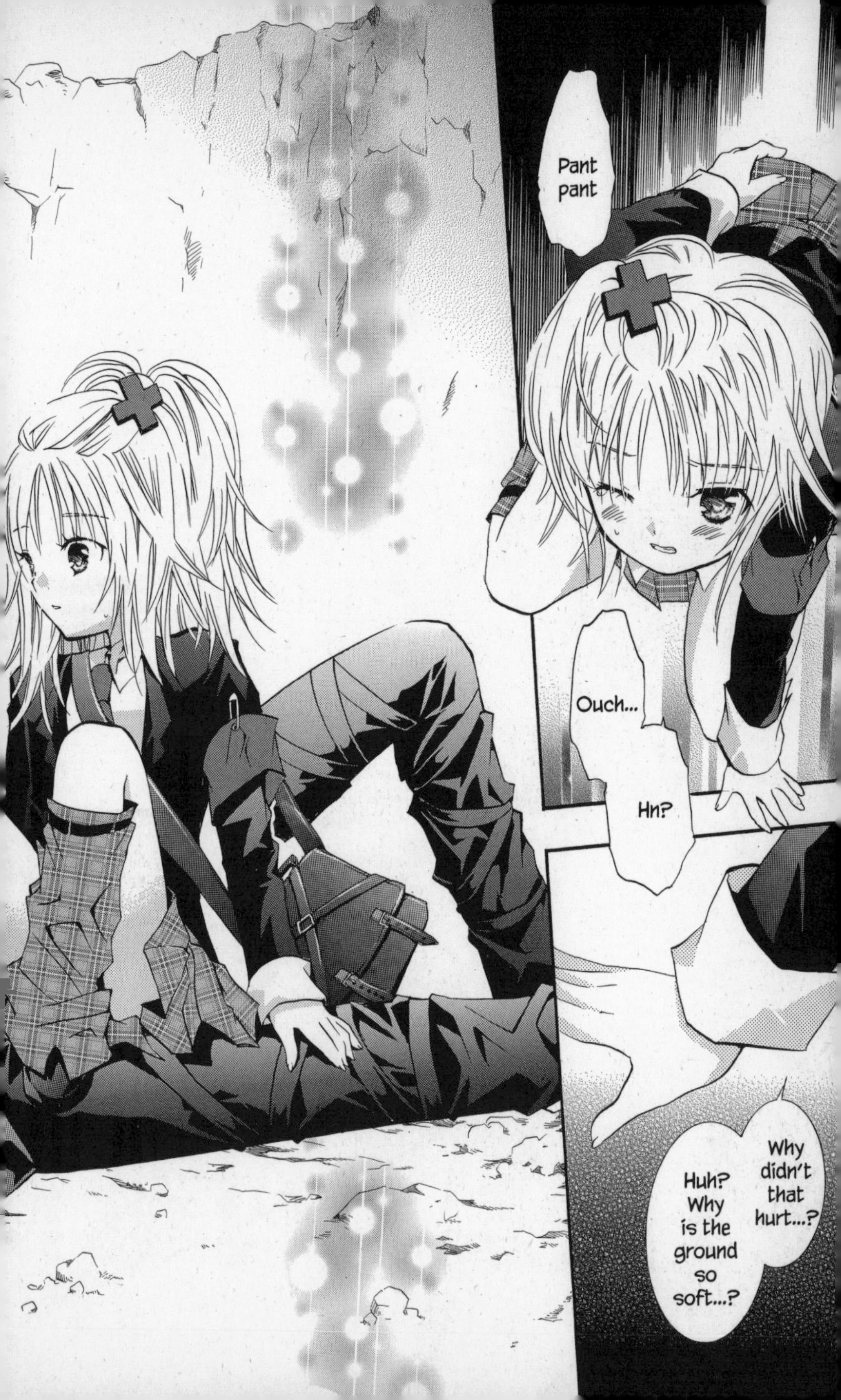
Pant pant
Ouch...
Hn?
Why didn't that hurt...?
Huh? Why is the ground so soft...?

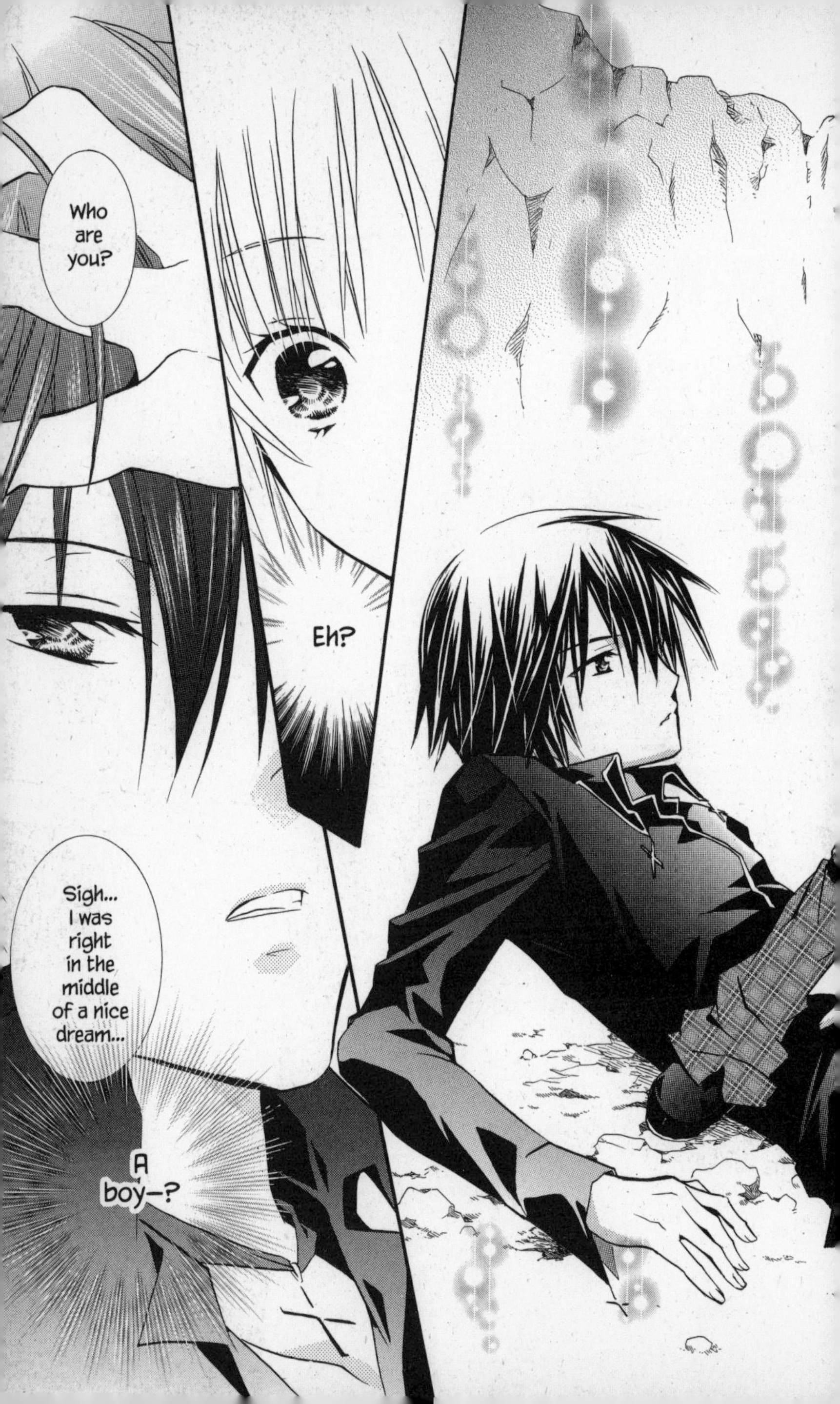
Eh?
Who are you?
Sigh... I was right in the middle of a nice dream...
A boy—?

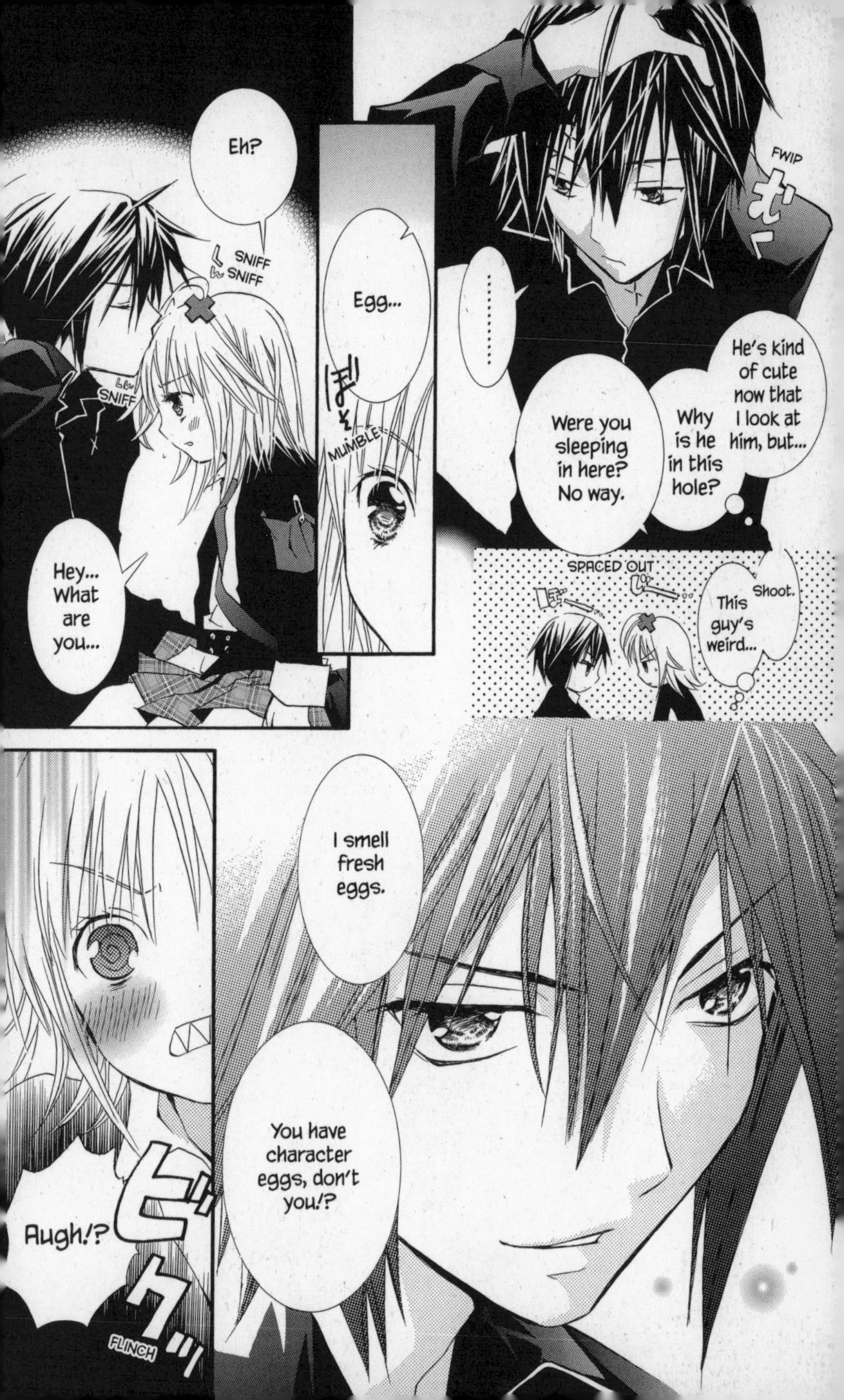
FWIP
......
He's kind of cute now that I look at him, but...
Why is he in this hole?
Were you sleeping in here? No way.
Shoot.
This guy's weird...
SPACED OUT
Egg...
MUMBLE
Eh?
SNIFF SNIFF
SNIFF
Hey... What are you...
I smell fresh eggs.
You have character eggs, don't you!?
FLINCH
Augh!?

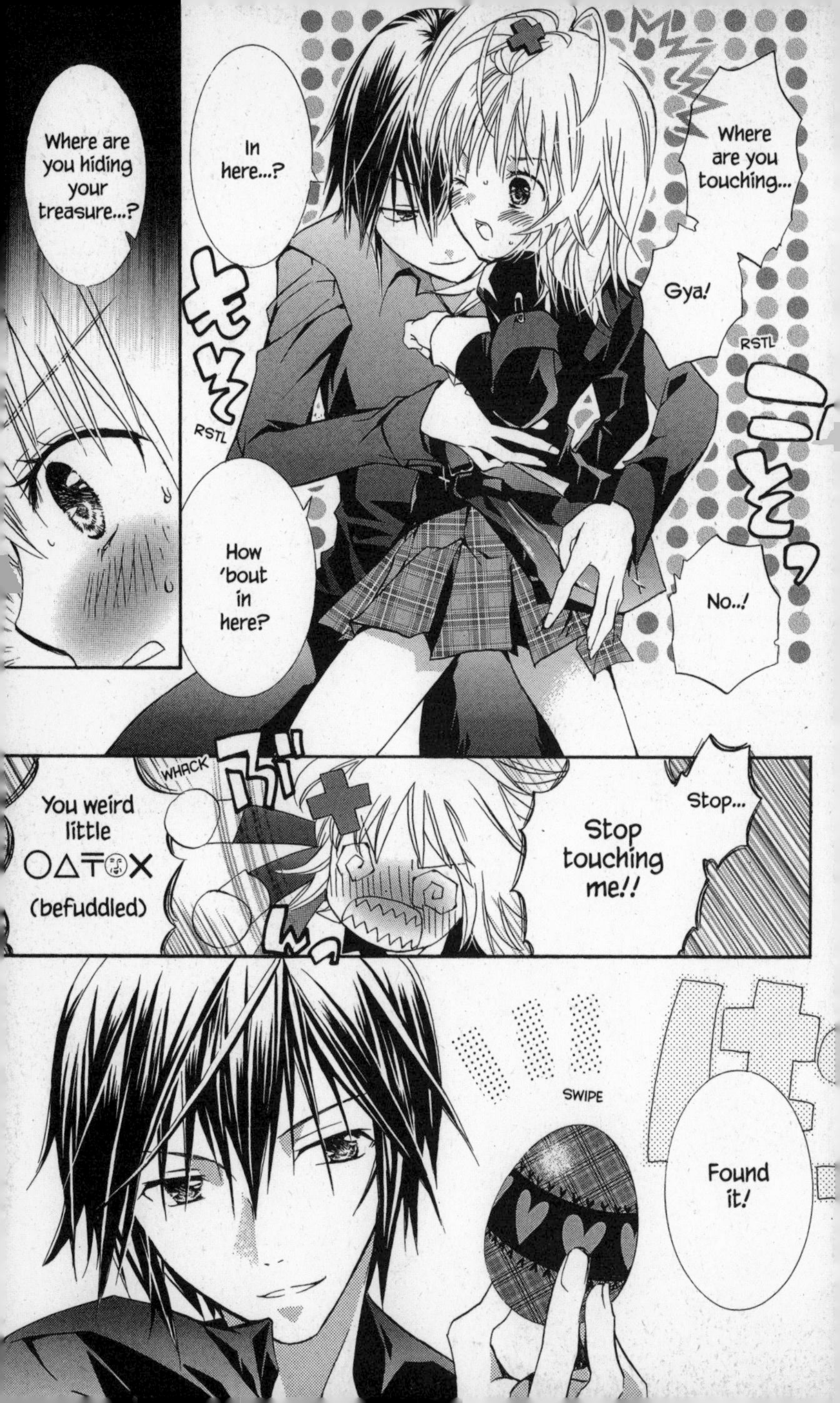
Where are you touching...
Gya!
RSTL
In here...?
RSTL
No..!
How 'bout in here?
Where are you hiding your treasure...?
Stop...
Stop touching me!!
WHACK
You weird little ○△〒☺✕ (befuddled)
SWIPE
Found it!

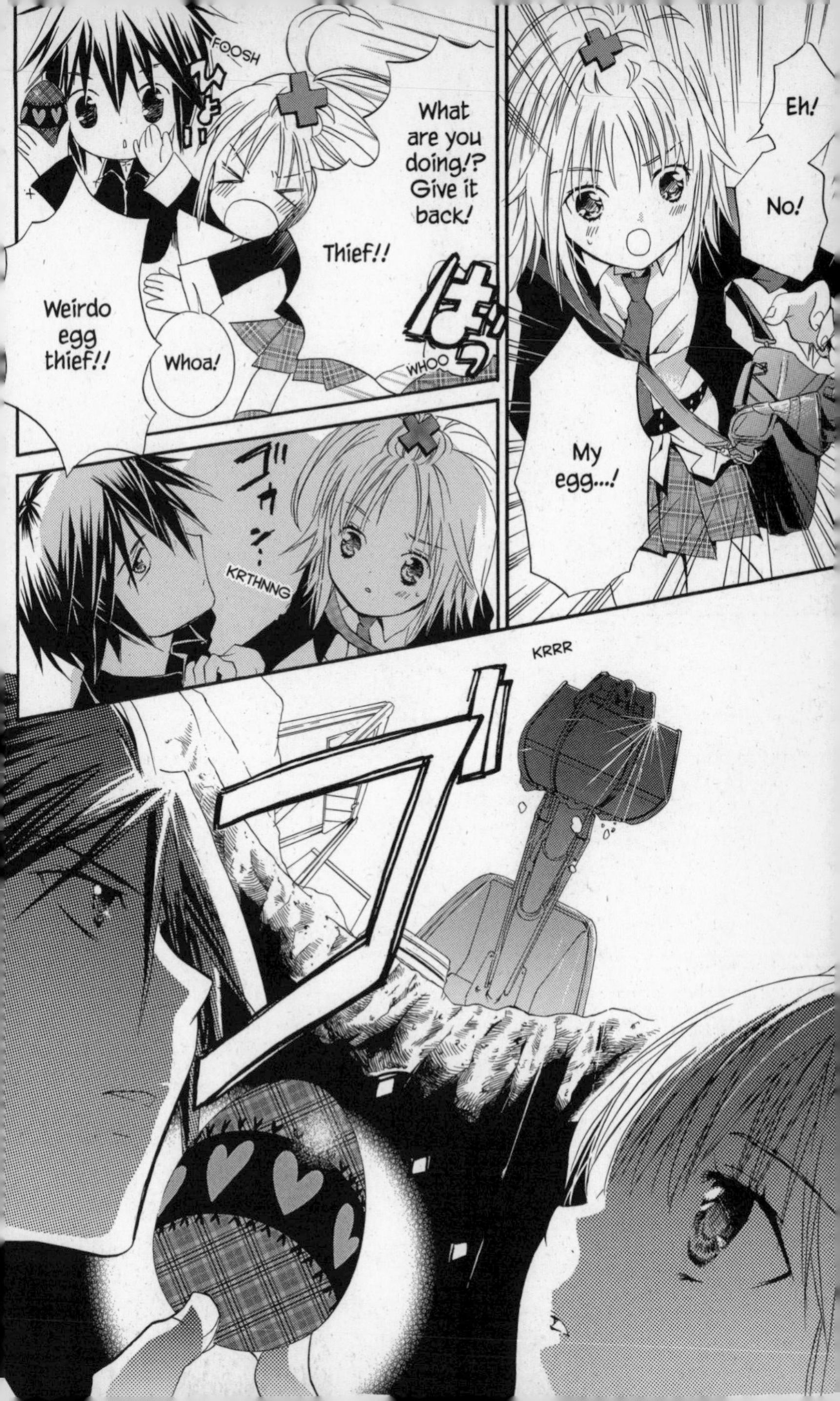
Eh!
No!
My egg...!
What are you doing!? Give it back!
FOOSH
Thief!!
WHOO
Whoa!
Weirdo egg thief!!
KRTHNNG
KRRR

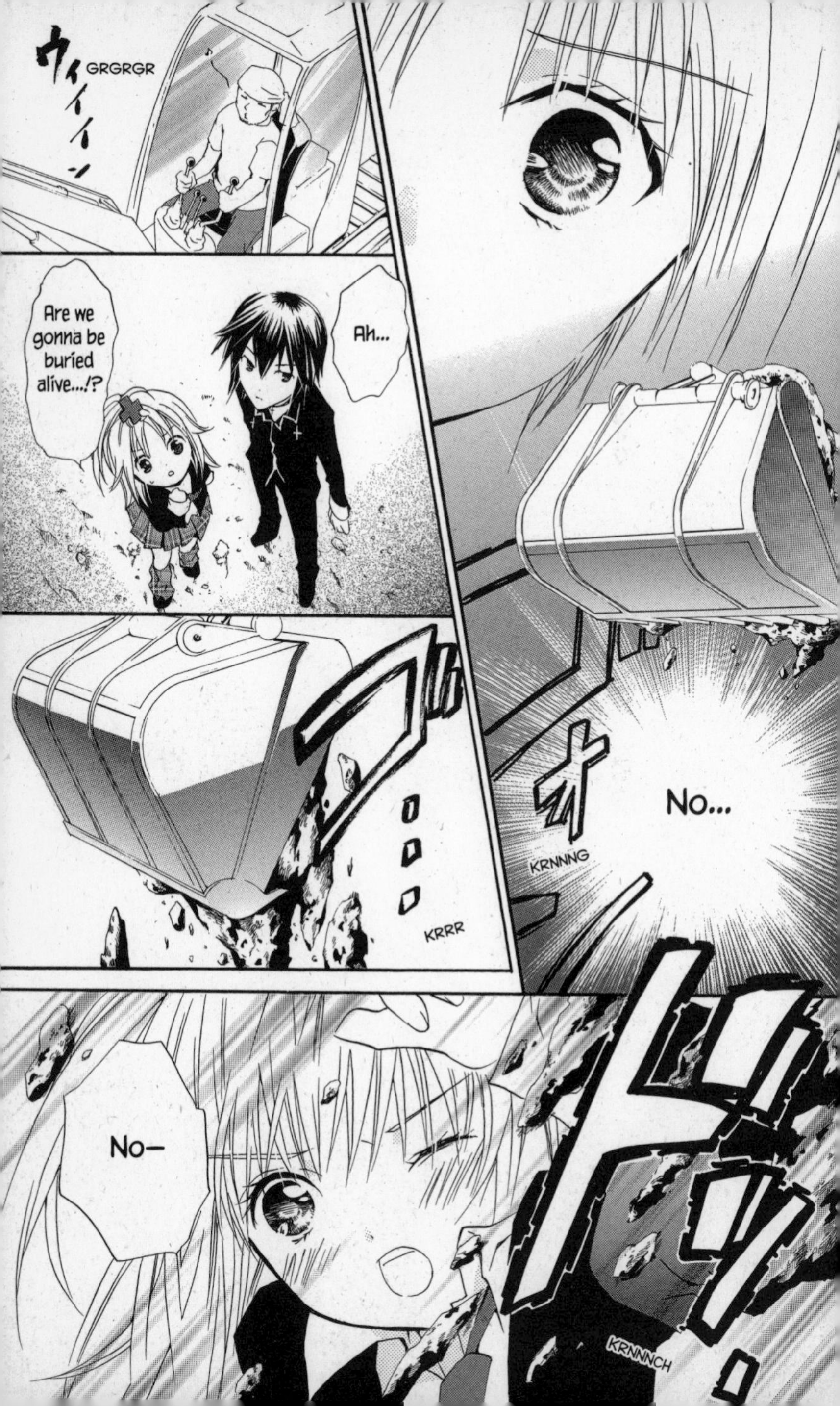

No...
KRNNNG
GRGRGR
Ah...
Are we gonna be buried alive...!?
KRRR
No–
KRNNNCH

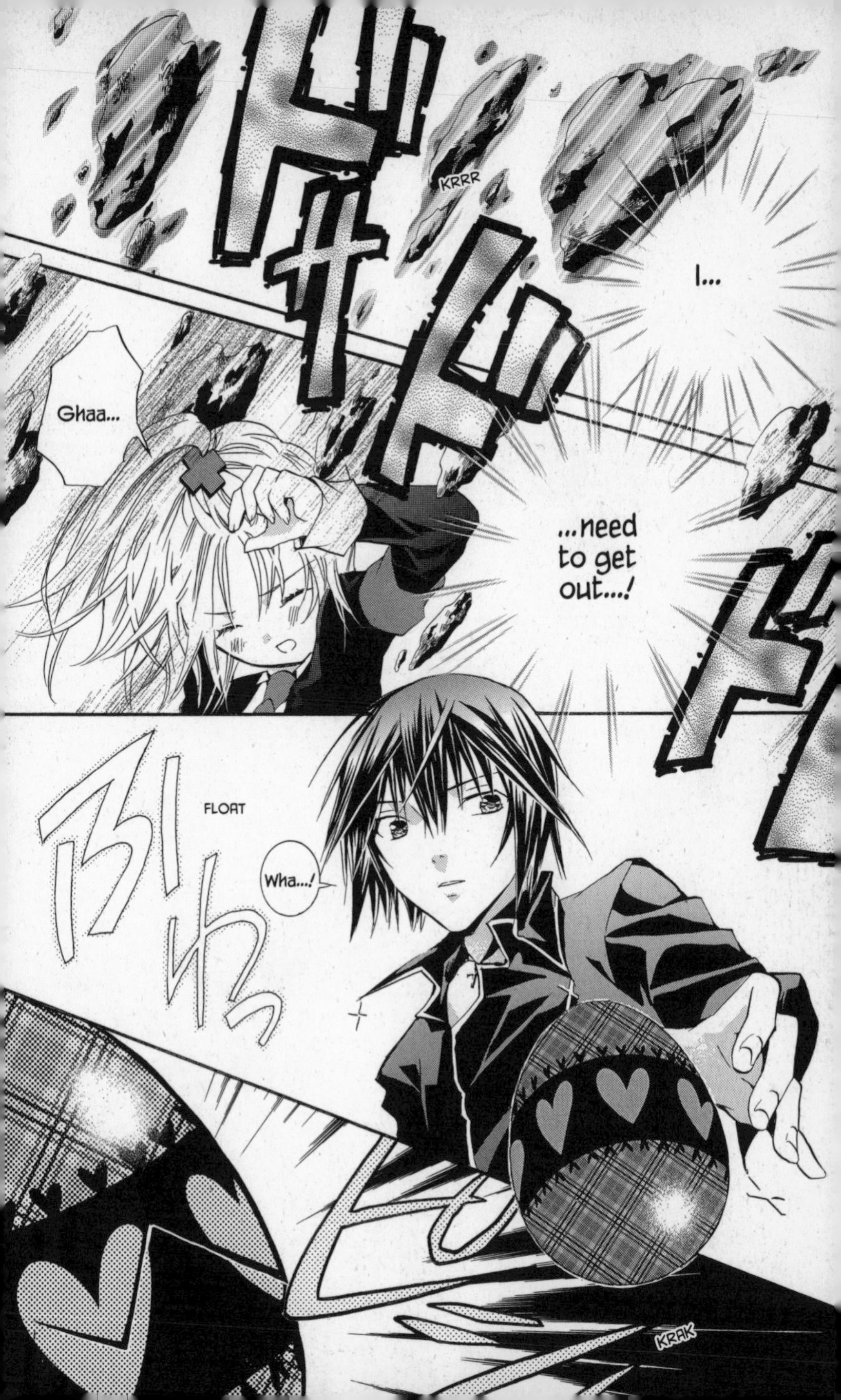
KRRR
I...
...need to get out...!
Ghaa...
FLOAT
Wha...!
KRAK

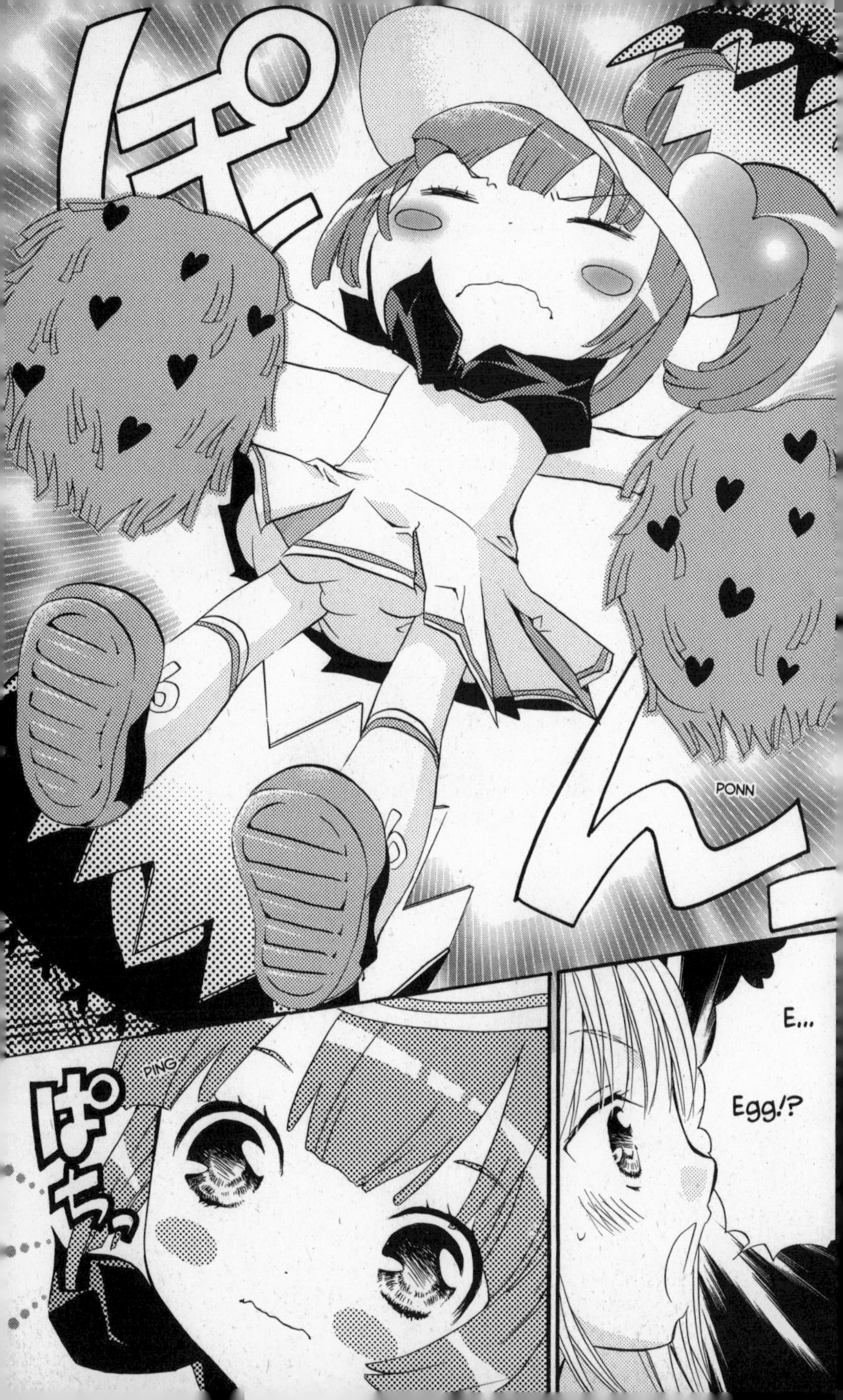
PONN
E...
Egg!?
ぱちっ
PING

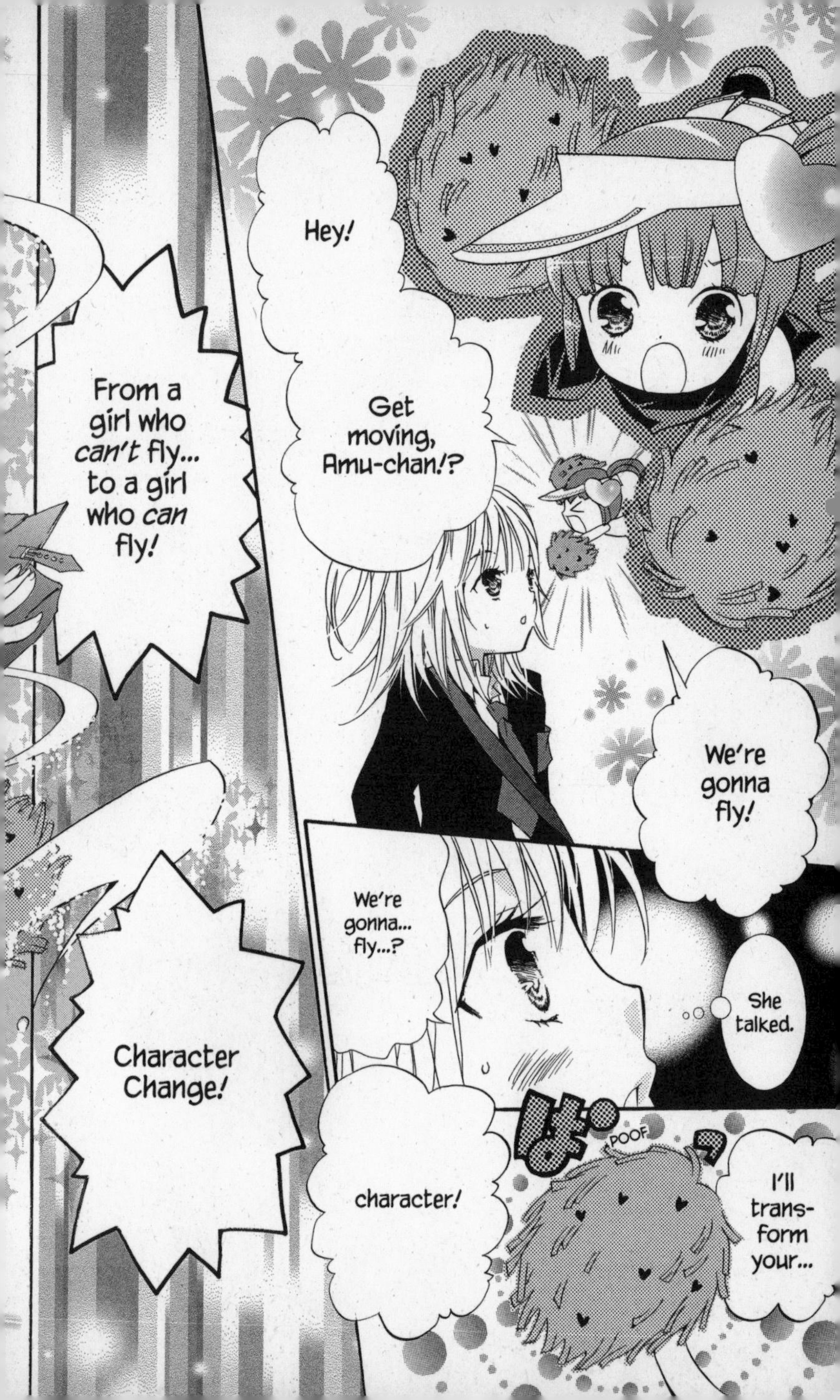
Hey!
Get moving, Amu-chan!?
We're gonna fly!
We're gonna... fly...?
She talked.
POOF
I'll trans-form your...
character!
From a girl who *can't* fly... to a girl who *can* fly!
Character Change!

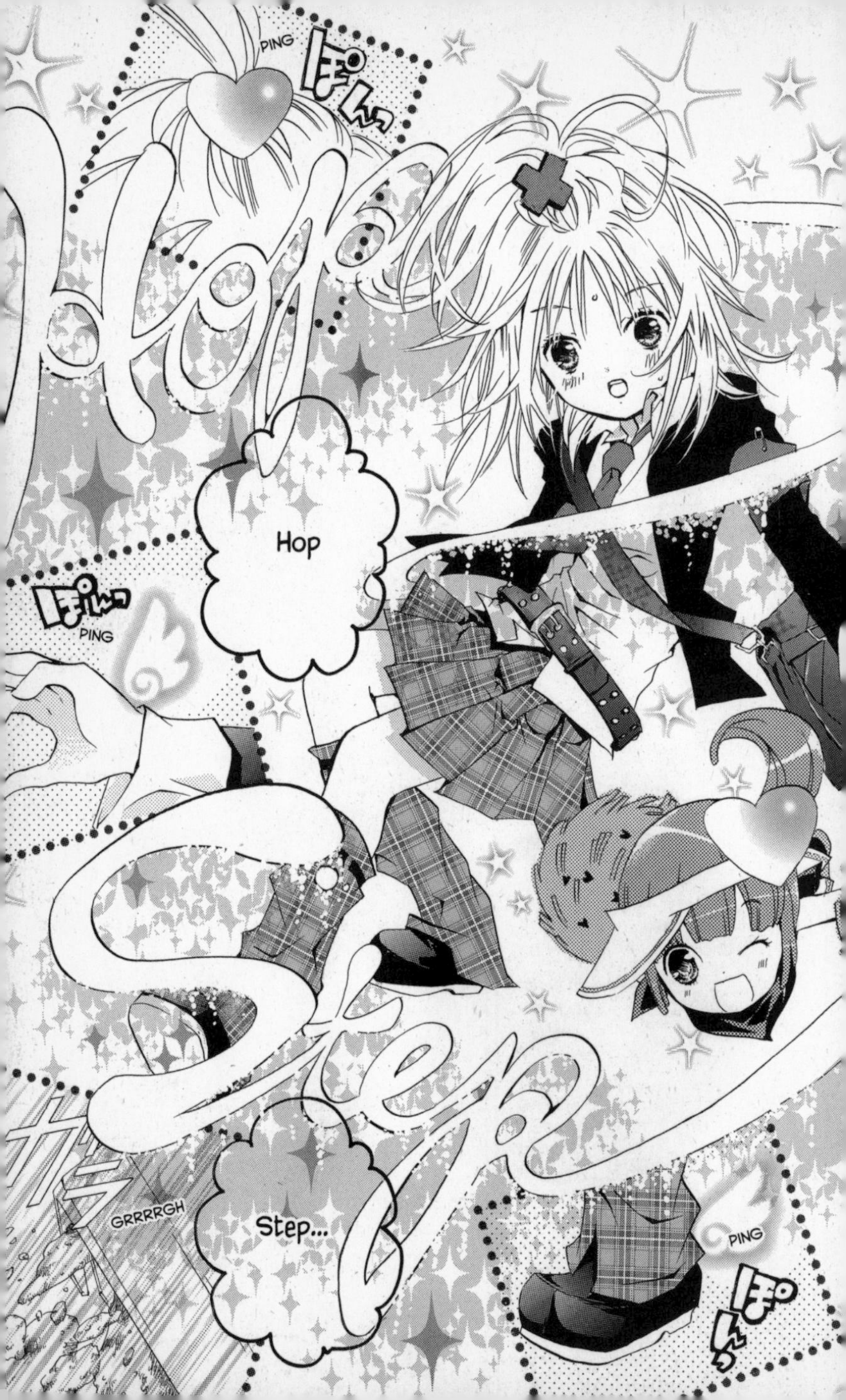
ぽんっ
PING
Hop
ぽんっ
PING
Step...
GRRRRGH
ぽんっ
PING

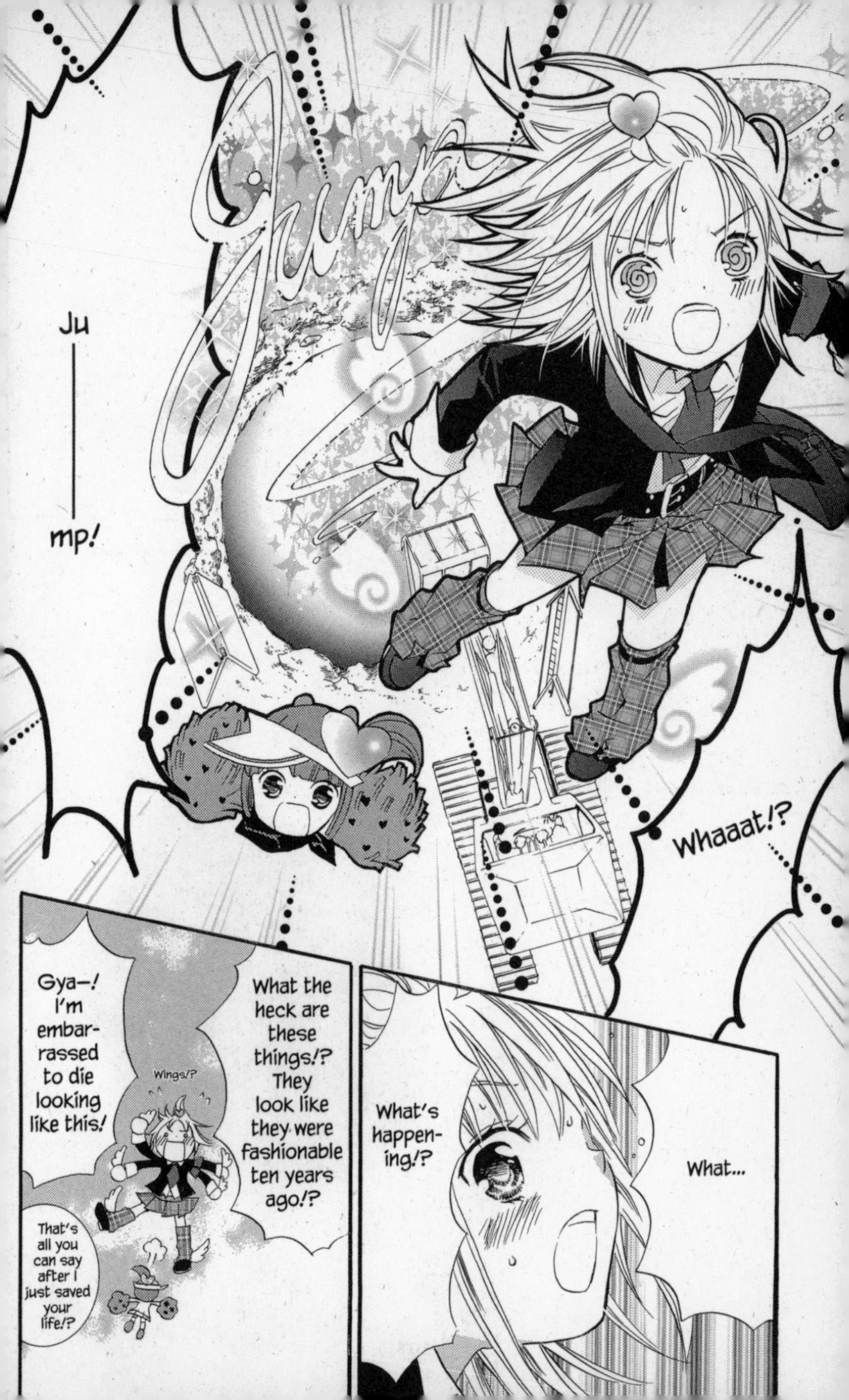
Ju— mp!
Whaaat!?
What...
What's happen-ing!?
What the heck are these things!? They look like they were fashionable ten years ago!?
Gya—! I'm embar-rassed to die looking like this!
Wings!?
That's all you can say after I just saved your life!?

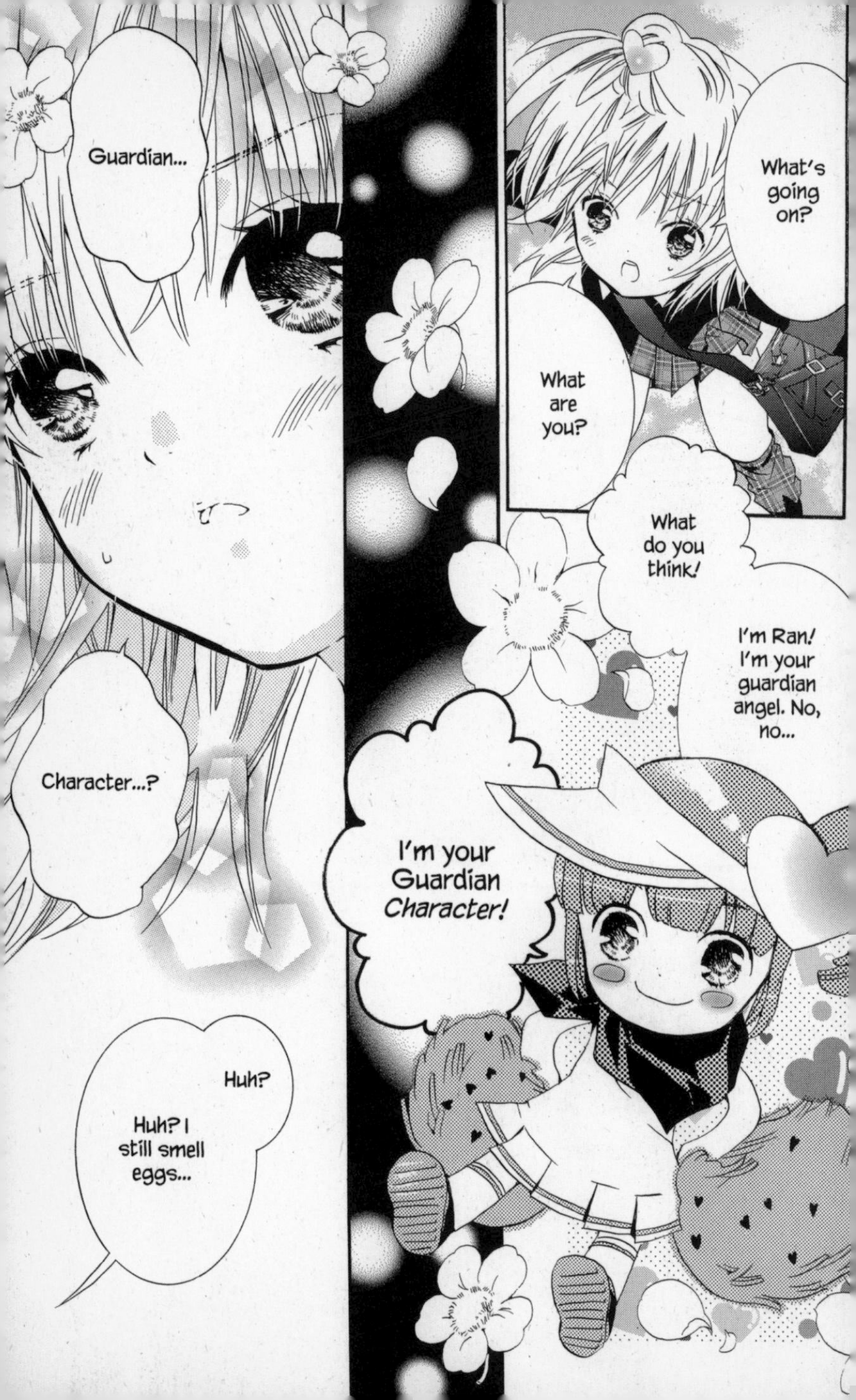
What's going on?
What are you?
What do you think!
I'm Ran! I'm your guardian angel. No, no...
I'm your Guardian *Character!*
Guardian...
Character...?
Huh? Huh? I still smell eggs...

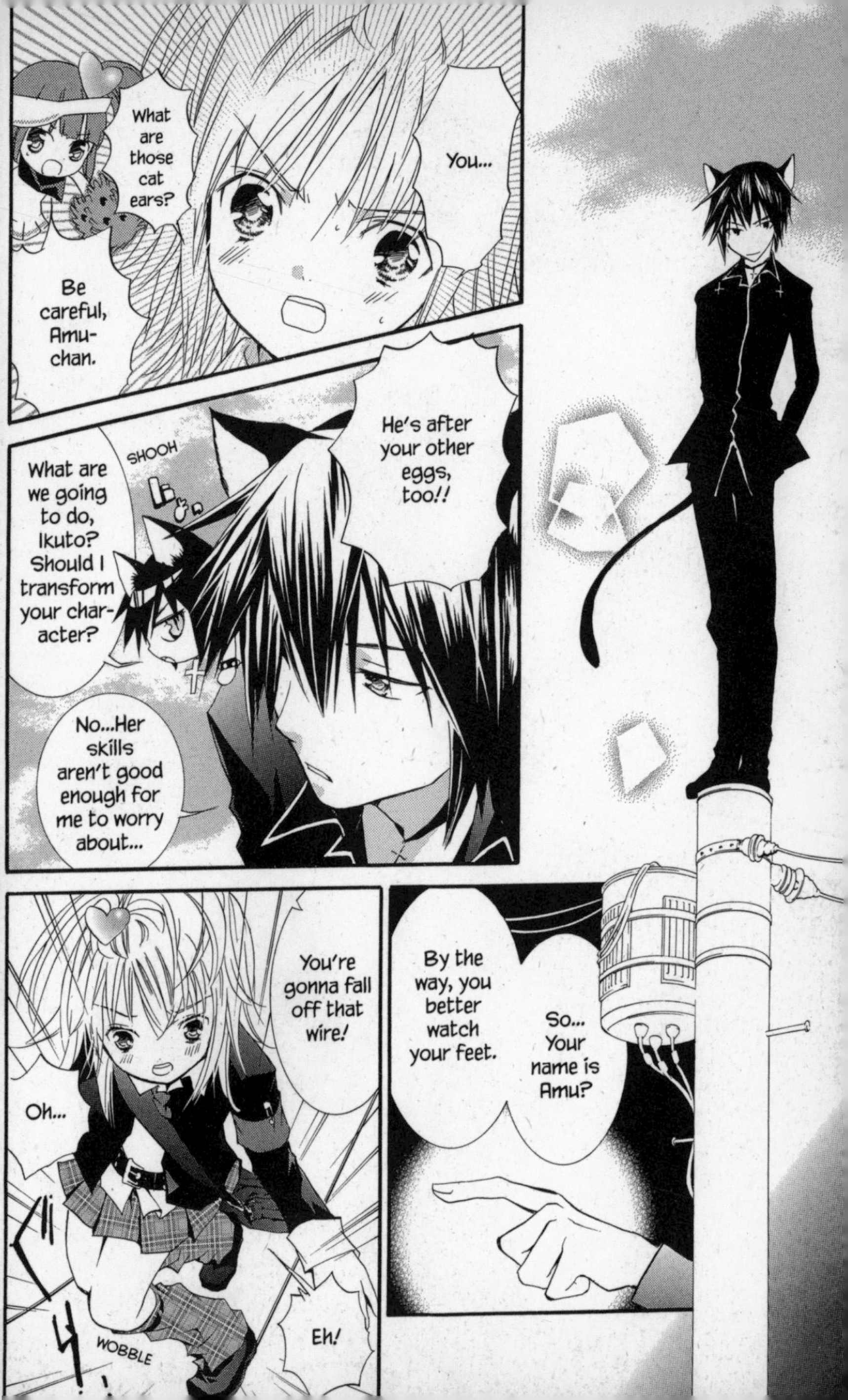
You...
What are those cat ears?
Be careful, Amu-chan.
He's after your other eggs, too!!
SHOOH
What are we going to do, Ikuto? Should I transform your character?
No...Her skills aren't good enough for me to worry about...
So... Your name is Amu?
By the way, you better watch your feet.
You're gonna fall off that wire!
Eh!
Oh...
WOBBLE

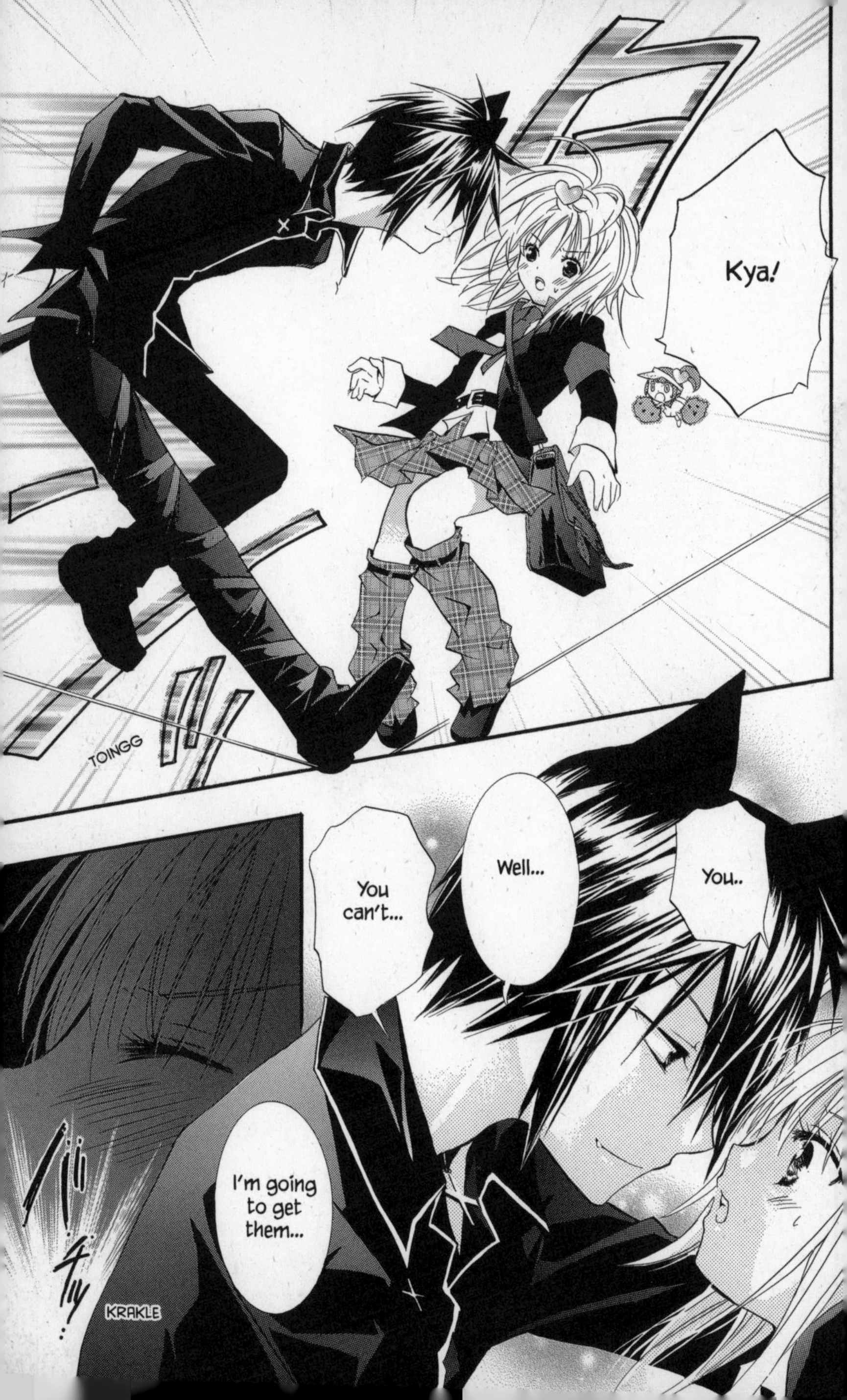
Kya!
TOINGG
You..
Well...
You can't...
I'm going to get them...
KRAKLE

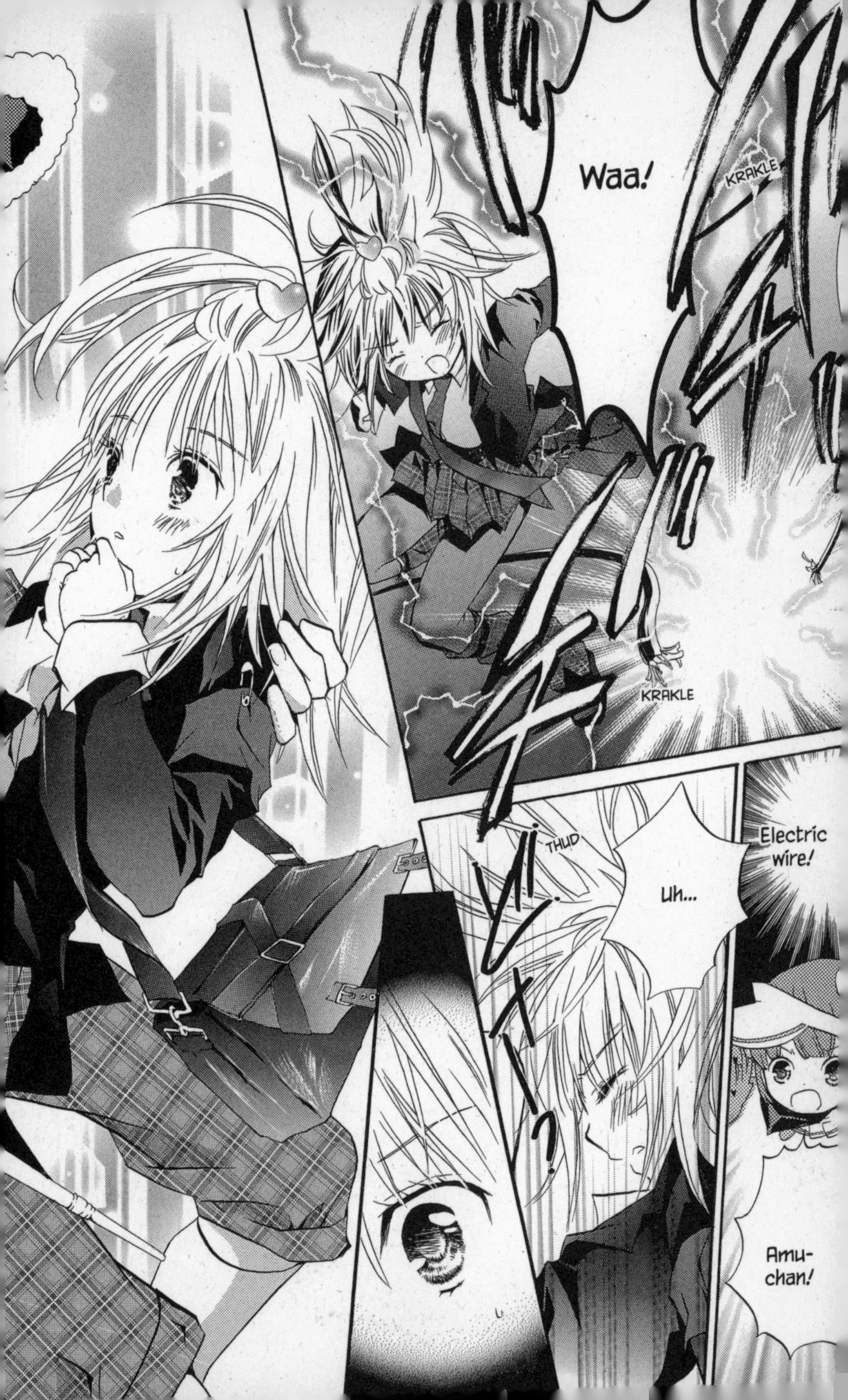
KRAKLE
Waa!
KRAKLE
Electric wire!
Amu-chan!
Uh...
THUD

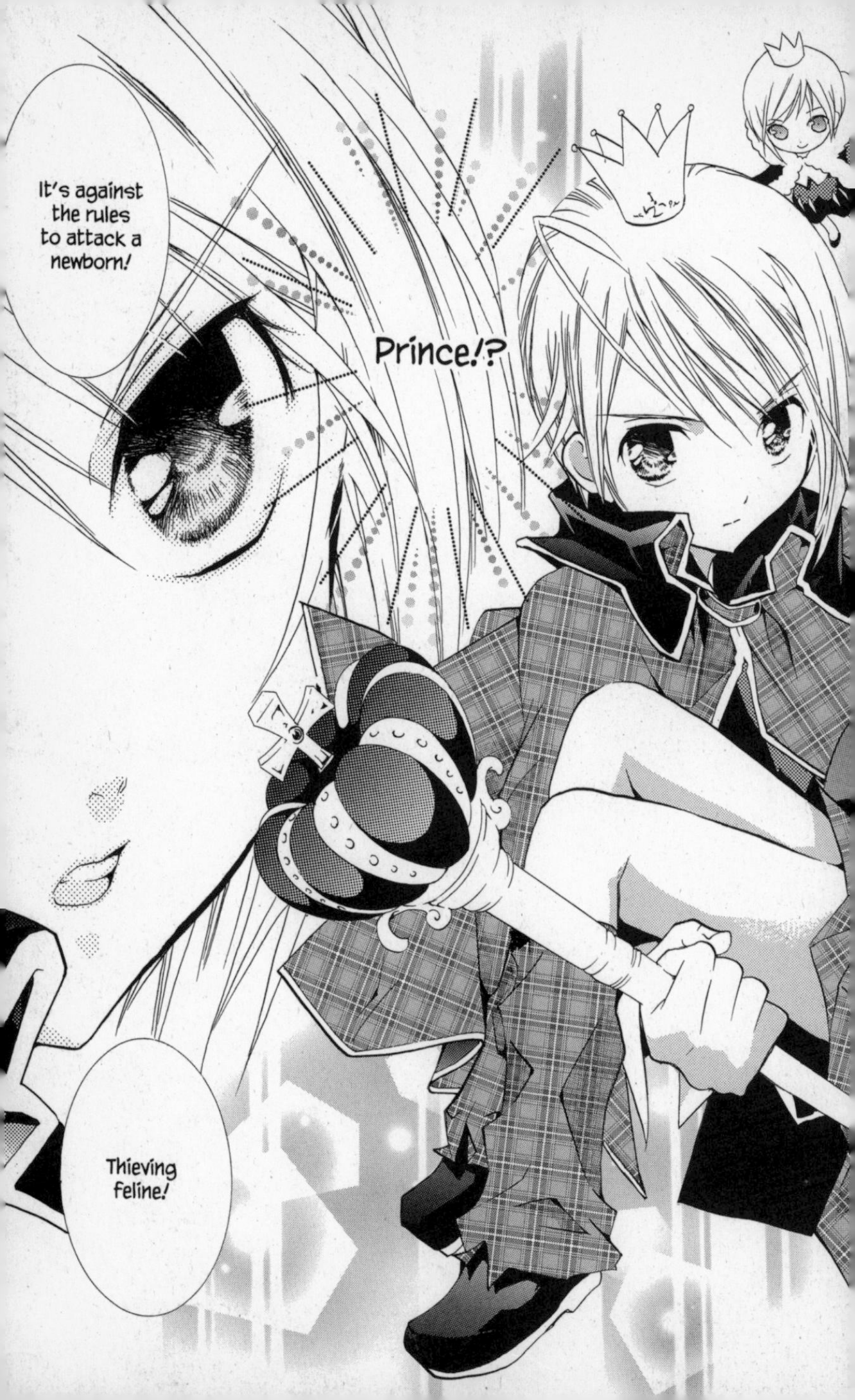
Prince!?
It's against the rules to attack a newborn!
Thieving feline!

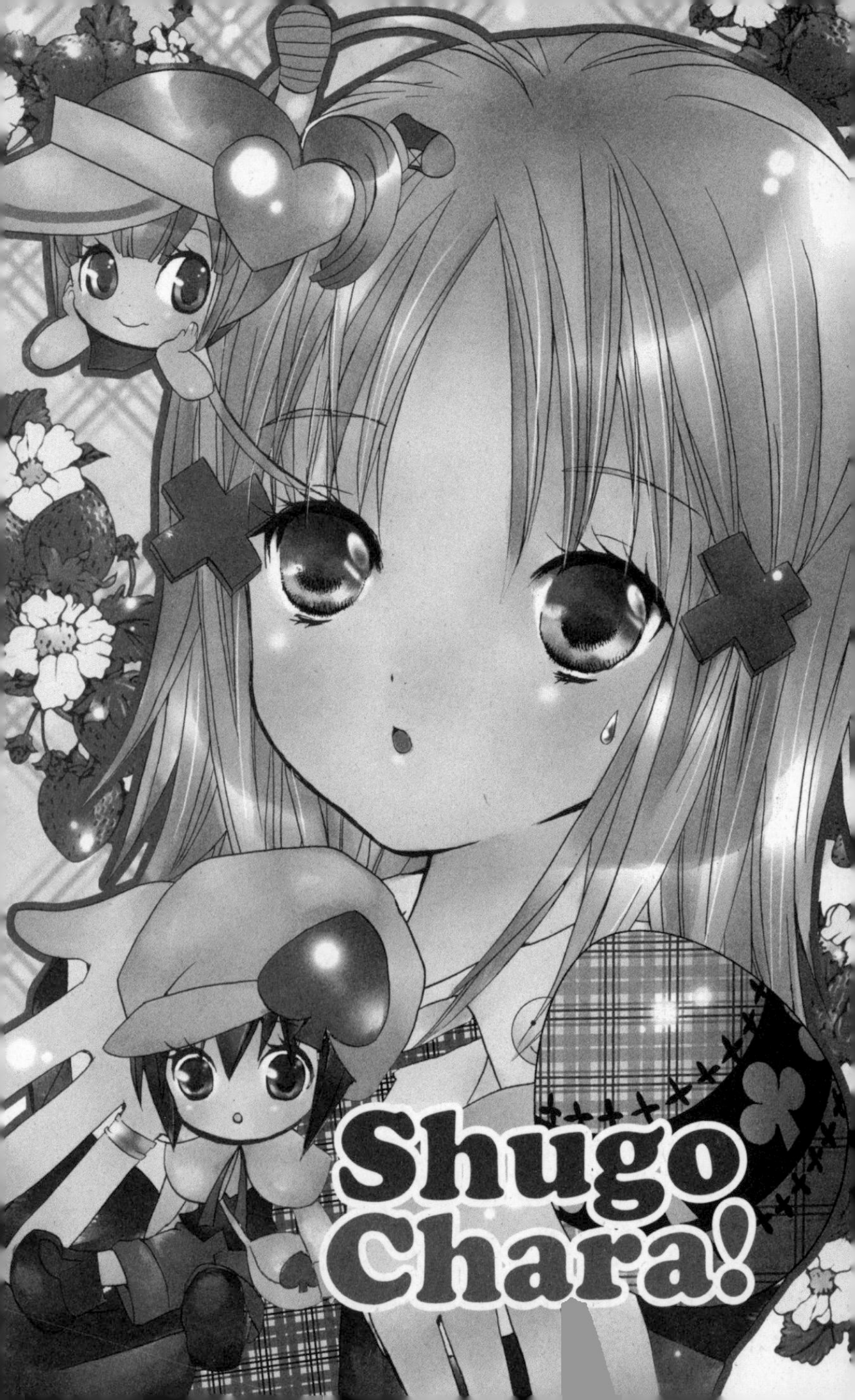
Shugo
Chara!

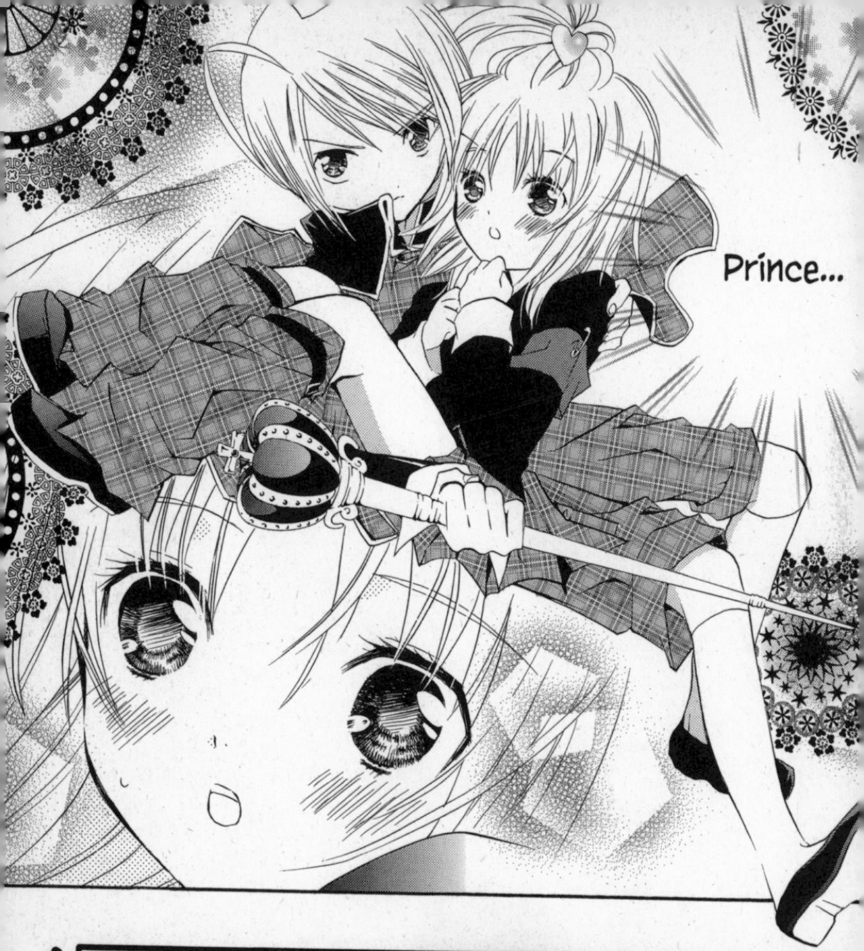
Prince...

Nice to meet you, everyone! We're PEACH-PIT.
We'd like to thank you for purchasing "Shugo Chara!" This is a free space we've been dreaming about having. We're very excited and hope you enjoy reading up to the end. ♡

We're thinking of using this free space to answer frequently asked questions from our fan mail (by the way...thank you for them!) or to just freely talk about whatever is on our mind.
Those of you who think, "the print's too small, I can't read it!" we apologize for that...please blow it up on a copy machine!

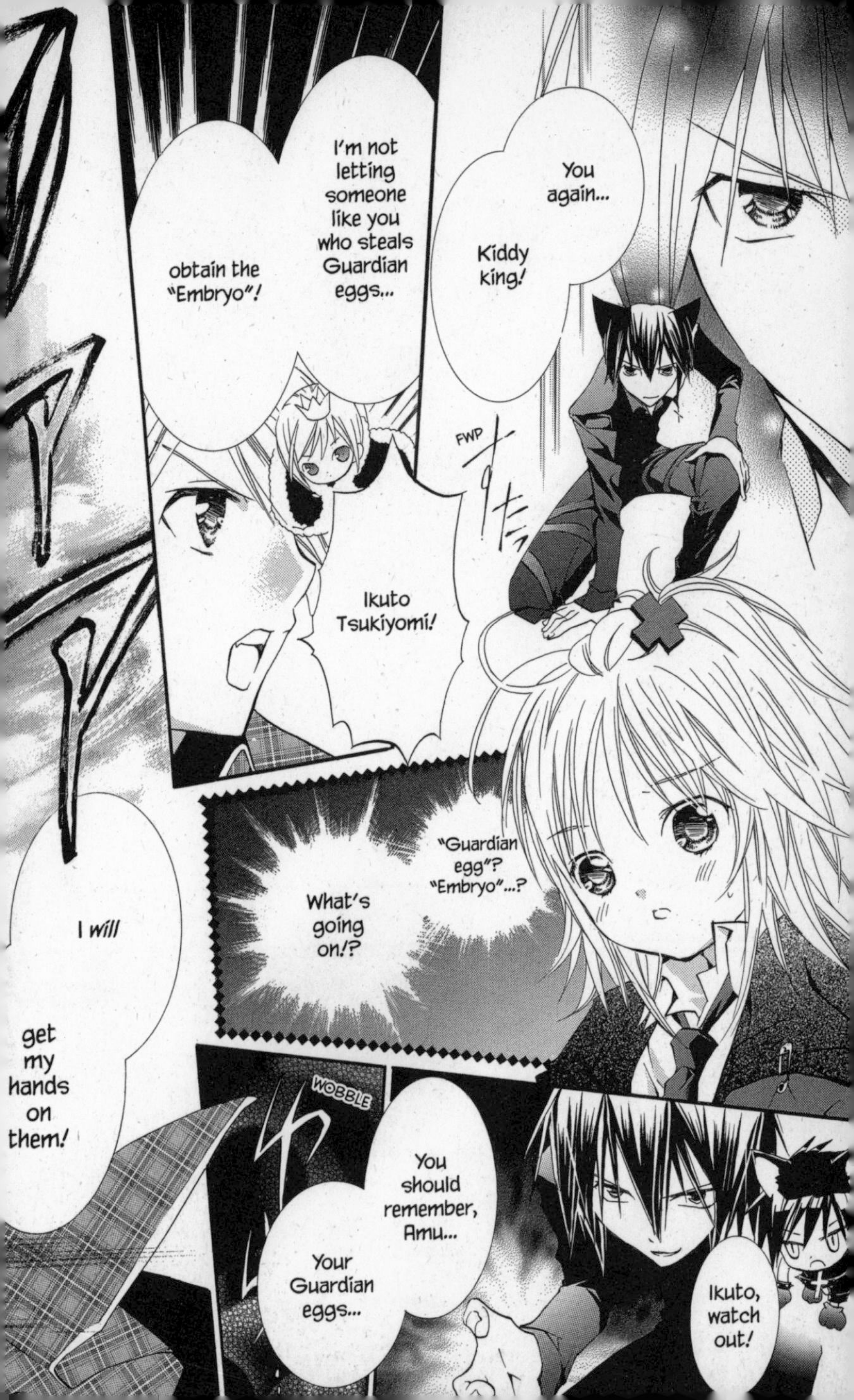
You again...
Kiddy king!
FWP
I'm not letting someone like you who steals Guardian eggs...
obtain the "Embryo"!
Ikuto Tsukiyomi!
"Guardian egg"? "Embryo"...?
What's going on!?
Ikuto, watch out!
You should remember, Amu...
Your Guardian eggs...
WOBBLE
I will
get my hands on them!

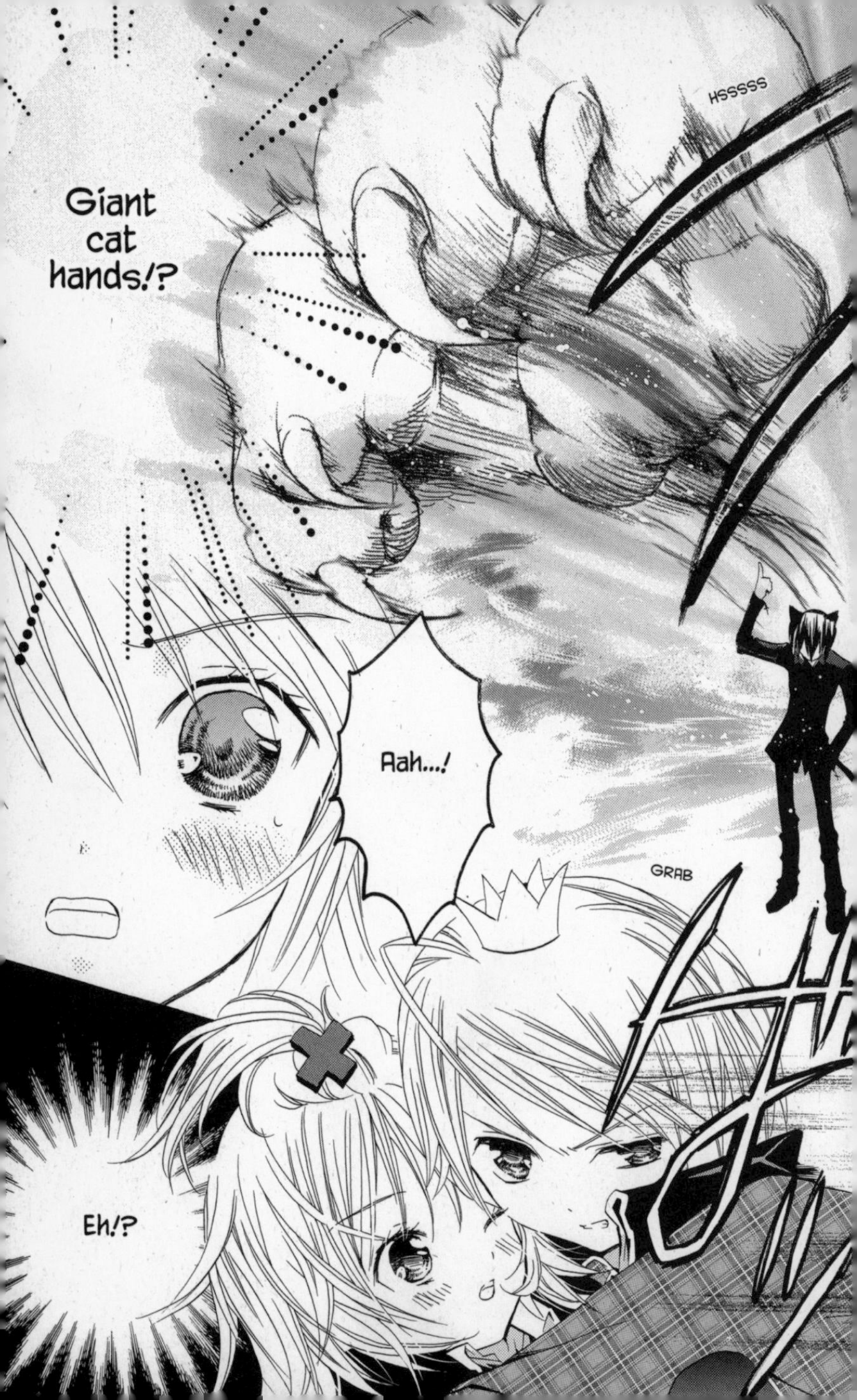
HSSSSS
Giant cat hands!?
Aah...!
GRAB
Eh!?

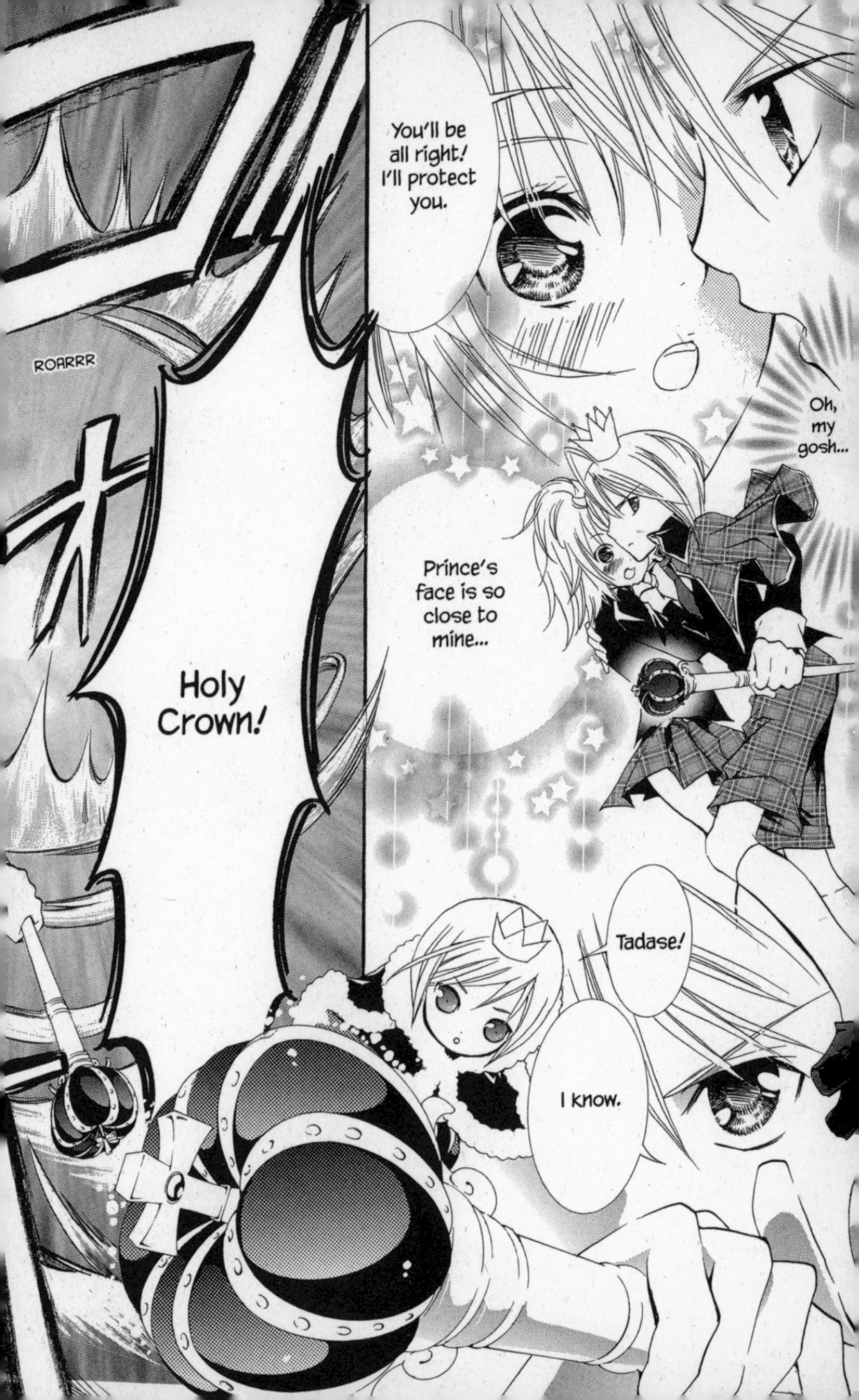
You'll be all right! I'll protect you.
Oh, my gosh...
Prince's face is so close to mine...
Tadase!
I know.
ROARRR
Holy Crown!

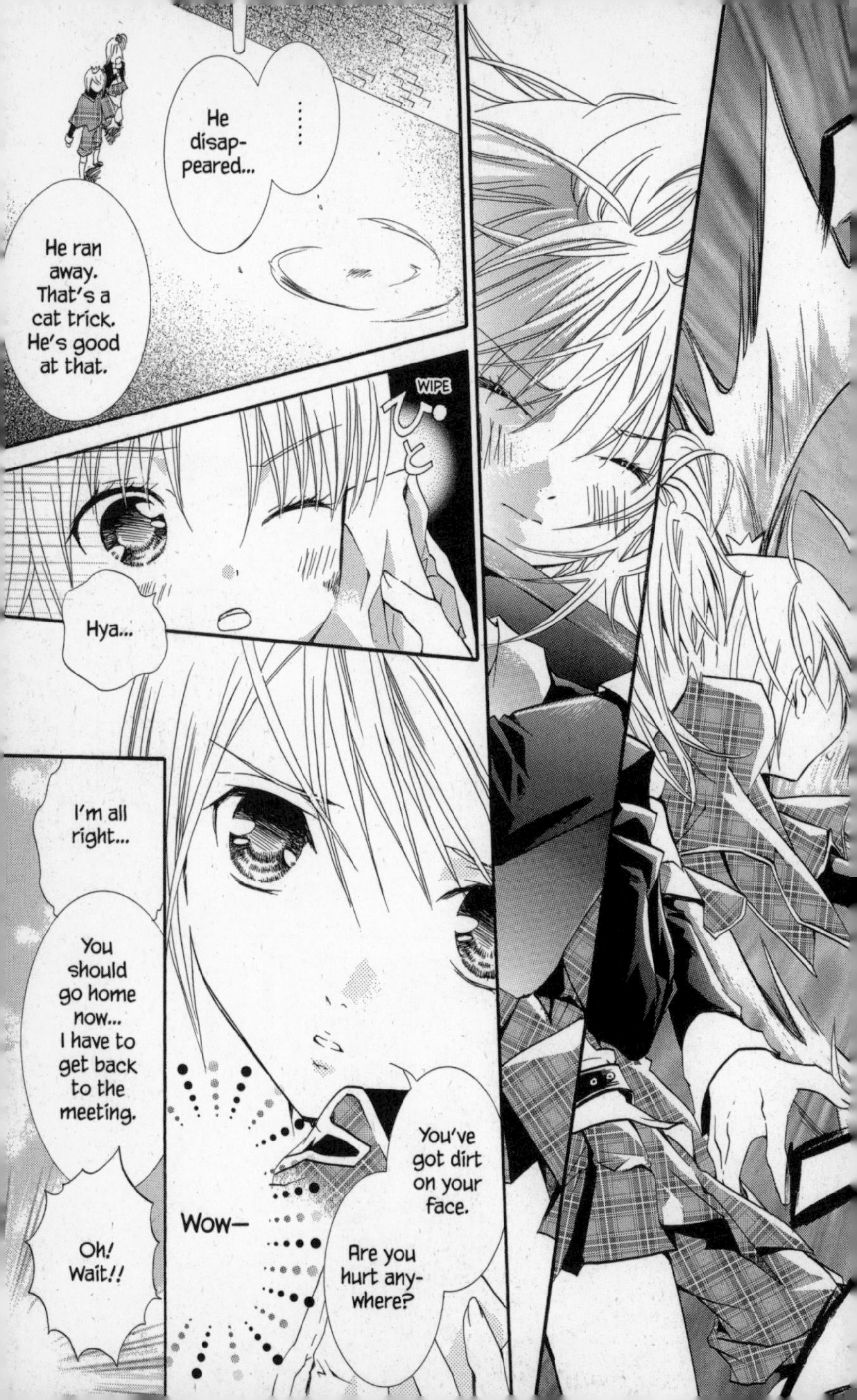
......
He disappeared...
He ran away. That's a cat trick. He's good at that.
ひと
WIPE
Hya...
You've got dirt on your face.
Are you hurt anywhere?
Wow—
I'm all right...
You should go home now... I have to get back to the meeting.
Oh! Wait!!

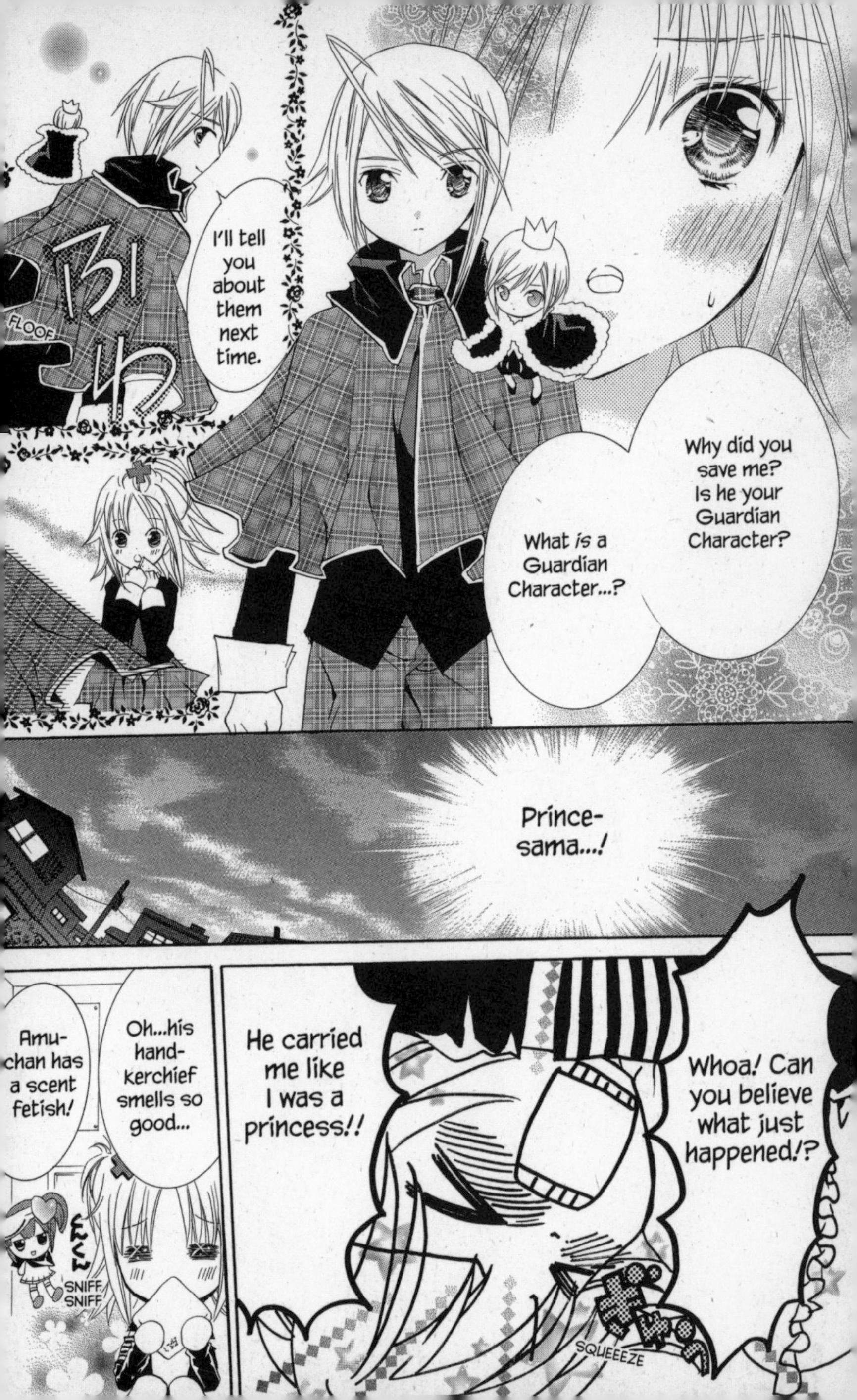
Why did you save me? Is he your Guardian Character?
What *is* a Guardian Character...?
I'll tell you about them next time.
FLOOF
Prince-sama...!
Whoa! Can you believe what just happened!?
He carried me like I was a princess!!
SQUEEEZE
Oh...his handkerchief smells so good...
Amu-chan has a scent fetish!
SNIFF SNIFF

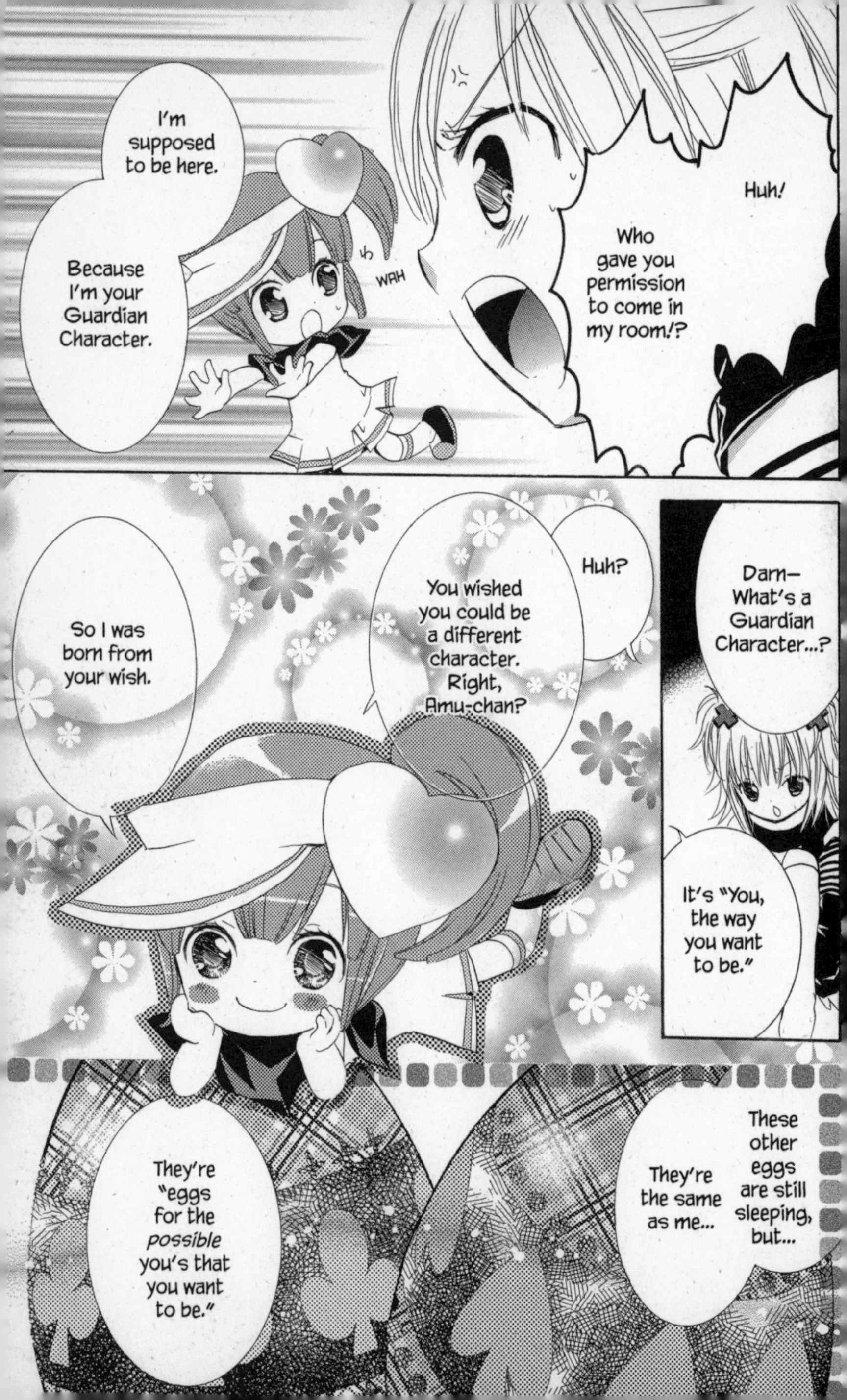
Huh!
Who gave you permission to come in my room!?
WAH
I'm supposed to be here.
Because I'm your Guardian Character.
Darn— What's a Guardian Character...?
It's "You, the way you want to be."
Huh?
You wished you could be a different character. Right, Amu-chan?
So I was born from your wish.
These other eggs are still sleeping, but...
They're the same as me...
They're "eggs for the *possible* you's that you want to be."

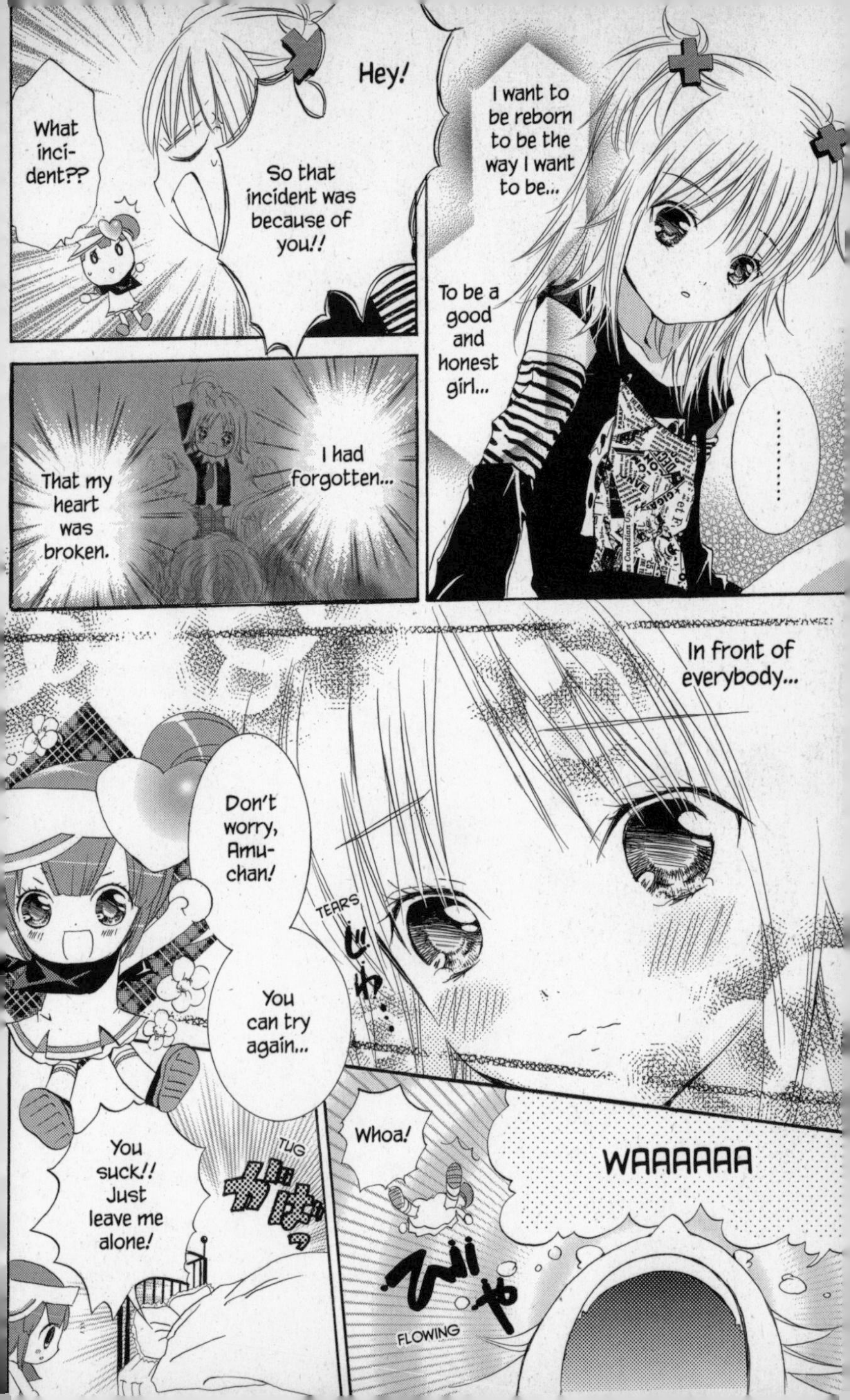
I want to be reborn to be the way I want to be...
To be a good and honest girl...
......
Hey!
So that incident was because of you!!
What incident??
I had forgotten...
That my heart was broken.
In front of everybody...
TEARS
Don't worry, Amu-chan!
You can try again...
WAAAAAA
FLOWING
Whoa!
TUG
You suck!! Just leave me alone!

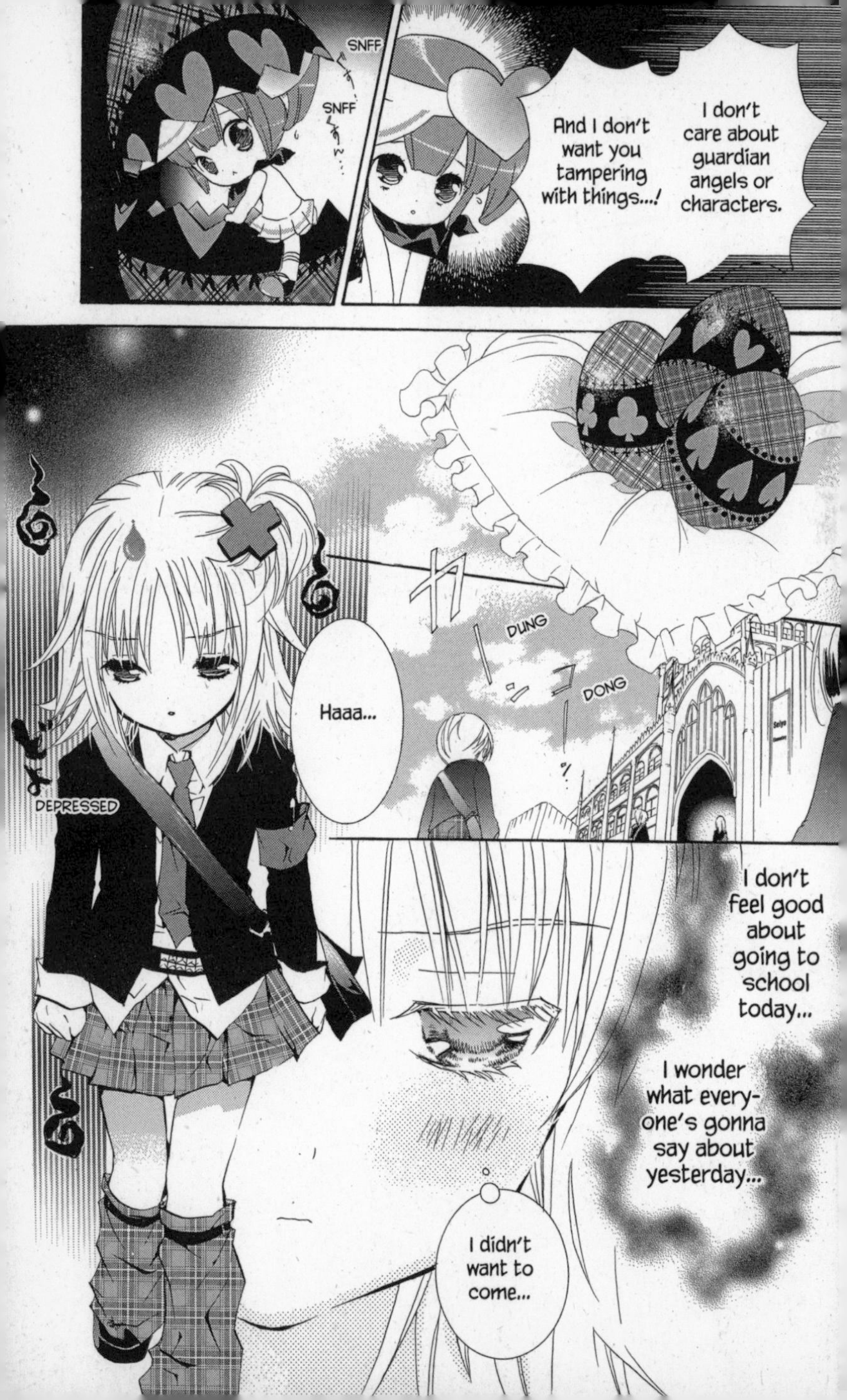
I don't care about guardian angels or characters.
And I don't want you tampering with things...!
SNFF
SNFF
DUNG
DONG
I don't feel good about going to school today...
I wonder what every-one's gonna say about yesterday...
I didn't want to come...
Haaa...
DEPRESSED

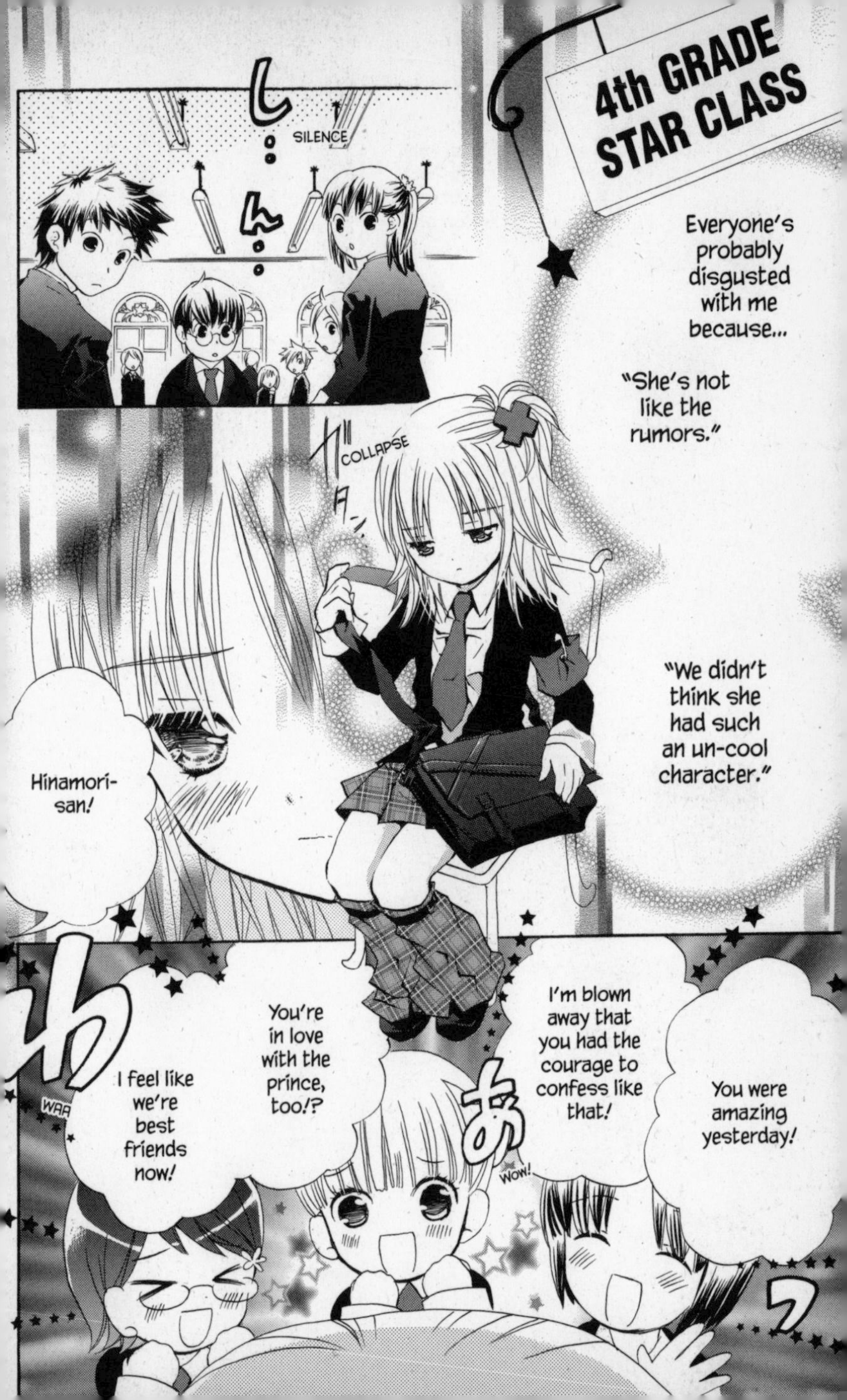
4th GRADE STAR CLASS
SILENCE
Everyone's probably disgusted with me because...
"She's not like the rumors."
"We didn't think she had such an un-cool character."
COLLAPSE
Hinamori-san!
You were amazing yesterday!
I'm blown away that you had the courage to confess like that!
WOW!
You're in love with the prince, too!?
I feel like we're best friends now!
WAA

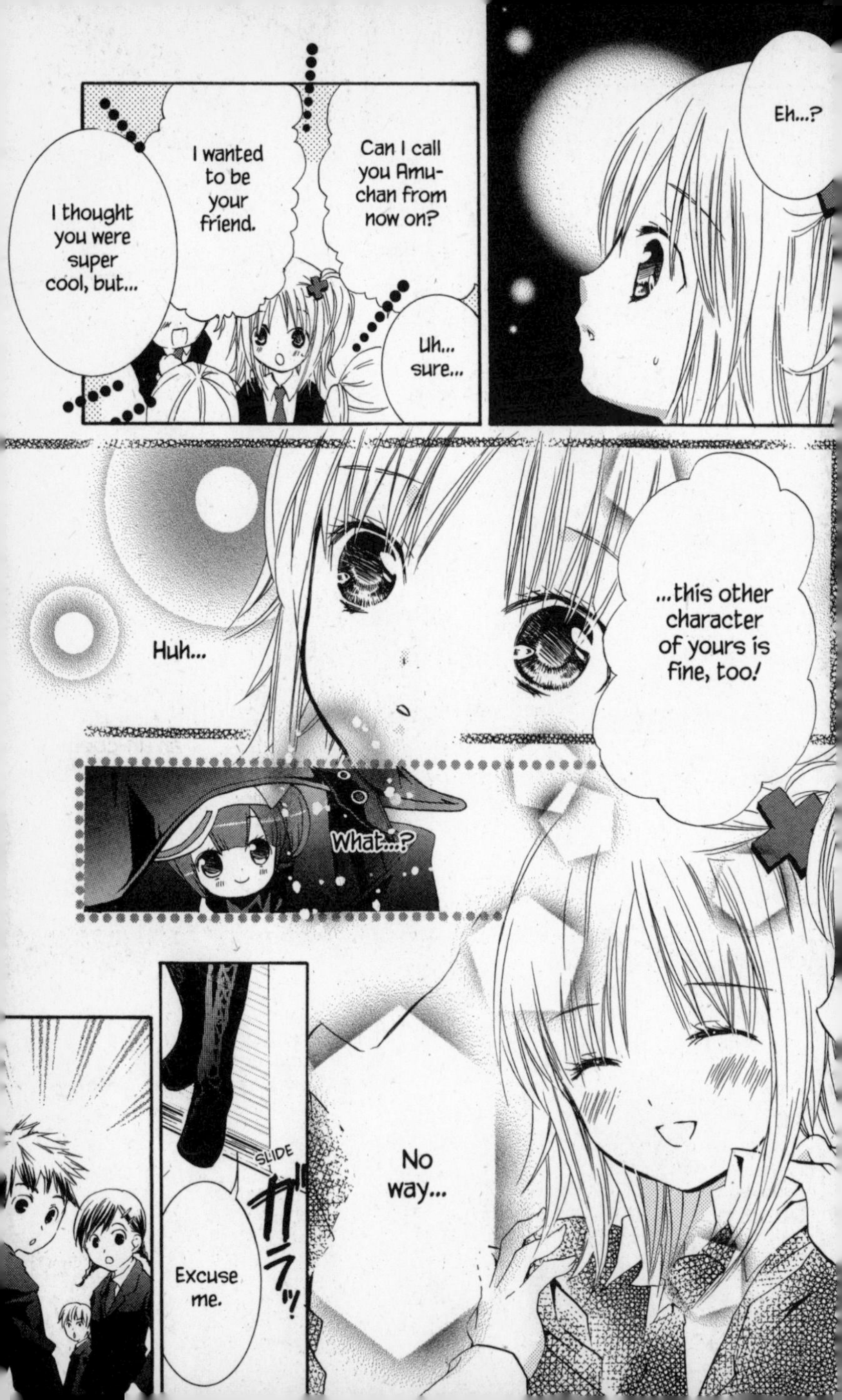

Eh...?
Can I call you Amu-chan from now on?
Uh... sure...
I wanted to be your friend.
I thought you were super cool, but...
...this other character of yours is fine, too!
Huh...
What...?
No way...
SLIDE
ガラッ
Excuse me.

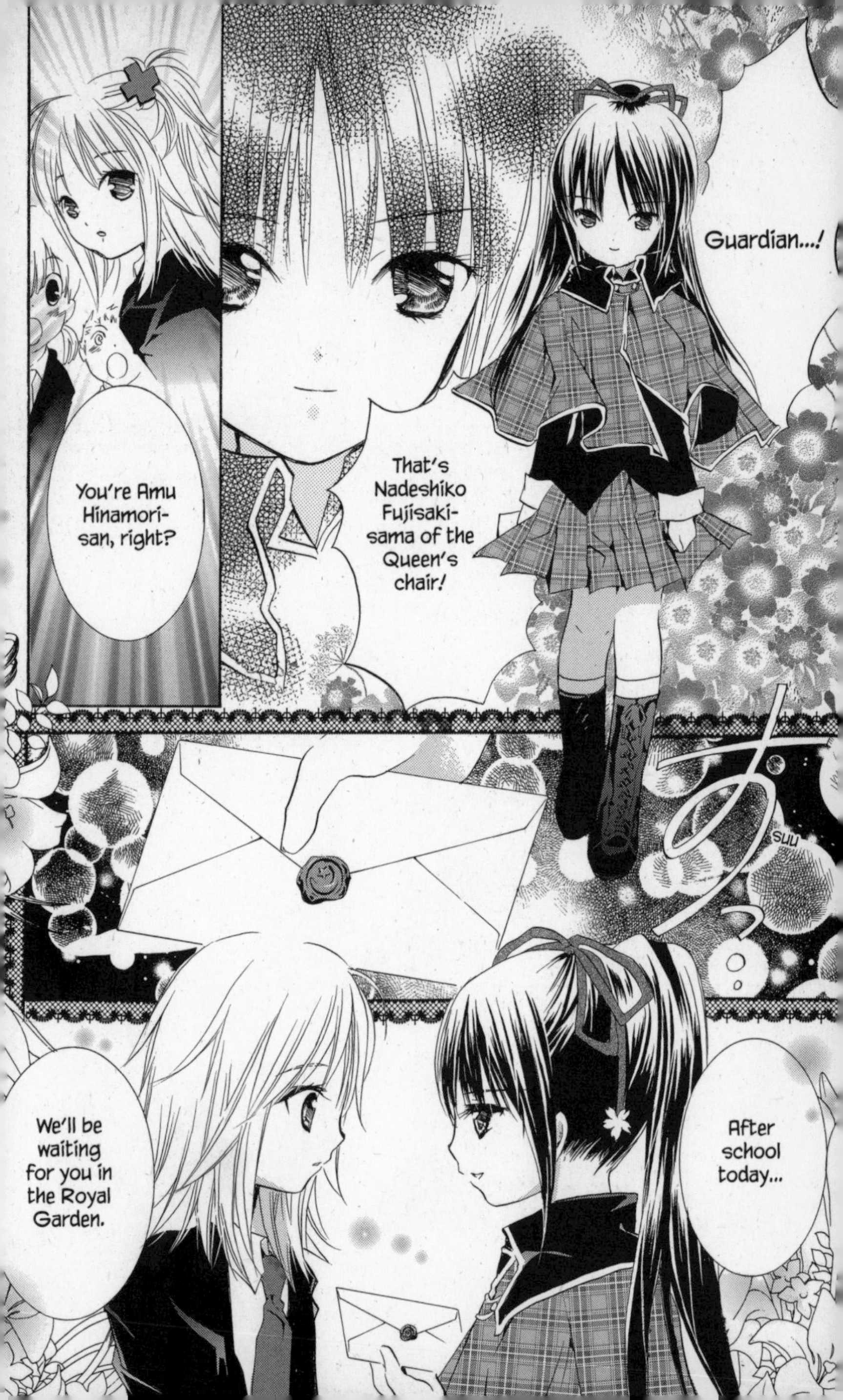
Guardian...!
That's Nadeshiko Fujisaki-sama of the Queen's chair!
You're Amu Hinamori-san, right?
SUU
After school today...
We'll be waiting for you in the Royal Garden.

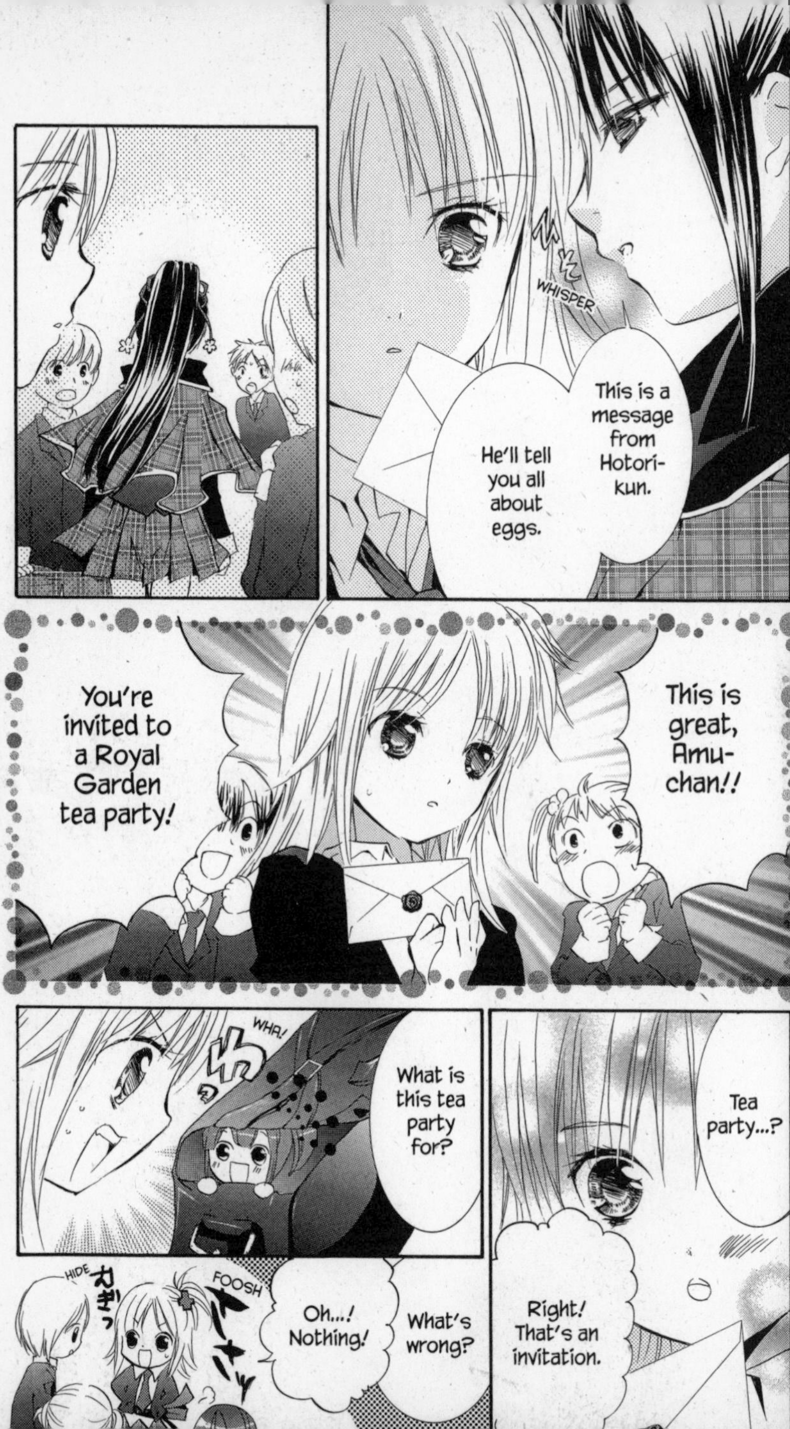
WHISPER
This is a message from Hotori-kun.
He'll tell you all about eggs.
This is great, Amu-chan!!
You're invited to a Royal Garden tea party!
Tea party...?
Right! That's an invitation.
WHA!
What is this tea party for?
What's wrong?
Oh...! Nothing!
FOOSH
HIDE

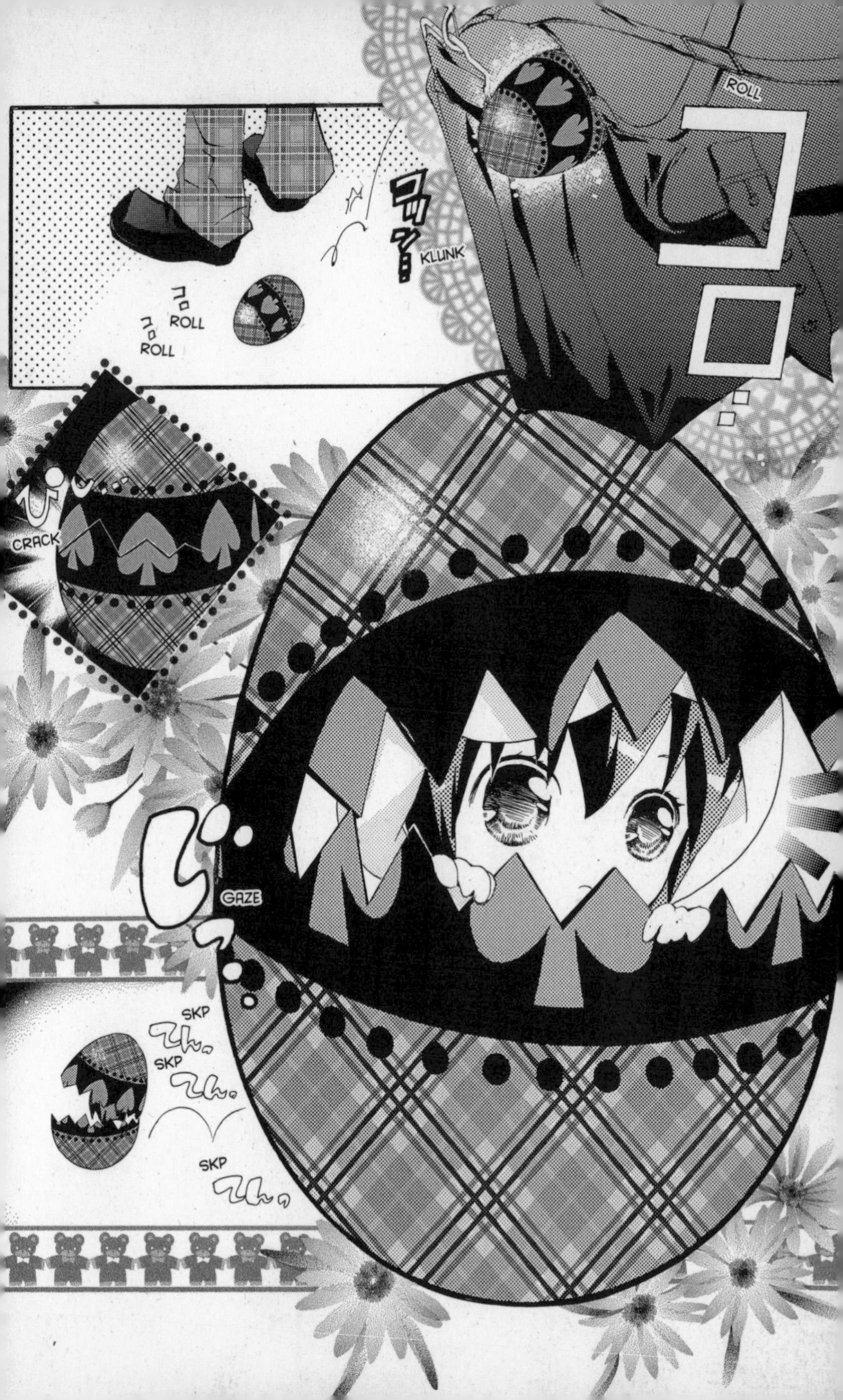
ROLL
KLUNK
ROLL
ROLL
CRACK
GAZE
SKP
SKP
SKP

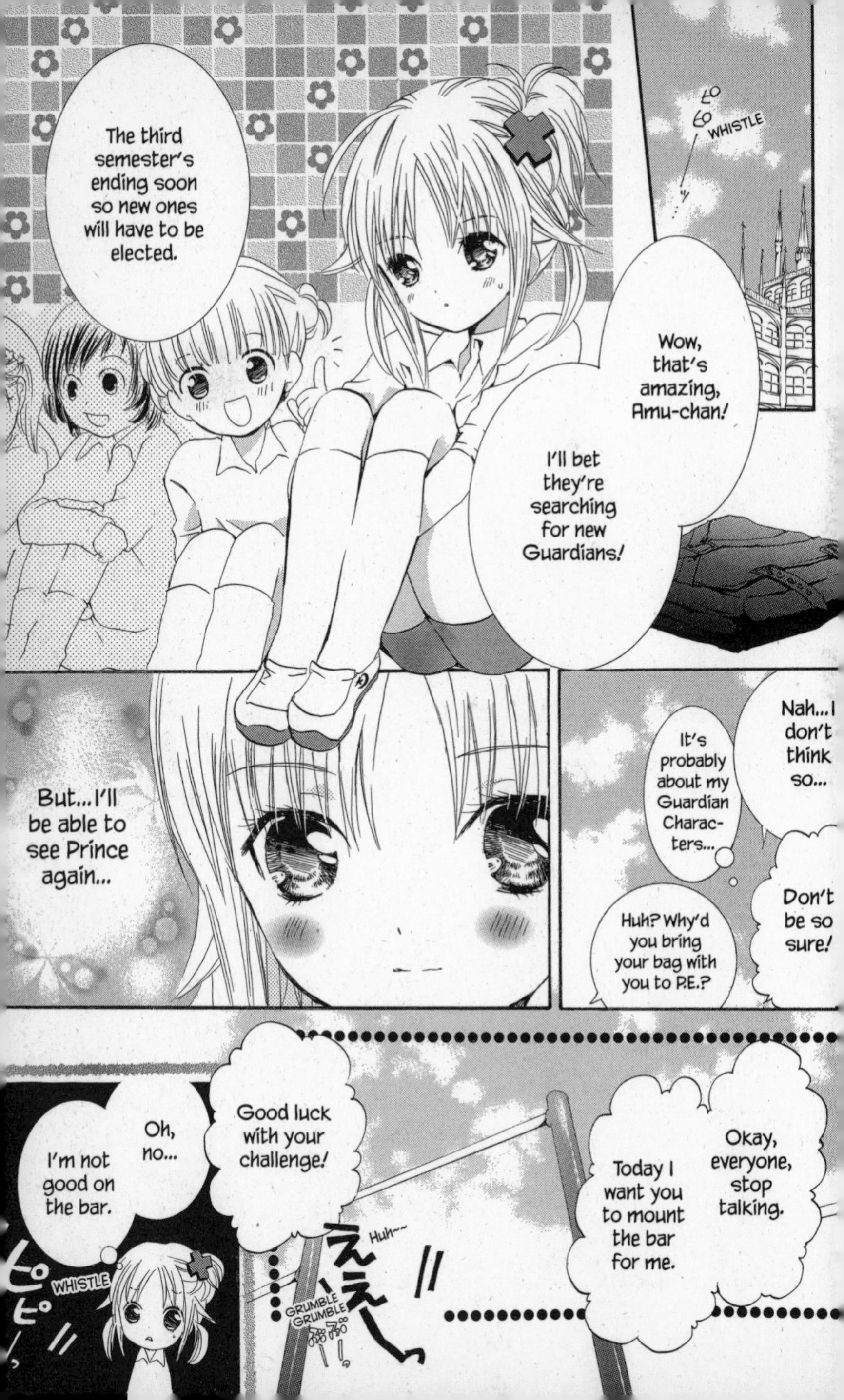
WHISTLE
Wow, that's amazing, Amu-chan!
I'll bet they're searching for new Guardians!
The third semester's ending soon so new ones will have to be elected.
Nah...I don't think so...
It's probably about my Guardian Characters...
Don't be so sure!
Huh? Why'd you bring your bag with you to P.E.?
But...I'll be able to see Prince again...
Okay, everyone, stop talking.
Today I want you to mount the bar for me.
Huh~~
GRUMBLE GRUMBLE
Good luck with your challenge!
Oh, no...
I'm not good on the bar.
WHISTLE

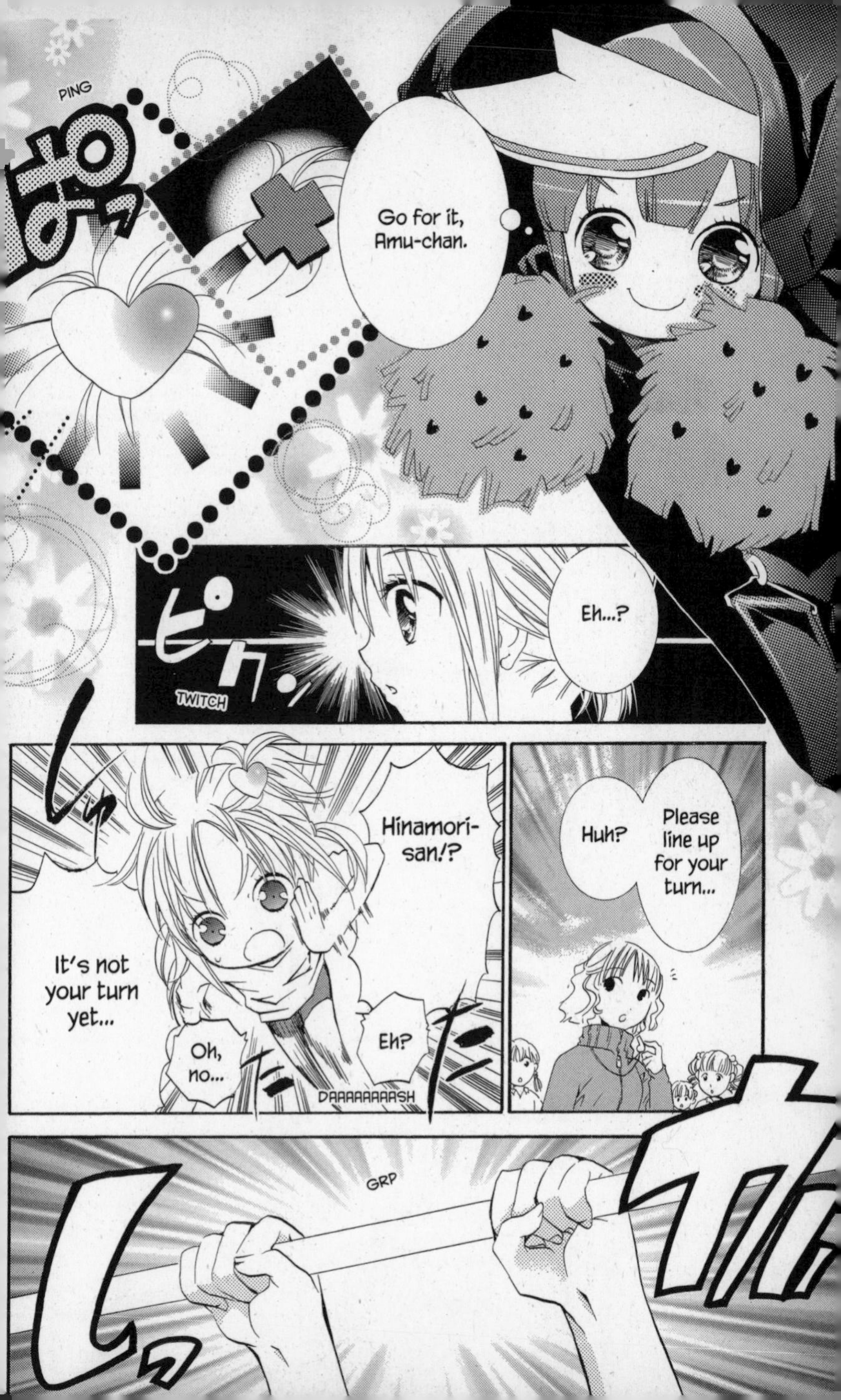

Go for it, Amu-chan.
PING
Eh...?
TWITCH
Hinamori-san!?
It's not your turn yet...
Eh?
Oh, no...
DAAAAAAAASH
Please line up for your turn...
Huh?
GRP

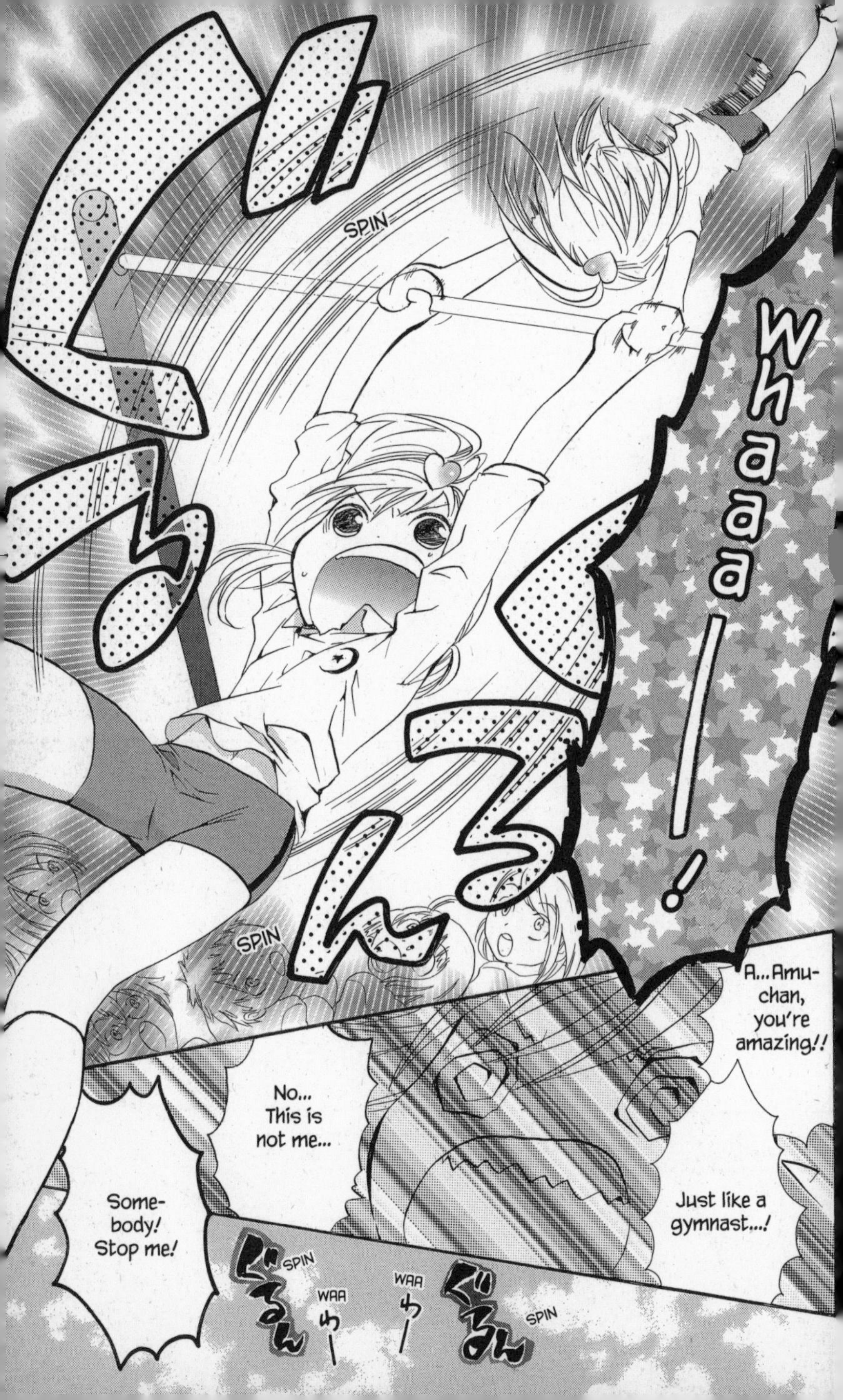

Whaaaa—!
SPIN
SPIN
A...Amu-chan, you're amazing!!
Just like a gymnast...!
No... This is not me...
Some-body! Stop me!
SPIN
WAA
WAA
SPIN

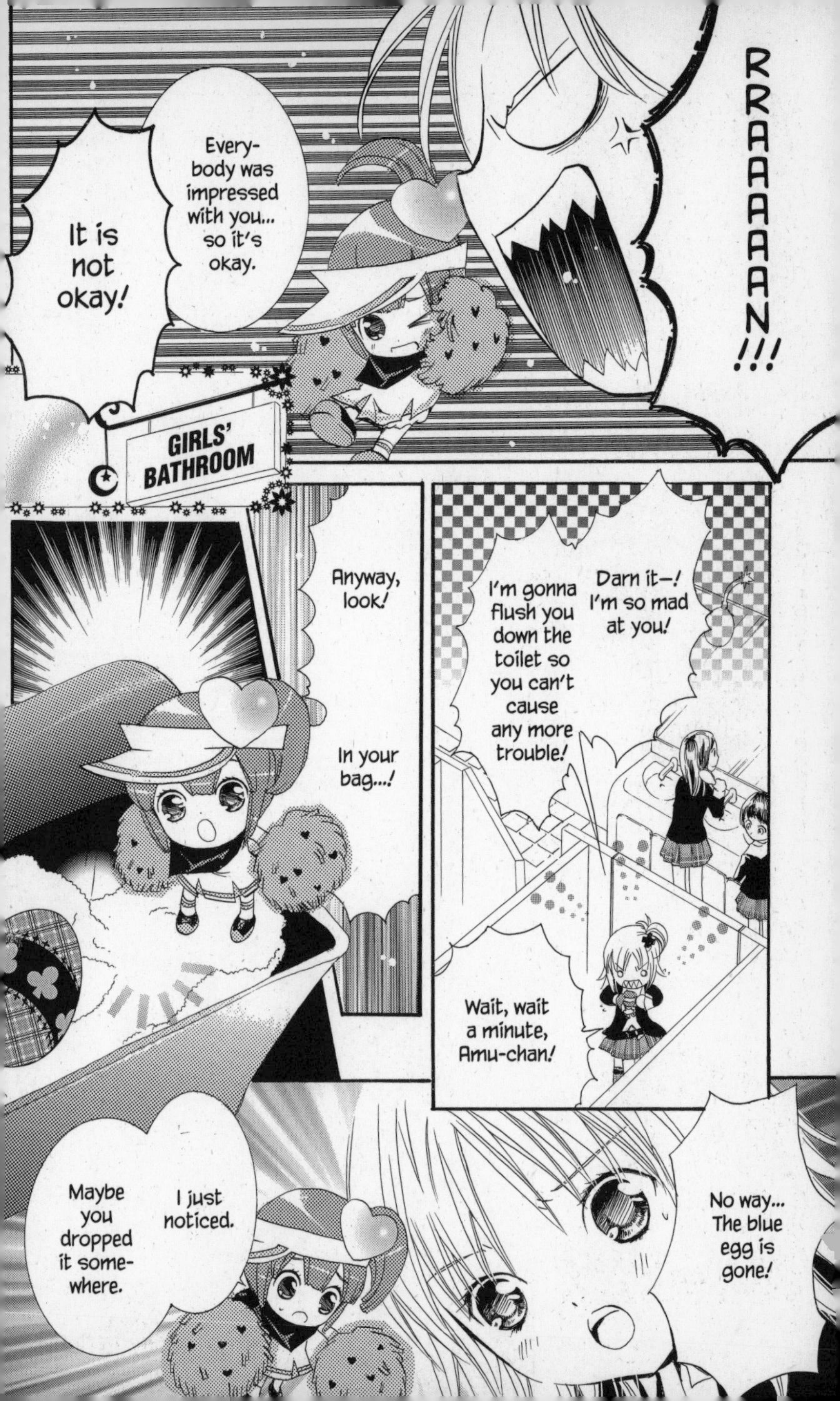
RRAAAAAN!!!
Every-body was impressed with you... so it's okay.
It is not okay!
GIRLS' BATHROOM
Darn it—! I'm so mad at you!
I'm gonna flush you down the toilet so you can't cause any more trouble!
Wait, wait a minute, Amu-chan!
Anyway, look!
In your bag...!
No way... The blue egg is gone!
I just noticed.
Maybe you dropped it some-where.

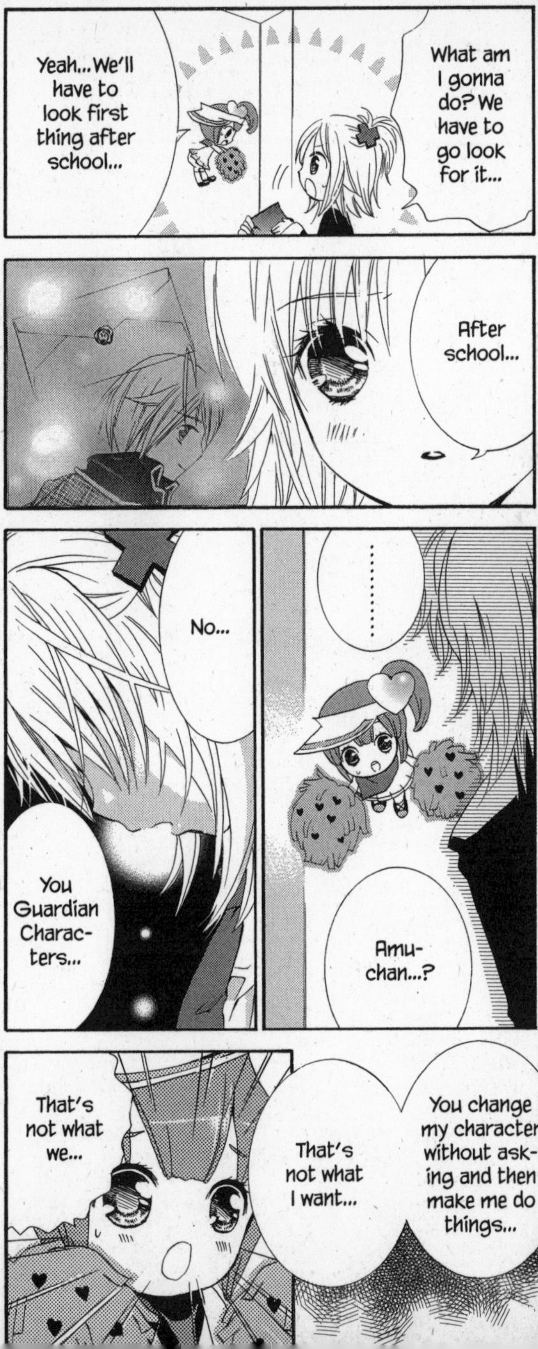
What am I gonna do? We have to go look for it...
Yeah...We'll have to look first thing after school...
After school...
......
Amu-chan...?
No...
You Guardian Characters...
You change my character without asking and then make me do things...
That's not what I want...
That's not what we...

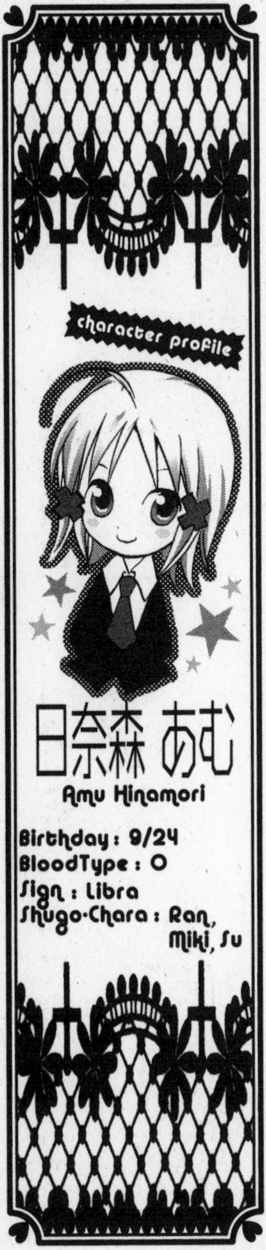
character profile
日奈森 あむ
Amu Hinamori
Birthday : 9/24
BloodType : O
Sign : Libra
Shugo-Chara : Ran, Miki, Su

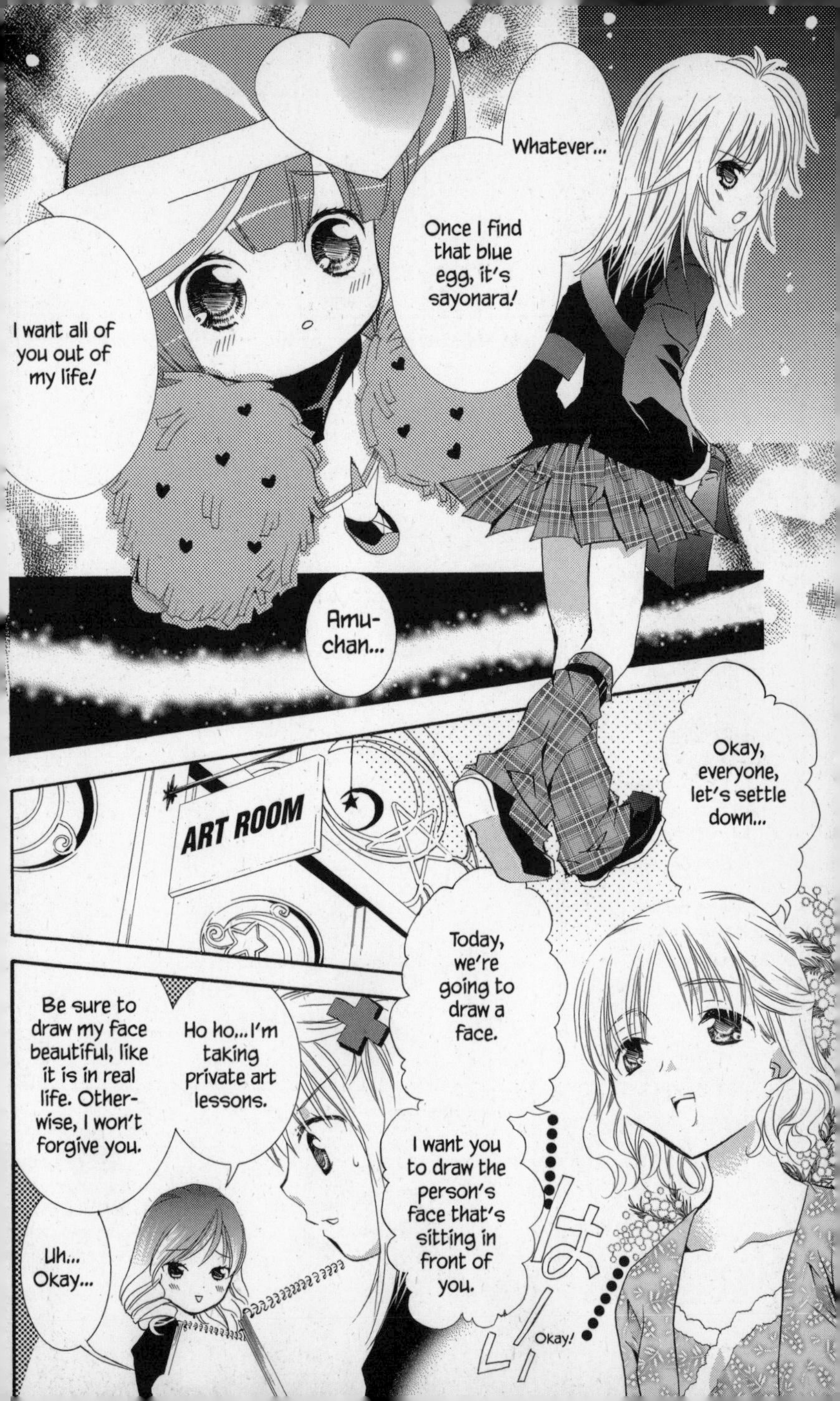

Whatever...
Once I find that blue egg, it's sayonara!
I want all of you out of my life!
Amu-chan...
Okay, everyone, let's settle down...
ART ROOM
Today, we're going to draw a face.
I want you to draw the person's face that's sitting in front of you.
はーい
Okay!
Ho ho...I'm taking private art lessons.
Be sure to draw my face beautiful, like it is in real life. Otherwise, I won't forgive you.
Uh... Okay...

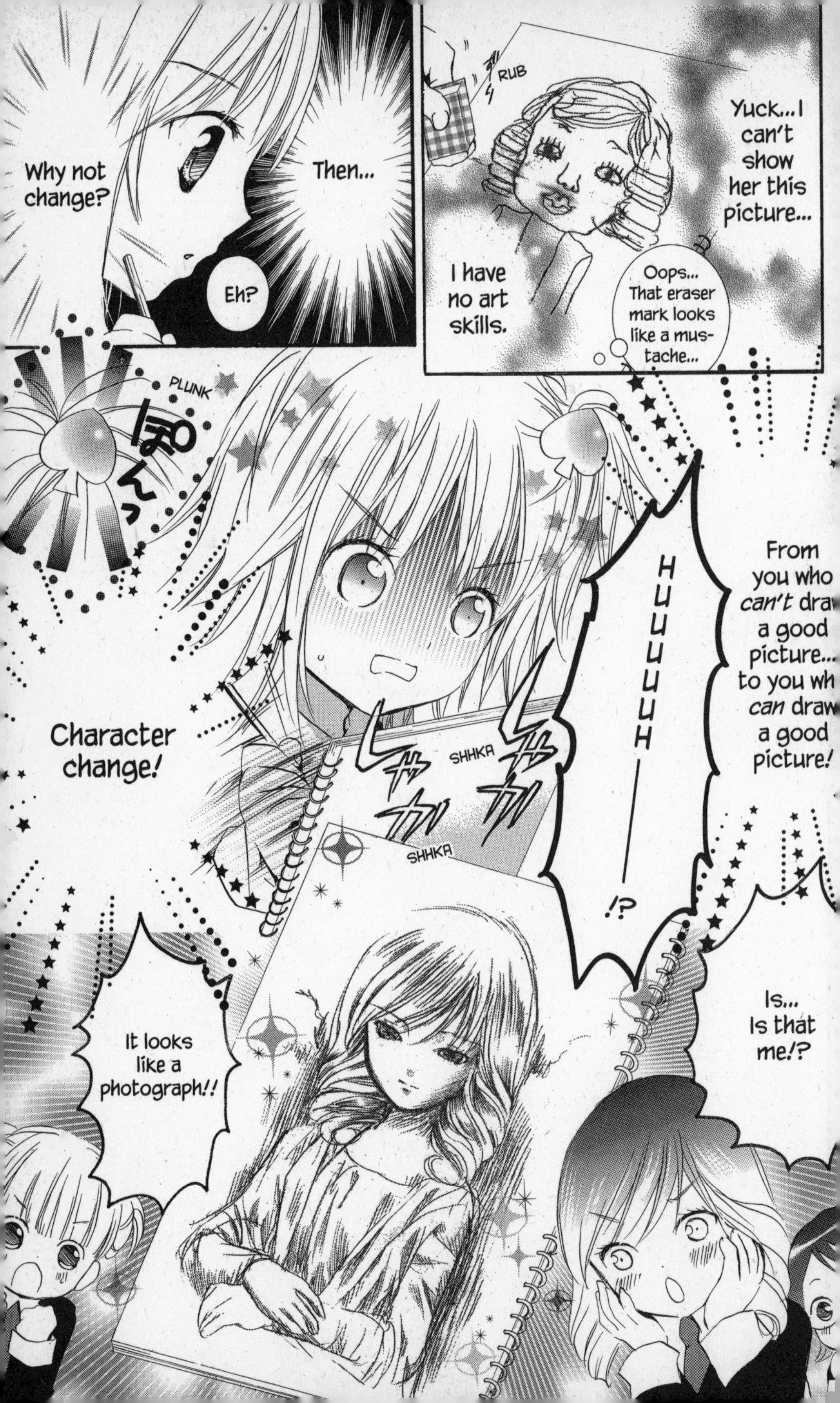
RUB
Yuck...I can't show her this picture...
I have no art skills.
Oops... That eraser mark looks like a mustache...
Then...
Why not change?
Eh?
From you who *can't* dra a good picture... to you wh *can* draw a good picture!
HUUUUUUH——!?
SHHKA
SHHKA
PLUNK
Character change!
Is... Is that me!?
It looks like a photograph!!

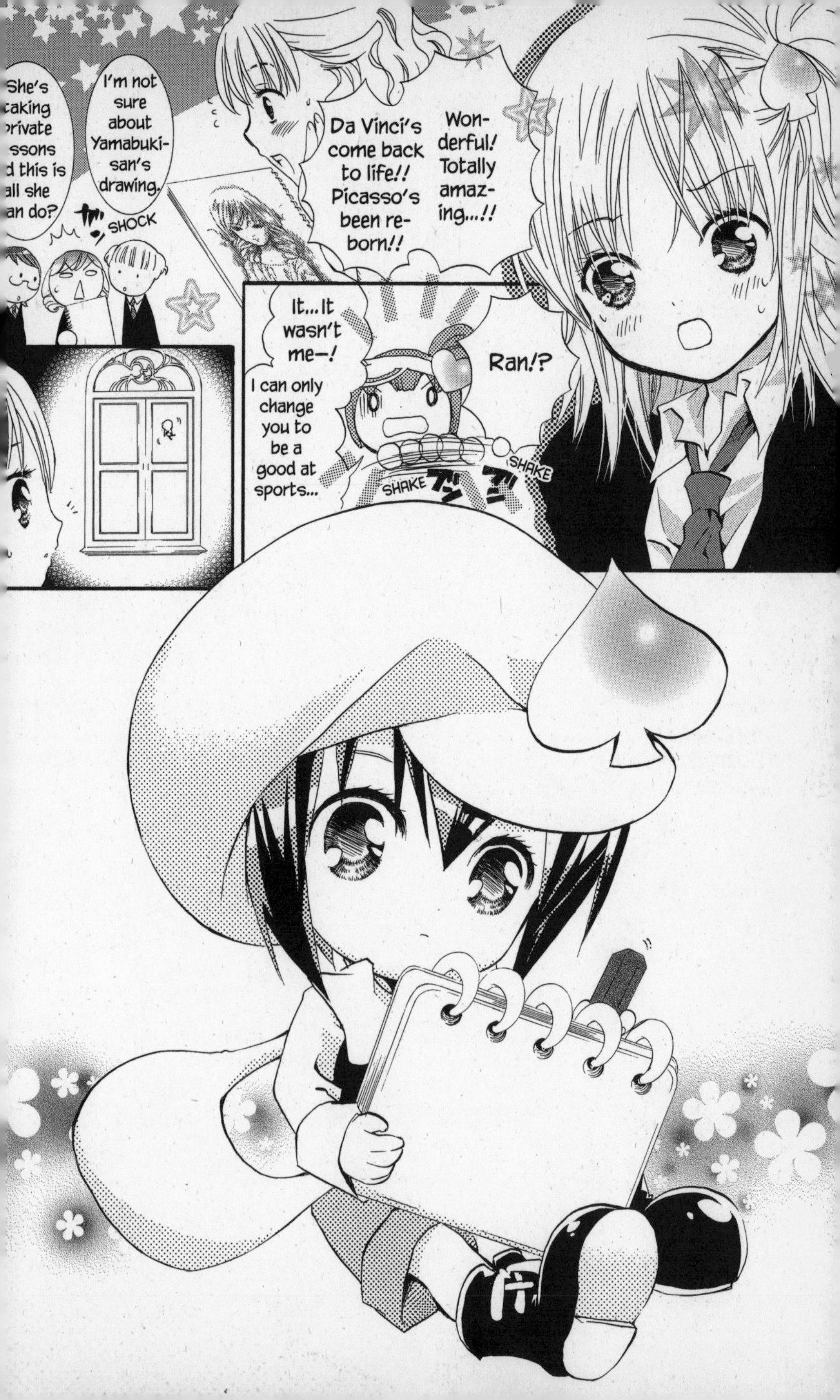

Wonderful! Totally amazing...!!
Da Vinci's come back to life!! Picasso's been reborn!!
I'm not sure about Yamabuki-san's drawing.
She's aking rivate ssons d this is all she an do?
SHOCK
Ran!?
It...It wasn't me—!
I can only change you to be a good at sports...
SHAKE
SHAKE

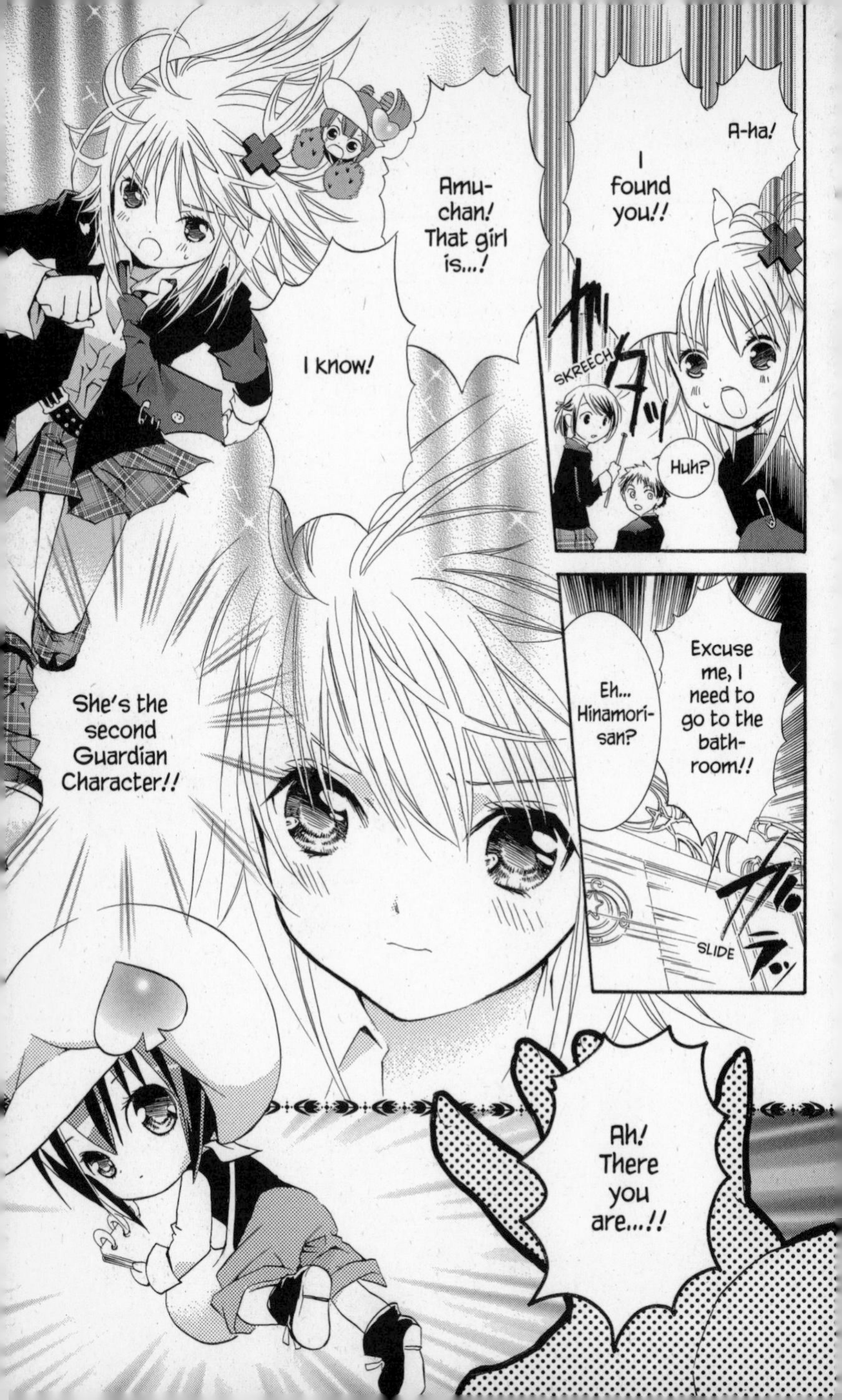
A-ha!
I found you!!
SKREECH
Huh?
Amu-chan! That girl is...!
I know!
Excuse me, I need to go to the bathroom!!
Eh... Hinamori-san?
SLIDE
She's the second Guardian Character!!
Ah! There you are...!!

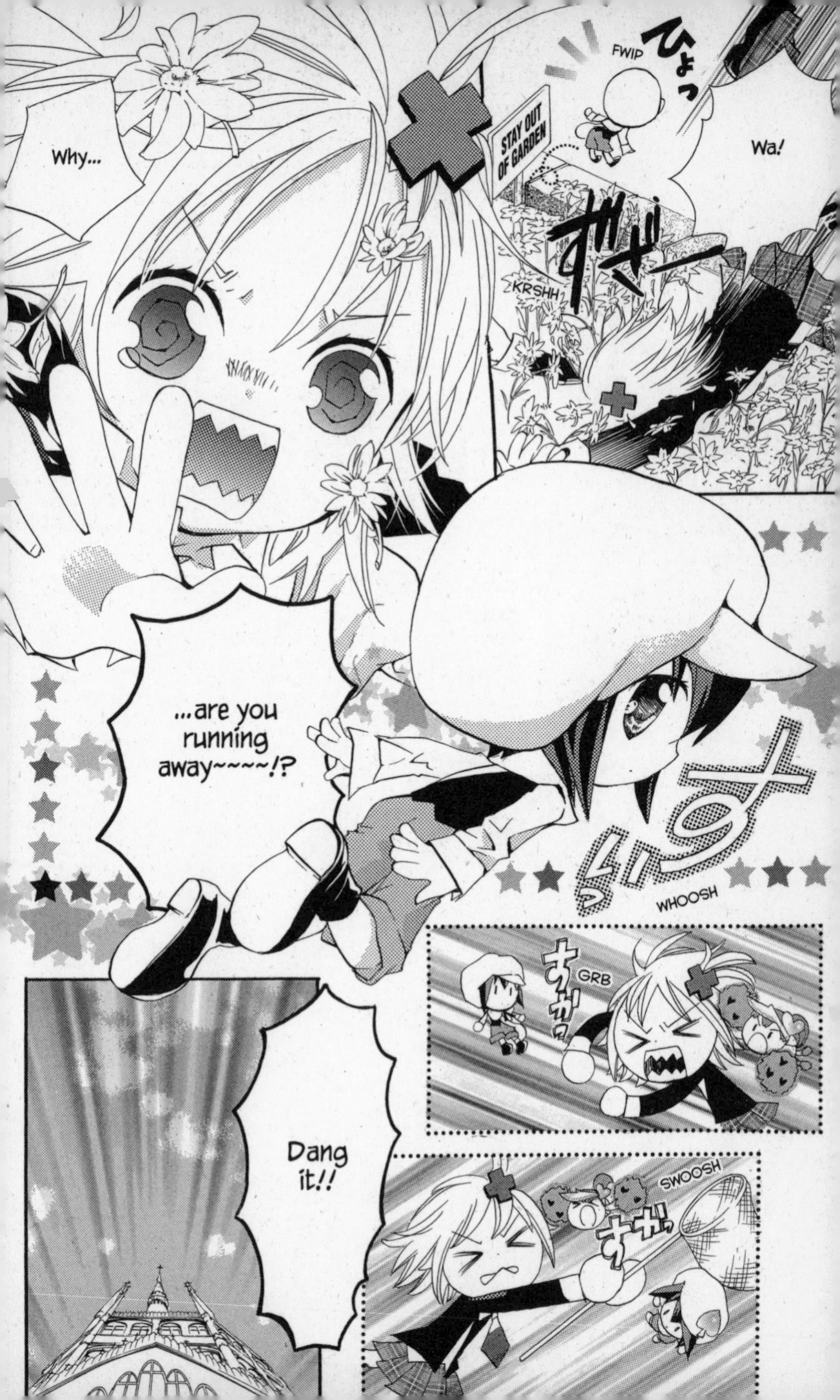
FWIP
ひょっ
Wa!
STAY OUT OF GARDEN
ずざー
KRSHH
Why...
...are you running away~~~~!?
WHOOSH
GRB
SWOOSH
すかっ
Dang it!!

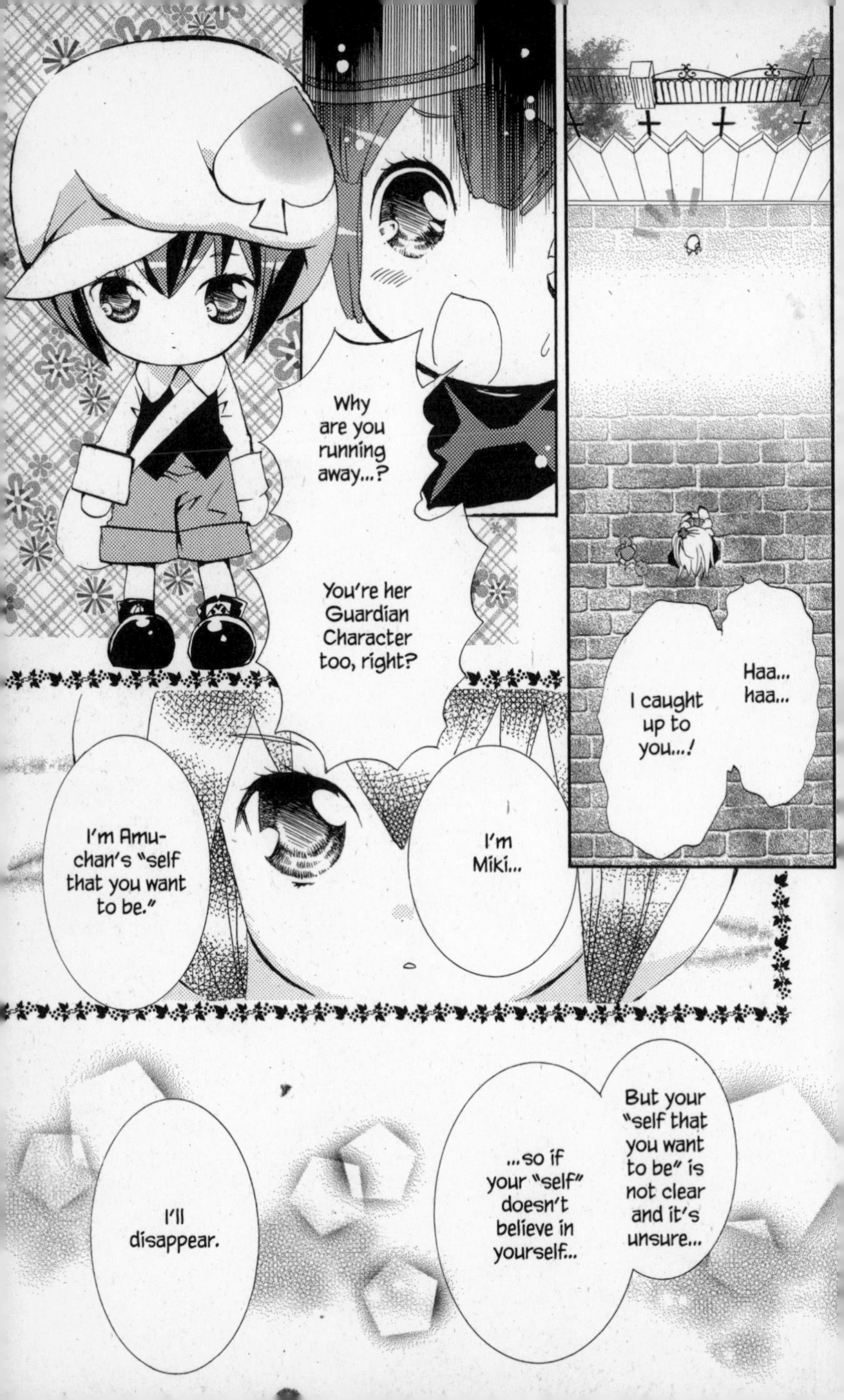
Haa... haa...
I caught up to you...!
Why are you running away...?
You're her Guardian Character too, right?
I'm Miki...
I'm Amu-chan's "self that you want to be."
But your "self that you want to be" is not clear and it's unsure...
...so if your "self" doesn't believe in yourself...
I'll disappear.

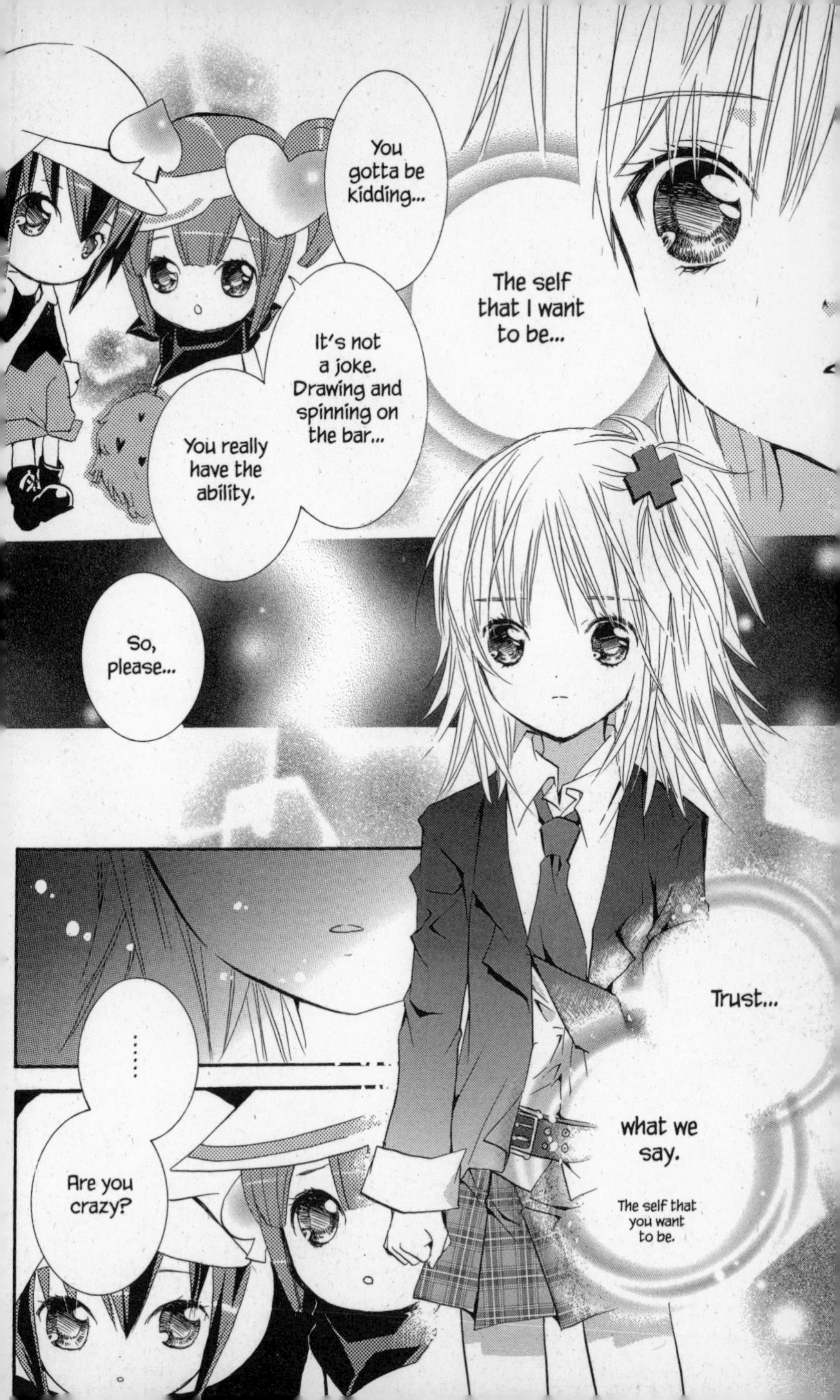
The self that I want to be...
You gotta be kidding...
It's not a joke. Drawing and spinning on the bar...
You really have the ability.
Trust...
what we say.
The self that you want to be.
So, please...
......
Are you crazy?

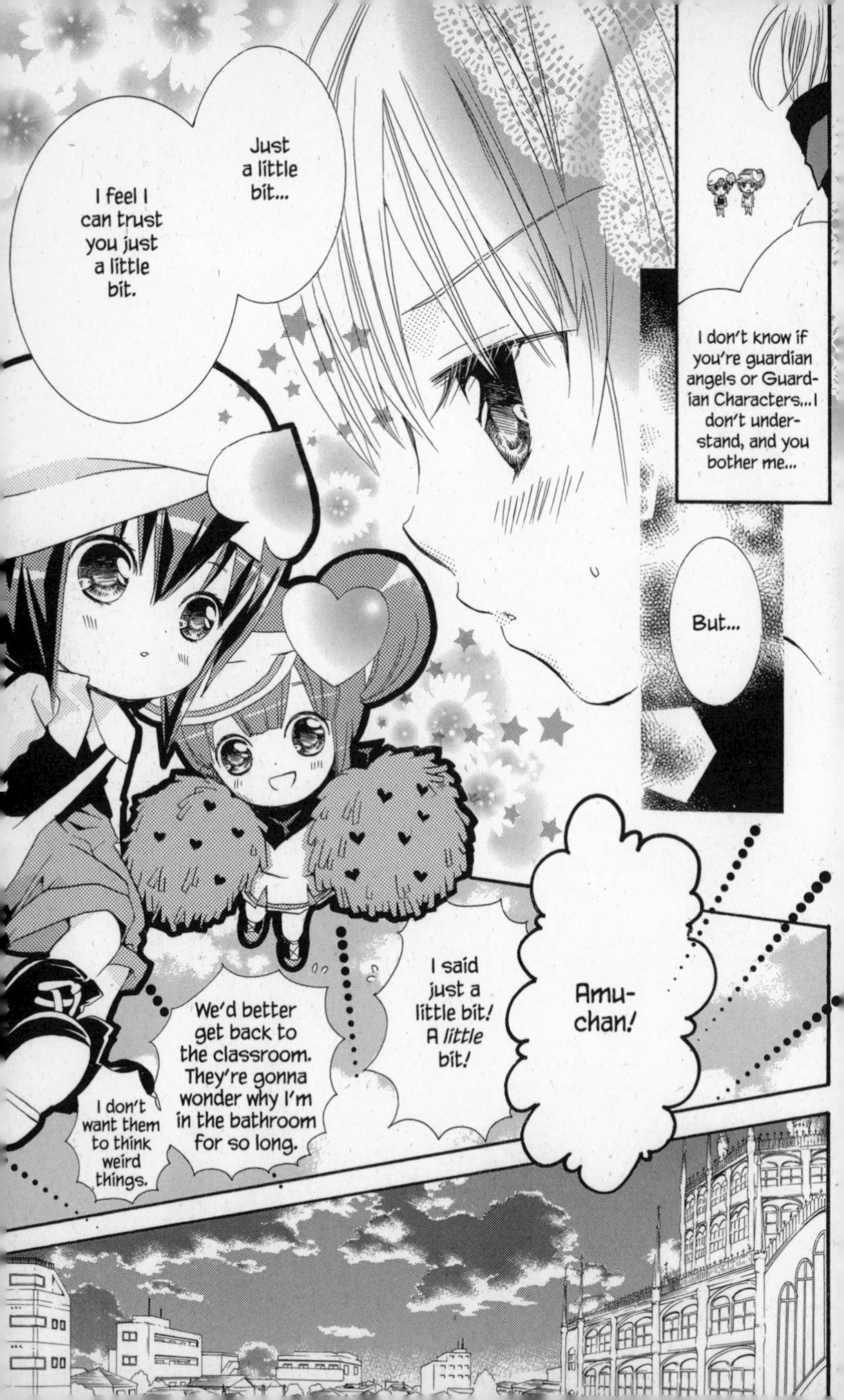

I don't know if you're guardian angels or Guardian Characters...I don't understand, and you bother me...
But...
Just a little bit...
I feel I can trust you just a little bit.
Amu-chan!
I said just a little bit! A *little* bit!
We'd better get back to the classroom. They're gonna wonder why I'm in the bathroom for so long.
I don't want them to think weird things.

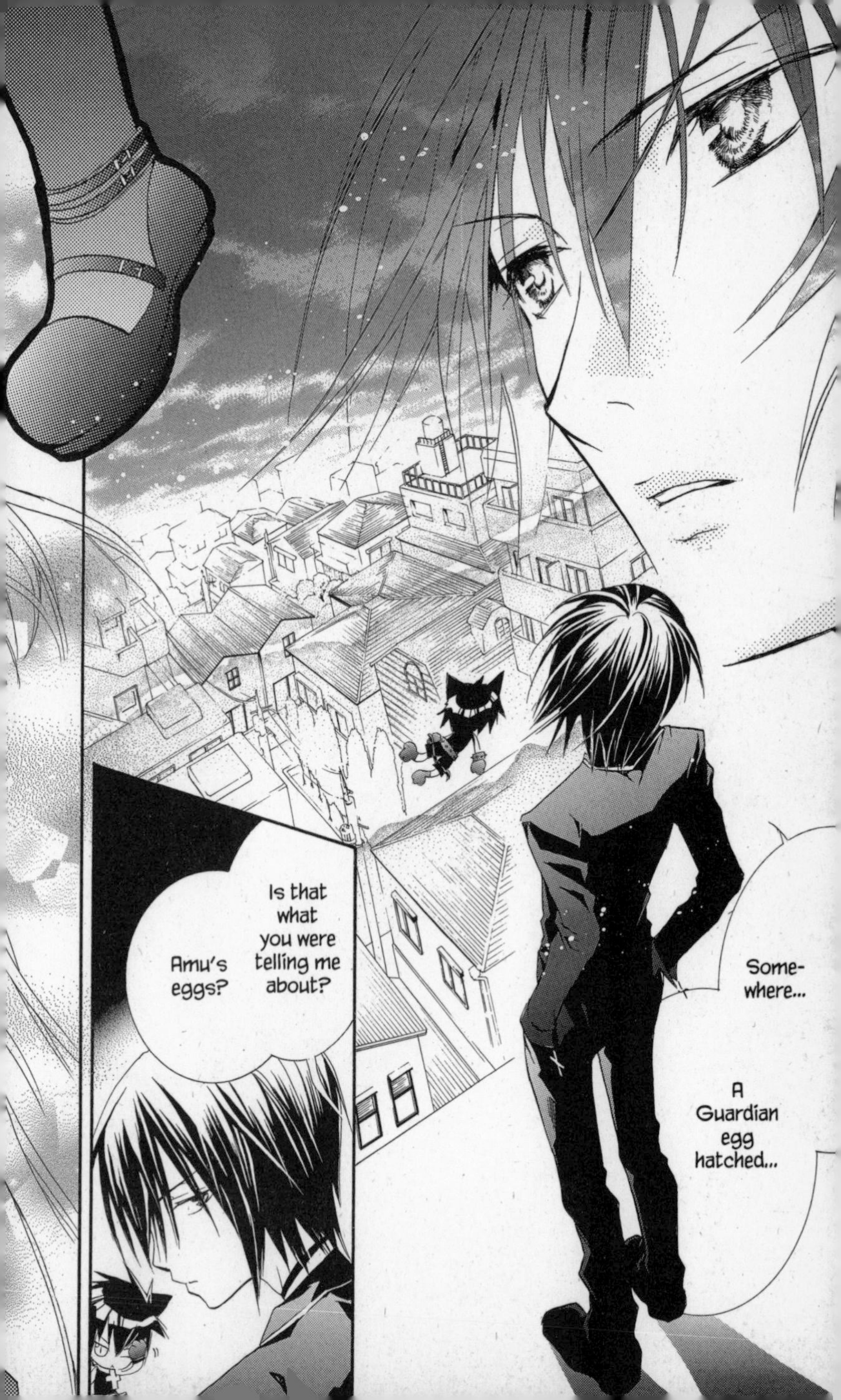
Some-where...
A Guardian egg hatched...
Is that what you were telling me about?
Amu's eggs?

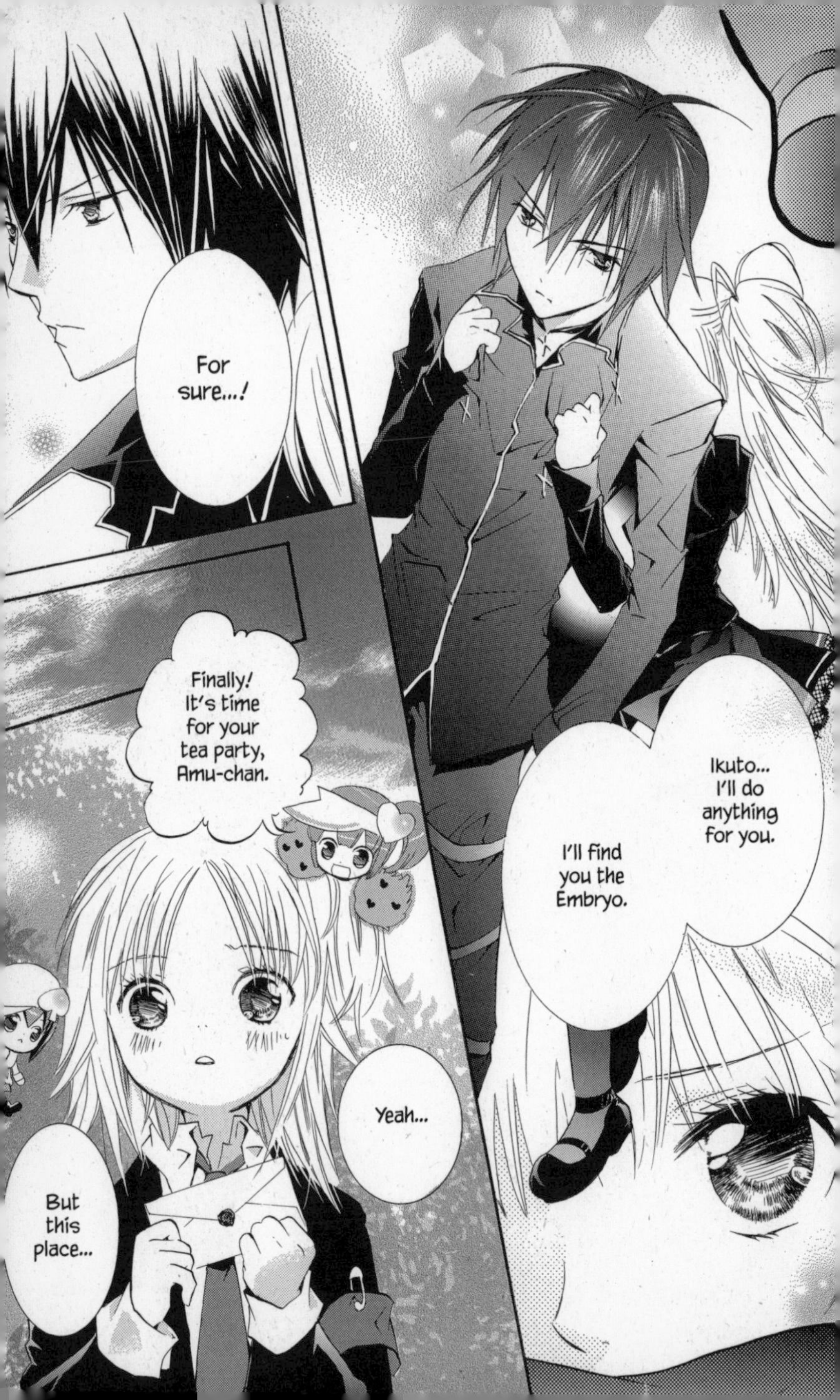
Ikuto... I'll do anything for you.
I'll find you the Embryo.
For sure...!
Finally! It's time for your tea party, Amu-chan.
Yeah...
But this place...

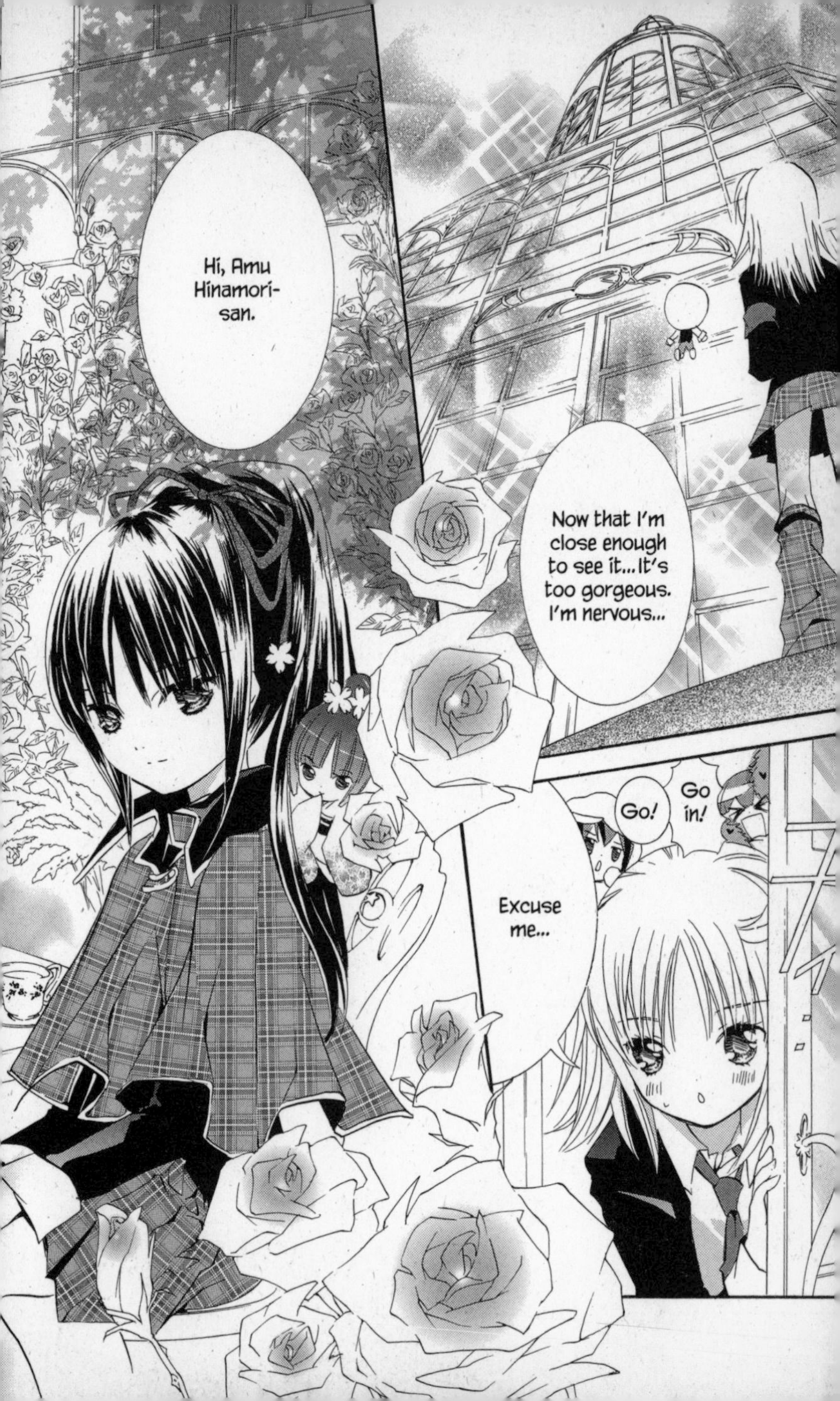
Now that I'm close enough to see it... It's too gorgeous. I'm nervous...
Go in!
Go!
Excuse me...
Hi, Amu Hinamori-san.

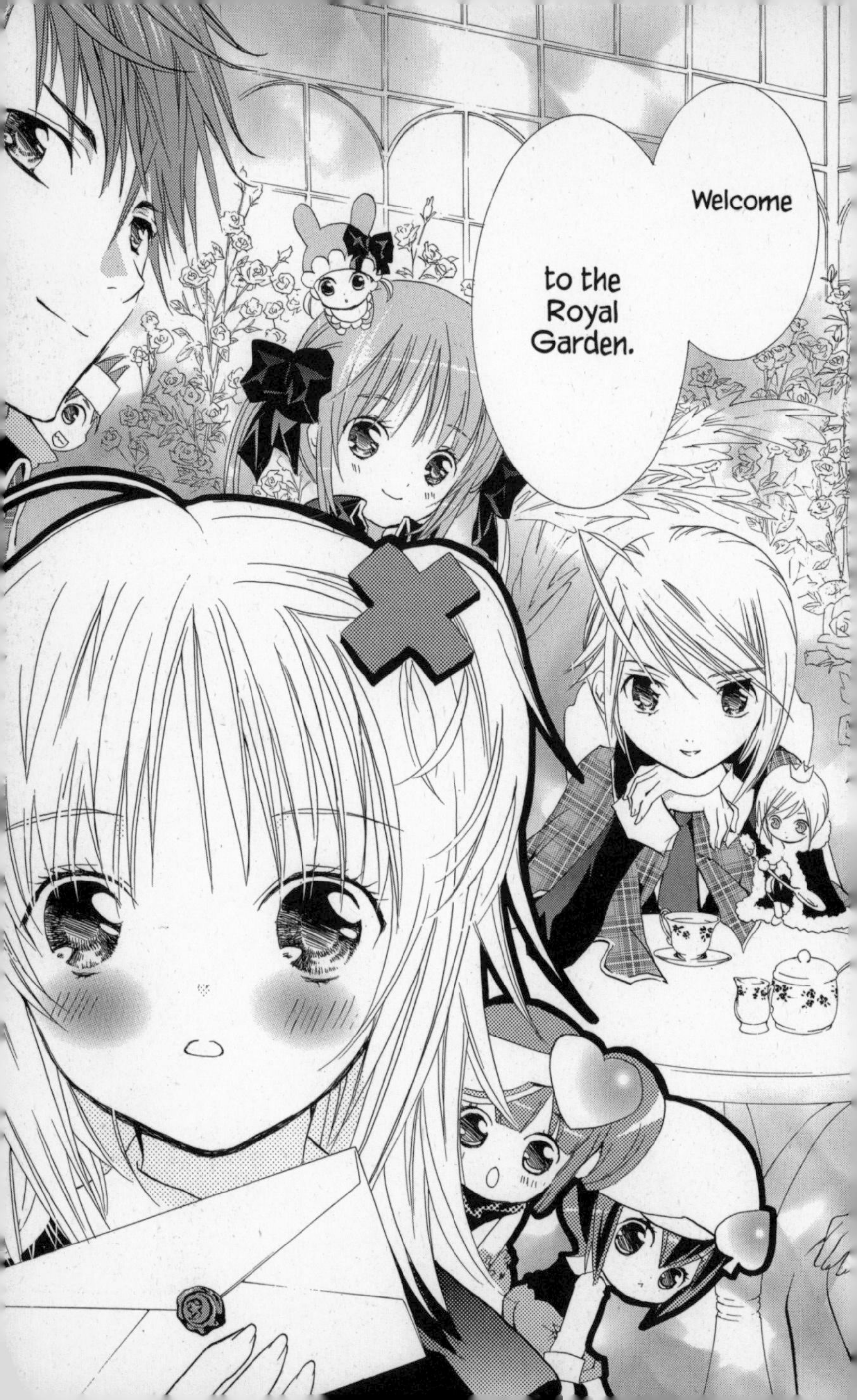
Welcome
to the Royal Garden.

Shugo Chara!

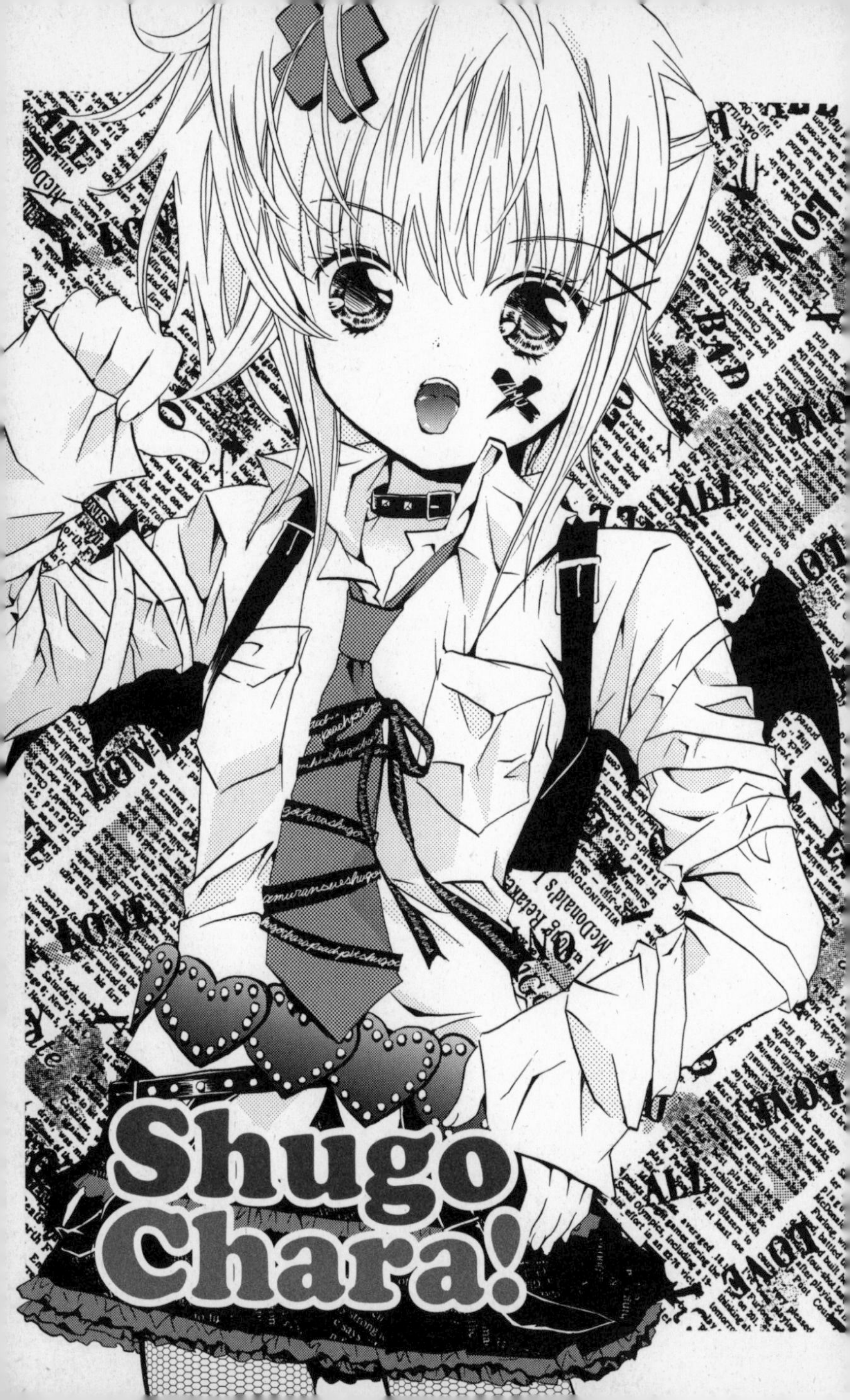
Shugo
Chara!

Please come in, Hinamori-san.

Being invited to the Royal Garden...

was already surprising.

But... what?

I'll answer your questions!

This is Ebara answering:

Q 1: Is PEACH-PIT-sensei a man or a woman?
A 1: Uhh...I...guess you can call us women. Yeah, biologically speaking, we're...probably women. Both of us.
Q 2: How do you draw manga together?
A 2: Banri-san creates the story, then we both draw our assigned characters.
Amu, Nadeshiko, Yaya, Ami, Guardian Characters...Shibuko Ebara
Tadase, Ikuto, Utau, Kukai...Banri Sendou
Can you tell the difference in our drawing styles?

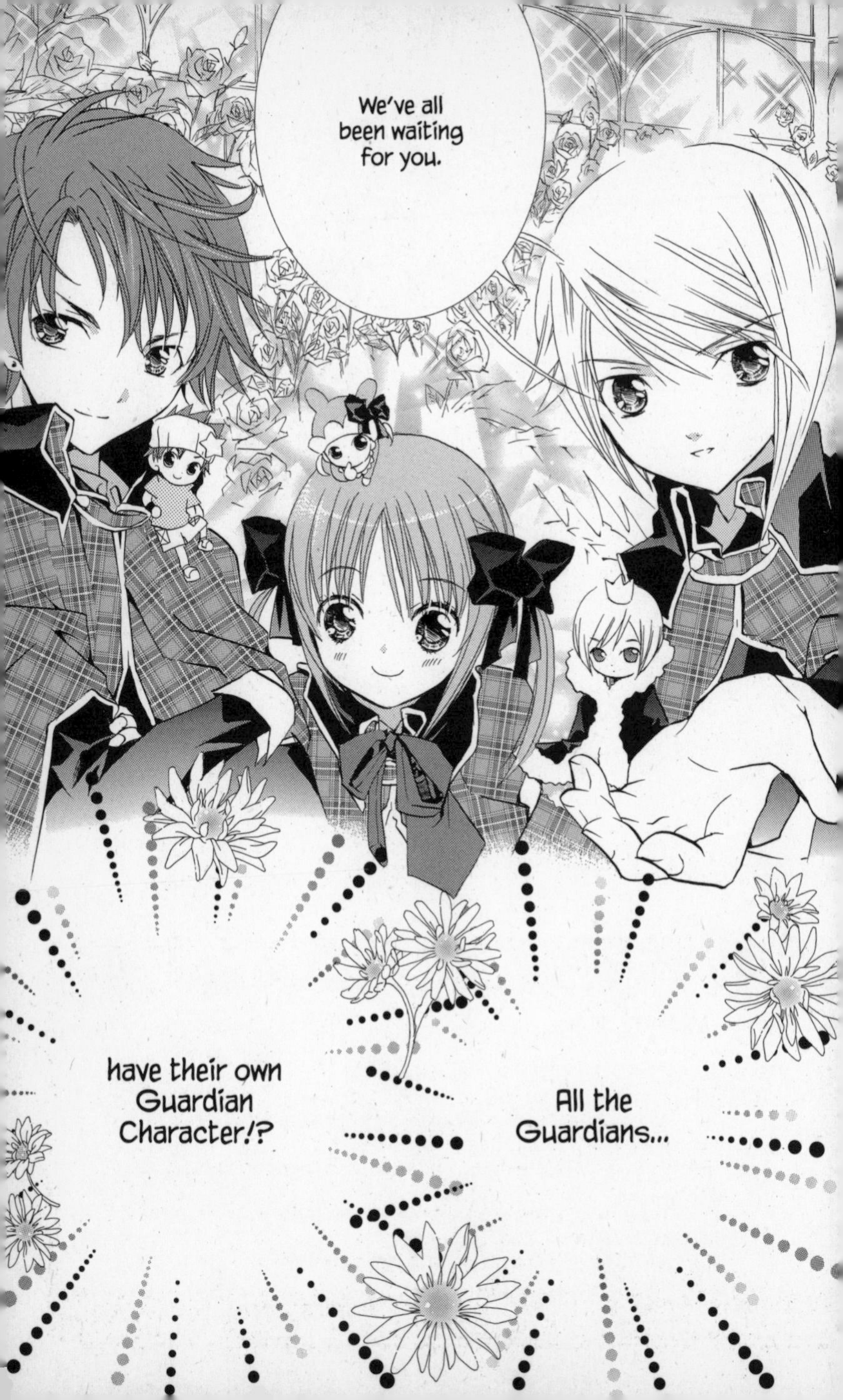
We've all been waiting for you.
All the Guardians...
have their own Guardian Character!?

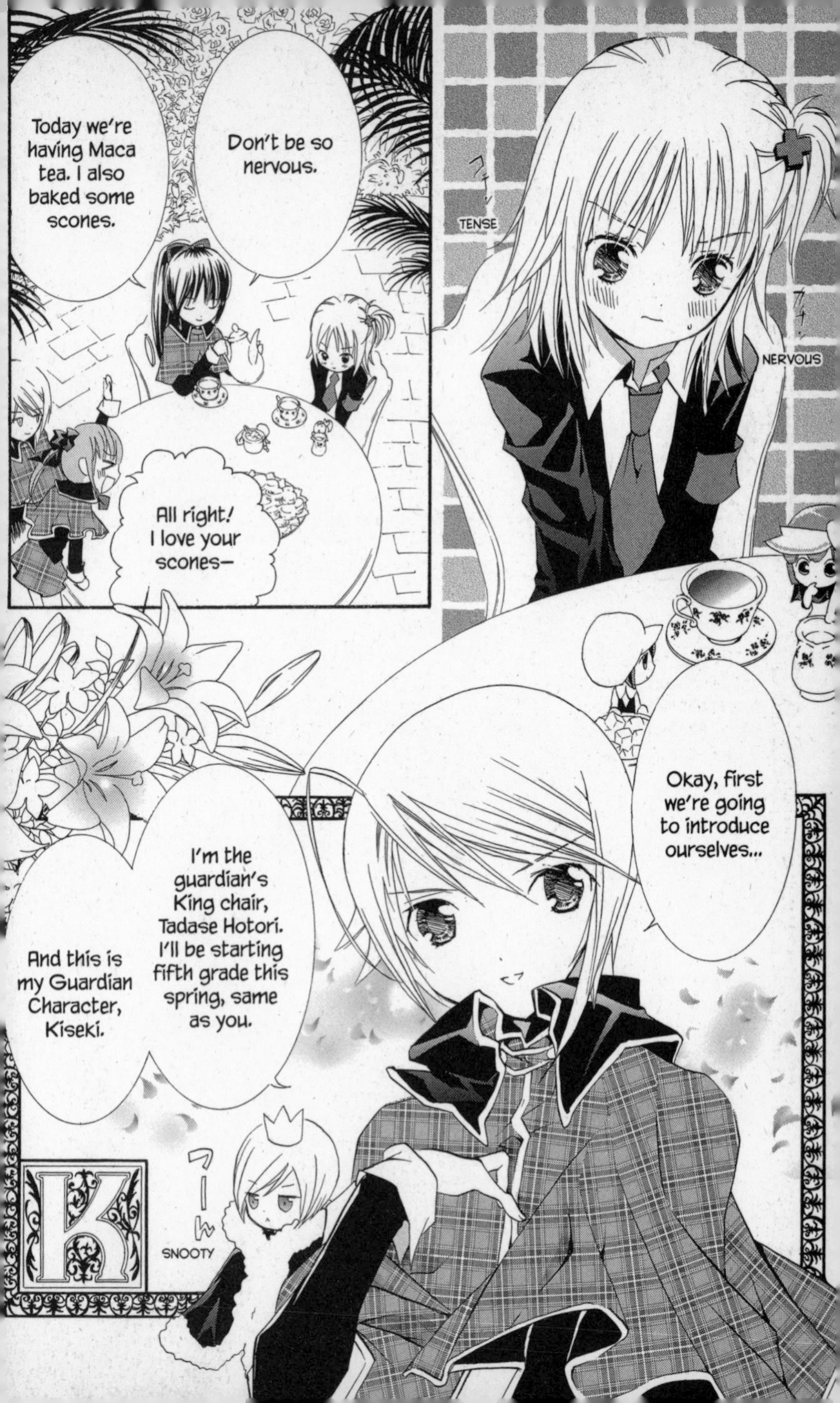
TENSE
NERVOUS
Don't be so nervous.
Today we're having Maca tea. I also baked some scones.
All right! I love your scones—
Okay, first we're going to introduce ourselves...
I'm the guardian's King chair, Tadase Hotori. I'll be starting fifth grade this spring, same as you.
And this is my Guardian Character, Kiseki.
SNOOTY
K

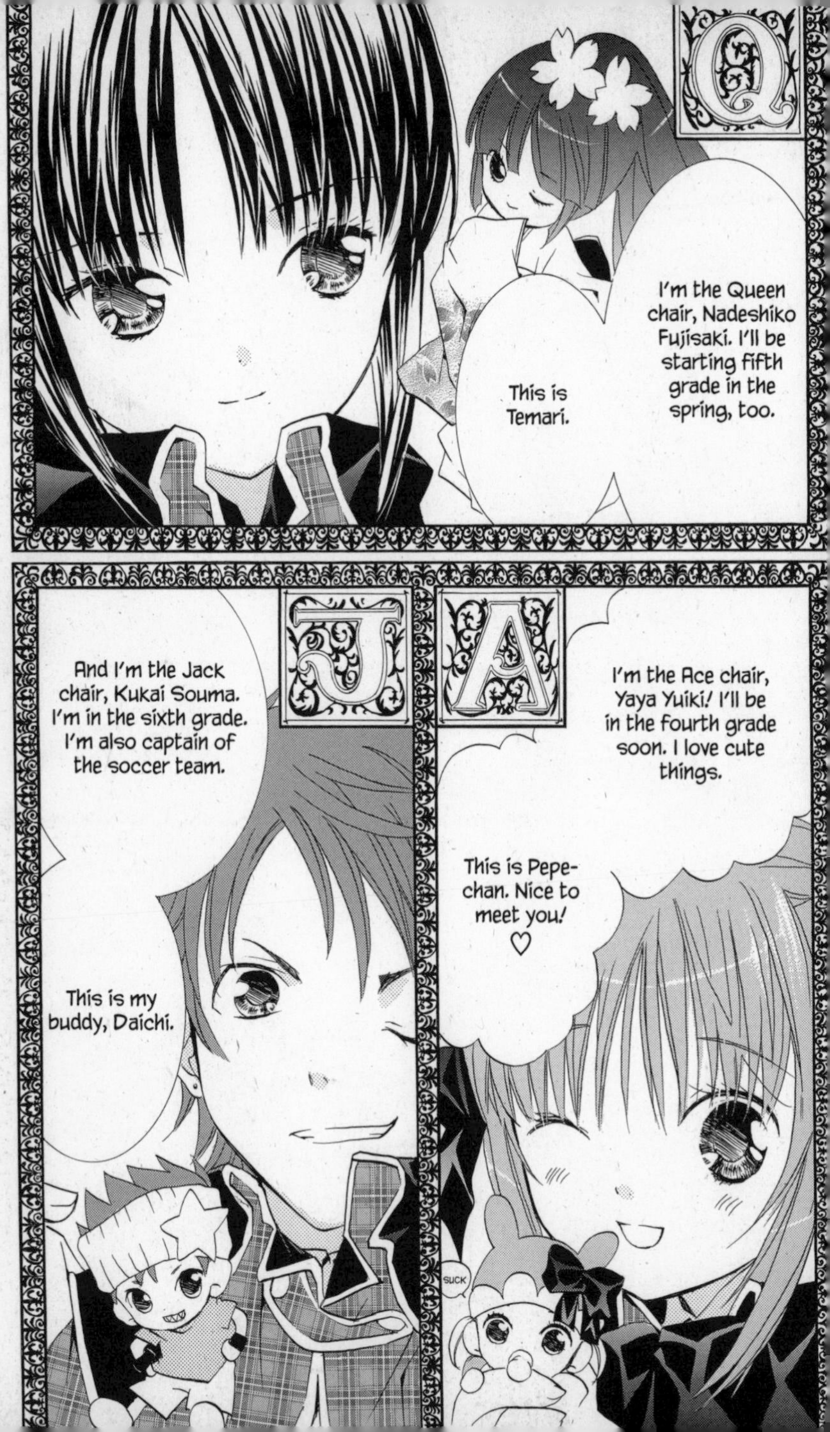
I'm the Queen chair, Nadeshiko Fujisaki. I'll be starting fifth grade in the spring, too.
This is Temari.
I'm the Ace chair, Yaya Yuiki! I'll be in the fourth grade soon. I love cute things.
This is Pepe-chan. Nice to meet you! ♡
SUCK
And I'm the Jack chair, Kukai Souma. I'm in the sixth grade. I'm also captain of the soccer team.
This is my buddy, Daichi.

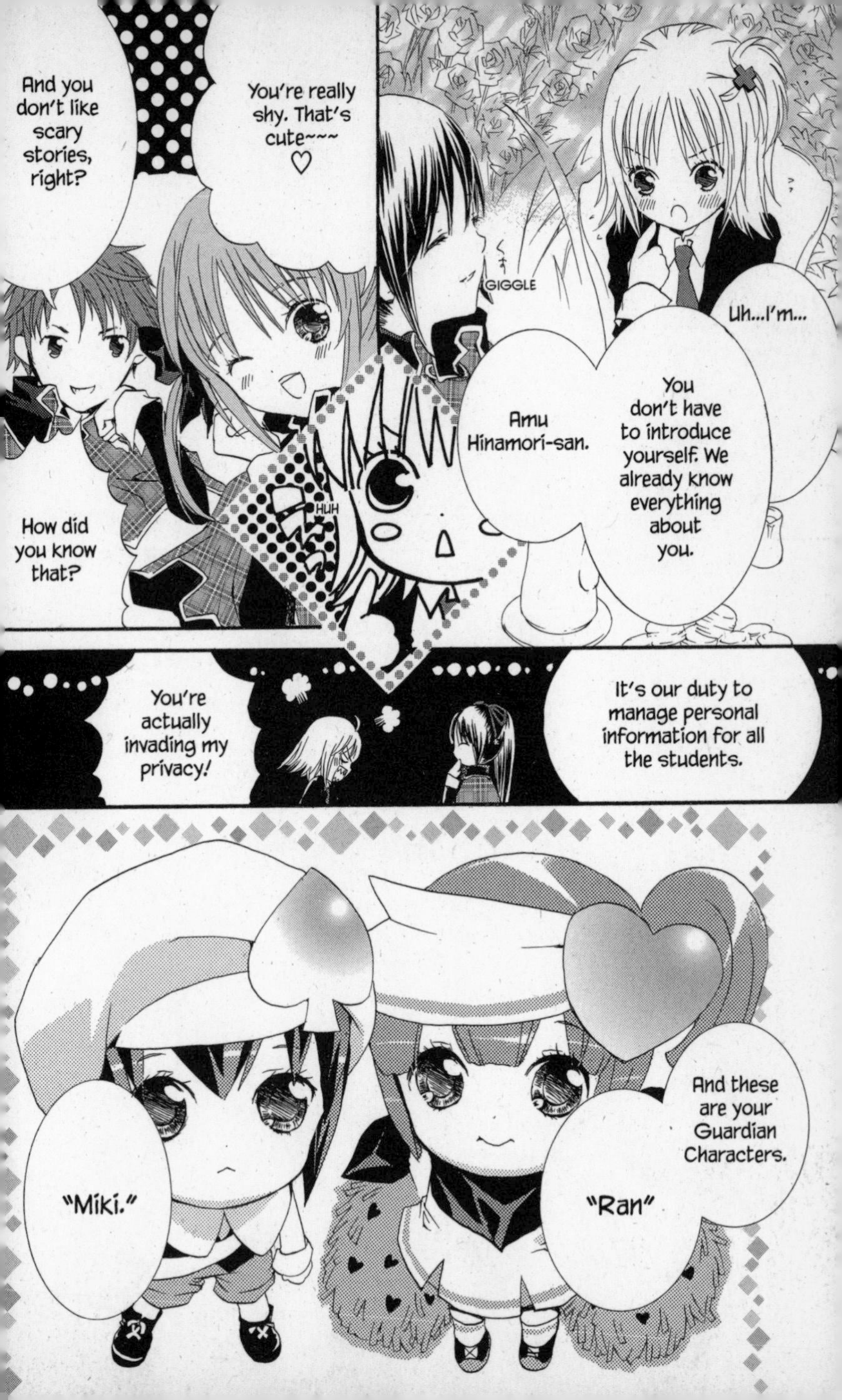
Uh...I'm...
GIGGLE
You don't have to introduce yourself. We already know everything about you.
Amu Hinamori-san.
You're really shy. That's cute~~~ ♡
And you don't like scary stories, right?
HUH
How did you know that?
It's our duty to manage personal information for all the students.
You're actually invading my privacy!
And these are your Guardian Characters.
"Ran"
"Miki."

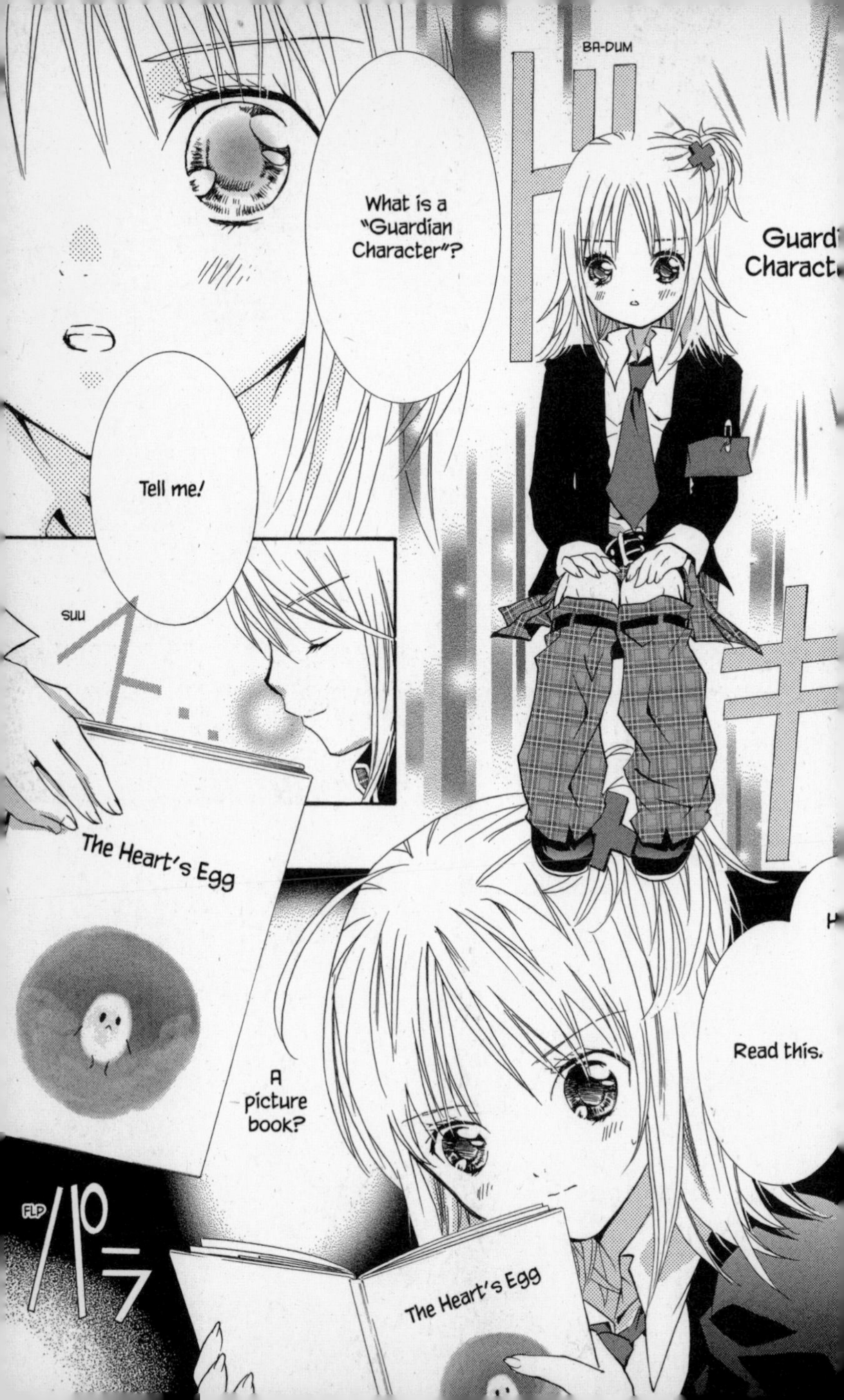

BA-DUM
Guardi Charact
What is a "Guardian Character"?
Tell me!
SUU
The Heart's Egg
Read this.
A picture book?
FLIP
The Heart's Egg

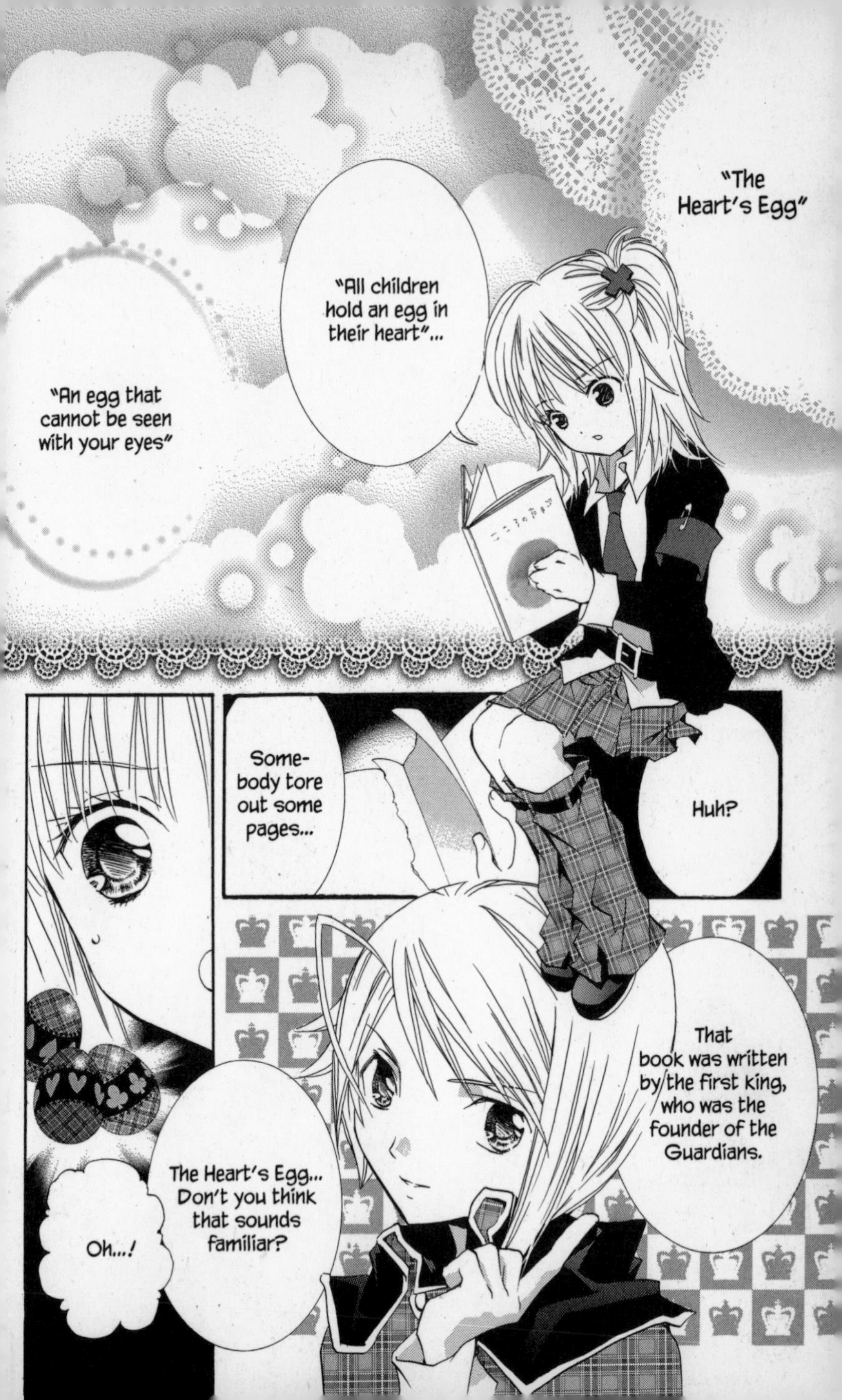
"The Heart's Egg"
"All children hold an egg in their heart"...
"An egg that cannot be seen with your eyes"
Huh?
Some-body tore out some pages...
That book was written by the first king, who was the founder of the Guardians.
The Heart's Egg... Don't you think that sounds familiar?
Oh...!

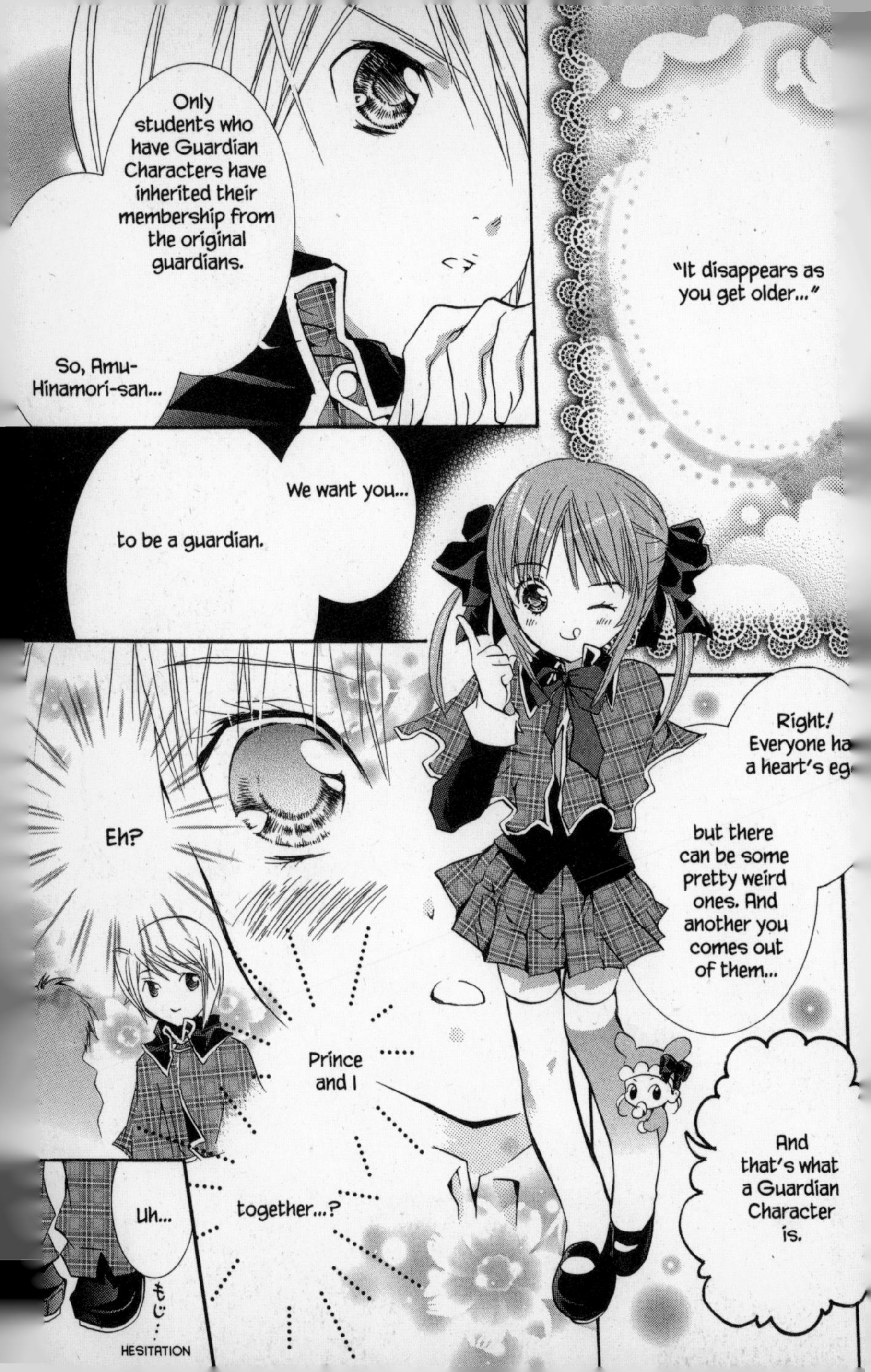
"It disappears as you get older..."
Right! Everyone ha a heart's eg
but there can be some pretty weird ones. And another you comes out of them...
And that's what a Guardian Character is.
Only students who have Guardian Characters have inherited their membership from the original guardians.
So, Amu-Hinamori-san...
We want you...
to be a guardian.
Eh?
Prince and I
together...?
Uh...
もじ
HESITATION

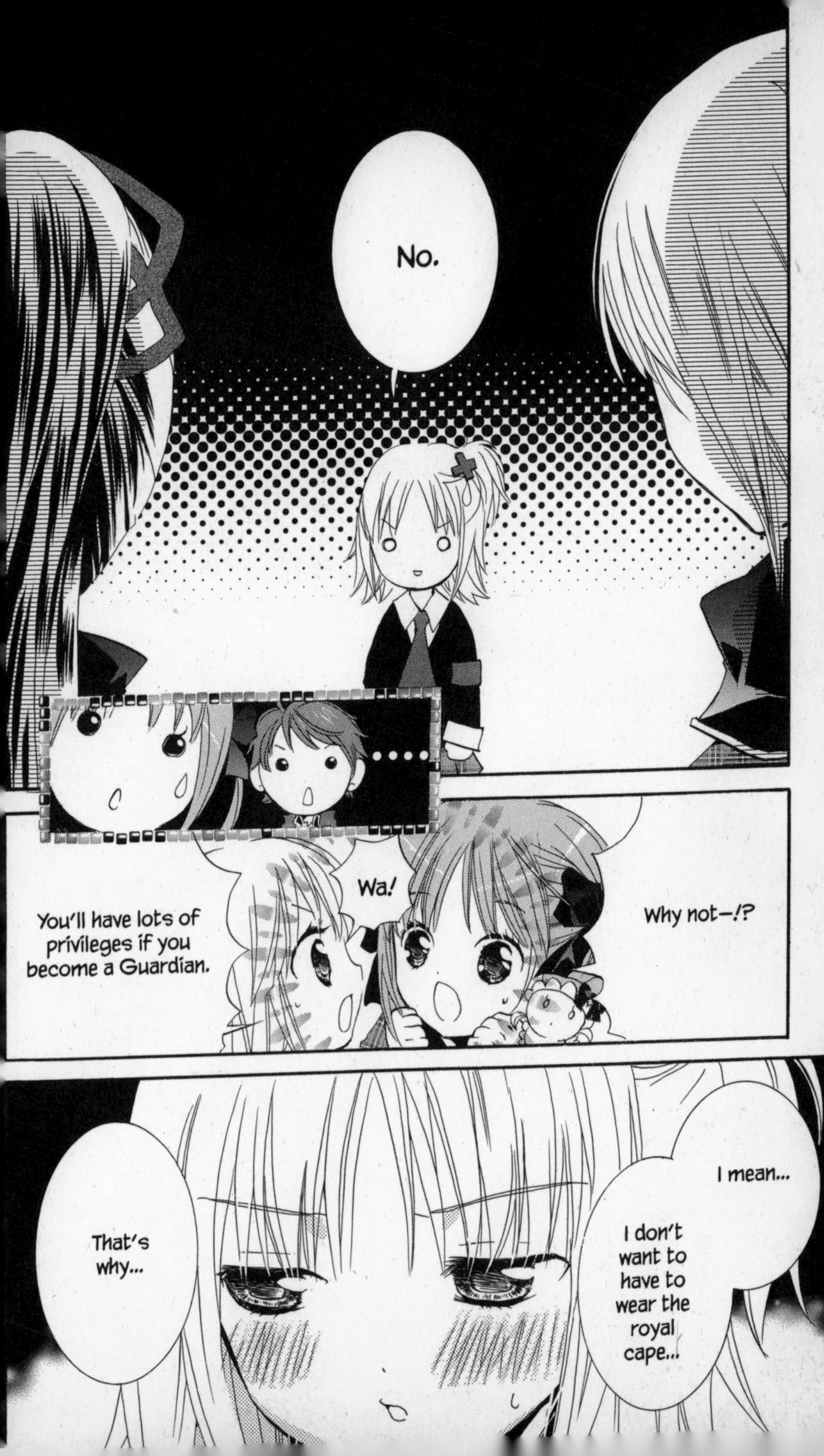
No.
.....
Why not–!?
Wa!
You'll have lots of privileges if you become a Guardian.
I mean...
I don't want to have to wear the royal cape...
That's why...

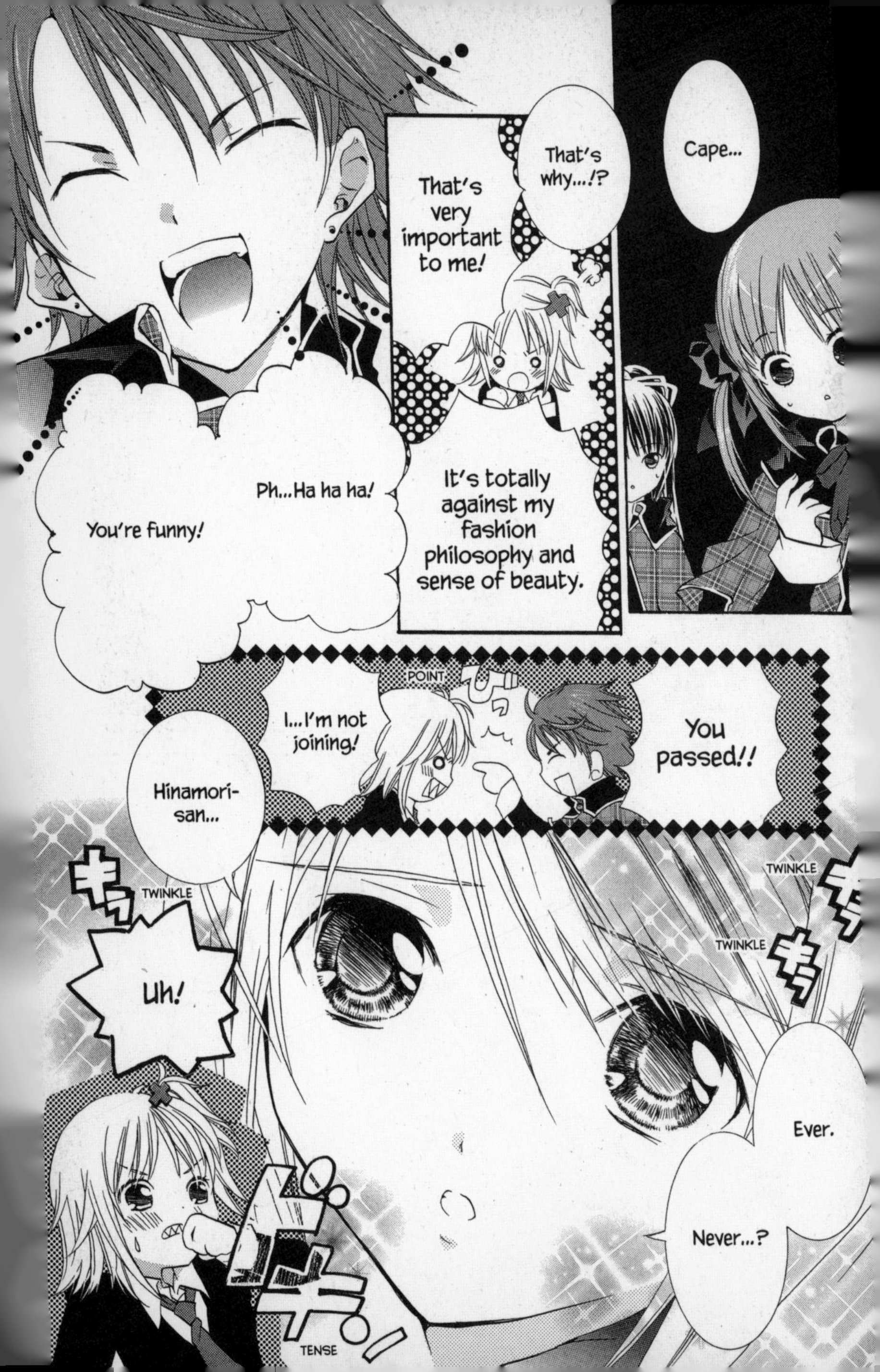
Cape...
That's why...!?
That's very important to me!
It's totally against my fashion philosophy and sense of beauty.
Ph...Ha ha ha!
You're funny!
You passed!!
POINT
I...I'm not joining!
TWINKLE
TWINKLE
Hinamori-san...
Never...?
Ever.
TWINKLE
Uh!
TENSE

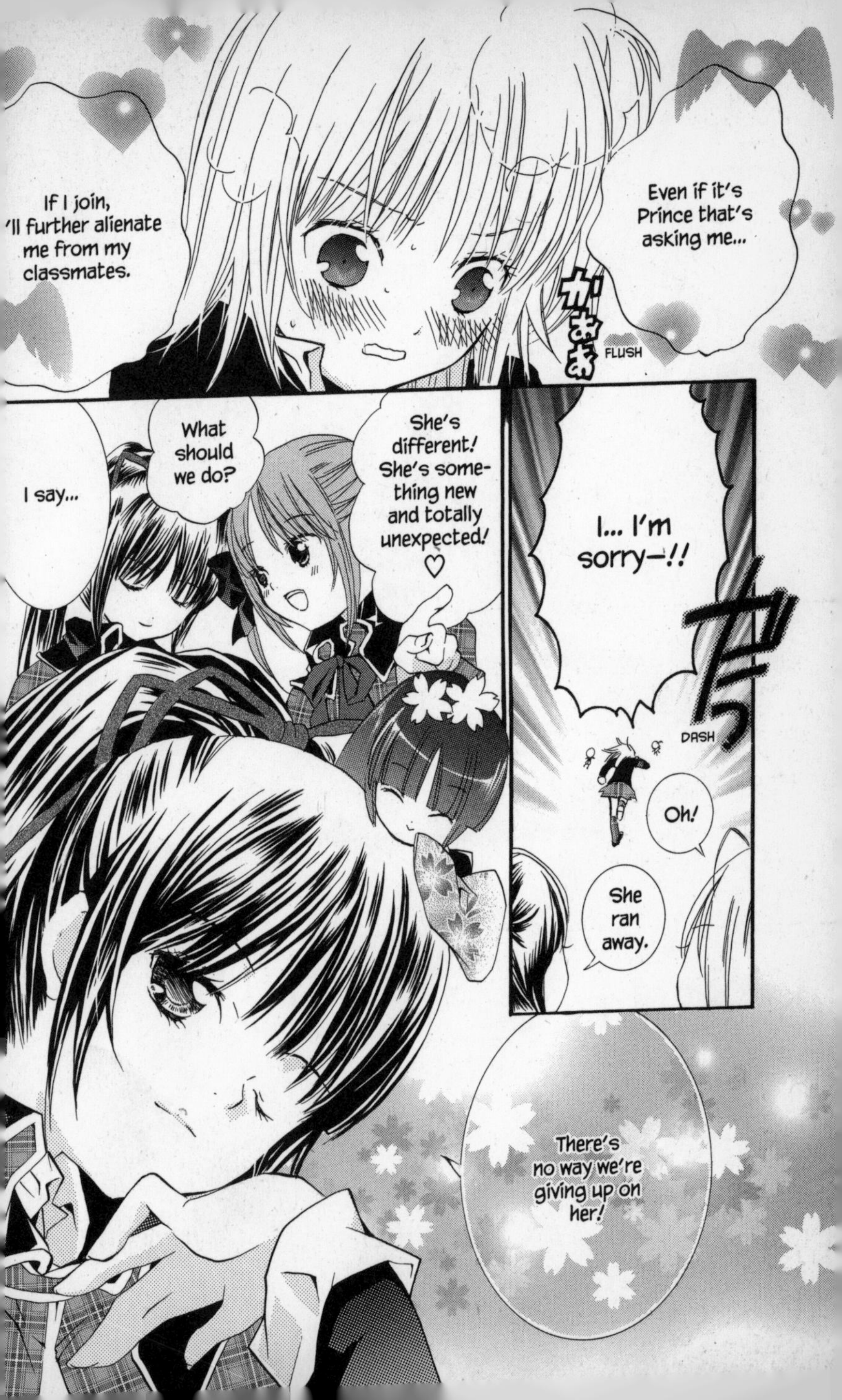

Even if it's Prince that's asking me...
FLUSH
If I join, 'll further alienate me from my classmates.
I... I'm sorry—!!
DASH
Oh!
She ran away.
She's different! She's some-thing new and totally unexpected! ♡
What should we do?
I say...
There's no way we're giving up on her!

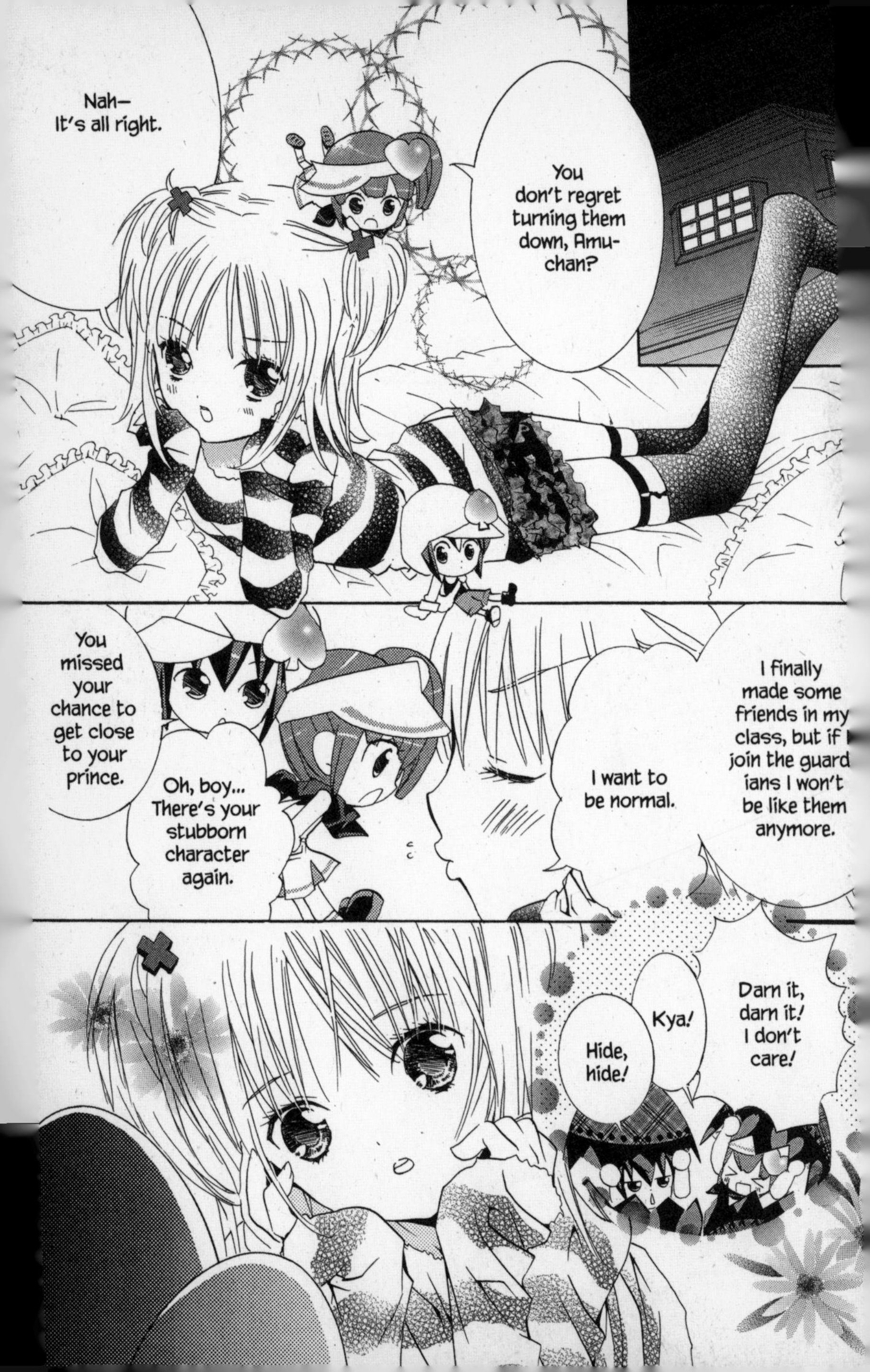
You don't regret turning them down, Amu-chan?
Nah— It's all right.
I finally made some friends in my class, but if I join the guardians I won't be like them anymore.
I want to be normal.
You missed your chance to get close to your prince.
Oh, boy... There's your stubborn character again.
Darn it, darn it! I don't care!
Kya!
Hide, hide!

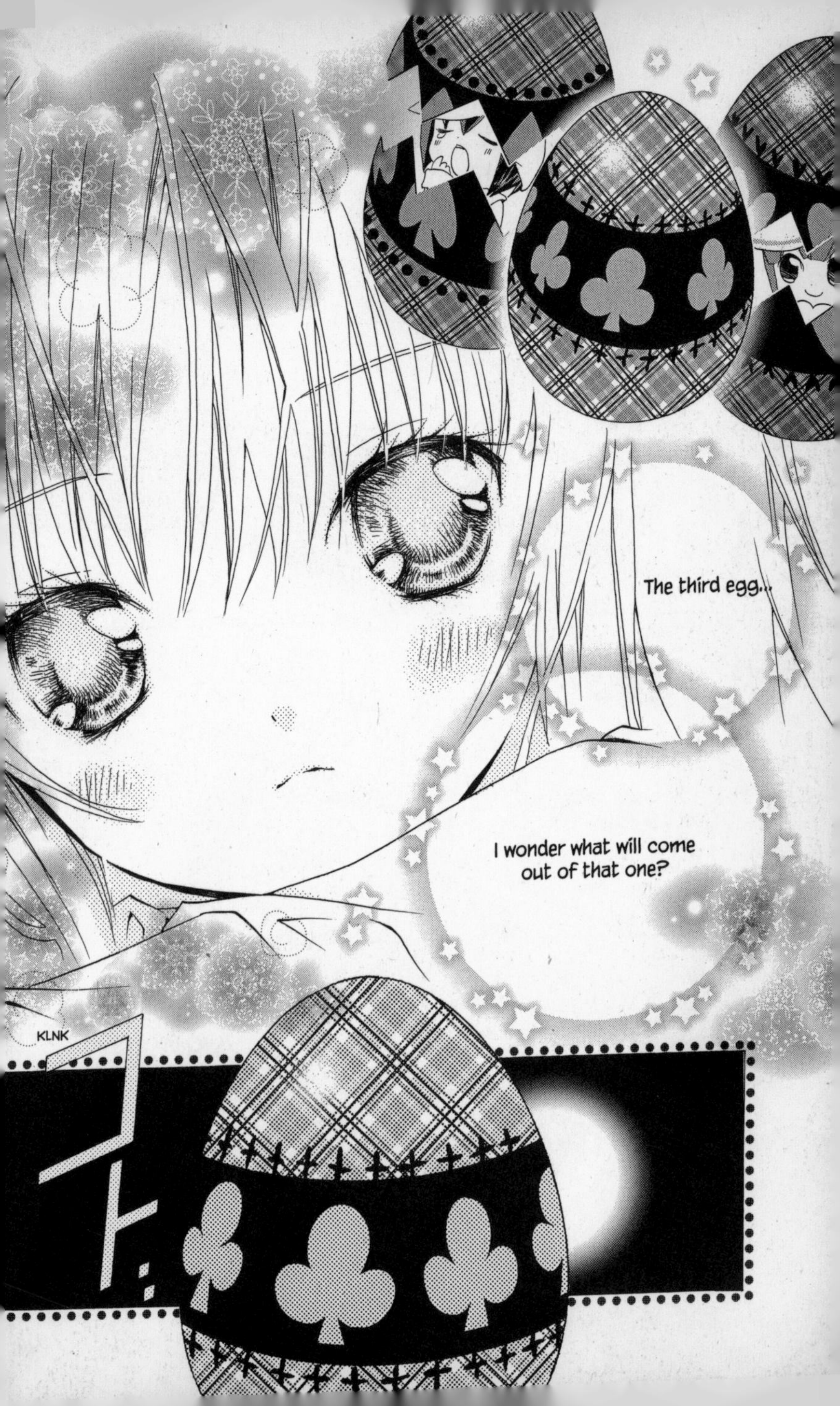
The third egg...
I wonder what will come out of that one?
KLNK

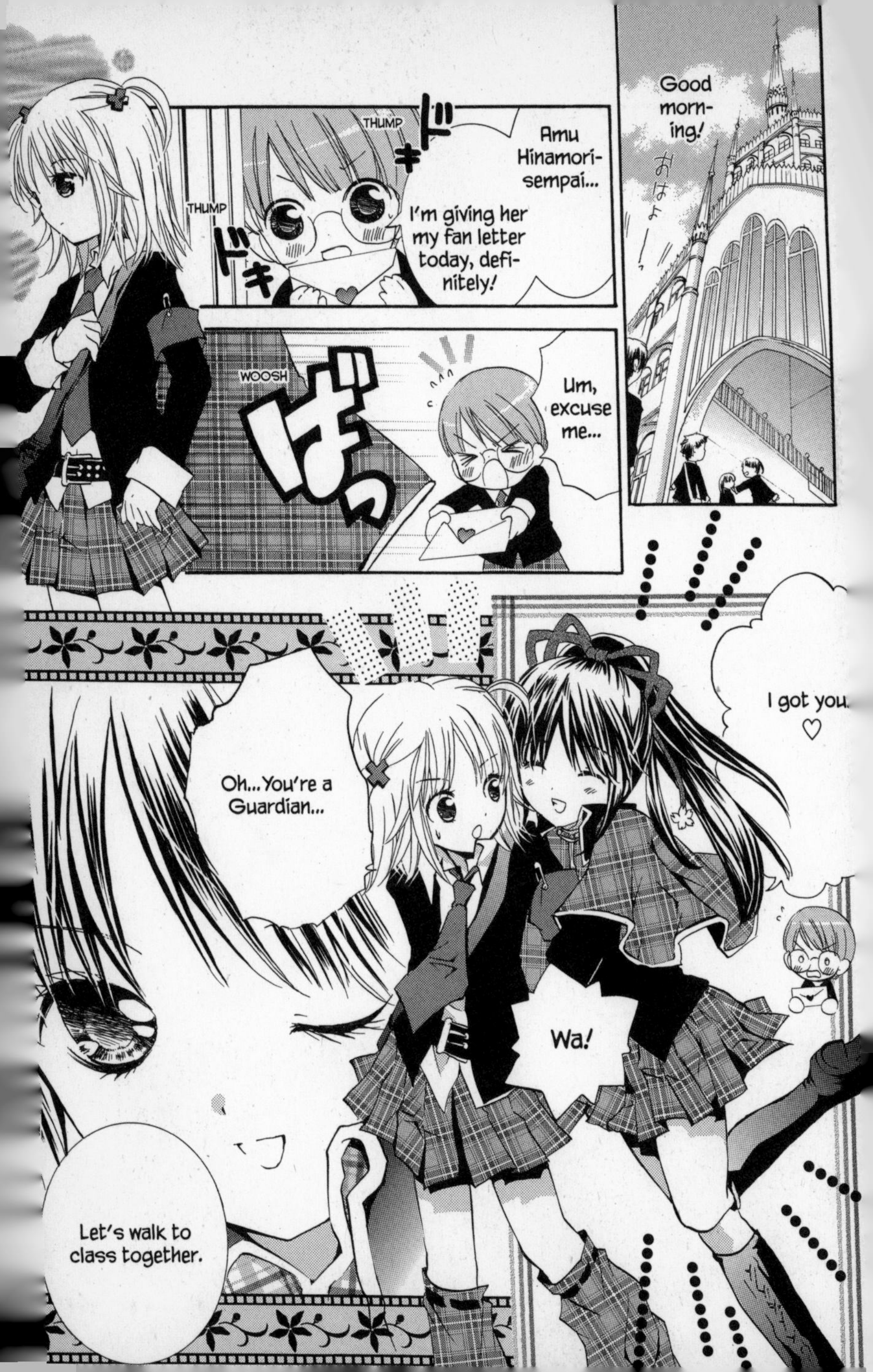
Good morning!
おはよー!!
THUMP
ドキ
Amu Hinamori-sempai...
I'm giving her my fan letter today, definitely!
THUMP
ドキ
Um, excuse me...
WOOSH
ばっ
I got you. ♡
Oh... You're a Guardian...
Wa!
Let's walk to class together.

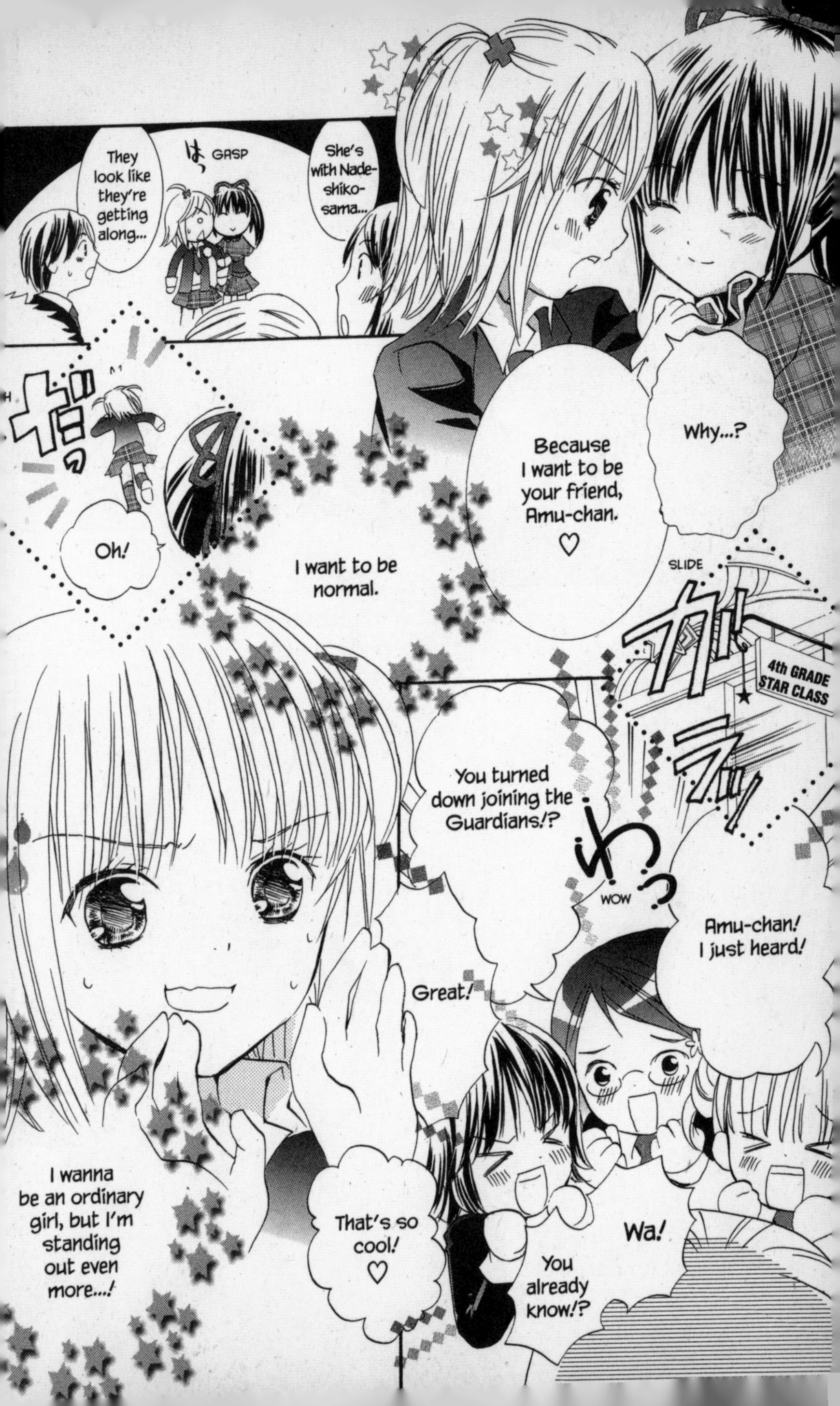
Why...?
Because I want to be your friend, Amu-chan. ♡
She's with Nade-shiko-sama...
GASP
They look like they're getting along...
Oh!
I want to be normal.
SLIDE
4th GRADE STAR CLASS
Amu-chan! I just heard!
WOW
You turned down joining the Guardians!?
Great!
Wa!
You already know!?
That's so cool! ♡
I wanna be an ordinary girl, but I'm standing out even more...!

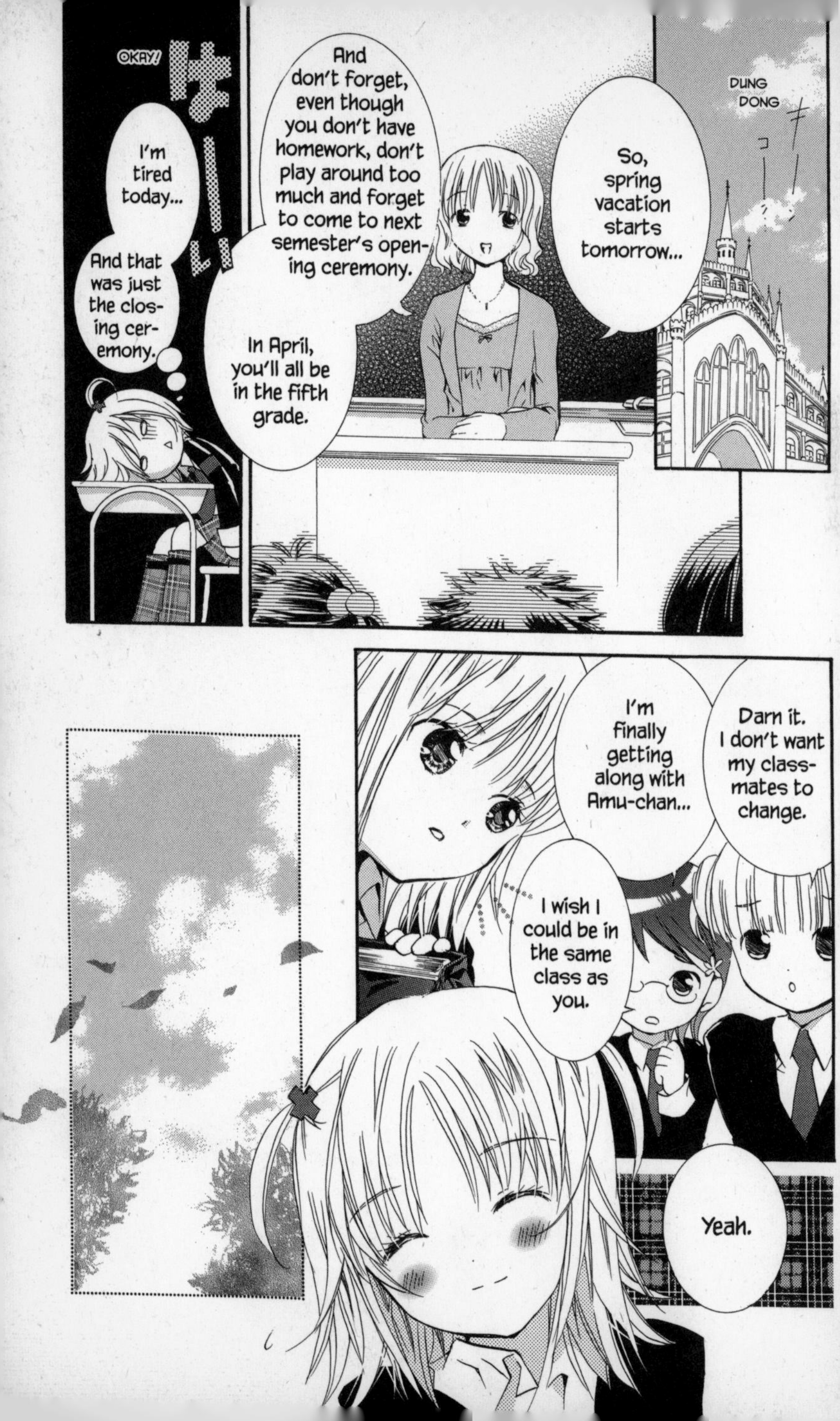

DUNG DONG
So, spring vacation starts tomorrow...
And don't forget, even though you don't have homework, don't play around too much and forget to come to next semester's opening ceremony.
In April, you'll all be in the fifth grade.
OKAY!
I'm tired today...
And that was just the closing ceremony.
Darn it. I don't want my classmates to change.
I'm finally getting along with Amu-chan...
I wish I could be in the same class as you.
Yeah.

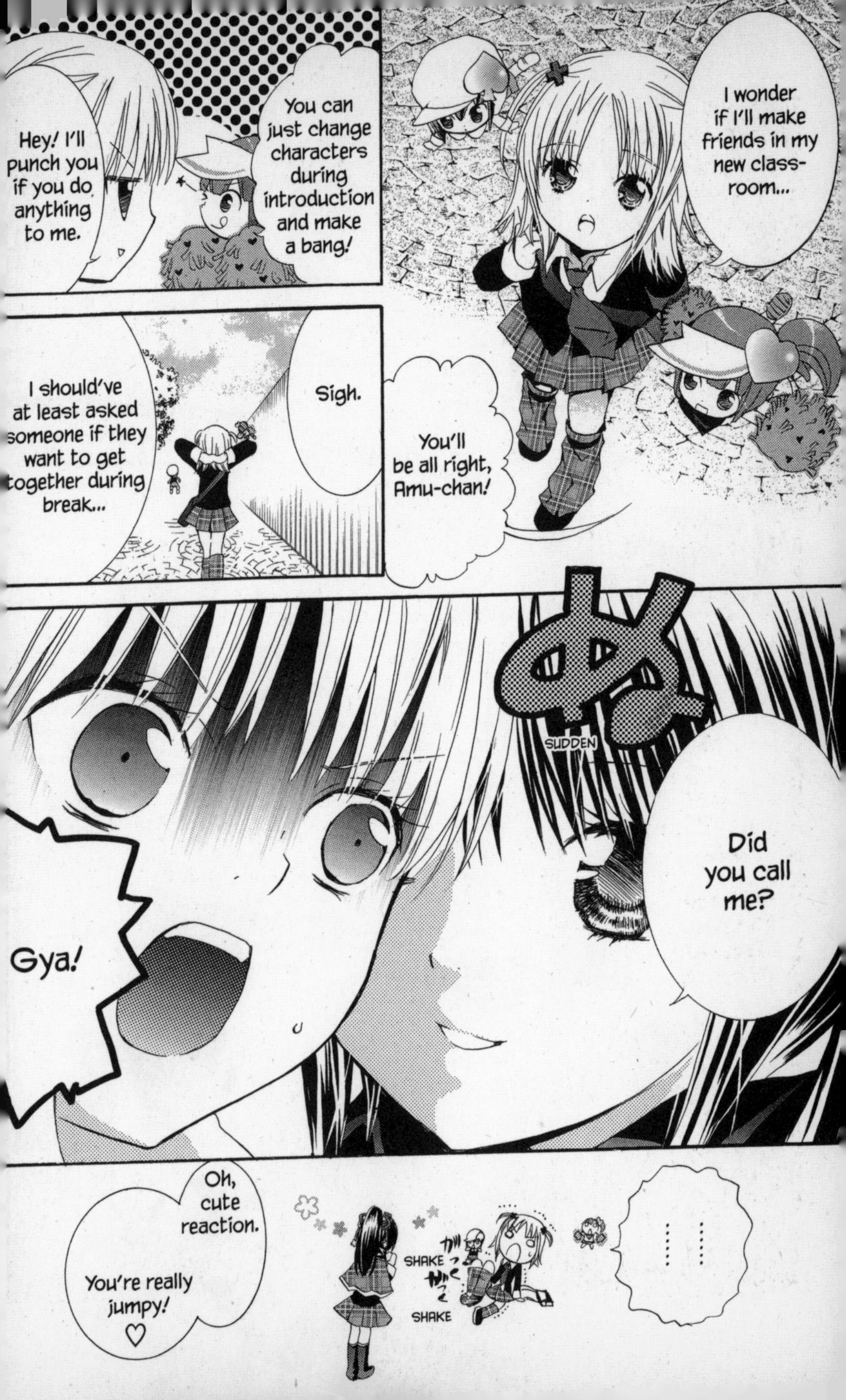
I wonder if I'll make friends in my new classroom...
You'll be all right, Amu-chan!
You can just change characters during introduction and make a bang!
Hey! I'll punch you if you do anything to me.
Sigh.
I should've at least asked someone if they want to get together during break...
SUDDEN
Did you call me?
Gya!
......
SHAKE
SHAKE
Oh, cute reaction.
You're really jumpy! ♡

character profile

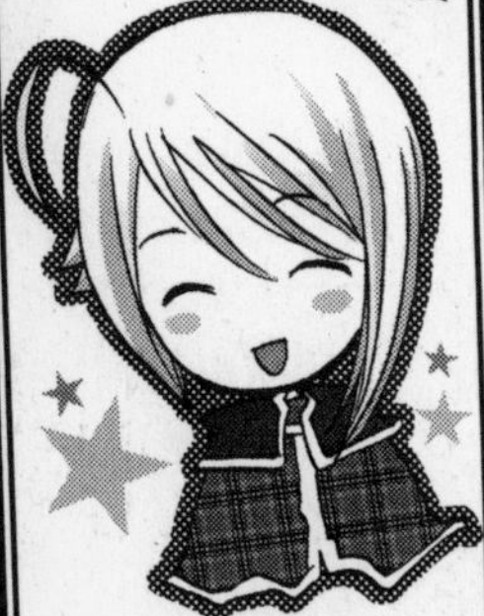

辺里 唯世

Tadase Hotori

Birthday : 3/29
BloodType : B
Sign : Aries
Shugo-Chara : Kiseki

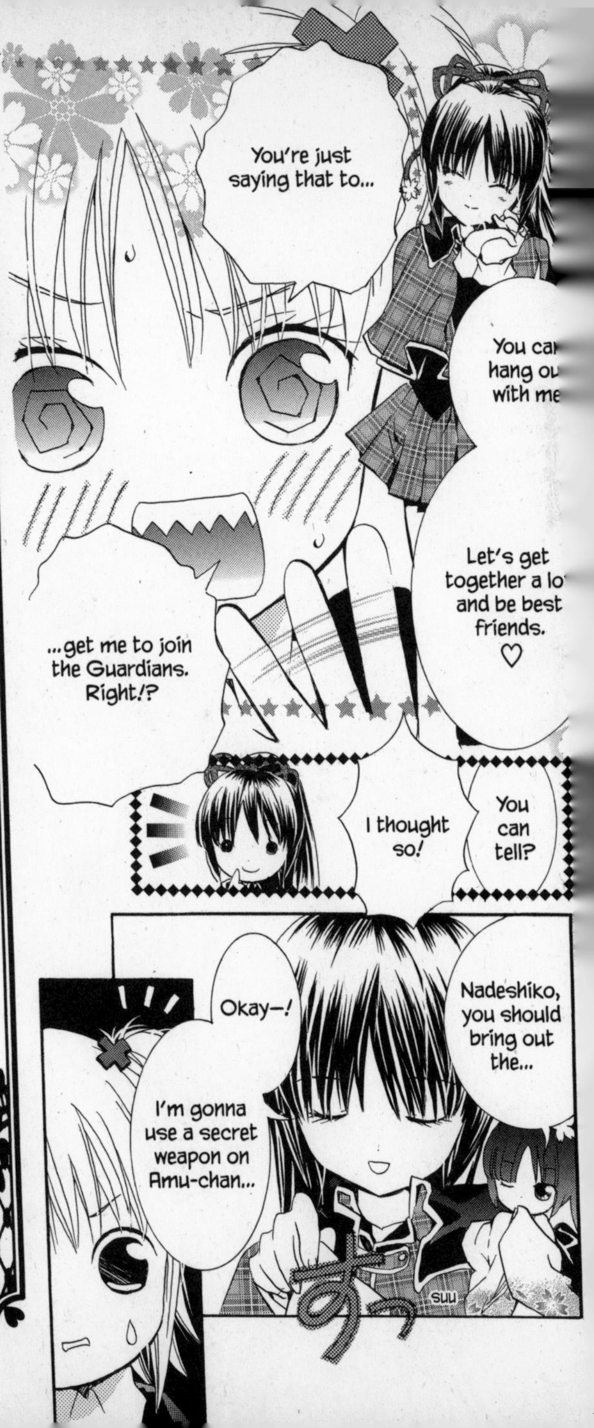
You ca
hang ou
with me
Let's get together a lo and be best friends. ♡
You're just saying that to...
...get me to join the Guardians. Right!?
You can tell?
I thought so!
Nadeshiko, you should bring out the...
Okay—!
I'm gonna use a secret weapon on Amu-chan...
SUU

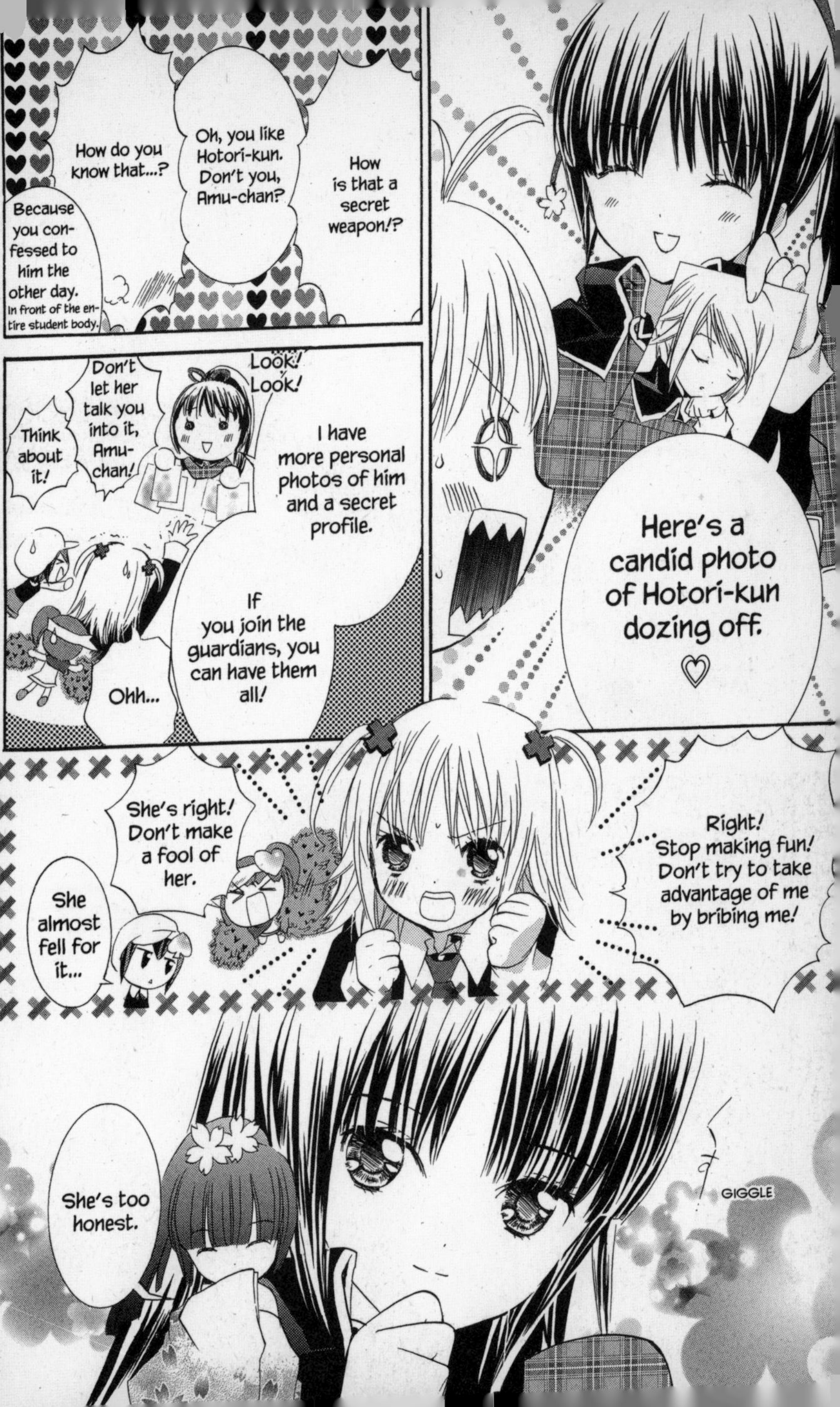
Here's a candid photo of Hotori-kun dozing off. ♡
How is that a secret weapon!?
Oh, you like Hotori-kun. Don't you, Amu-chan?
How do you know that...?
Because you confessed to him the other day. In front of the entire student body.
I have more personal photos of him and a secret profile.
Look! Look!
If you join the guardians, you can have them all!
Don't let her talk you into it, Amu-chan!
Think about it!
Ohh...
Right! Stop making fun! Don't try to take advantage of me by bribing me!
She's right! Don't make a fool of her.
She almost fell for it...
GIGGLE
She's too honest.

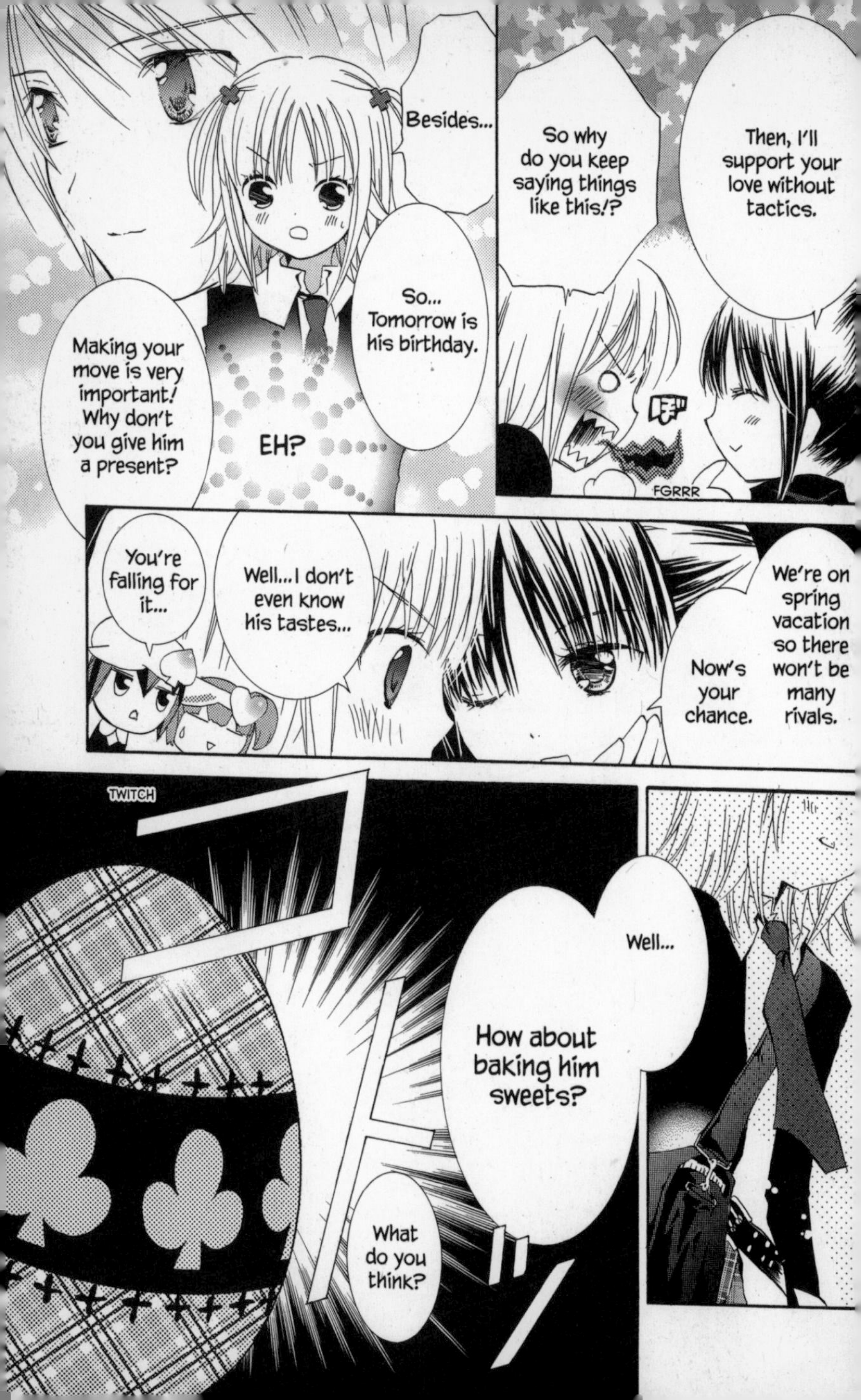

Then, I'll support your love without tactics.
So why do you keep saying things like this!?
FGRRR
Besides...
So... Tomorrow is his birthday.
EH?
Making your move is very important! Why don't you give him a present?
We're on spring vacation so there won't be many rivals.
Now's your chance.
Well...I don't even know his tastes...
You're falling for it...
Well...
How about baking him sweets?
TWITCH
What do you think?

Shugo Chara!

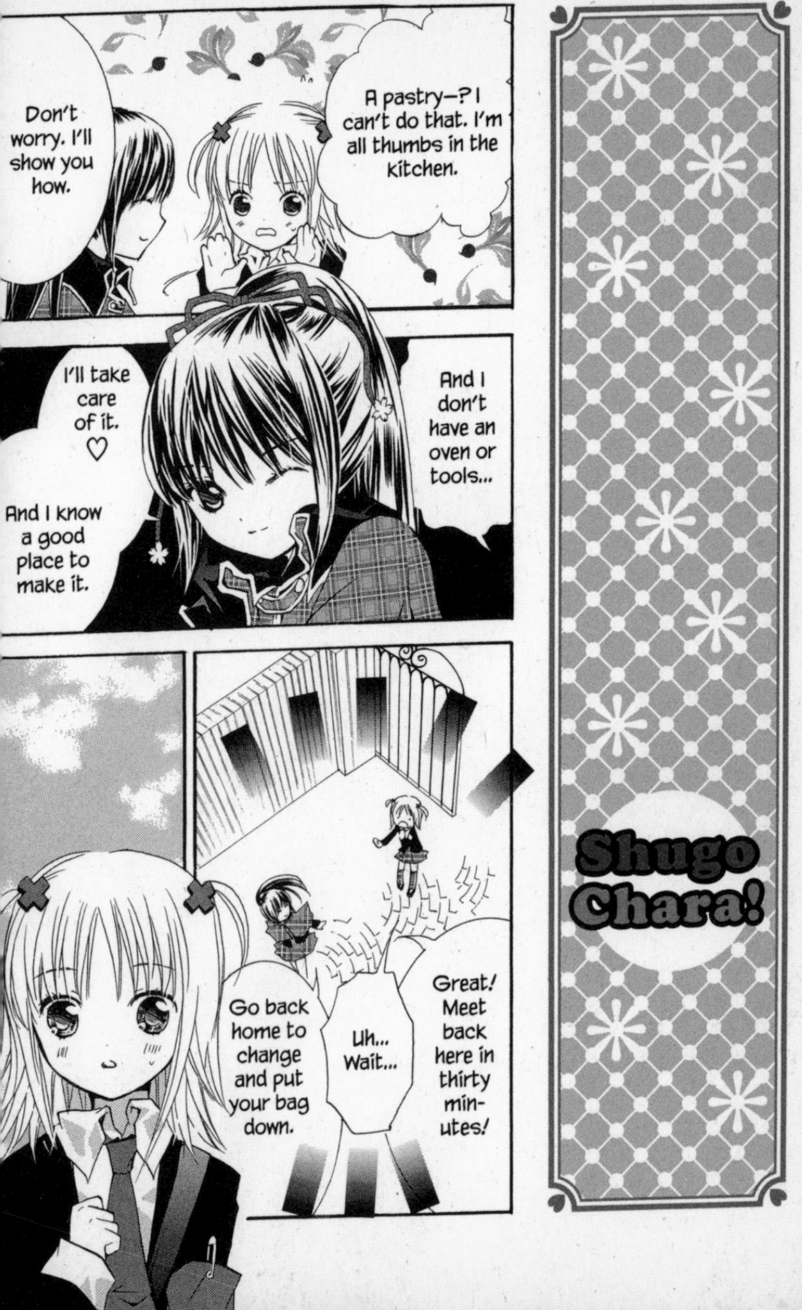
A pastry—? I can't do that. I'm all thumbs in the kitchen.
Don't worry. I'll show you how.
And I don't have an oven or tools...
I'll take care of it. ♡
And I know a good place to make it.
Great! Meet back here in thirty min-utes!
Uh... Wait...
Go back home to change and put your bag down.

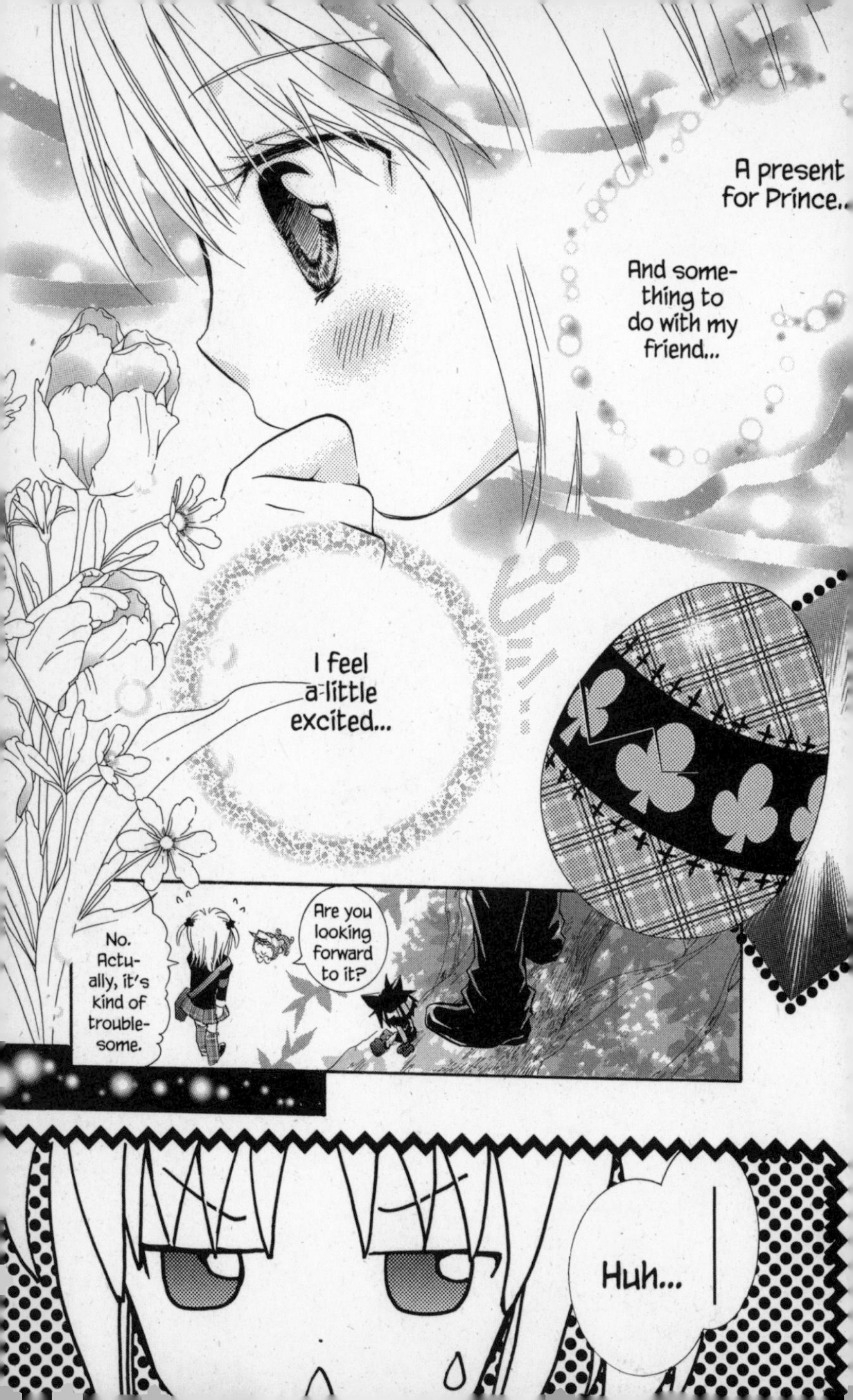
A present for Prince...
And something to do with my friend...
I feel a little excited...
Are you looking forward to it?
No. Actually, it's kind of troublesome.
Huh...

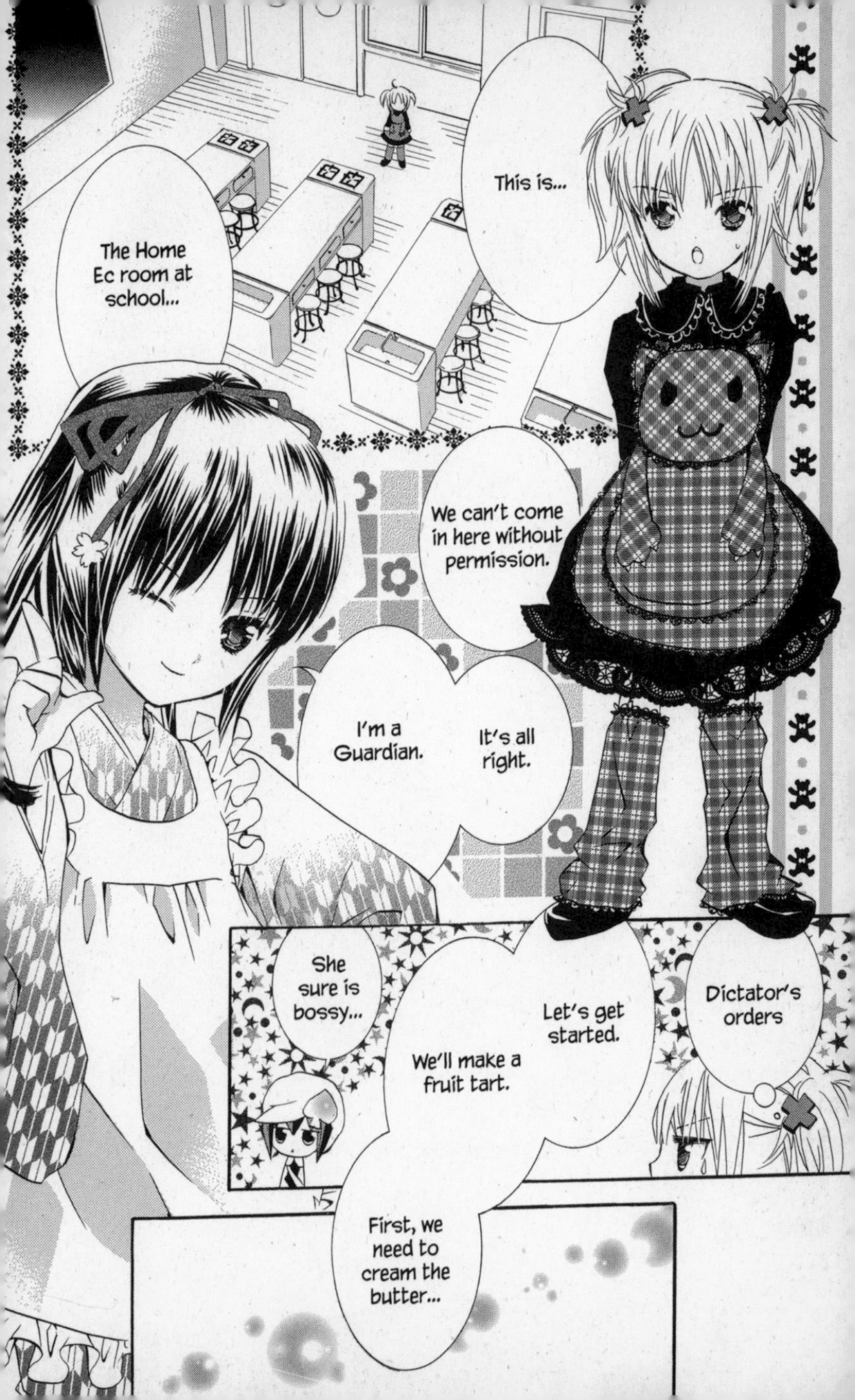
This is...
The Home Ec room at school...
We can't come in here without permission.
It's all right.
I'm a Guardian.
Let's get started.
We'll make a fruit tart.
Dictator's orders
She sure is bossy...
First, we need to cream the butter...

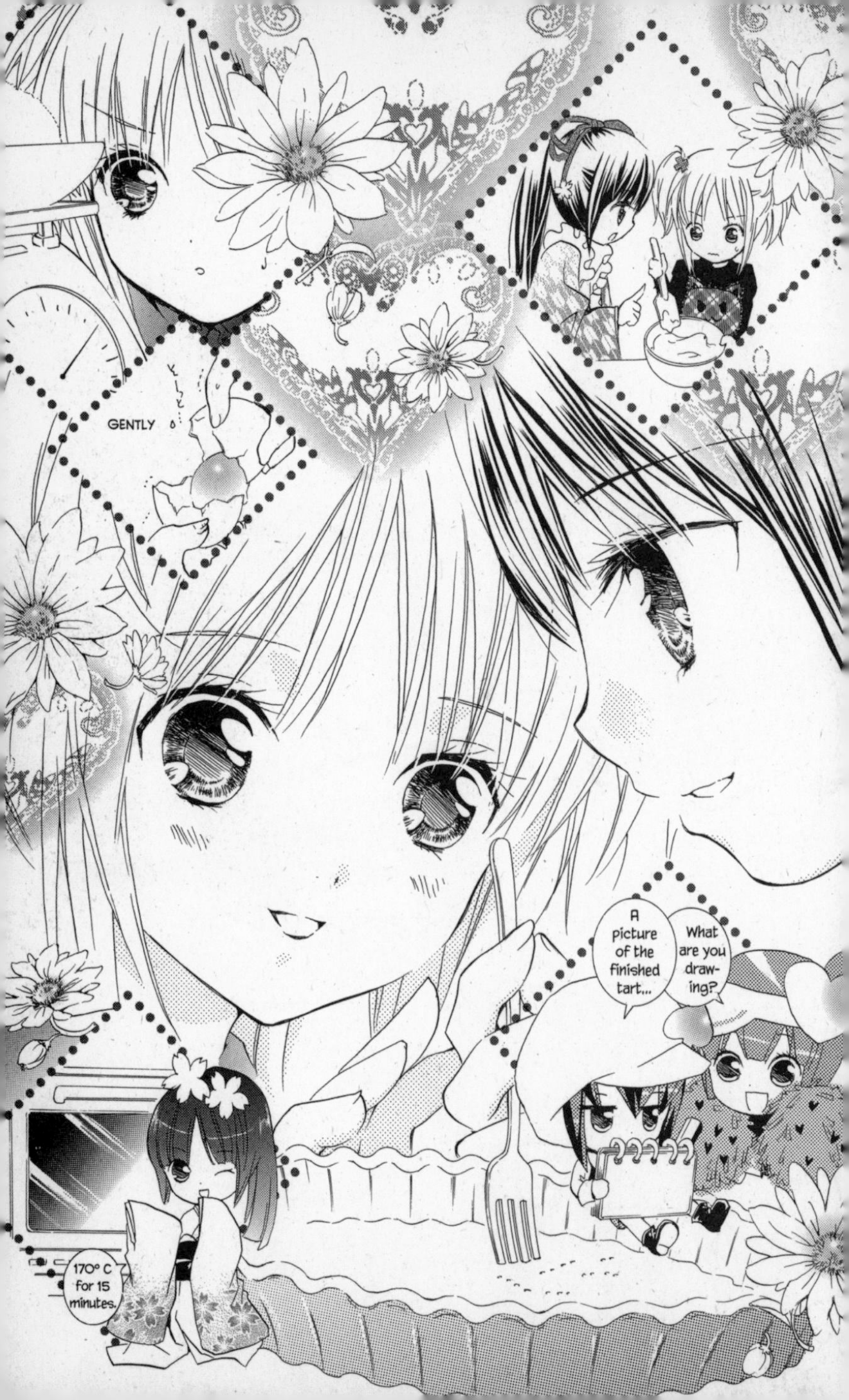
GENTLY
What are you draw-ing?
A picture of the finished tart...
170° C for 15 minutes.

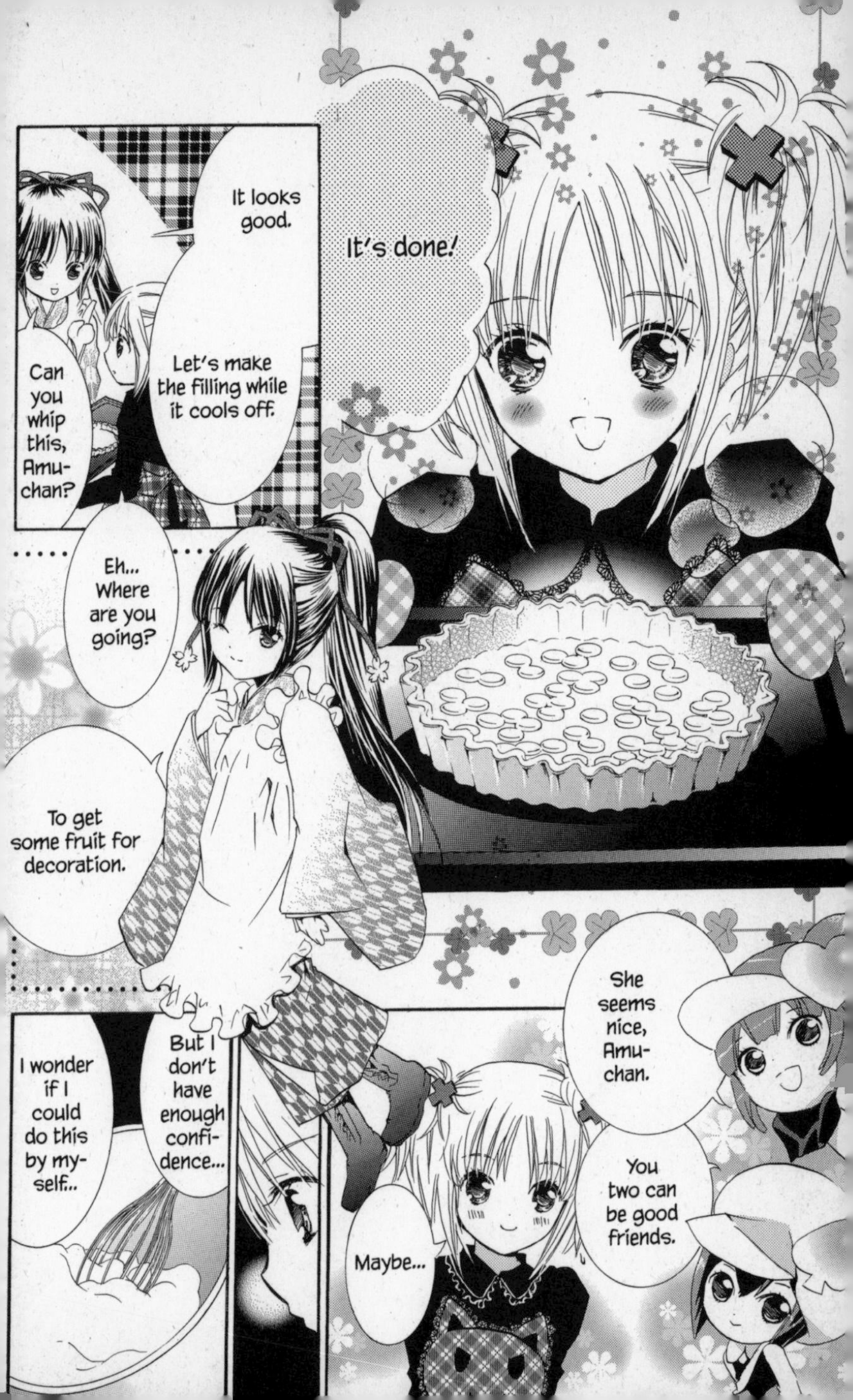

It's done!
It looks good.
Let's make the filling while it cools off.
Can you whip this, Amu-chan?
Eh... Where are you going?
To get some fruit for decoration.
She seems nice, Amu-chan.
You two can be good friends.
Maybe...
But I don't have enough confidence...
I wonder if I could do this by myself...

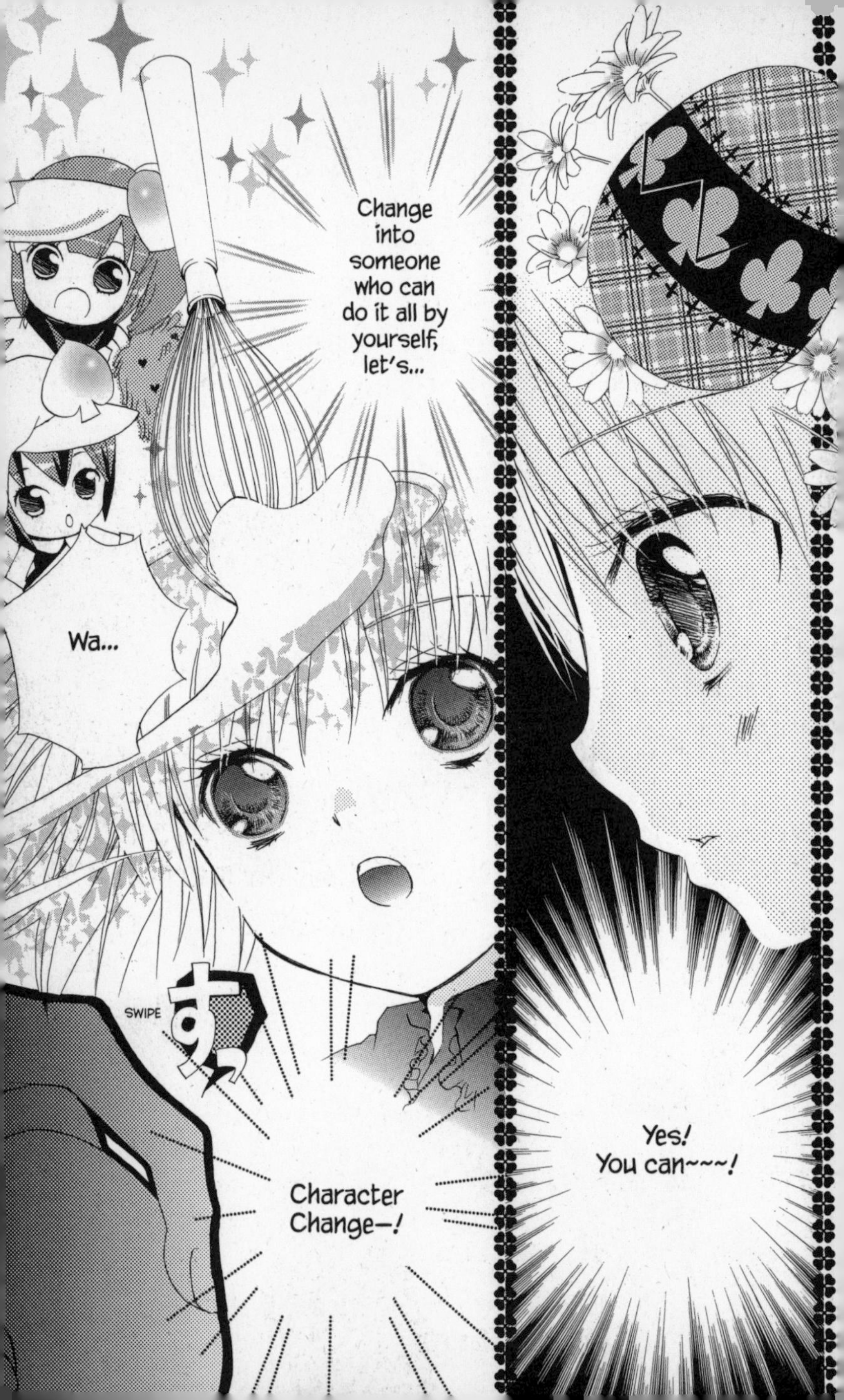
Yes!
You can~~~!
Change into someone who can do it all by yourself, let's...
Wa...
SWIPE
す
Character Change—!

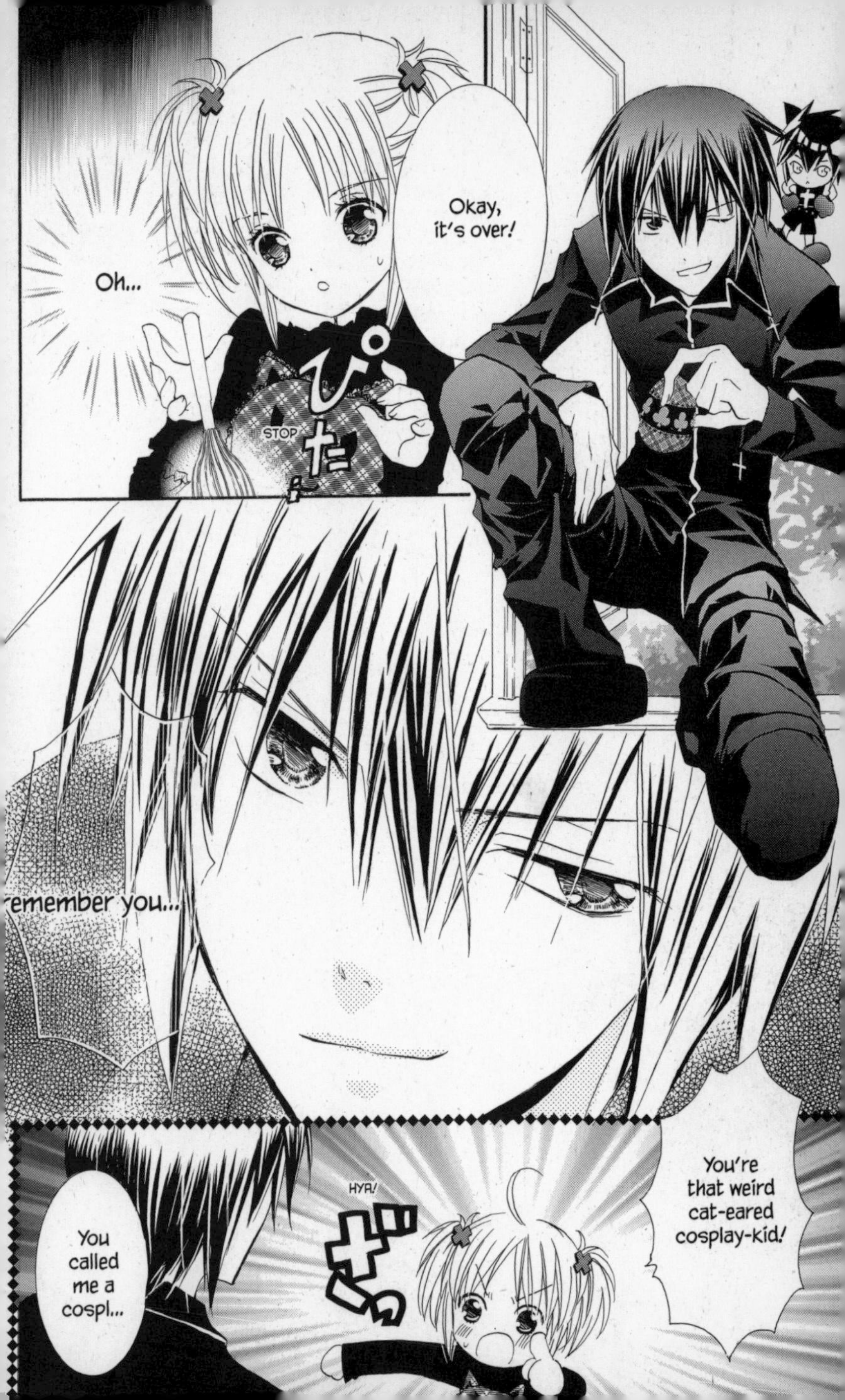
Okay, it's over!
Oh...
STOP
ぴた
remember you...
You're that weird cat-eared cosplay-kid!
HYA!
You called me a cospl...

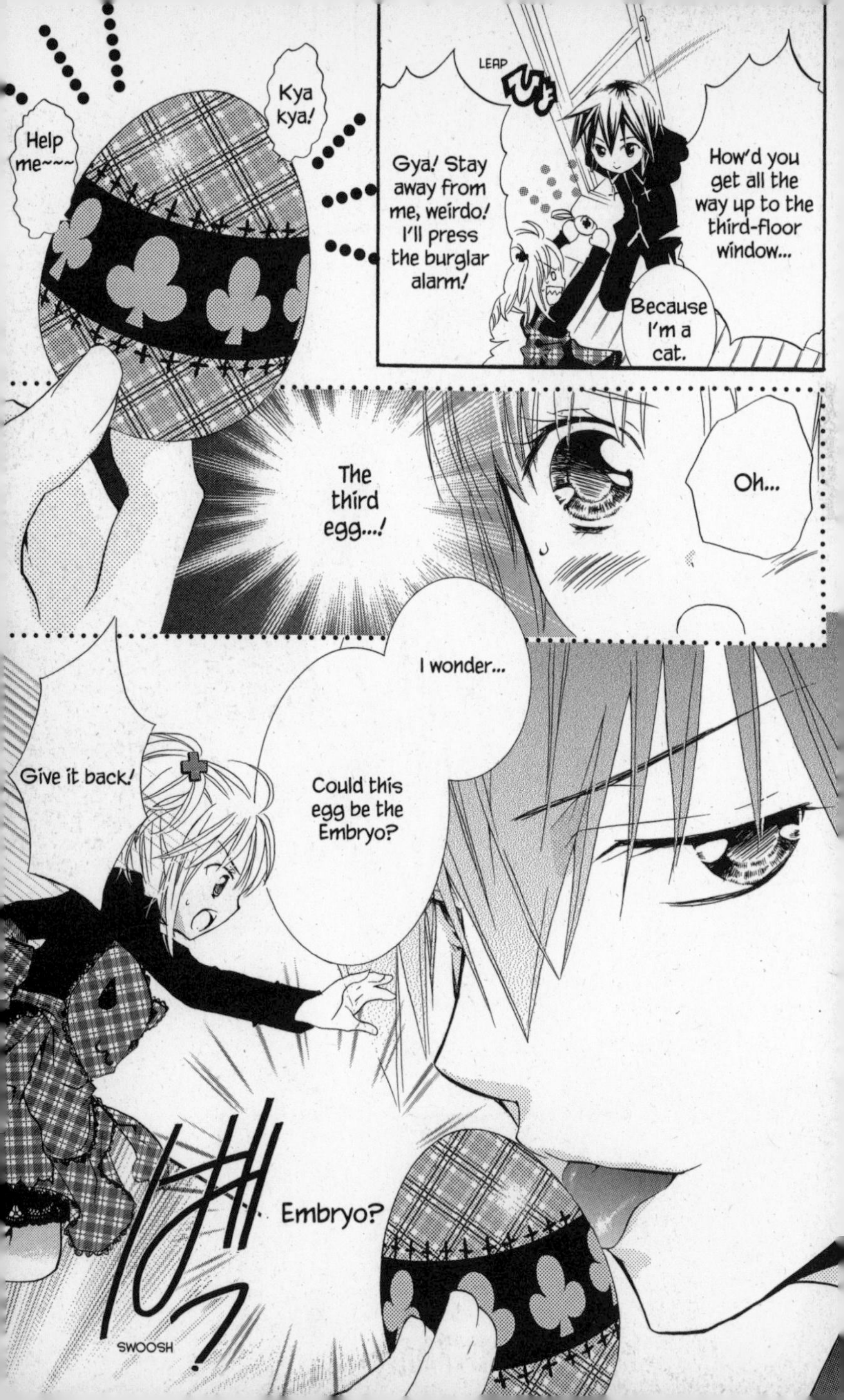
LEAP
How'd you get all the way up to the third-floor window...
Because I'm a cat.
Gya! Stay away from me, weirdo! I'll press the burglar alarm!
Kya kya!
Help me~~~
Oh...
The third egg...!
I wonder...
Could this egg be the Embryo?
Give it back!
Embryo?
SWOOSH

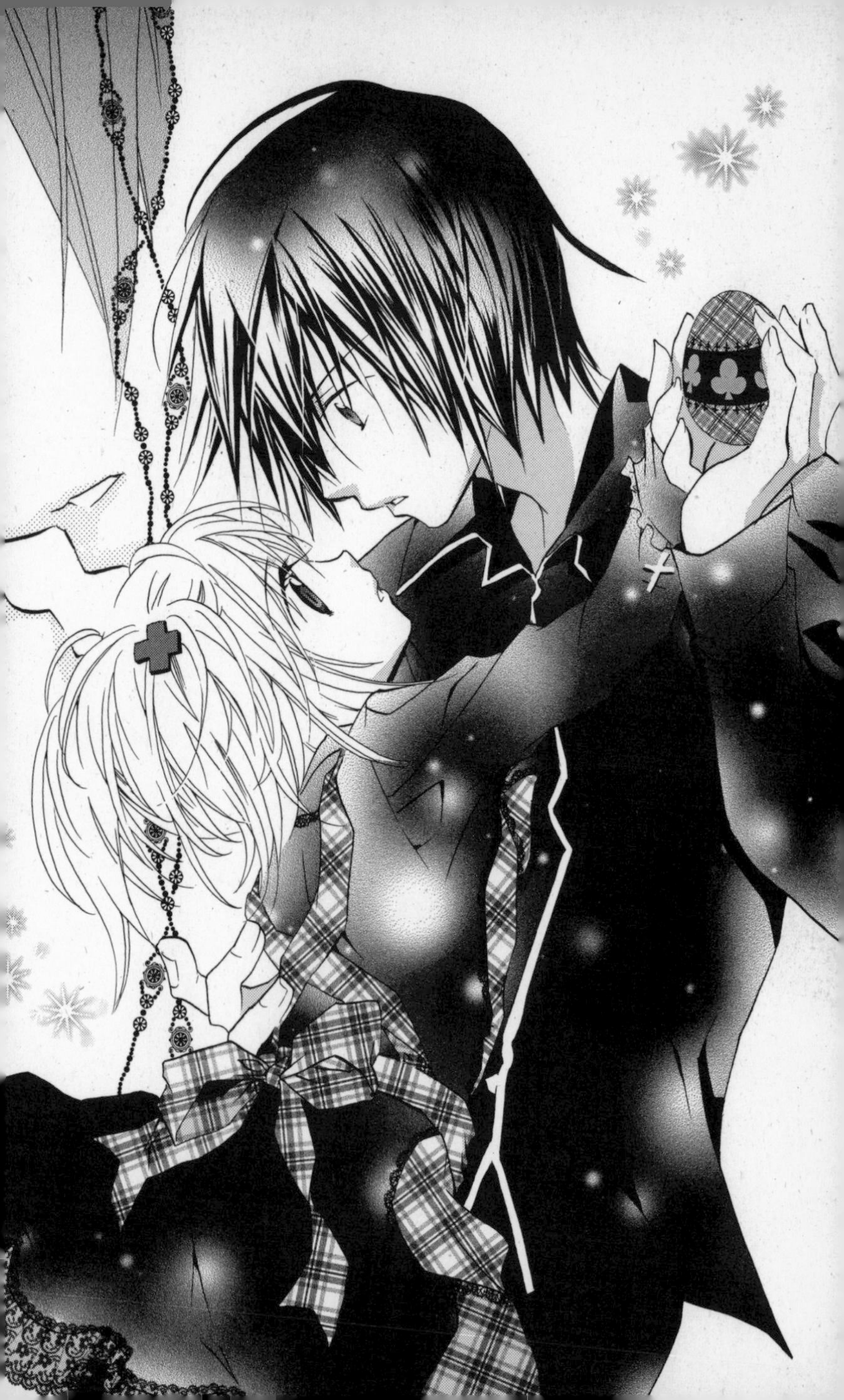

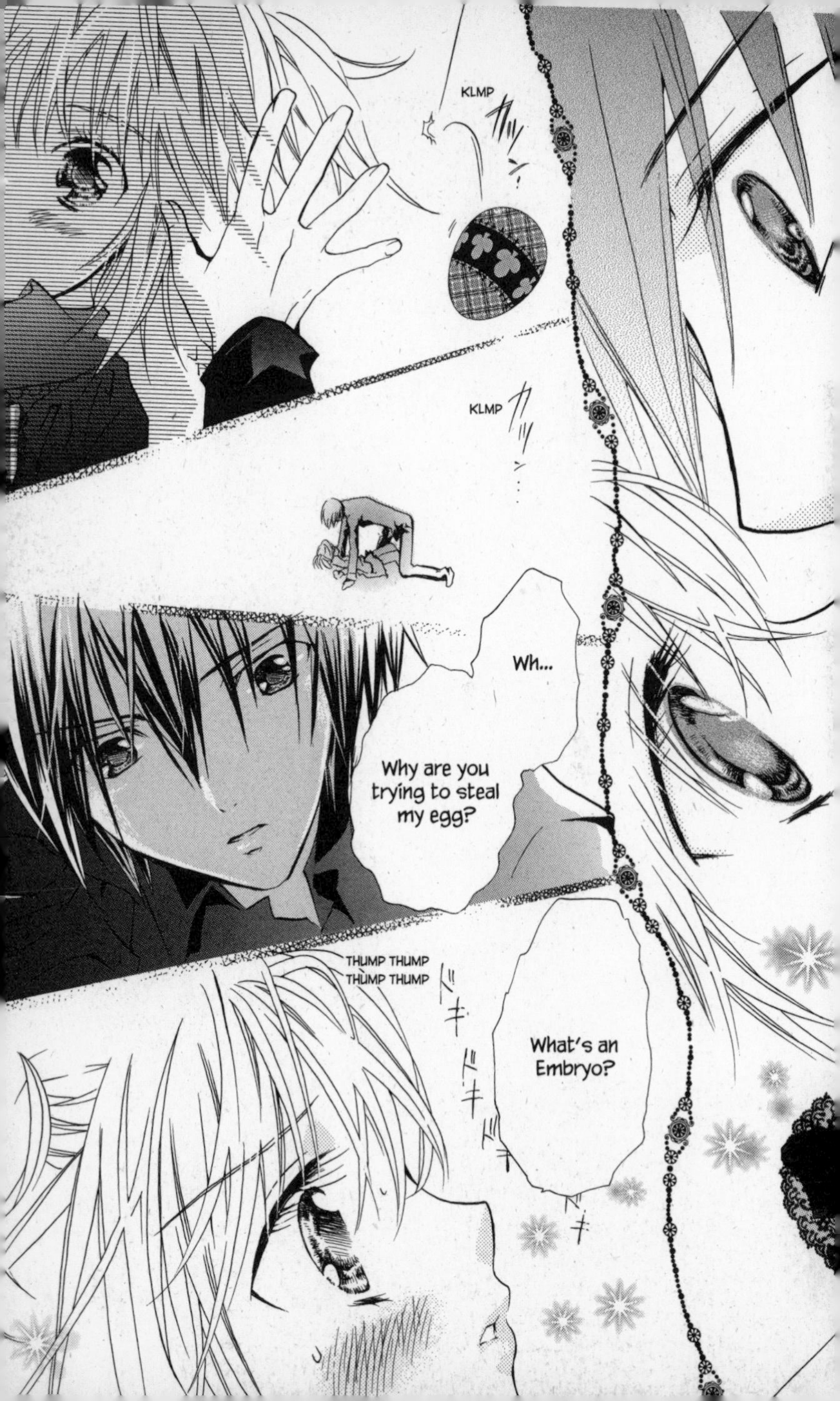

KLMP
KLMP
Wh...
Why are you trying to steal my egg?
THUMP THUMP
THUMP THUMP
What's an Embryo?

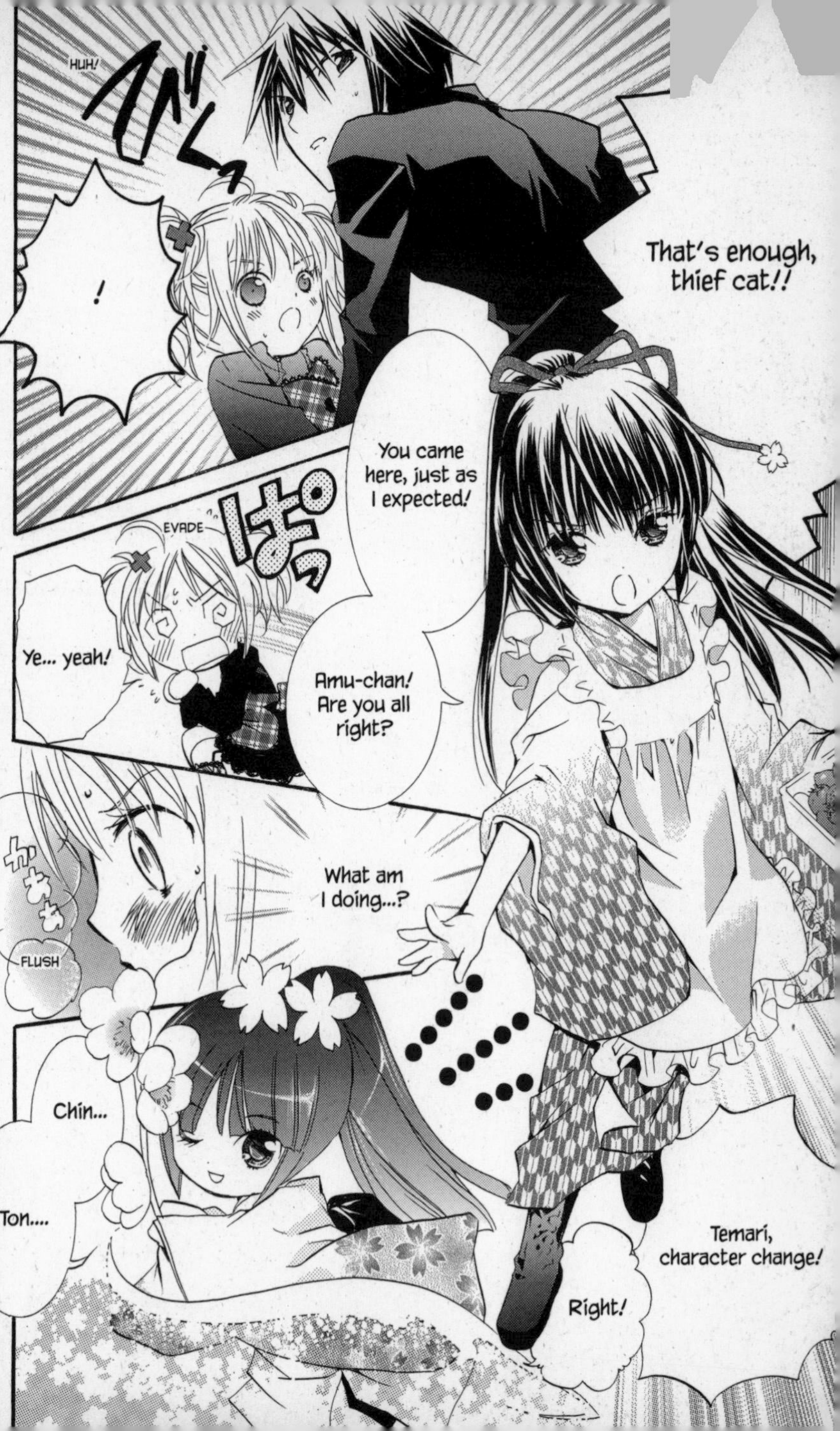
That's enough, thief cat!!
HUH!
!
You came here, just as I expected!
Amu-chan! Are you all right?
EVADE
Ye... yeah!
What am I doing...?
FLUSH
Temari, character change!
Right!
Chin...
Ton....

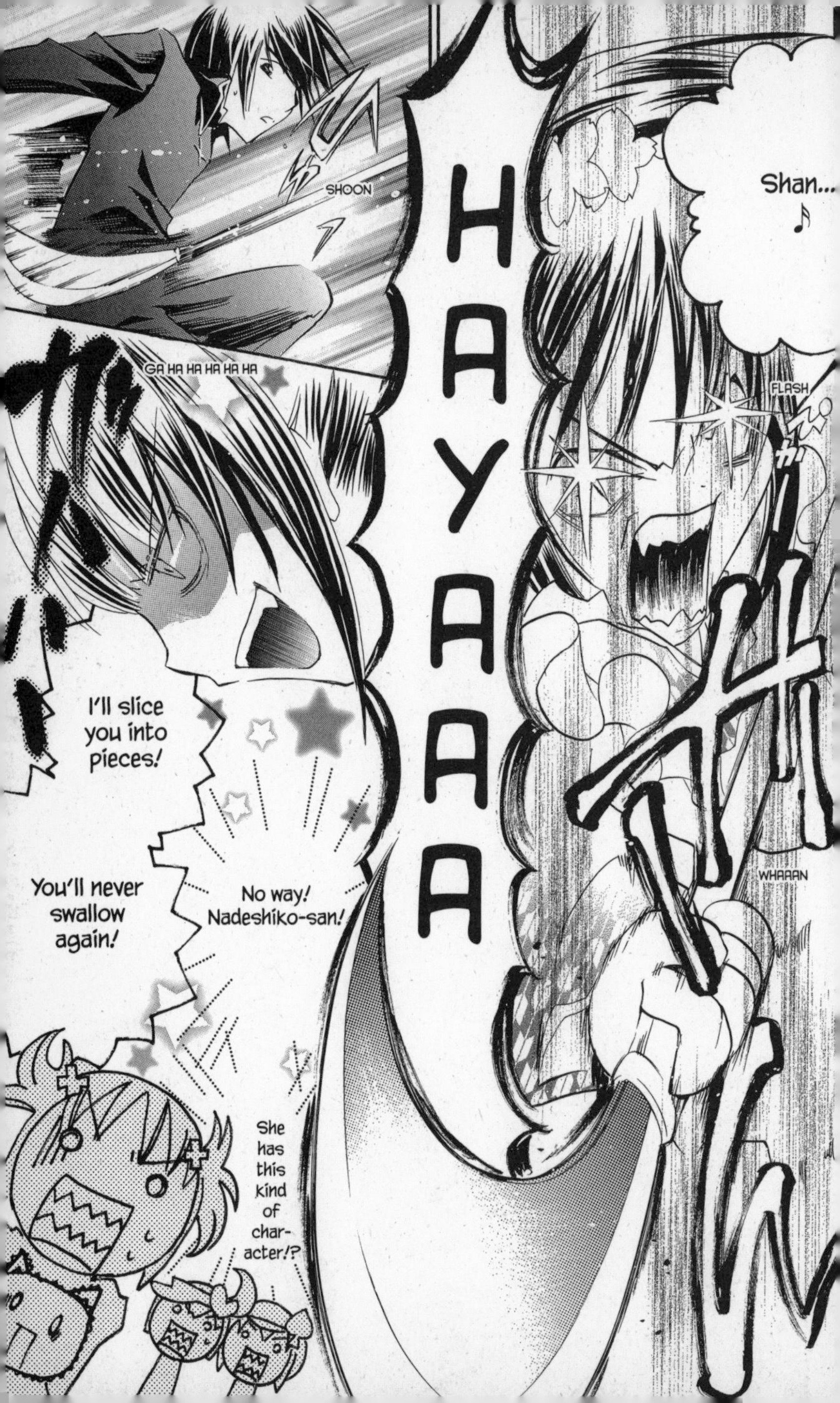
Shan... ♪
FLASH
HAYAAAA
WHAAAN
SHOON
GA HA HA HA HA HA
I'll slice you into pieces!
You'll never swallow again!
No way! Nadeshiko-san!
She has this kind of char-acter!?

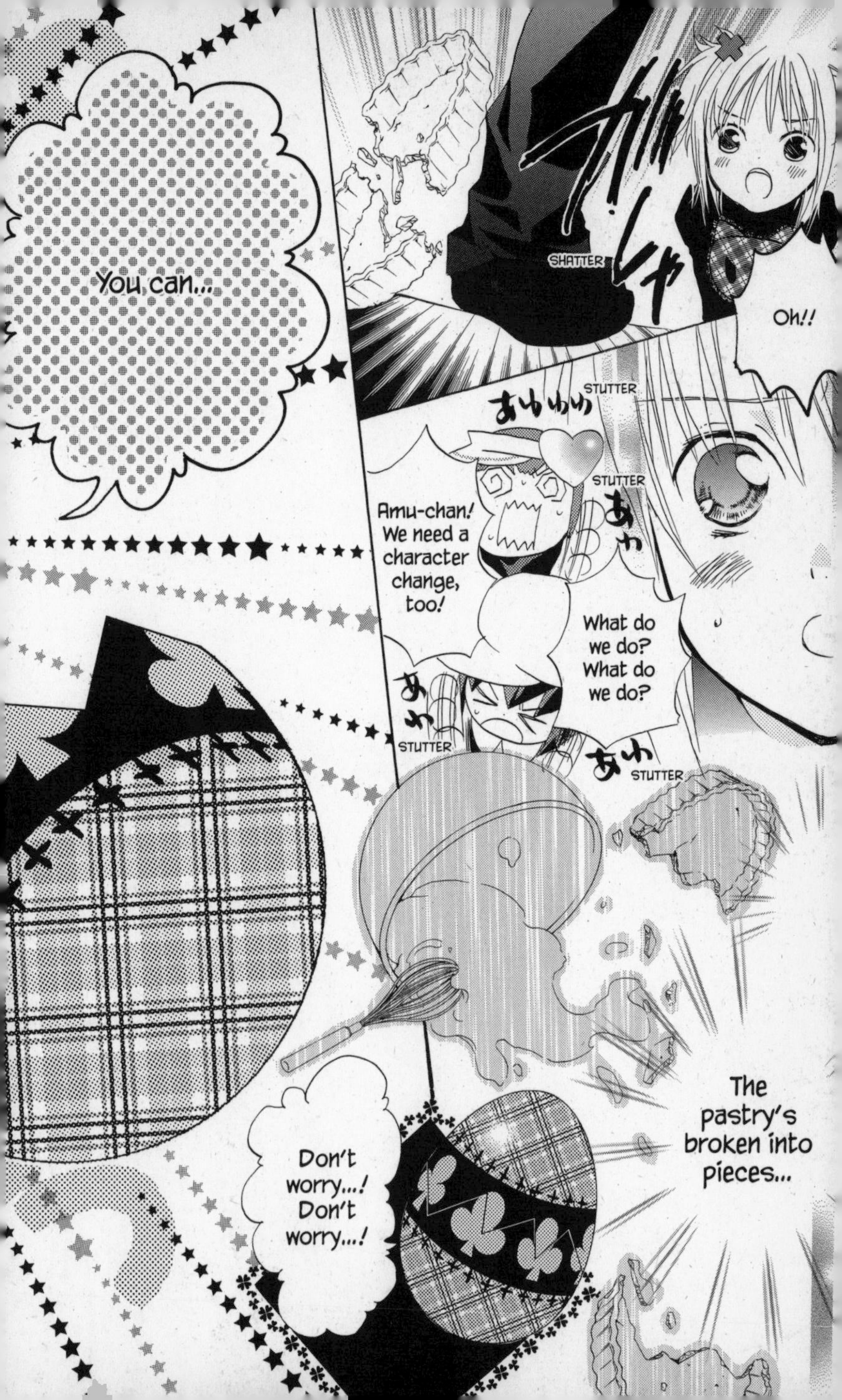

SHATTER
Oh!!
あわわわ
STUTTER
あわ
STUTTER
Amu-chan! We need a character change, too!
What do we do? What do we do?
あわ
STUTTER
あわ
STUTTER
The pastry's broken into pieces...
Don't worry...! Don't worry...!
You can...

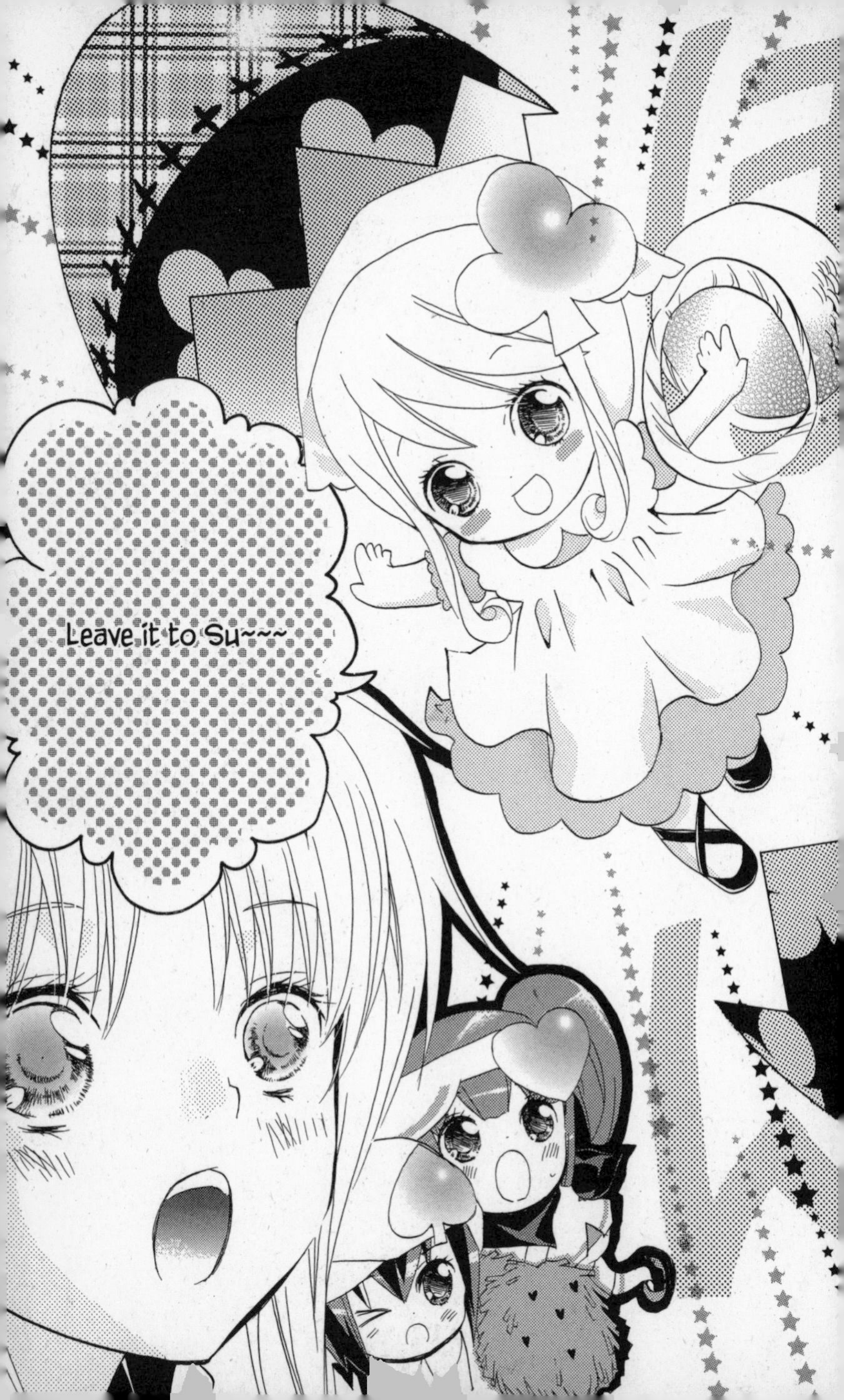
Leave it to Su~~~

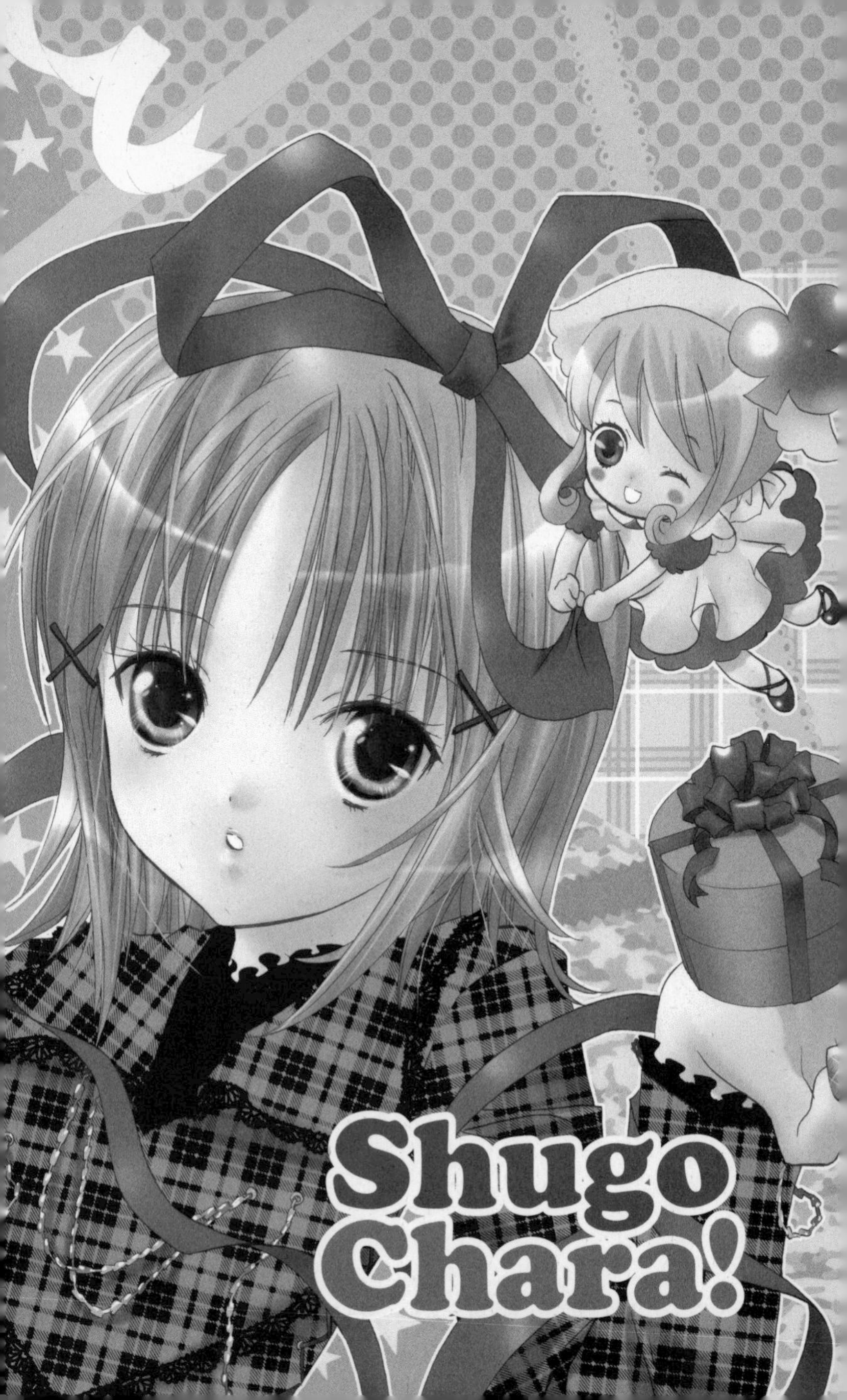
Shugo
Chara!

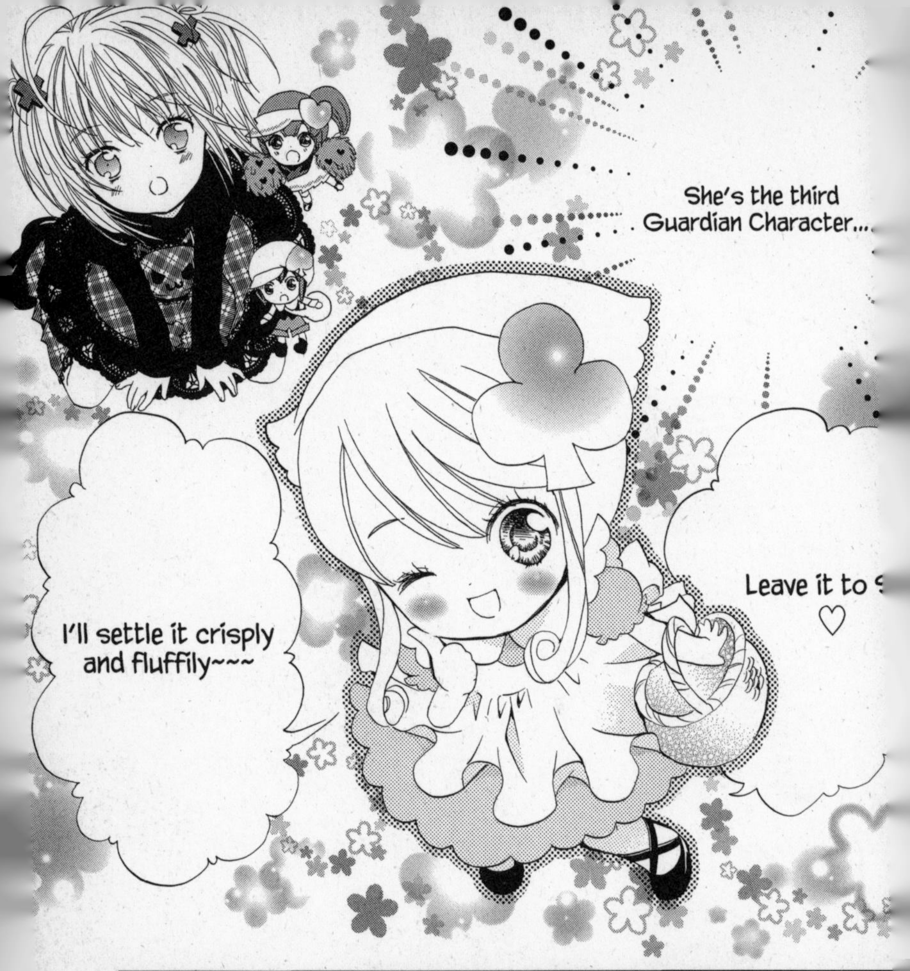
She's the third Guardian Character...
Leave it to
♡
I'll settle it crisply and fluffily~~~

Q 3. I want to be a manga artist. Do you have any suggestions?

A 3. Well...If you like manga and keep drawing it, maybe some day you might just naturally become a manga artist. But there's a lot more to it than just drawing pictures. So I suggest that for now, you hang out with your friends, fall in love with someone, and study hard. (I envy your youth!)

Q 4. Are you more of a Kamenashi-san fan or an Akanishi-kun fan?

A 4. Hm....Ebara is a fan of Kamenishi-kun and Banri-san is a fan of Yamapi. Akanishi-kun...?

That's all for now. See you in volume 2! ♡

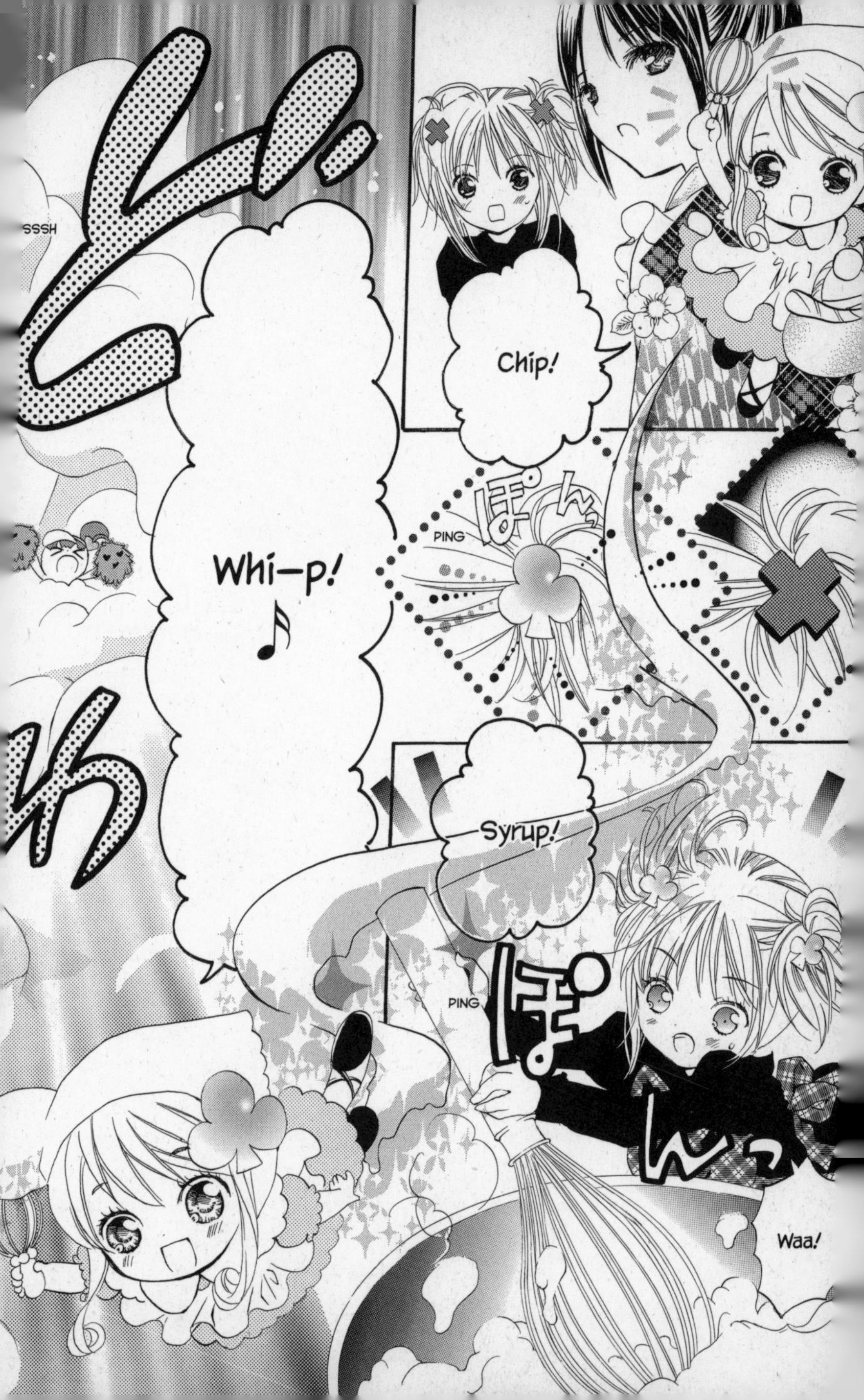

Chip!
PING
Syrup!
PING
Waa!
SSSH
Whi-p! ♪

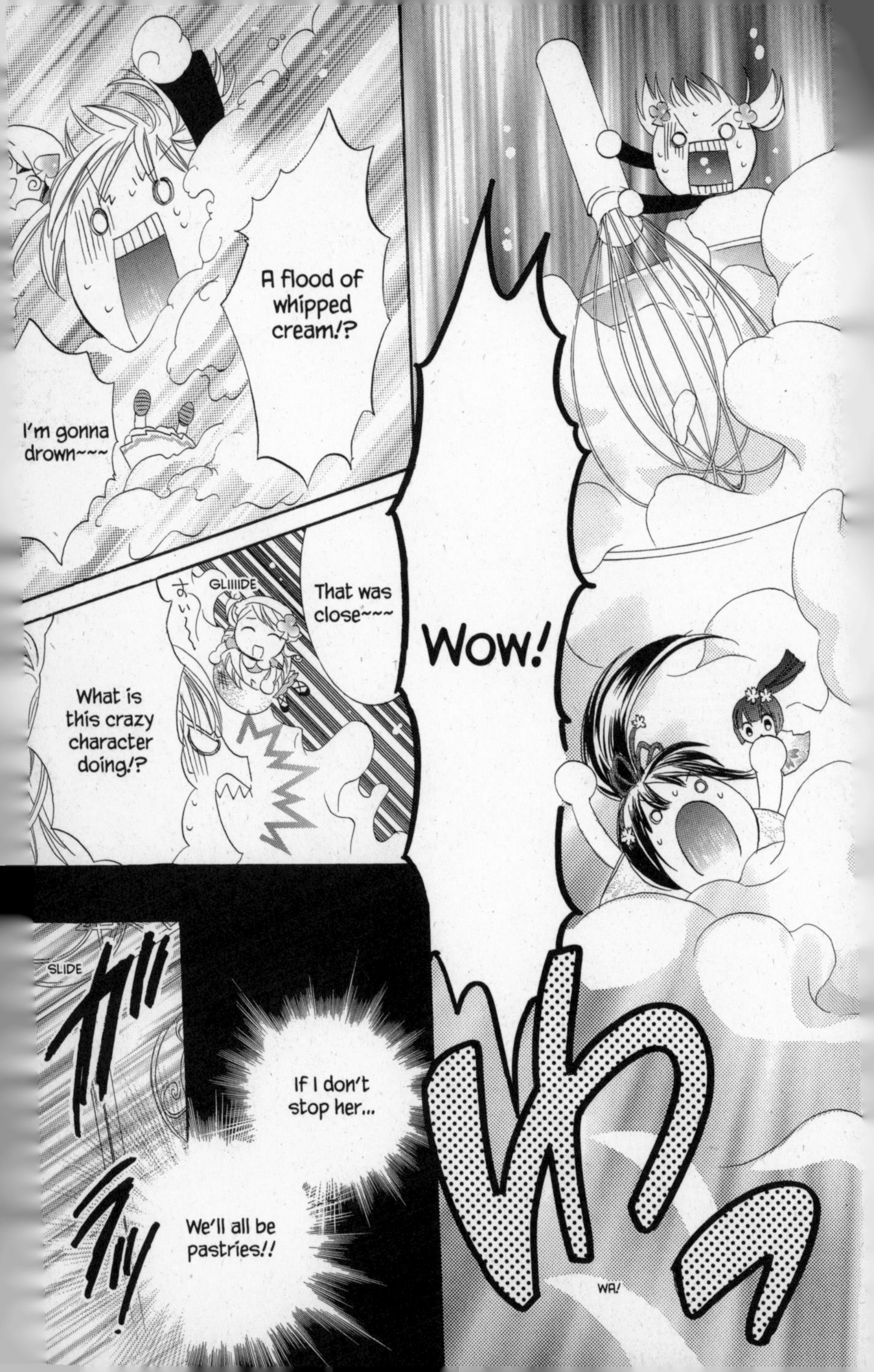
WOW!
WA!
A flood of whipped cream!?
I'm gonna drown~~~
GLIIIDE
That was close~~~
What is this crazy character doing!?
SLIDE
If I don't stop her...
We'll all be pastries!!

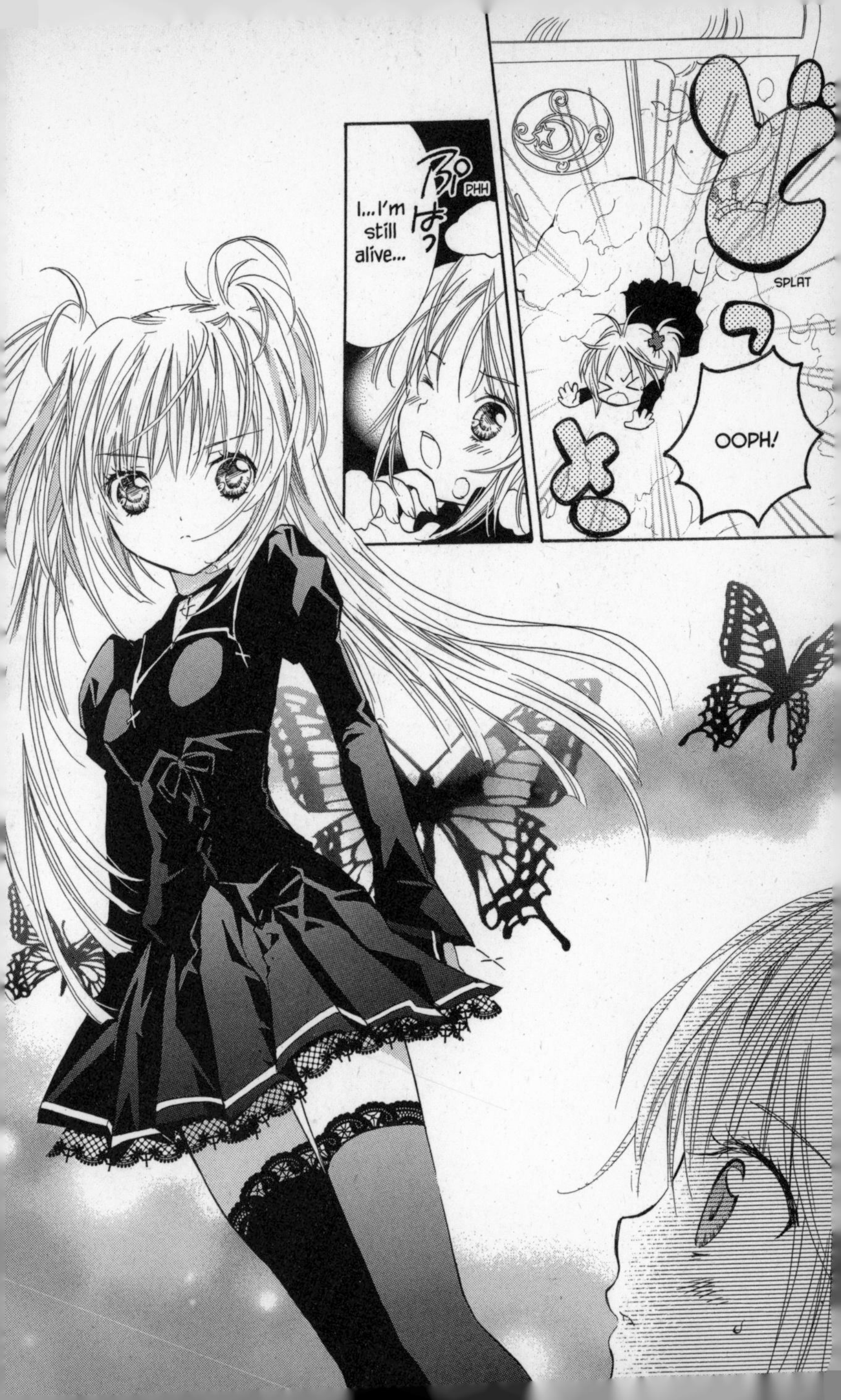
SPLAT
OOPH!
PHH
I...I'm still alive...

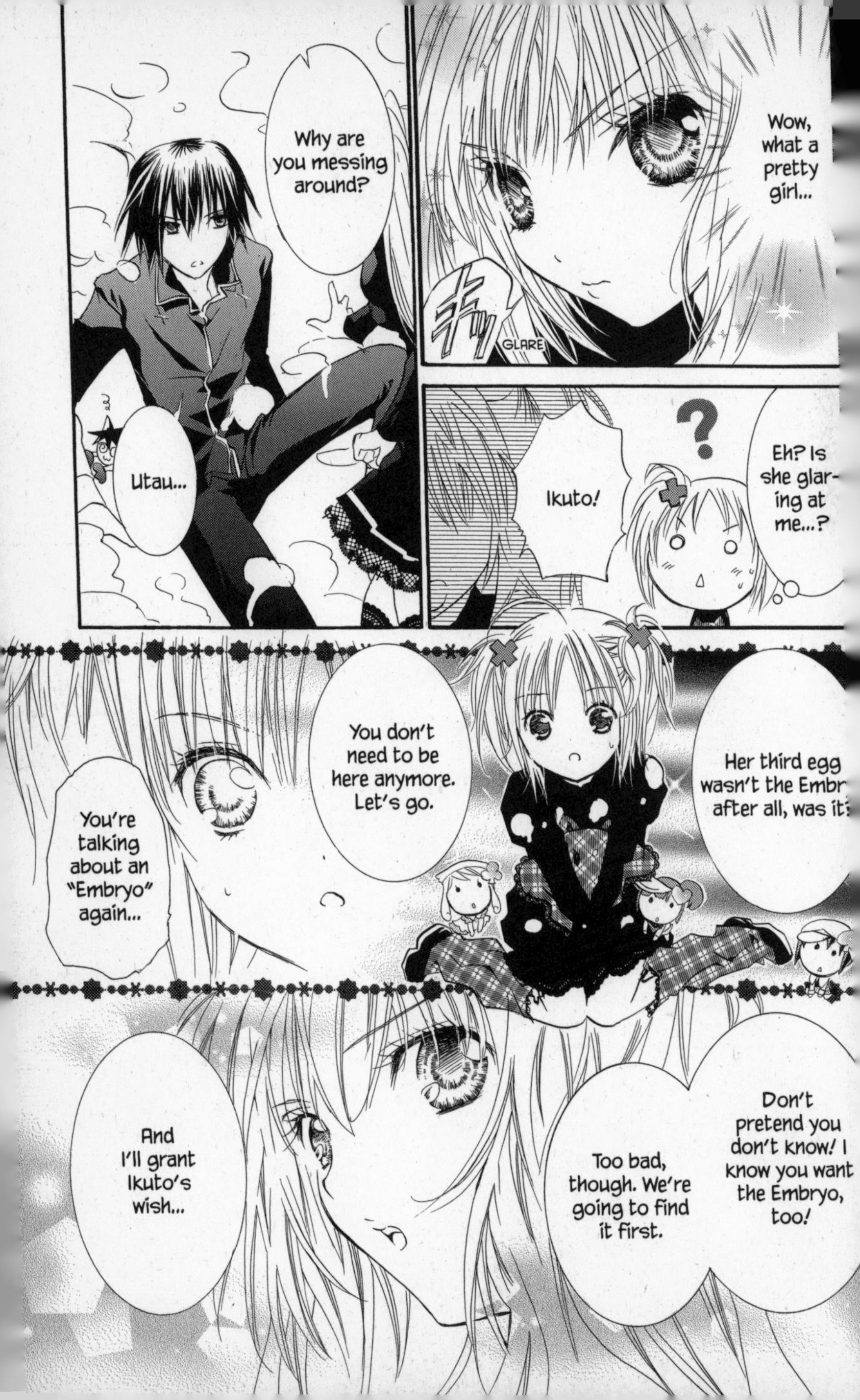
Wow, what a pretty girl...
GLARE
Eh? Is she glaring at me...?
Ikuto!
Why are you messing around?
Utau...
Her third egg wasn't the Embr after all, was it
You don't need to be here anymore. Let's go.
You're talking about an "Embryo" again...
Don't pretend you don't know! I know you want the Embryo, too!
Too bad, though. We're going to find it first.
And I'll grant Ikuto's wish...

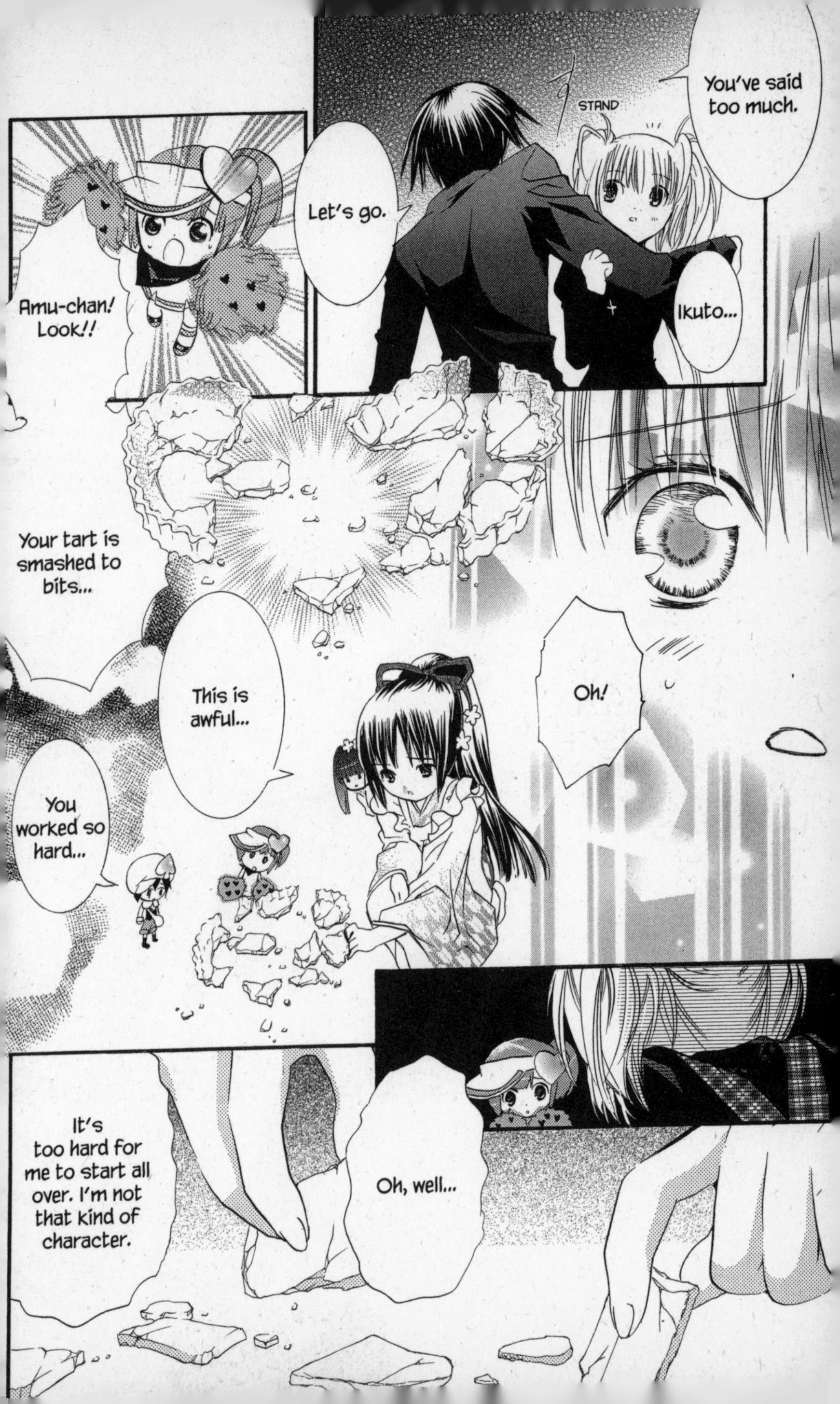

You've said too much.
STAND
Let's go.
Ikuto...
Amu-chan! Look!!
Oh!
Your tart is smashed to bits...
This is awful...
You worked so hard...
Oh, well...
It's too hard for me to start all over. I'm not that kind of character.

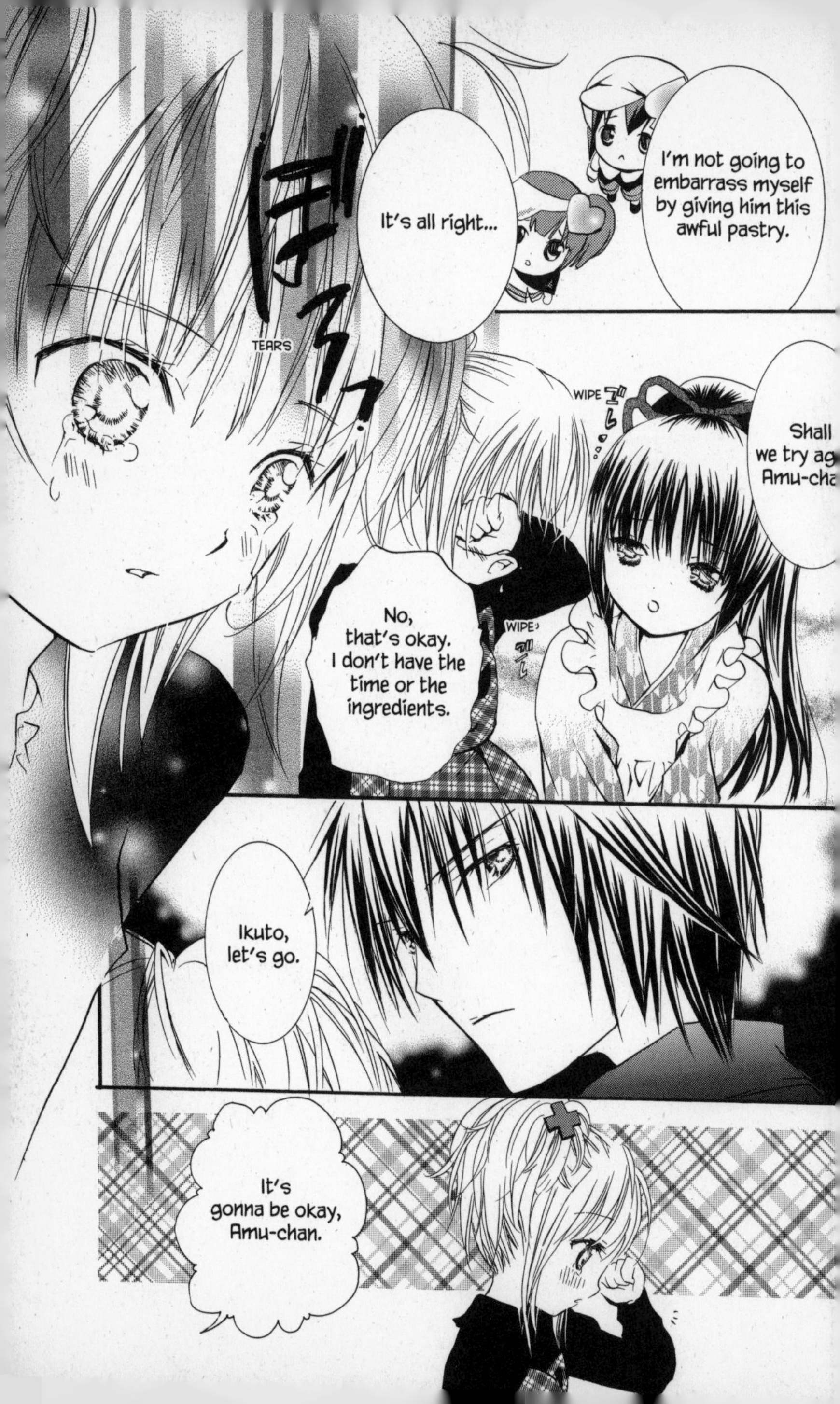

I'm not going to embarrass myself by giving him this awful pastry.
Shall we try ag Amu-cha
WIPE
WIPE
No, that's okay. I don't have the time or the ingredients.
Ikuto, let's go.
It's gonna be okay, Amu-chan.
TEARS
It's all right...

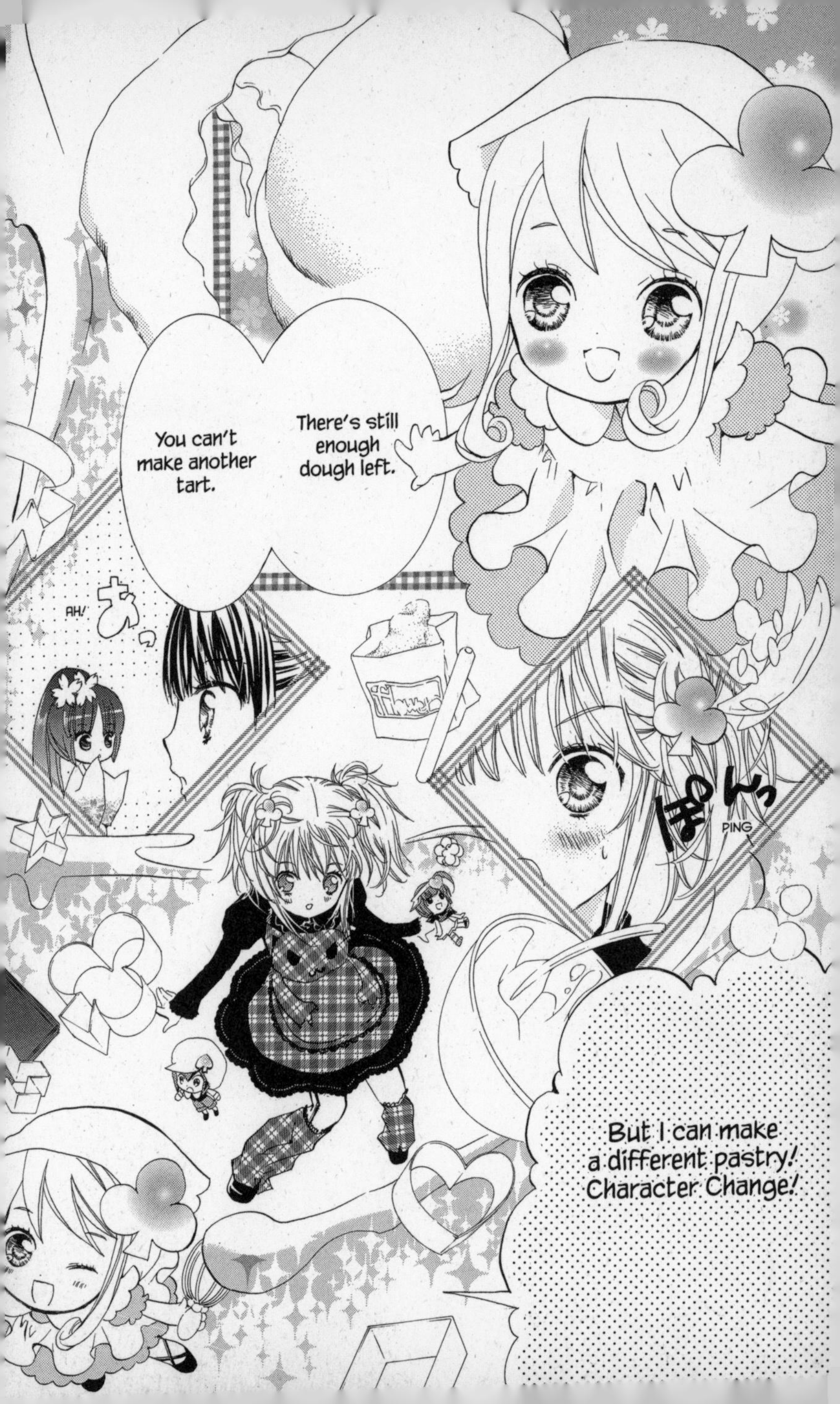
There's still enough dough left.
You can't make another tart.
あっ
AH!
ぽんっ
PING
But I can make a different pastry! Character Change!

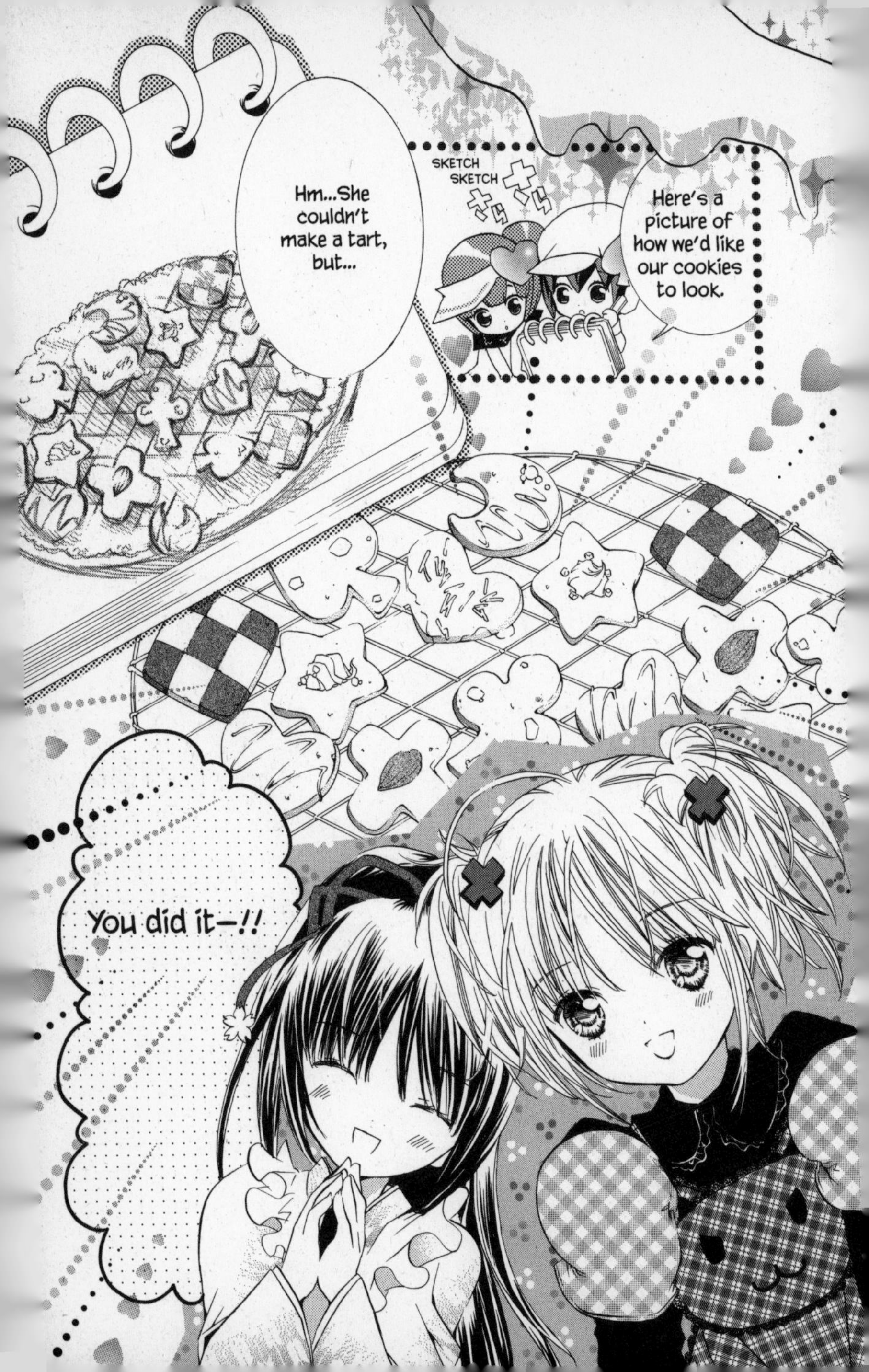
SKETCH SKETCH
Here's a picture of how we'd like our cookies to look.
Hm...She couldn't make a tart, but...
You did it—!!

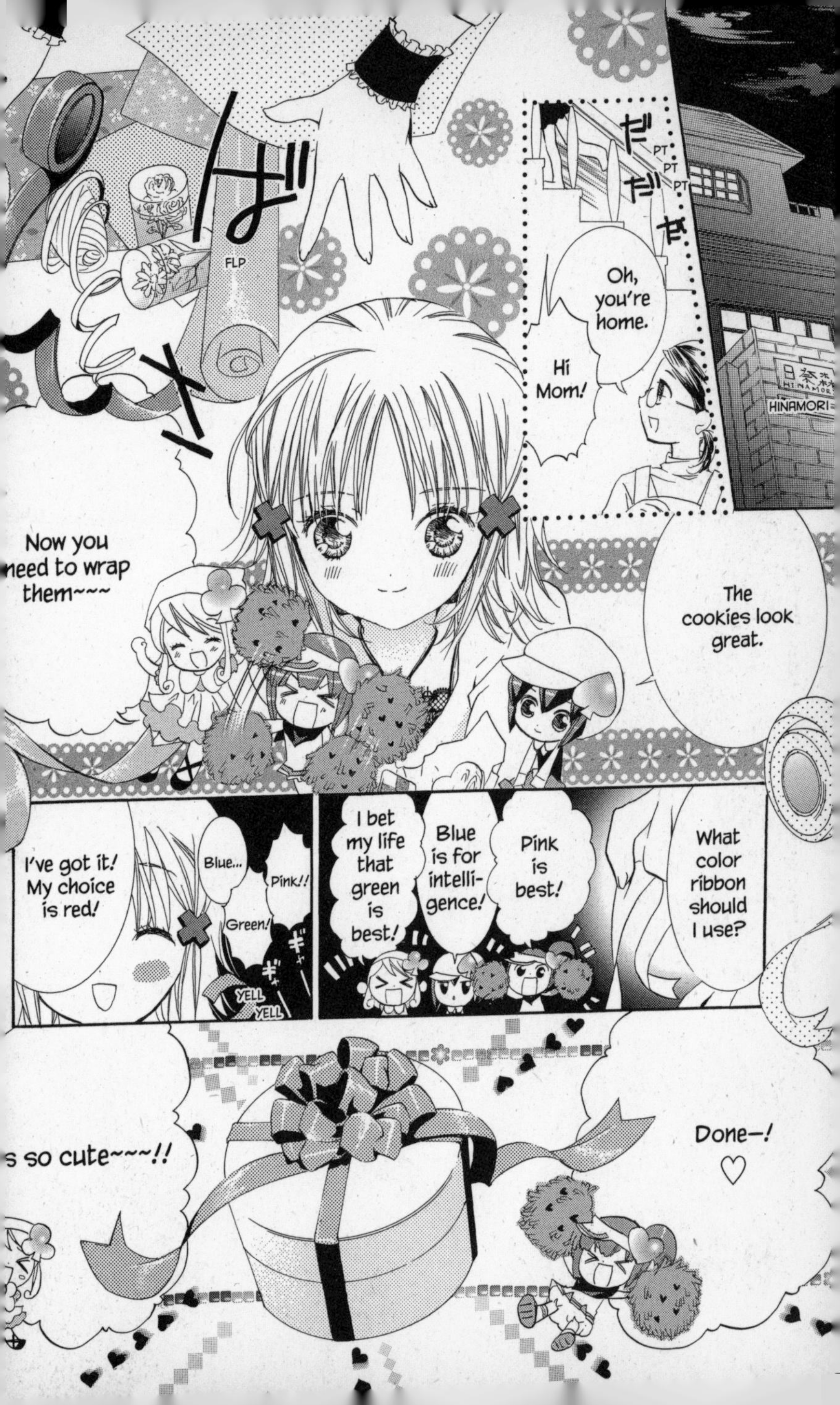

だだだ
PT PT PT
Oh, you're home.
Hi Mom!
HINAMORI
FLP
The cookies look great.
Now you need to wrap them~~~
What color ribbon should I use?
Pink is best!
Blue is for intelli-gence!
I bet my life that green is best!
Pink!!
Blue...
Green!
ギャ ギャ
YELL YELL
I've got it! My choice is red!
Done—! ♡
s so cute~~~!!

You need to put a card in it, too!

Good idea.

It's okay. Don't you guys dare touch it.

SWIPE

I'm a little concerned that the folds aren't even...

"Dea Prince sama.

I love you— Please eat these like they're me ☆

Yeah...

From the really shy girl, Amu Hinamori.

I'll be waiting forever for your text message. ♡

Ah ha.

We almost got her!

She set herself up.

I can't send him that!!

CHK

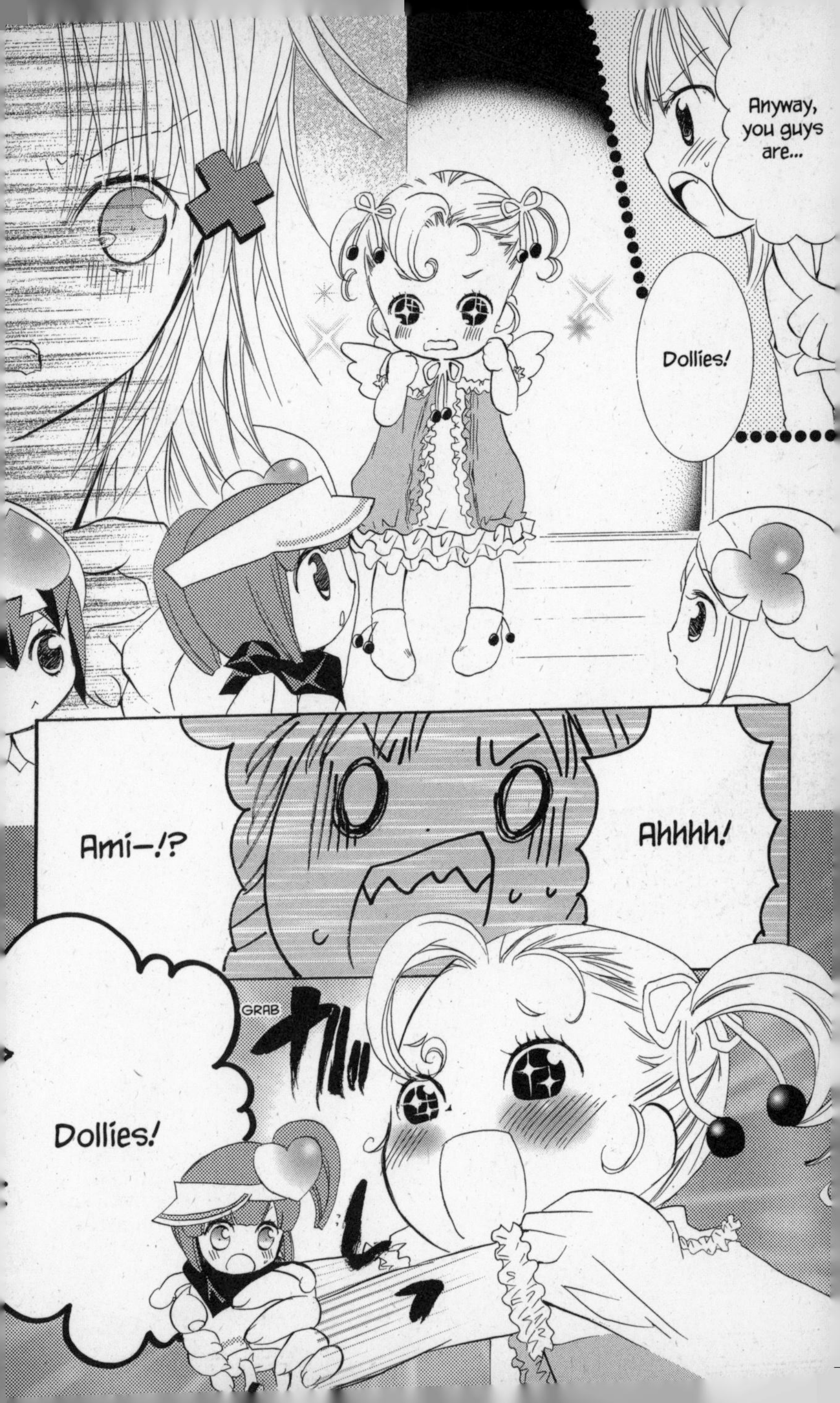
Anyway, you guys are...
Dollies!
Ahhhh!
Ami-!?
GRAB
Dollies!

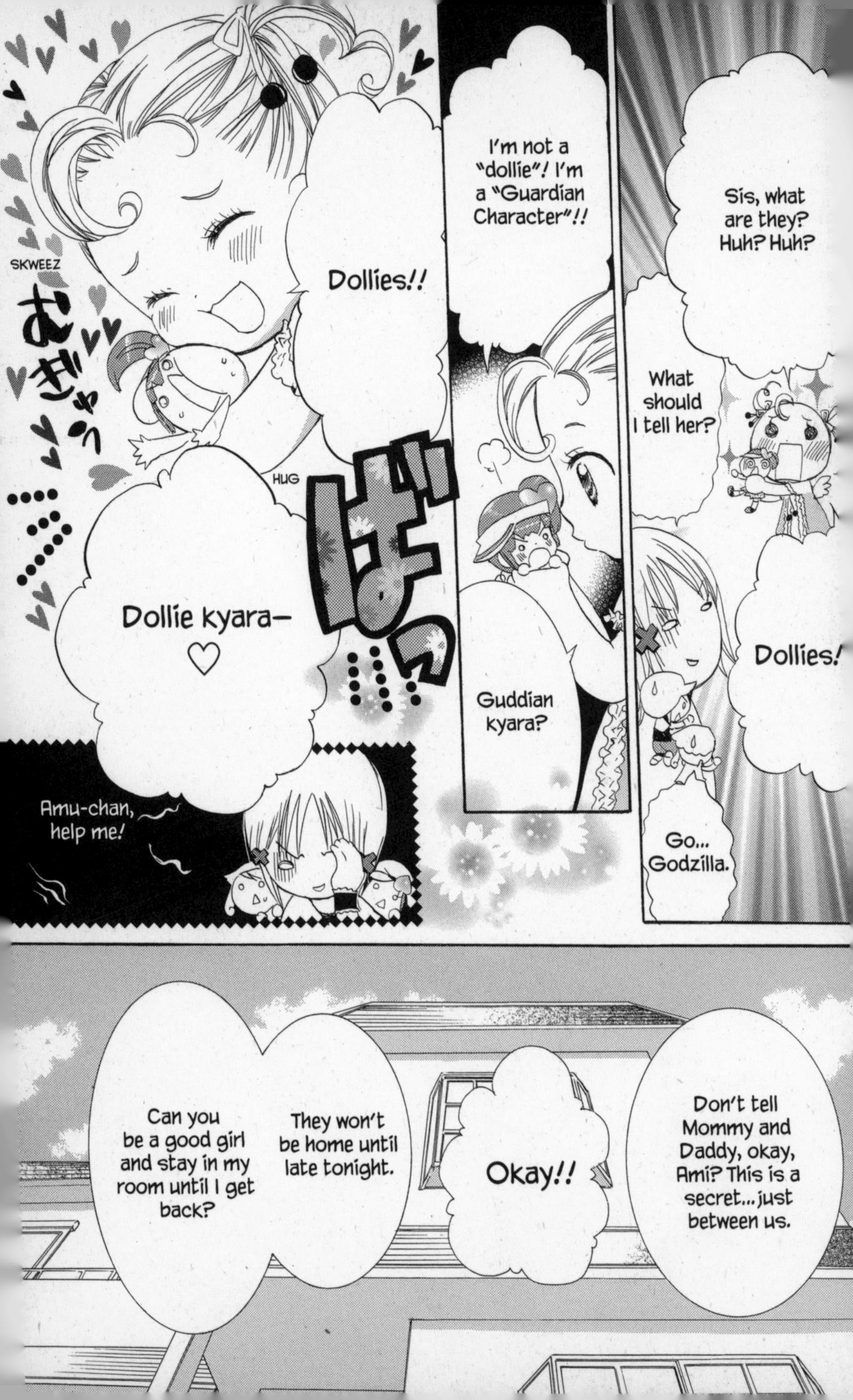
Sis, what are they? Huh? Huh?
What should I tell her?
Dollies!
Go... Godzilla.
I'm not a "dollie"! I'm a "Guardian Character"!!
Guddian kyara?
Dollies!!
SKWEEZ
HUG
Dollie kyara— ♡
Amu-chan, help me!
Don't tell Mommy and Daddy, okay, Ami? This is a secret...just between us.
Okay!!
They won't be home until late tonight.
Can you be a good girl and stay in my room until I get back?

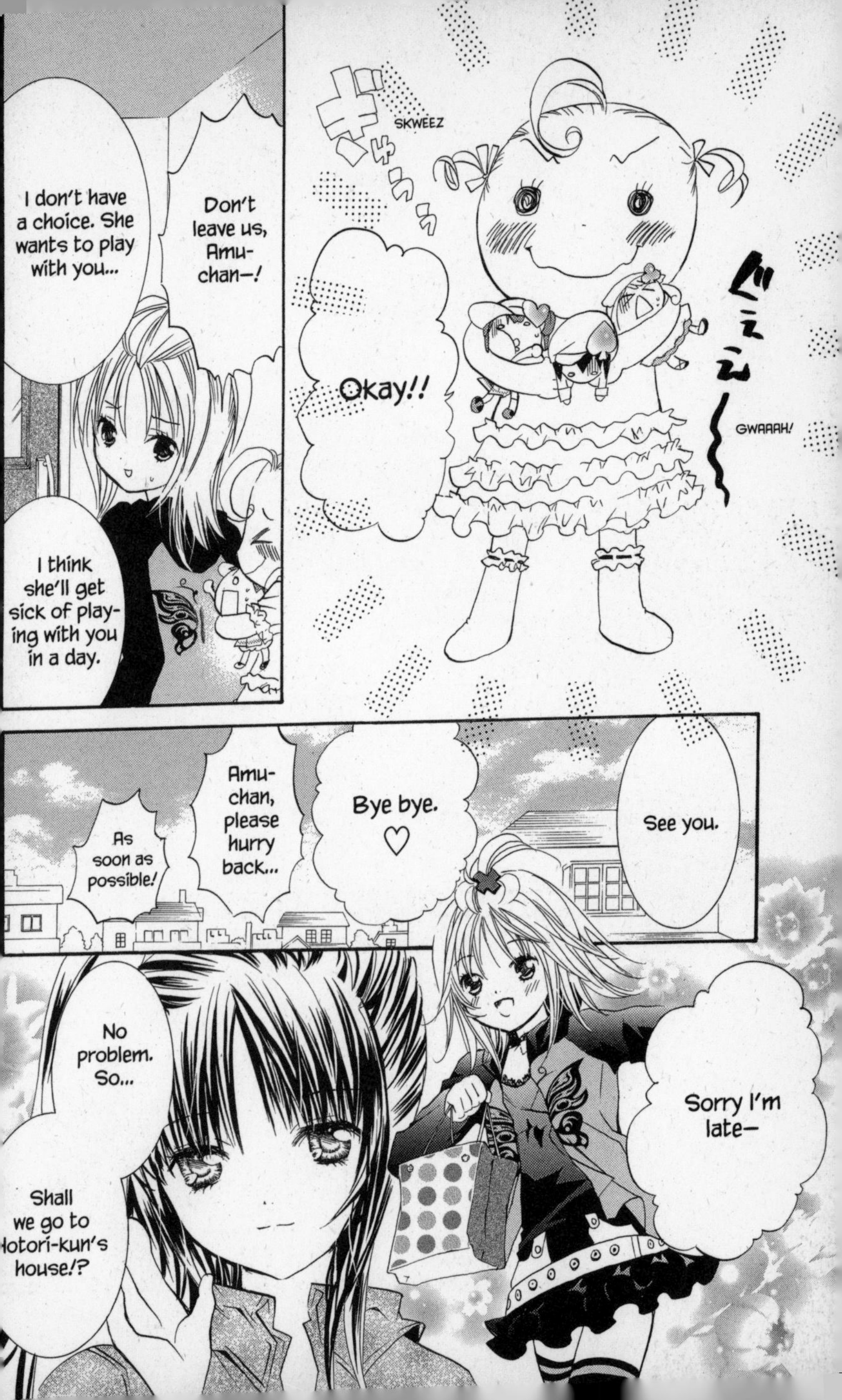
ぎゅううう
SKWEEZ
ぐえええ〜
GWAAAH!
Okay!!
Don't leave us, Amu-chan—!
I don't have a choice. She wants to play with you...
I think she'll get sick of playing with you in a day.
See you.
Bye bye. ♡
Amu-chan, please hurry back...
As soon as possible!
Sorry I'm late—
No problem. So...
Shall we go to Hotori-kun's house!?

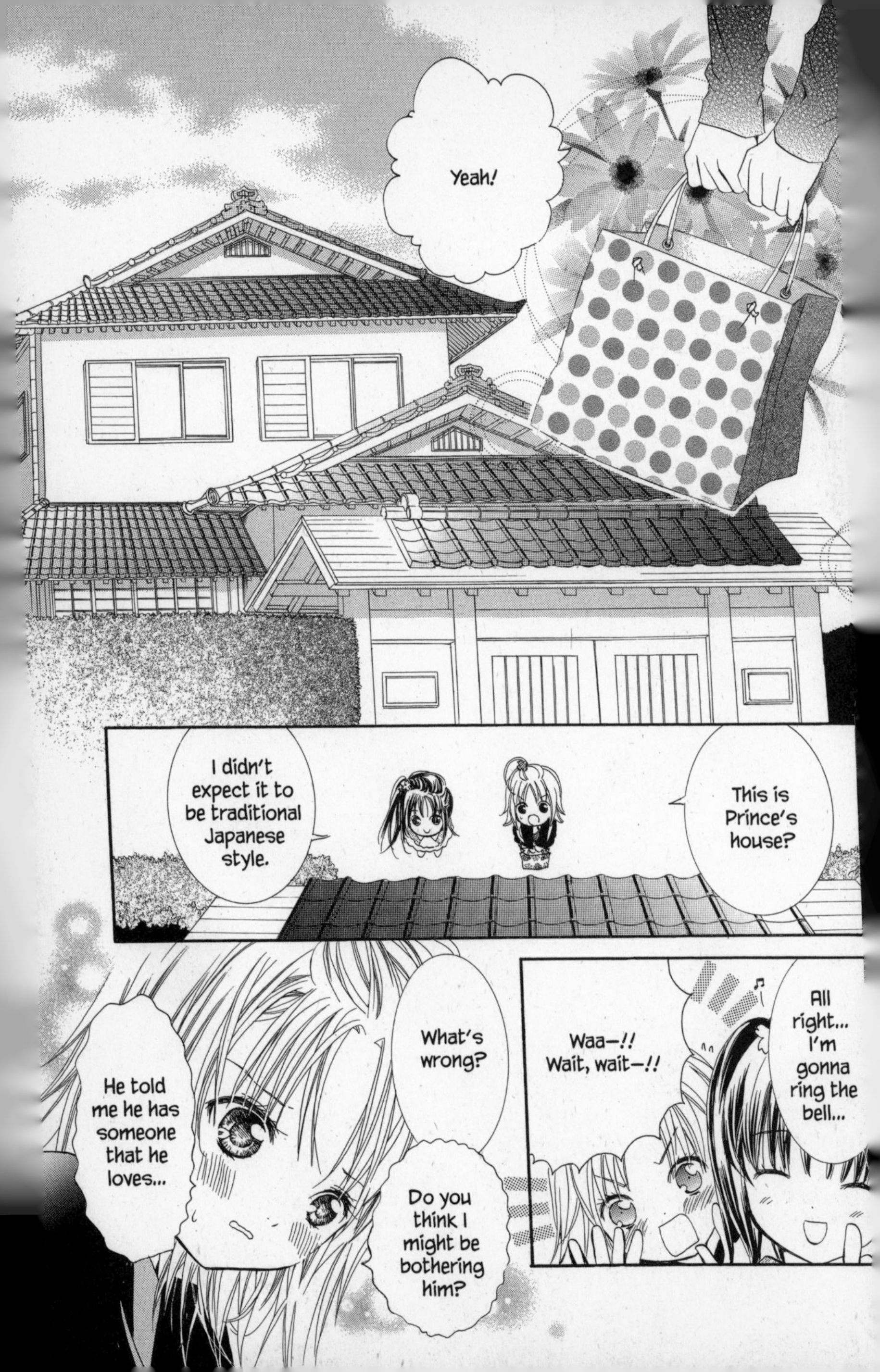
Yeah!
This is Prince's house?
I didn't expect it to be traditional Japanese style.
All right... I'm gonna ring the bell...
Waa-!! Wait, wait-!!
What's wrong?
He told me he has someone that he loves...
Do you think I might be bothering him?

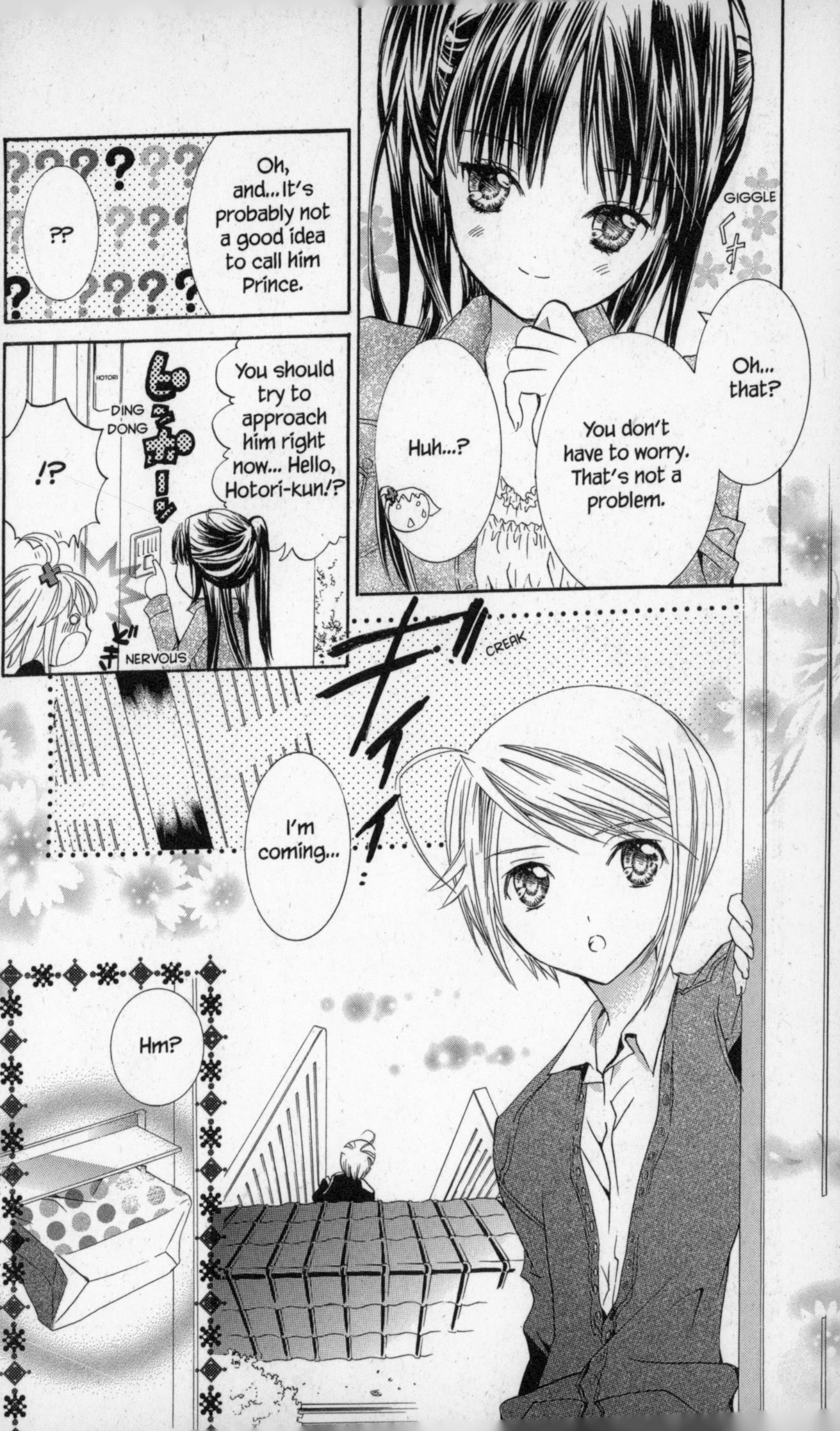
GIGGLE
Oh... that?
You don't have to worry. That's not a problem.
Huh...?
Oh, and...It's probably not a good idea to call him Prince.
??
You should try to approach him right now... Hello, Hotori-kun!?
HOTORI
DING DONG
!?
NERVOUS
CREAK
I'm coming...
Hm?

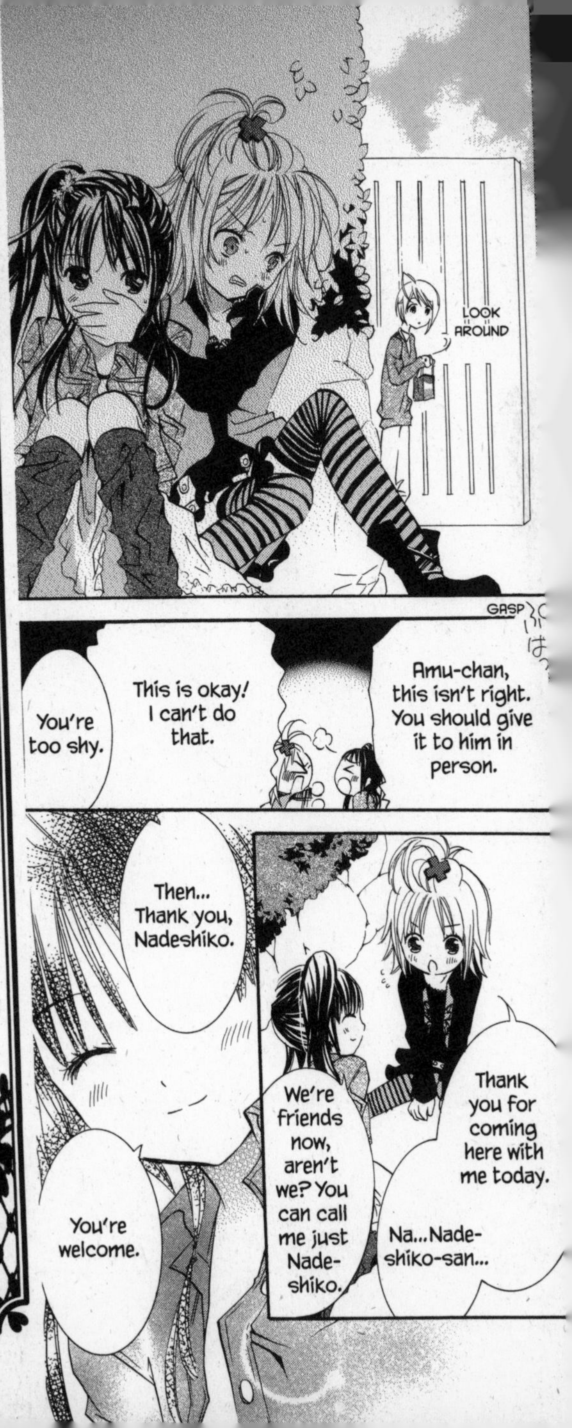
LOOK AROUND
GASP
Amu-chan, this isn't right. You should give it to him in person.
This is okay! I can't do that.
You're too shy.
Thank you for coming here with me today.
Na...Nade-shiko-san...
We're friends now, aren't we? You can call me just Nade-shiko.
Then... Thank you, Nadeshiko.
You're welcome.

character profile

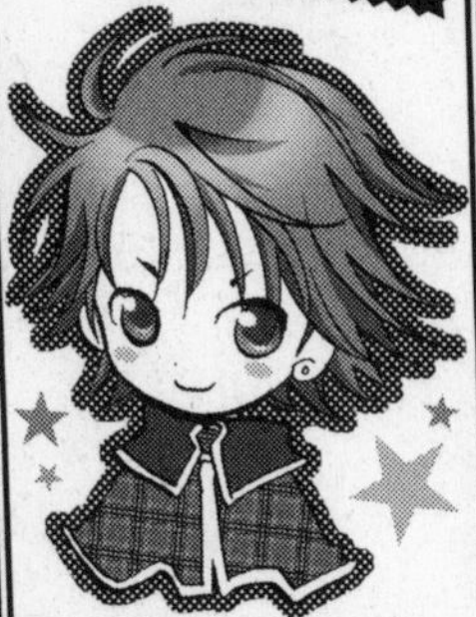

相馬 空海

Kukai Soma

Birthday : 8/17
BloodType : A
Sign : Leo
Shugo-Chara : Daichi

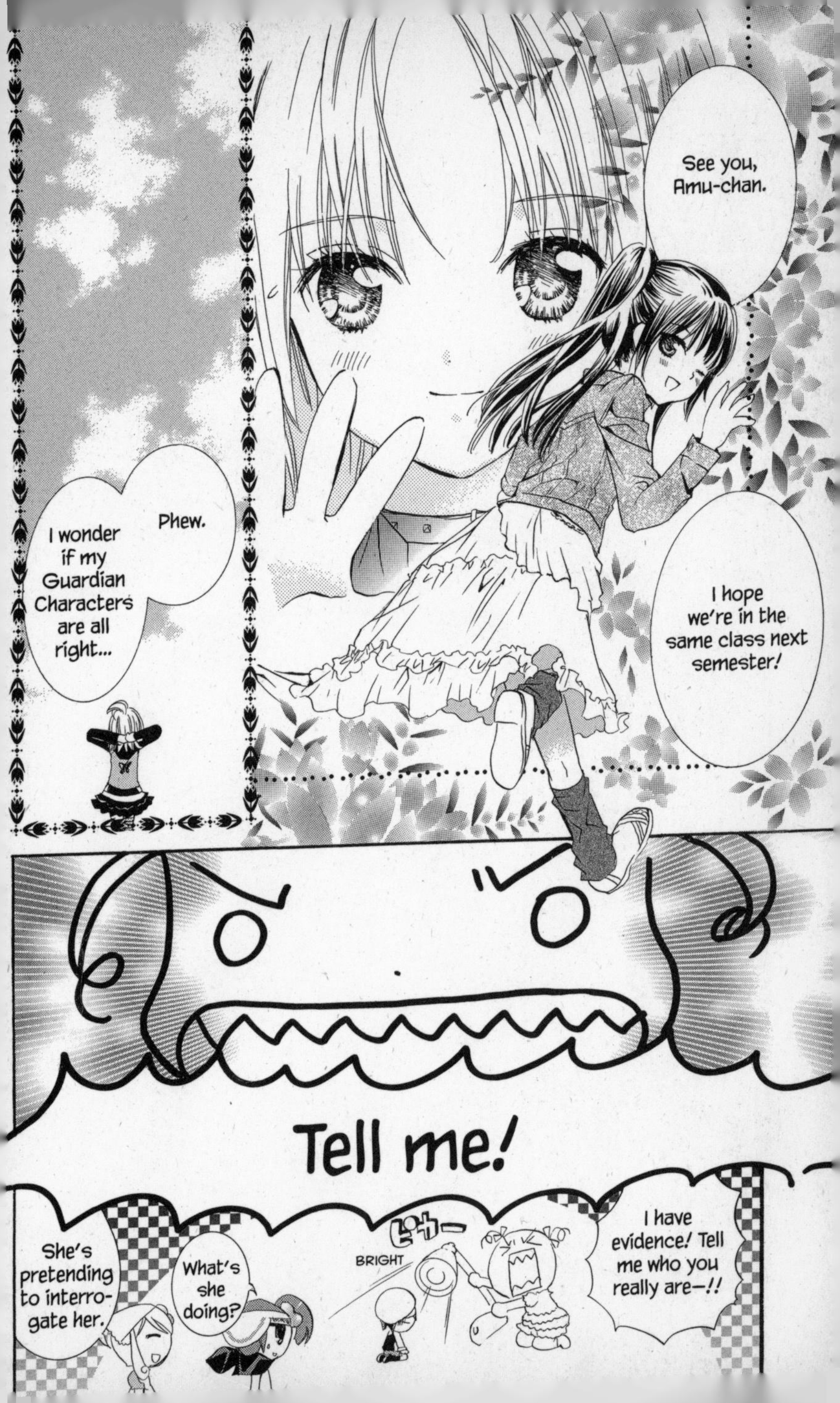
See you, Amu-chan.
I hope we're in the same class next semester!
Phew.
I wonder if my Guardian Characters are all right...
Tell me!
I have evidence! Tell me who you really are—!!
ピカー
BRIGHT
What's she doing?
She's pretending to interrogate her.

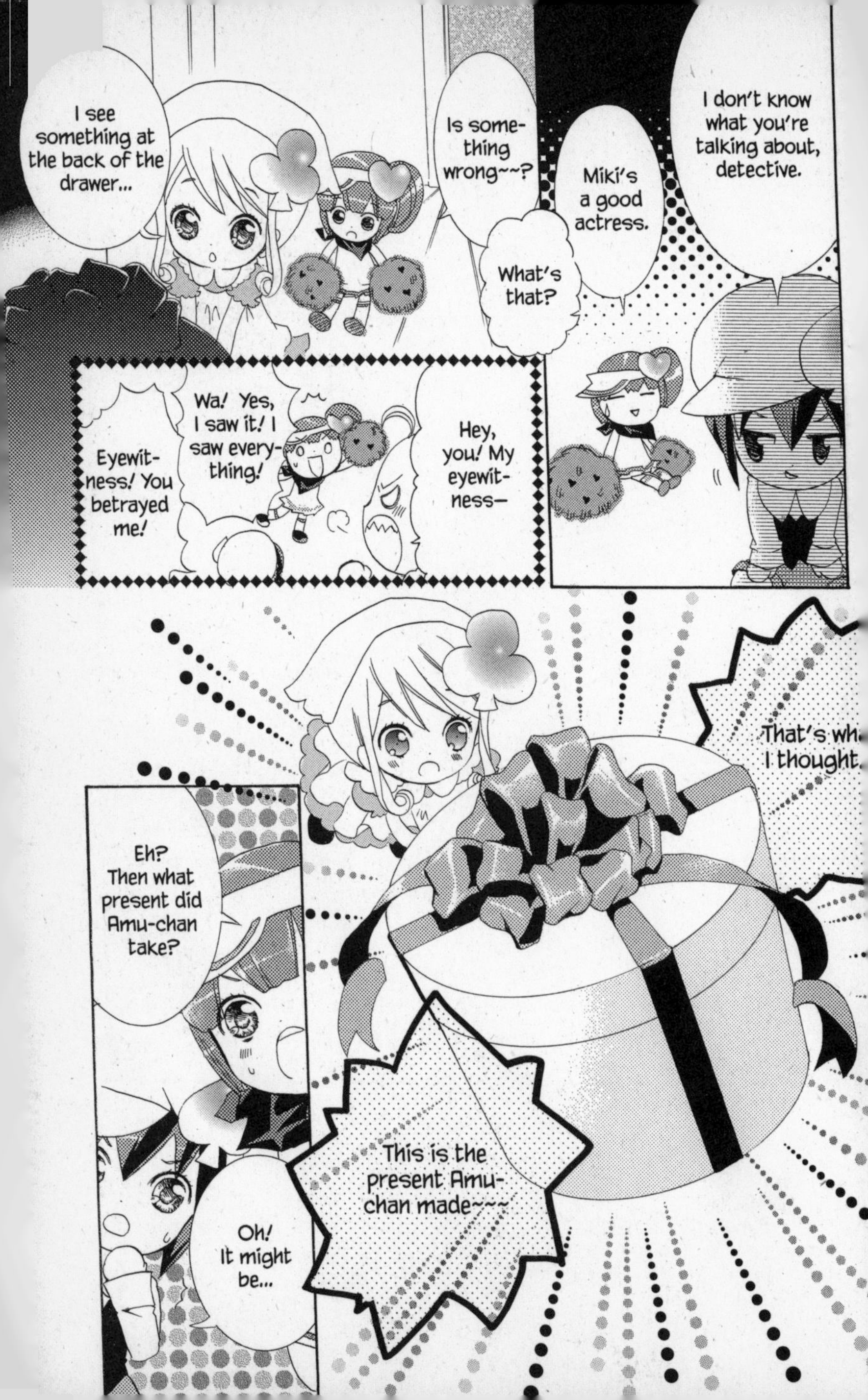
I don't know what you're talking about, detective.
Miki's a good actress.
What's that?
Is some-thing wrong~~?
I see something at the back of the drawer...
Hey, you! My eyewit-ness—
Wa! Yes, I saw it! I saw every-thing!
Eyewit-ness! You betrayed me!
That's wh
I thought
This is the present Amu-chan made~~~
Eh? Then what present did Amu-chan take?
Oh! It might be...

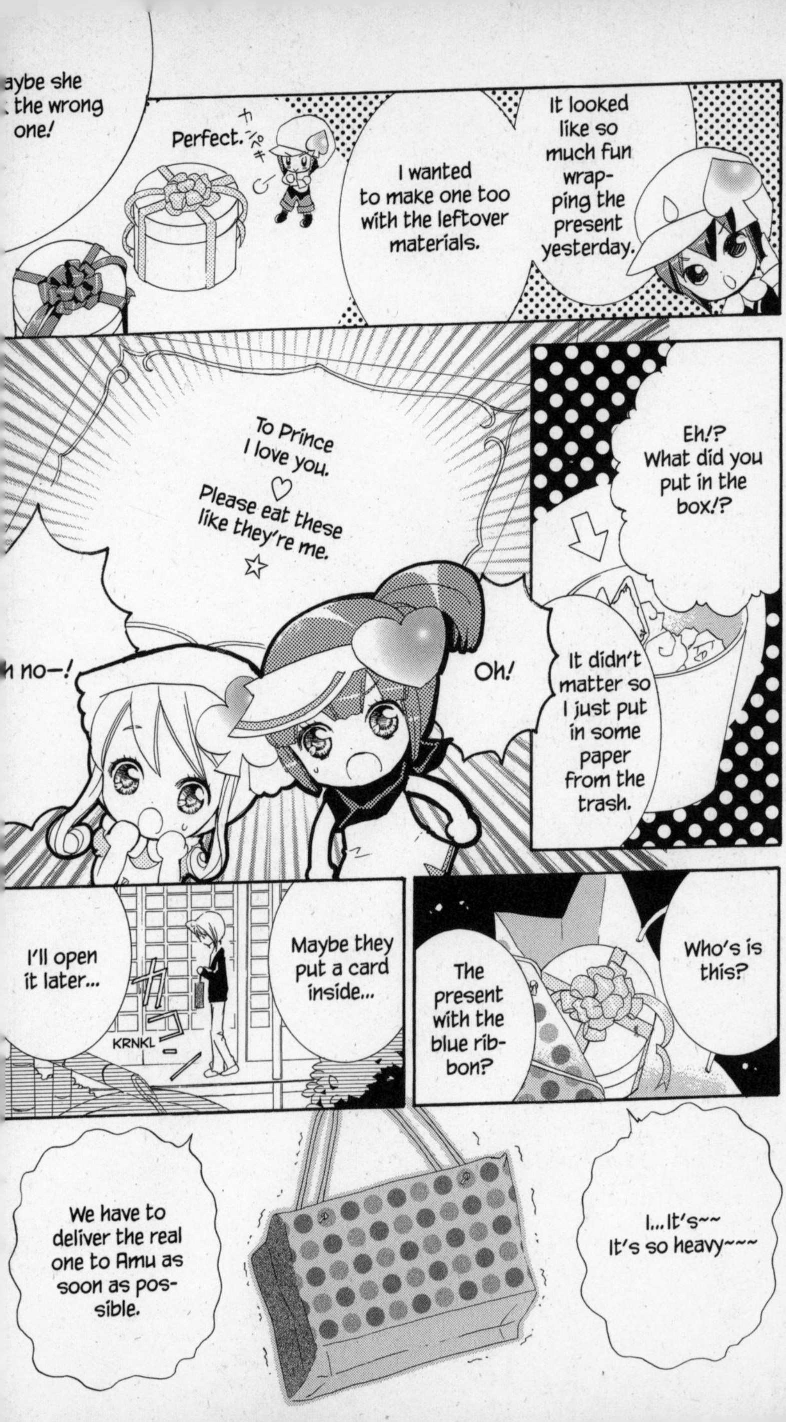
It looked like so much fun wrap-ping the present yesterday.
I wanted to make one too with the leftover materials.
Perfect.
aybe she
the wrong
one!
Eh!? What did you put in the box!?
It didn't matter so I just put in some paper from the trash.
Oh!
n no-!
To Prince
I love you. ♡
Please eat these like they're me. ☆
Who's is this?
The present with the blue rib-bon?
Maybe they put a card inside...
I'll open it later...
KRNKL
I...It's~~
It's so heavy~~~
We have to deliver the real one to Amu as soon as pos-sible.

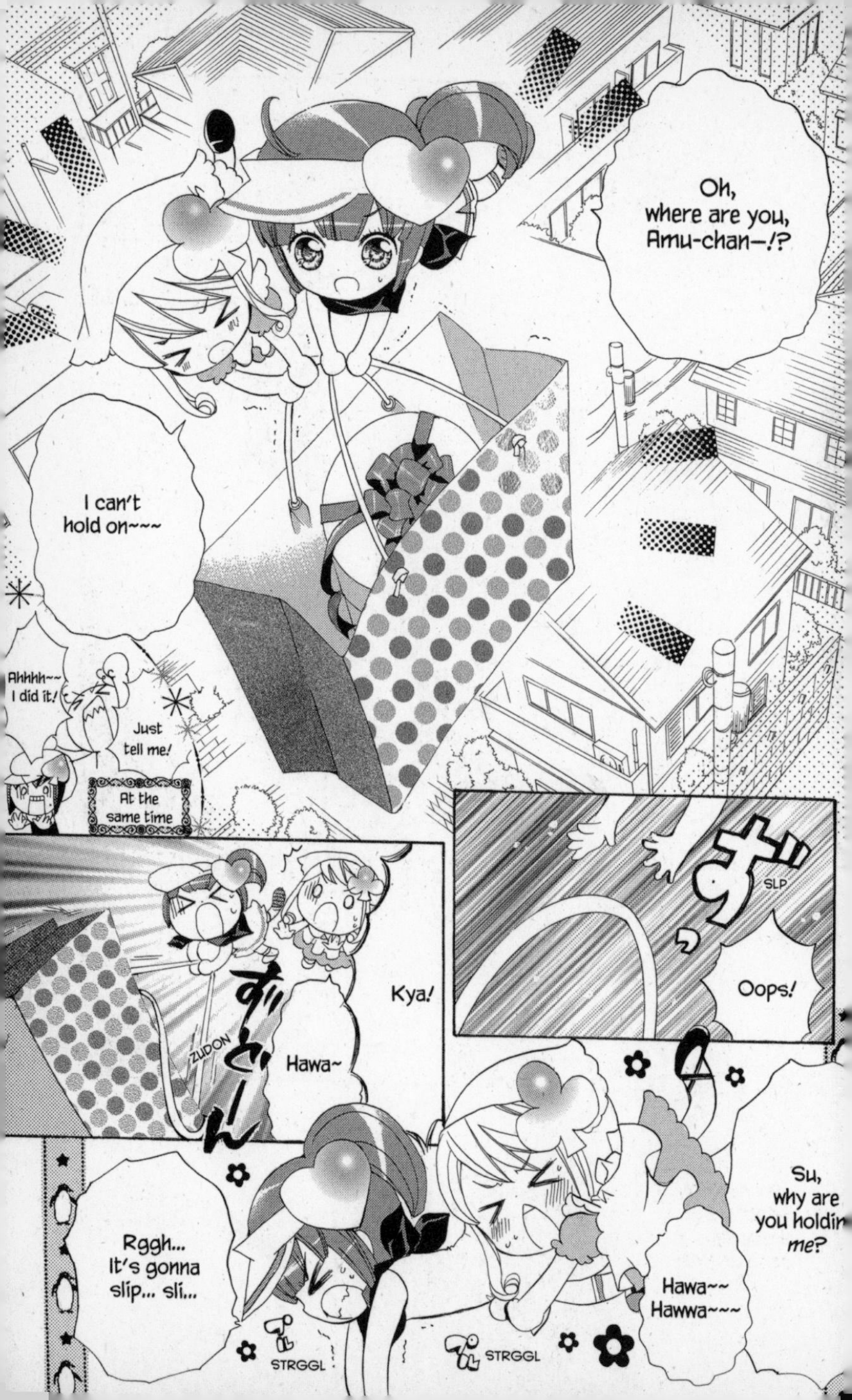

Oh, where are you, Amu-chan—!?
I can't hold on~~~
Ahhhh~~ I did it!
Just tell me!
At the same time
SLP
Oops!
Kya!
Hawa~
ZUDON
Su, why are you holdin *me*?
Hawa~~ Hawwa~~~
STRGGL
Rggh... It's gonna slip... sli...
STRGGL

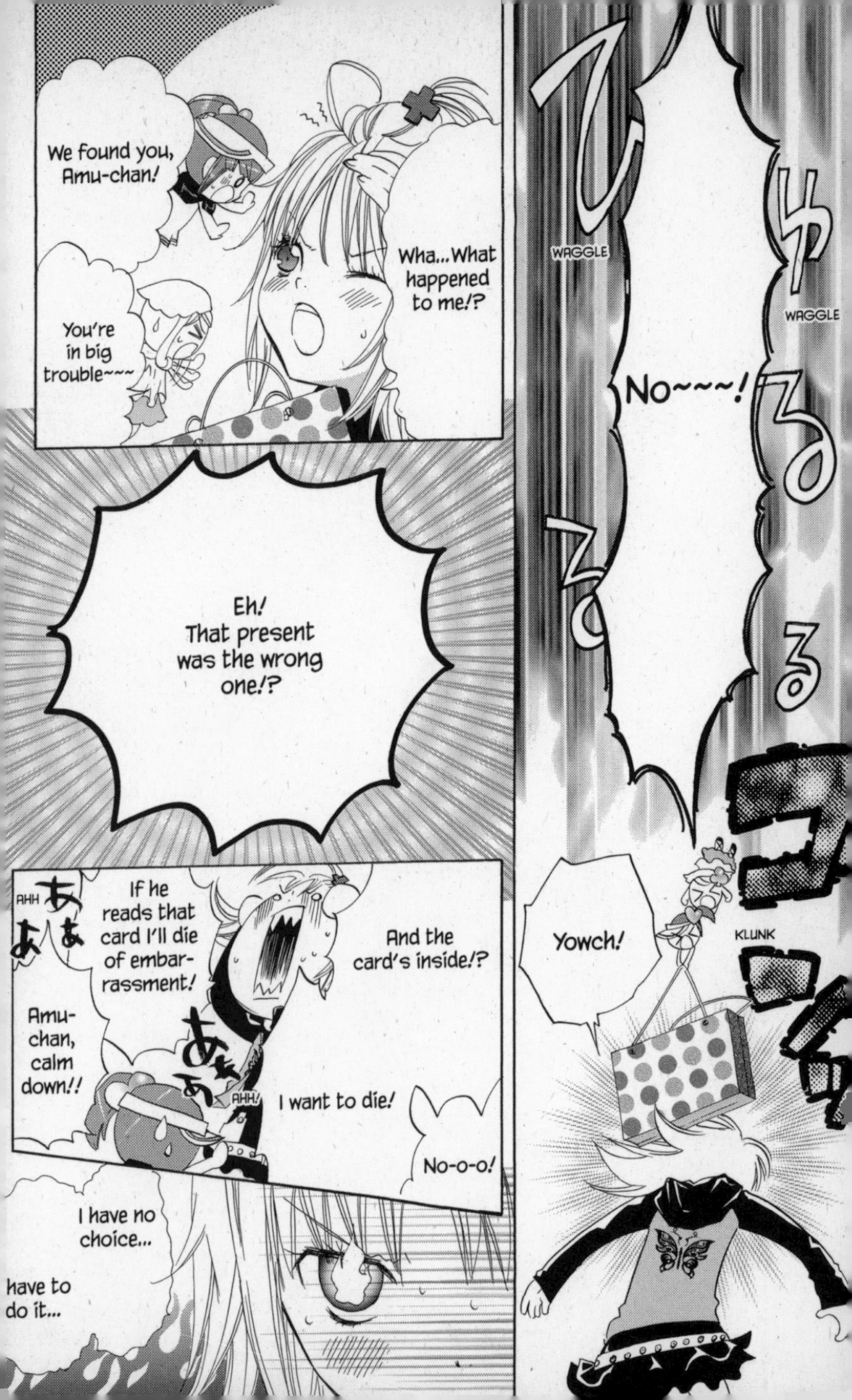
WAGGLE
WAGGLE
No~~~!
KLUNK
Yowch!
Wha...What happened to me!?
We found you, Amu-chan!
You're in big trouble~~~
Eh! That present was the wrong one!?
And the card's inside!?
If he reads that card I'll die of embarrassment!
AHH
Amu-chan, calm down!!
I want to die!
AHH!
No-o-o!
I have no choice...
have to do it...

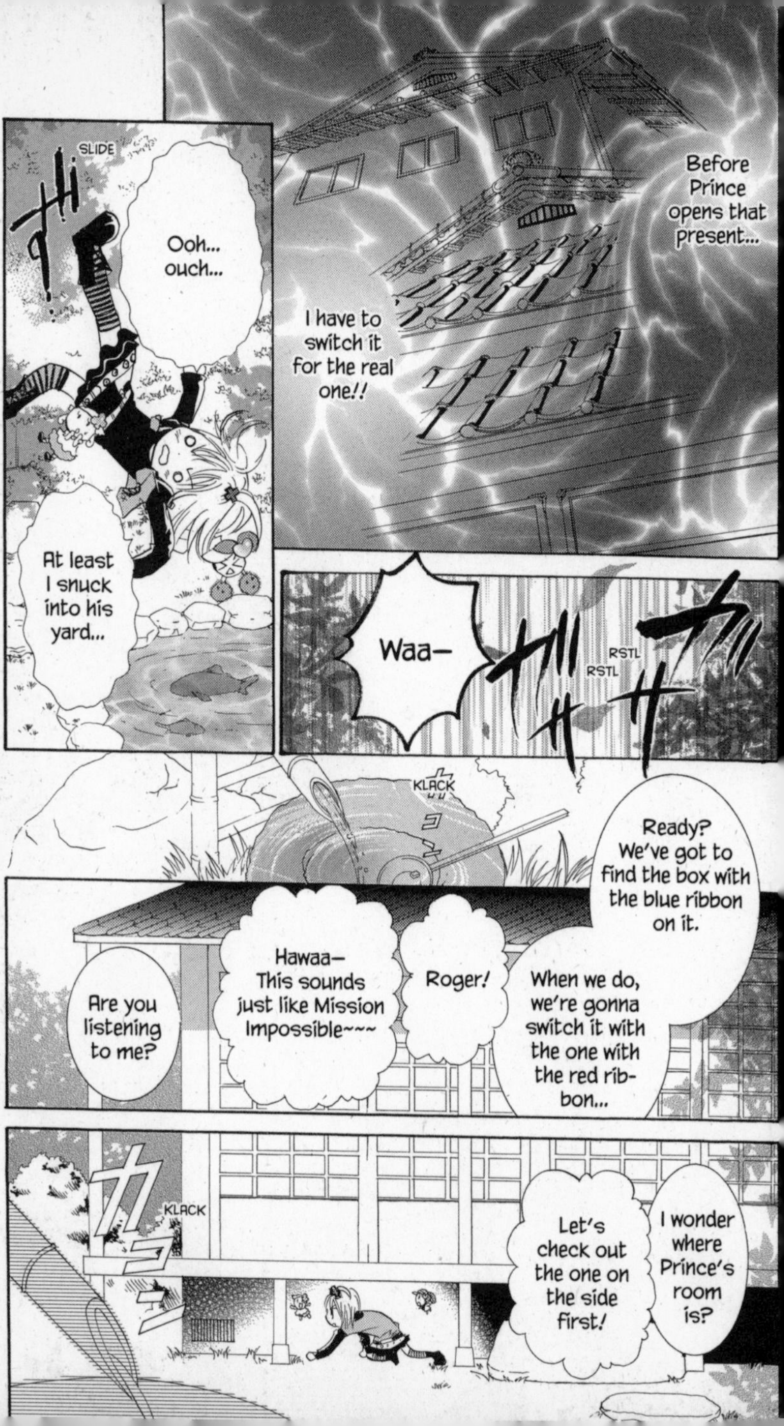
Before Prince opens that present...
I have to switch it for the real one!!
Waa-
RSTL
RSTL
SLIDE
Ooh... ouch...
At least I snuck into his yard...
KLACK
Ready? We've got to find the box with the blue ribbon on it.
When we do, we're gonna switch it with the one with the red rib-bon...
Roger!
Hawaa- This sounds just like Mission Impossible~~~
Are you listening to me?
I wonder where Prince's room is?
Let's check out the one on the side first!
KLACK

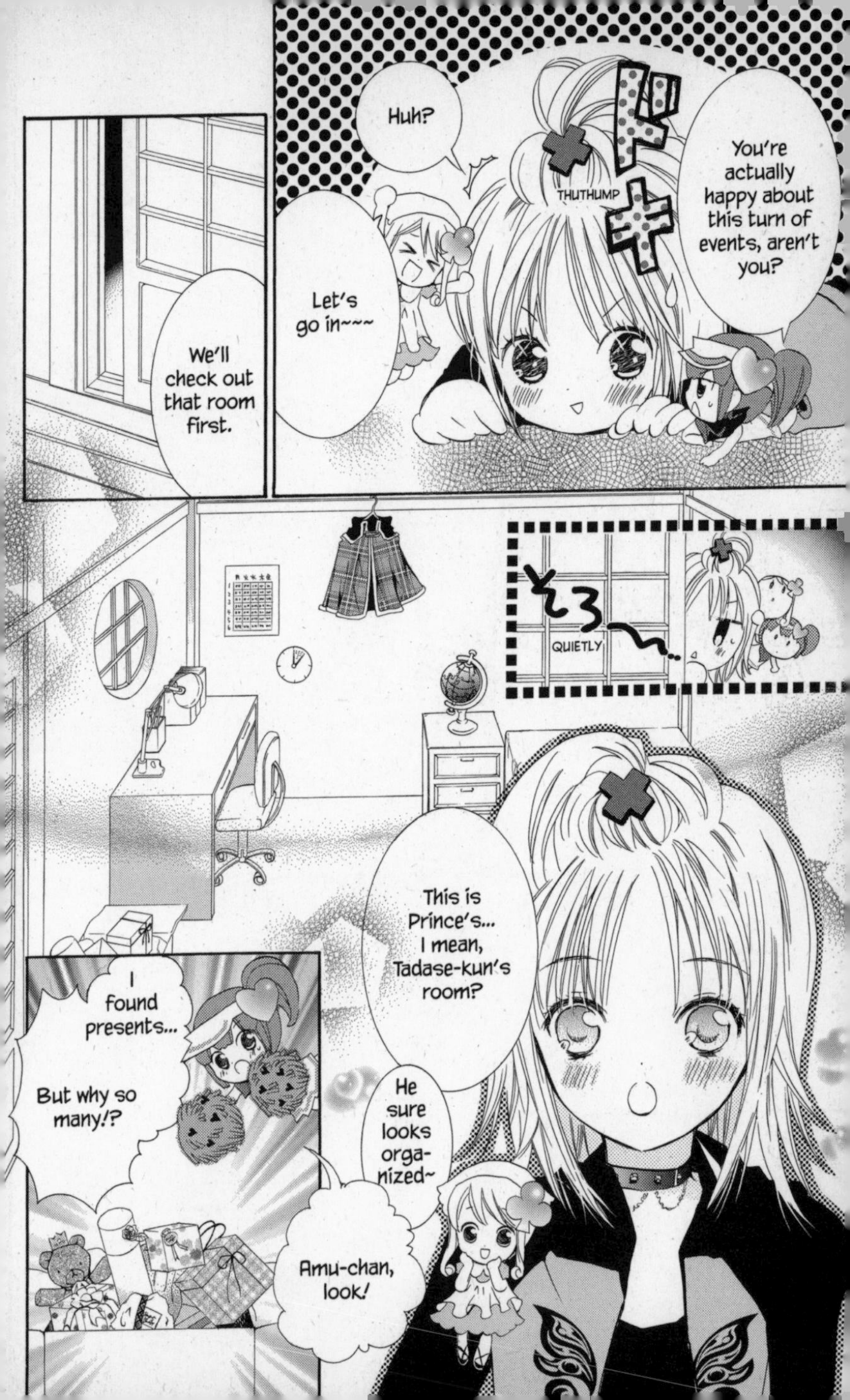

You're actually happy about this turn of events, aren't you?
THUTHUMP
Huh?
Let's go in~~~
We'll check out that room first.
QUIETLY
This is Prince's... I mean, Tadase-kun's room?
He sure looks orga-nized~
Amu-chan, look!
I found presents...
But why so many!?

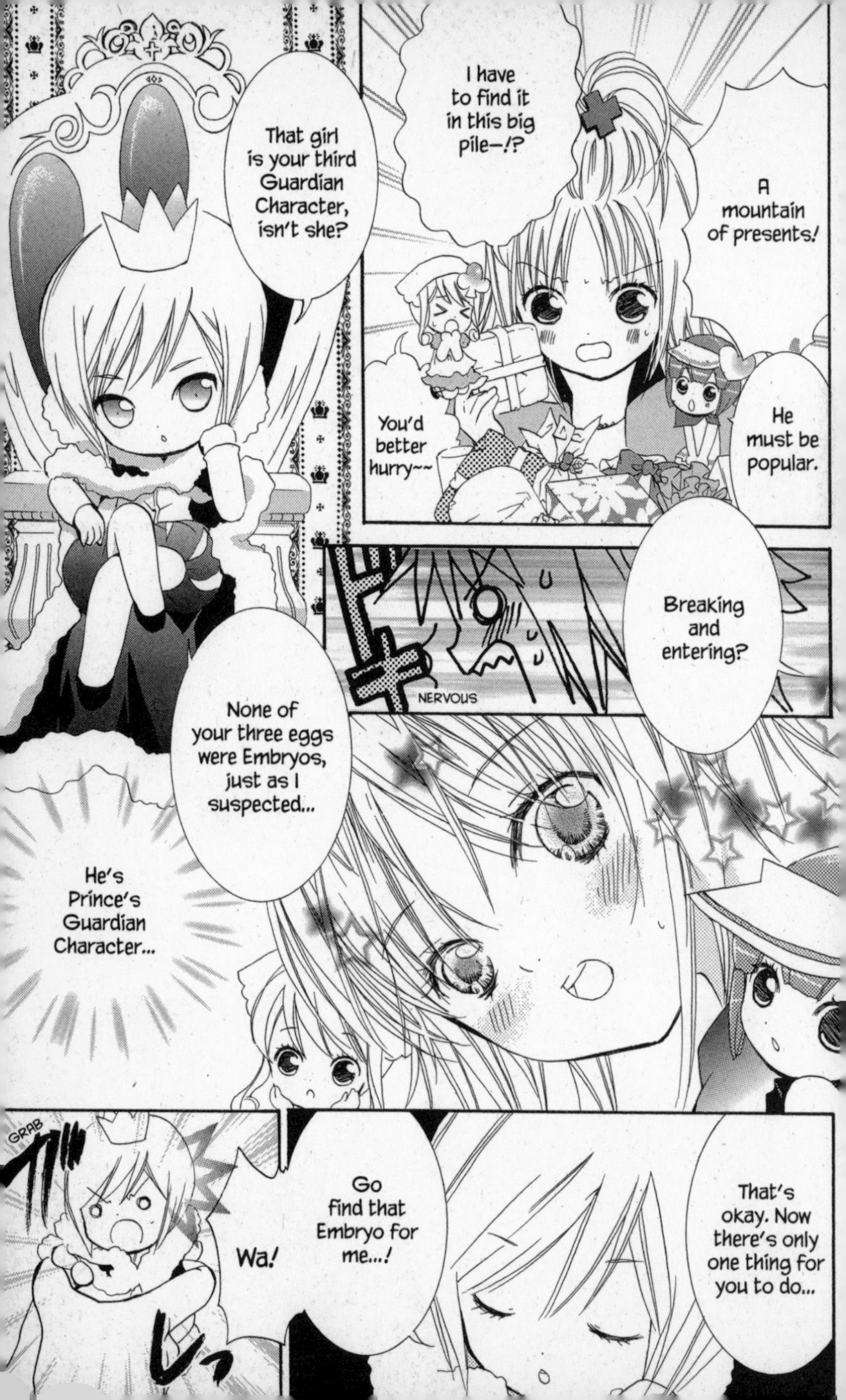
A mountain of presents!
I have to find it in this big pile—!?
He must be popular.
You'd better hurry~~
Breaking and entering?
NERVOUS
That girl is your third Guardian Character, isn't she?
None of your three eggs were Embryos, just as I suspected...
He's Prince's Guardian Character...
That's okay. Now there's only one thing for you to do...
Go find that Embryo for me...!
Wa!
GRAB

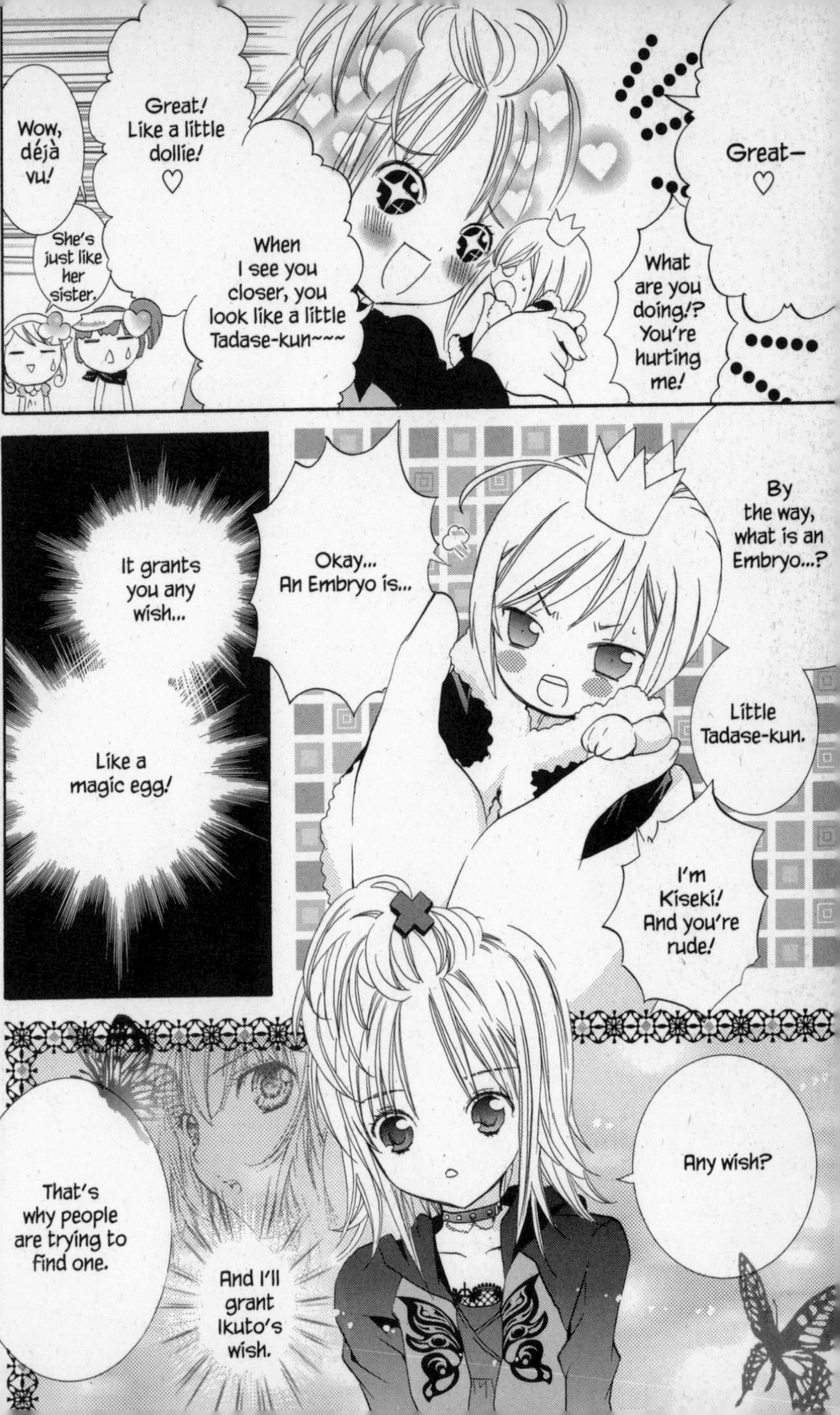

Great— ♡
What are you doing!? You're hurting me!
Great! Like a little dollie! ♡
When I see you closer, you look like a little Tadase-kun~~~
Wow, déjà vu!
She's just like her sister.
By the way, what is an Embryo...?
Little Tadase-kun.
I'm Kiseki! And you're rude!
Okay... An Embryo is...
It grants you any wish...
Like a magic egg!
Any wish?
And I'll grant Ikuto's wish.
That's why people are trying to find one.

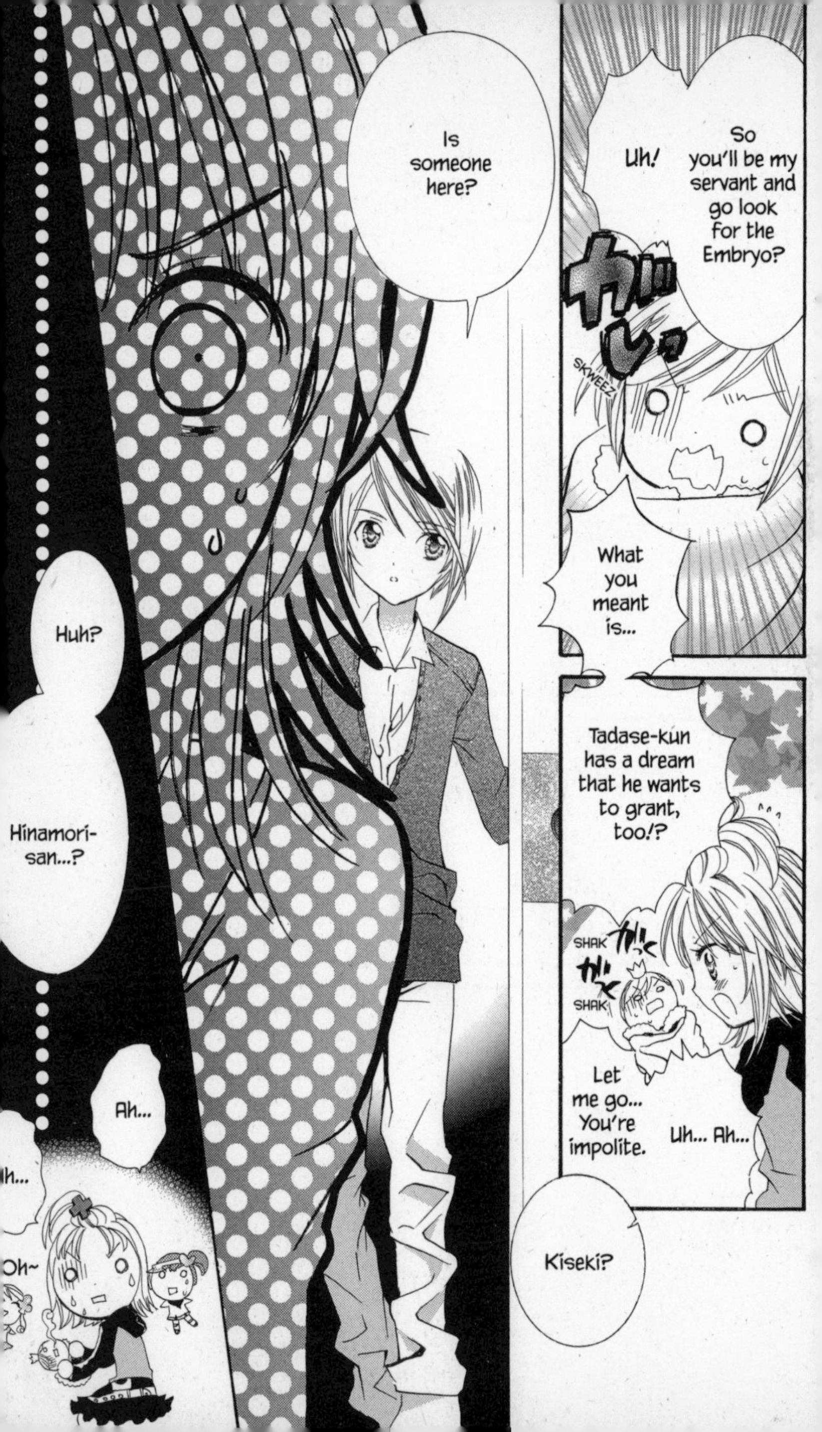
So you'll be my servant and go look for the Embryo?
Uh!
SKWEEZ
What you meant is...
Tadase-kun has a dream that he wants to grant, too!?
SHAK
SHAK
Let me go... You're impolite.
Uh... Ah...
Kiseki?
Is someone here?
Huh?
Hinamori-san...?
Ah...
h...
Oh~

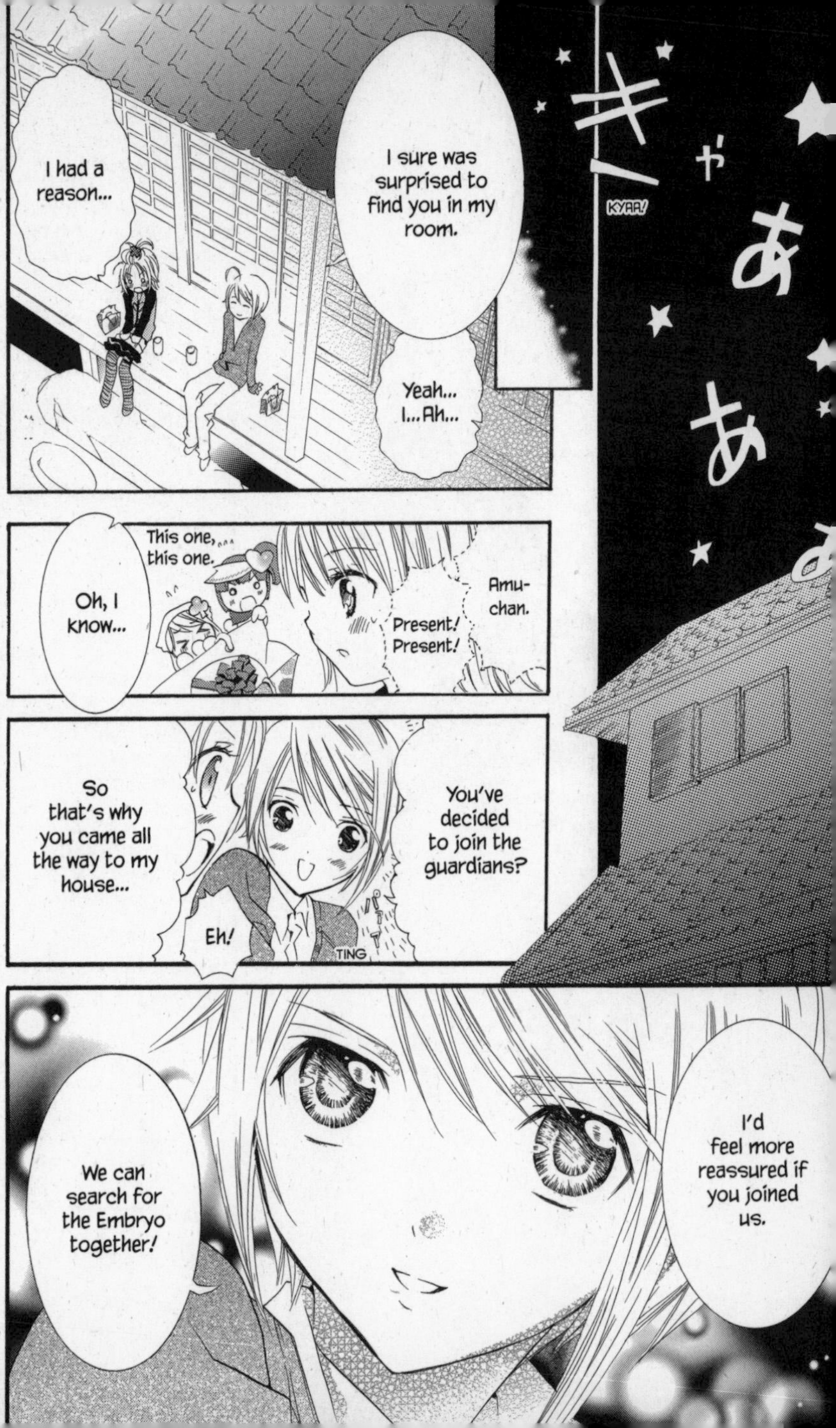
キャーあああ
KYAA!
I sure was surprised to find you in my room.
Yeah... I...Ah...
I had a reason...
Amu-chan.
Present! Present!
This one, this one.
Oh, I know...
You've decided to join the guardians?
TING
Eh!
So that's why you came all the way to my house...
I'd feel more reassured if you joined us.
We can search for the Embryo together!

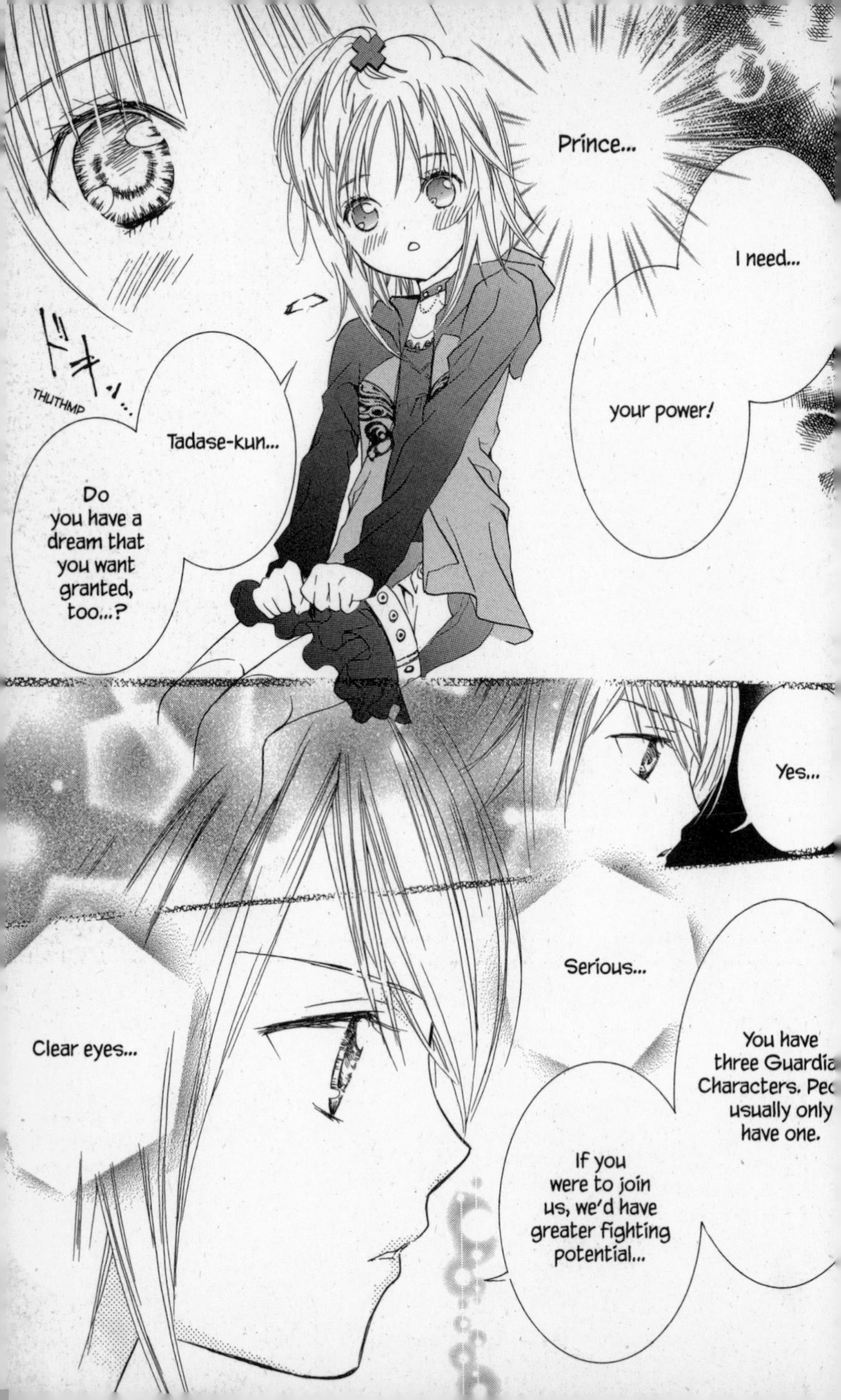

Prince...
I need...
your power!
ドキッ...
THUTHMP
Tadase-kun...
Do you have a dream that you want granted, too...?
Yes...
Serious...
Clear eyes...
You have three Guardia Characters. Peo usually only have one.
If you were to join us, we'd have greater fighting potential...

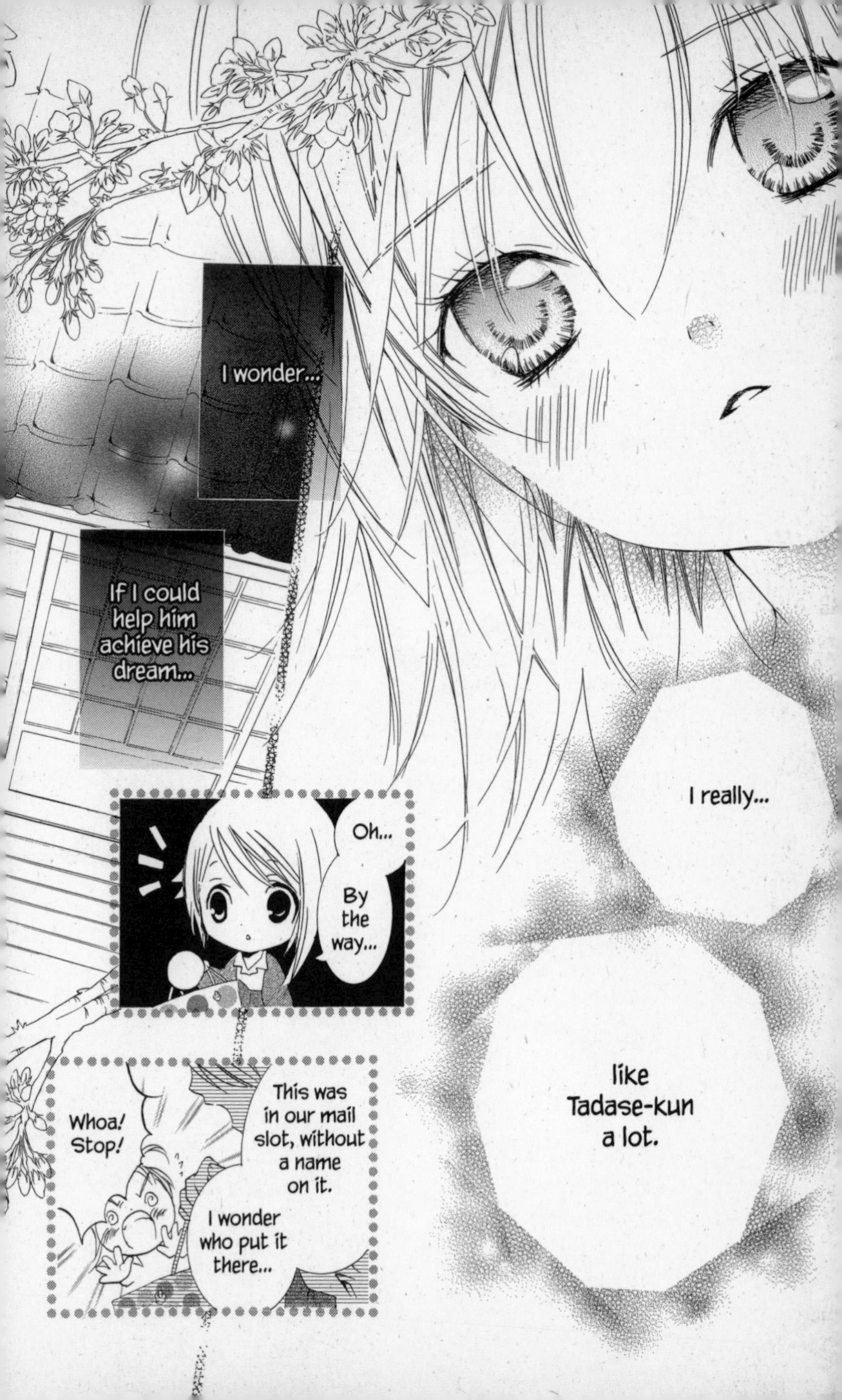
I wonder...
If I could help him achieve his dream...
I really...
like Tadase-kun a lot.
Oh...
By the way...
This was in our mail slot, without a name on it.
I wonder who put it there...
Whoa! Stop!

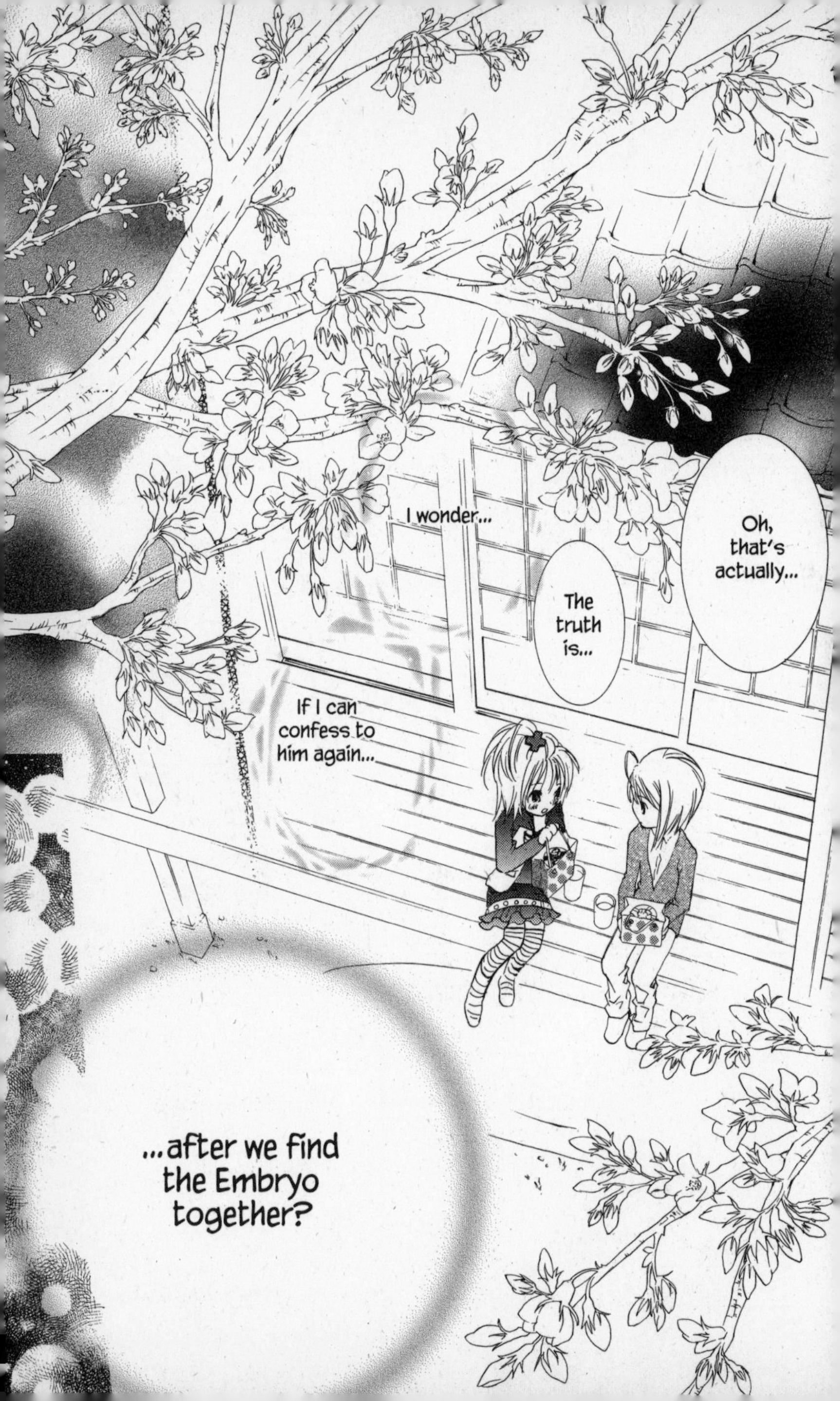
Oh, that's actually...
The truth is...
I wonder...
If I can confess to him again...
...after we find the Embryo together?

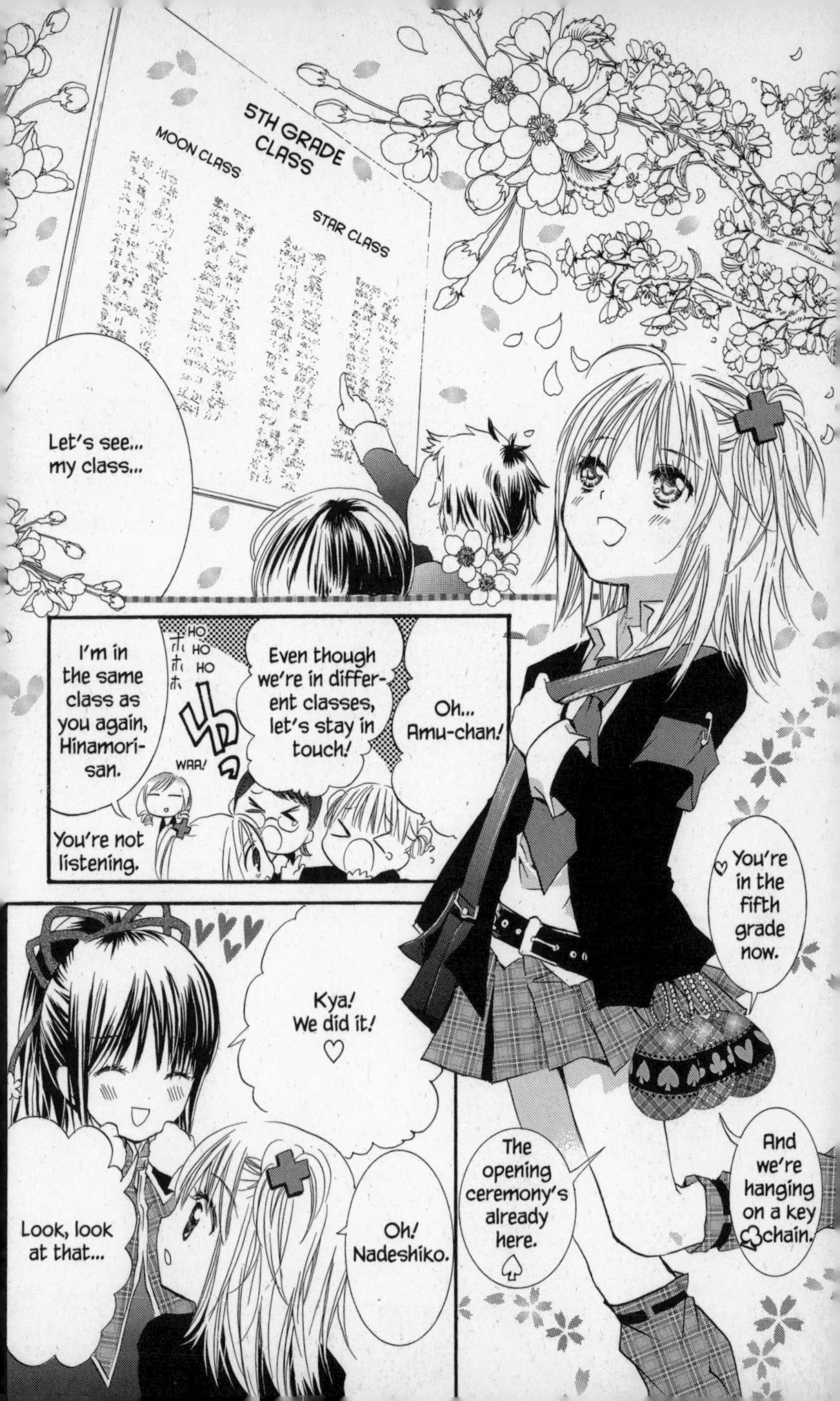
5TH GRADE CLASS
MOON CLASS
STAR CLASS
Let's see... my class...
You're in the fifth grade now.
And we're hanging on a key chain.
The opening ceremony's already here.
Oh... Amu-chan!
Even though we're in different classes, let's stay in touch!
HO HO HO
WAA!
I'm in the same class as you again, Hinamori-san.
You're not listening.
Kya! We did it!
Oh! Nadeshiko.
Look, look at that...

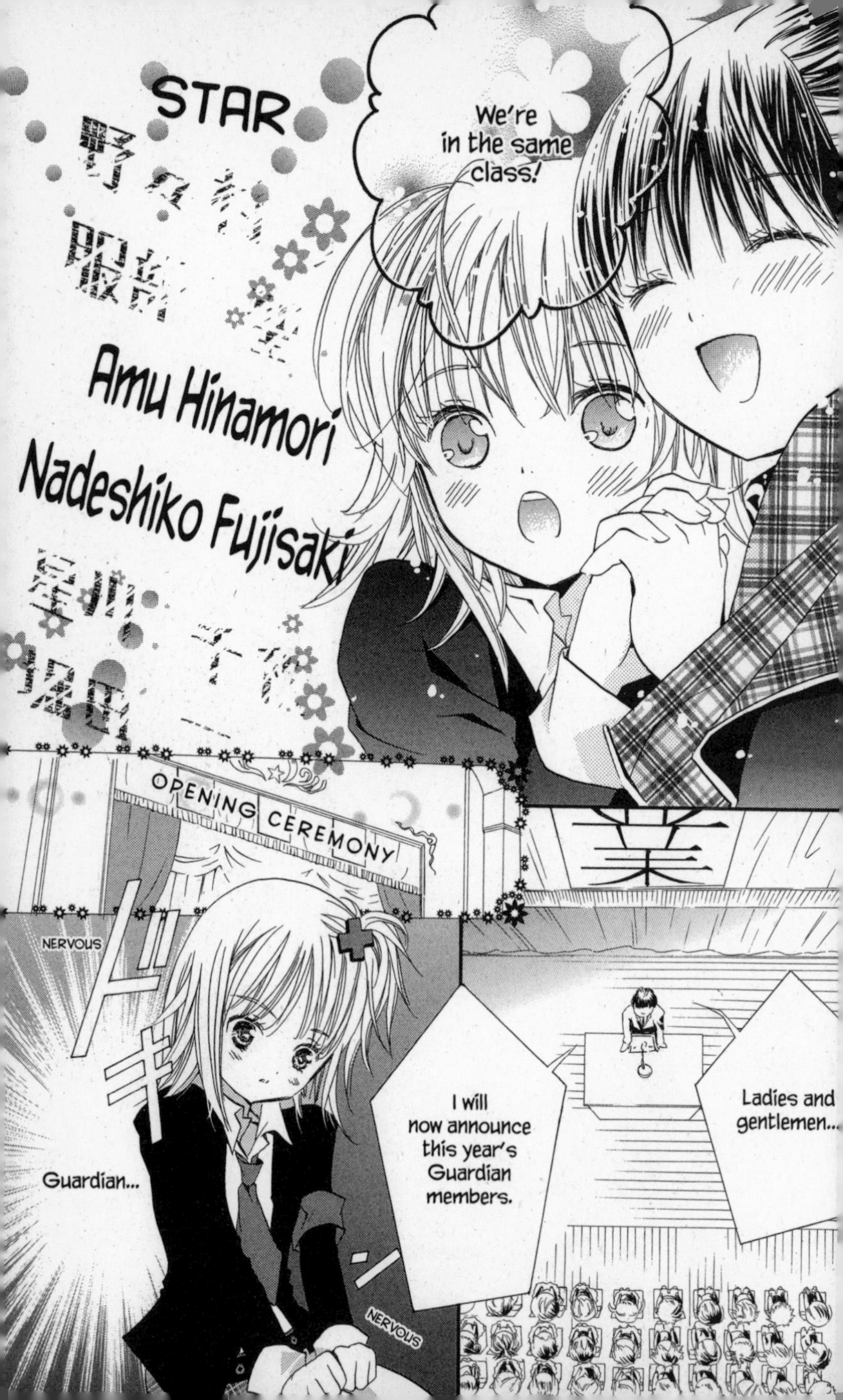

We're in the same class!
STAR
Amu Hinamori
Nadeshiko Fujisaki
OPENING CEREMONY
Ladies and gentlemen...
I will now announce this year's Guardian members.
NERVOUS
Guardian...
NERVOUS

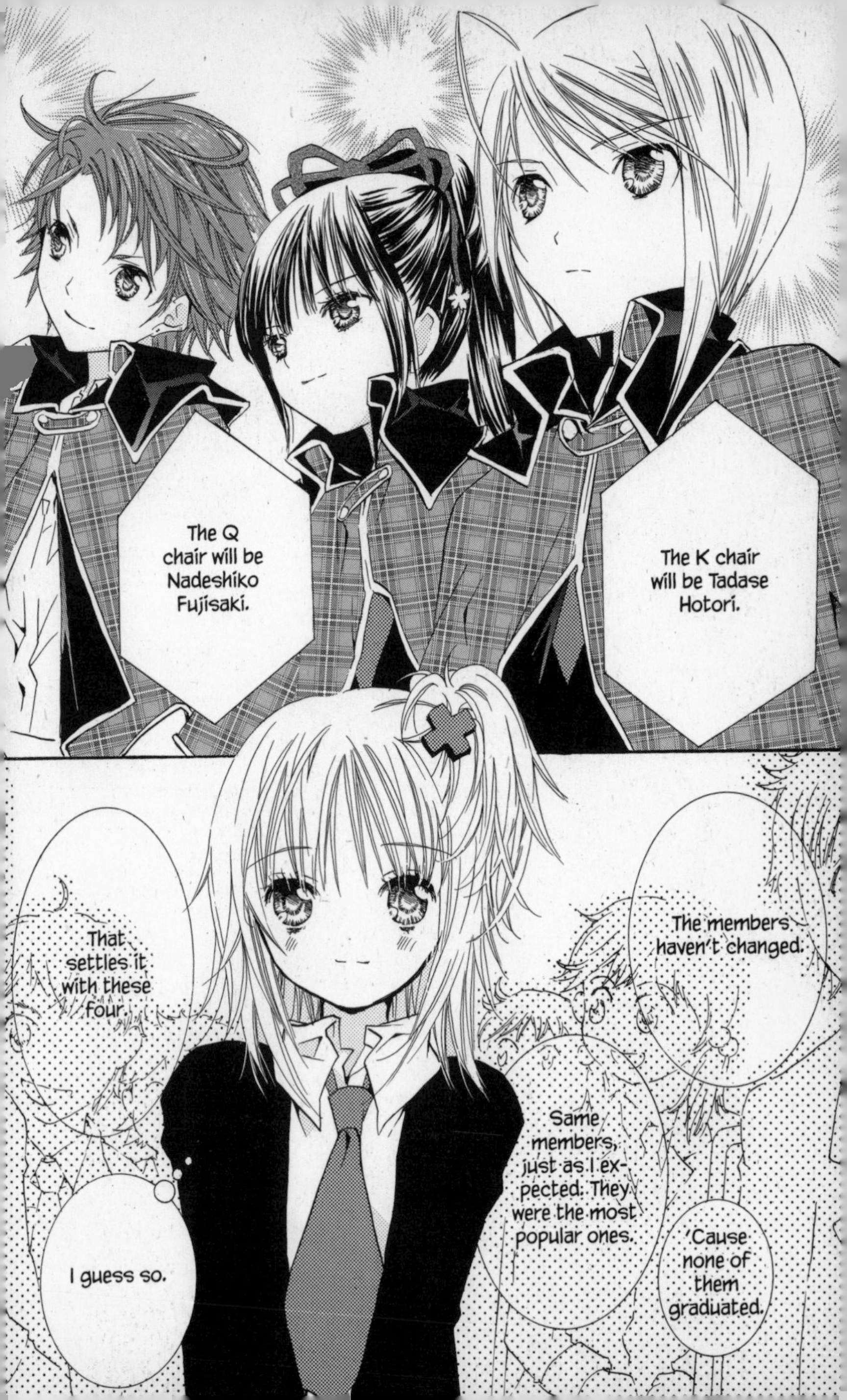
The K chair will be Tadase Hotori.
The Q chair will be Nadeshiko Fujisaki.
The members haven't changed.
That settles it with these four.
Same members, just as I ex-pected. They were the most popular ones.
'Cause none of them graduated.
I guess so.

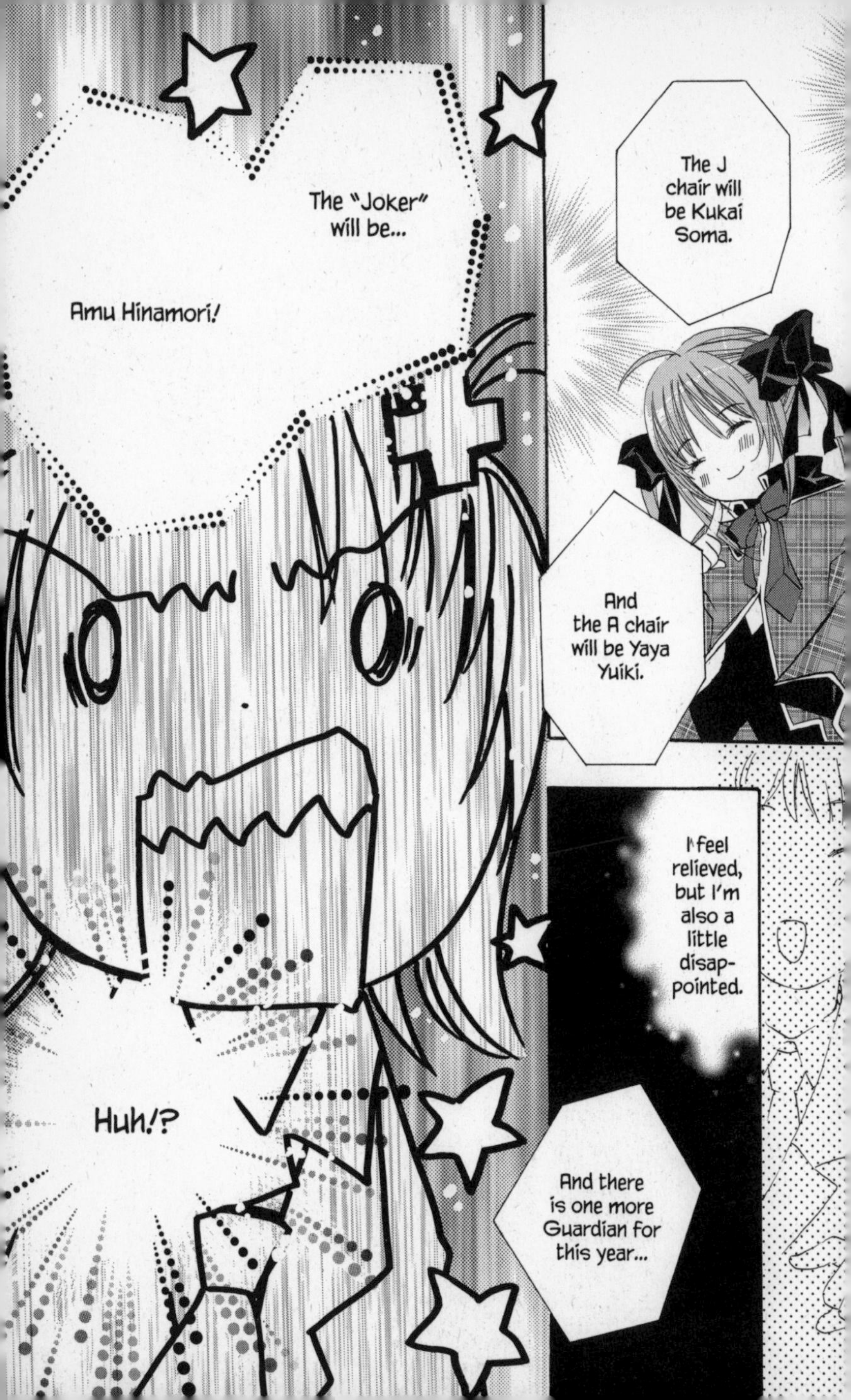
The J chair will be Kukai Soma.
And the A chair will be Yaya Yuiki.
I feel relieved, but I'm also a little disap-pointed.
And there is one more Guardian for this year...
The "Joker" will be...
Amu Hinamori!
Huh!?

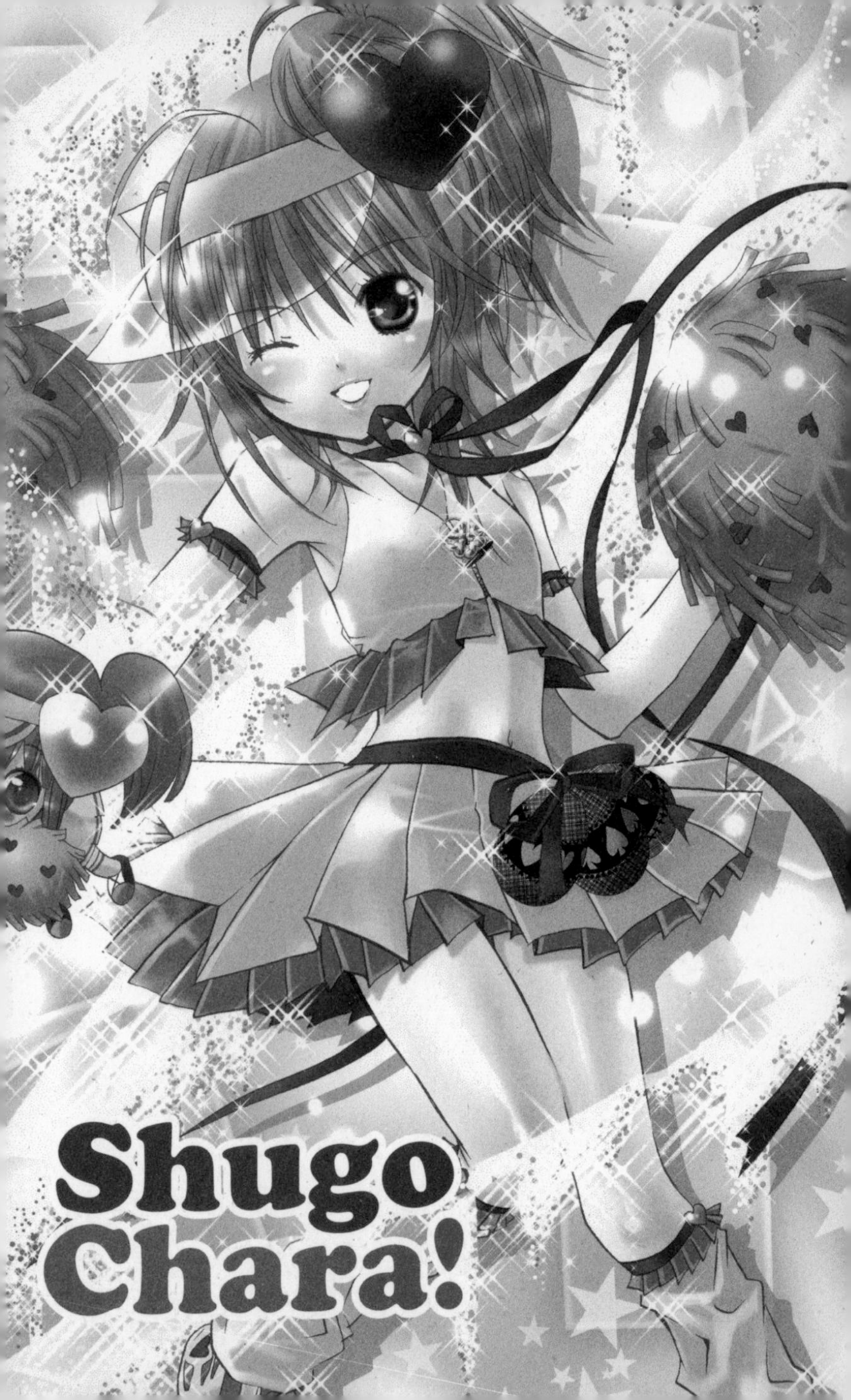
Shugo Chara!

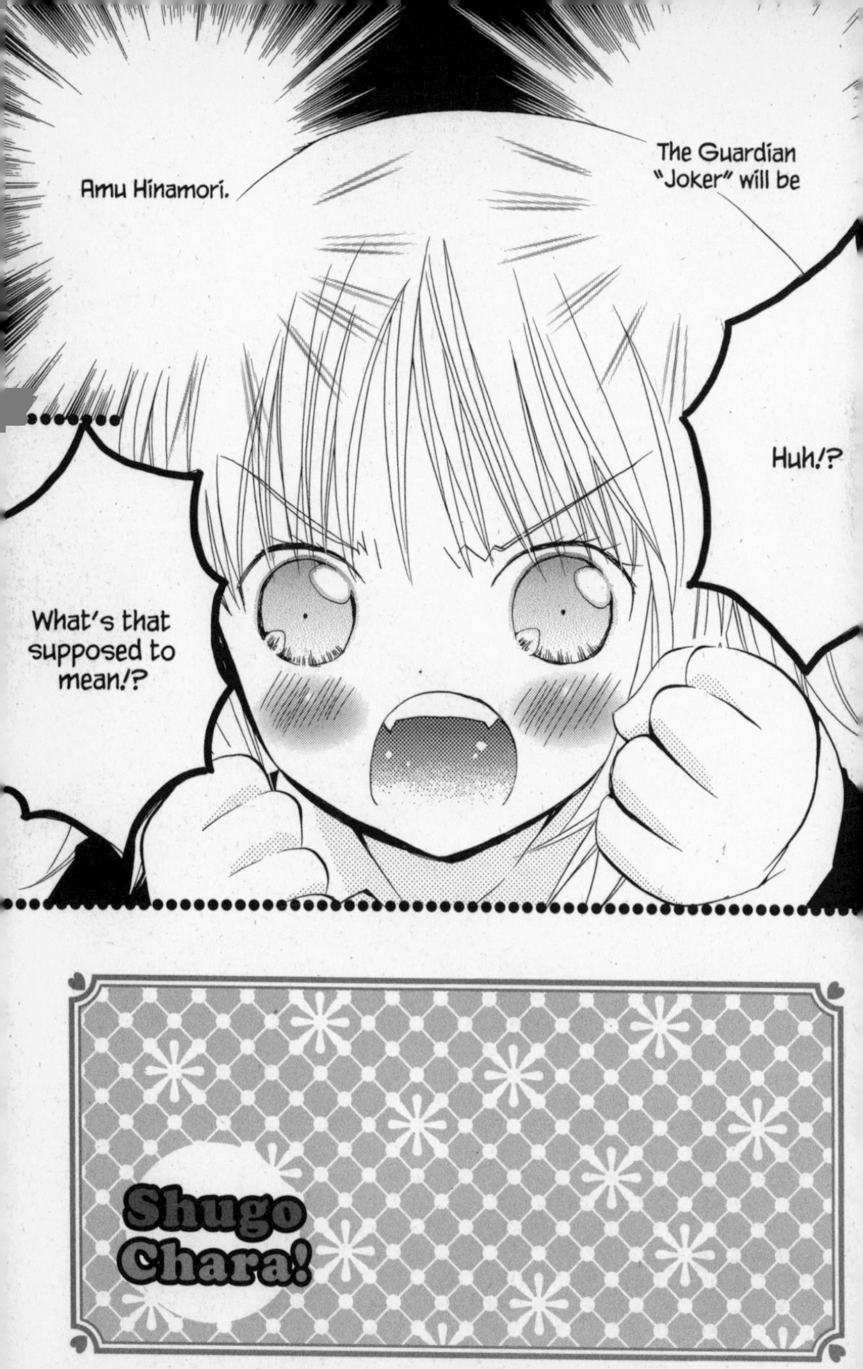
The Guardian "Joker" will be
Amu Hinamori.
Huh!?
....
What's that supposed to mean!?

Shugo Chara!

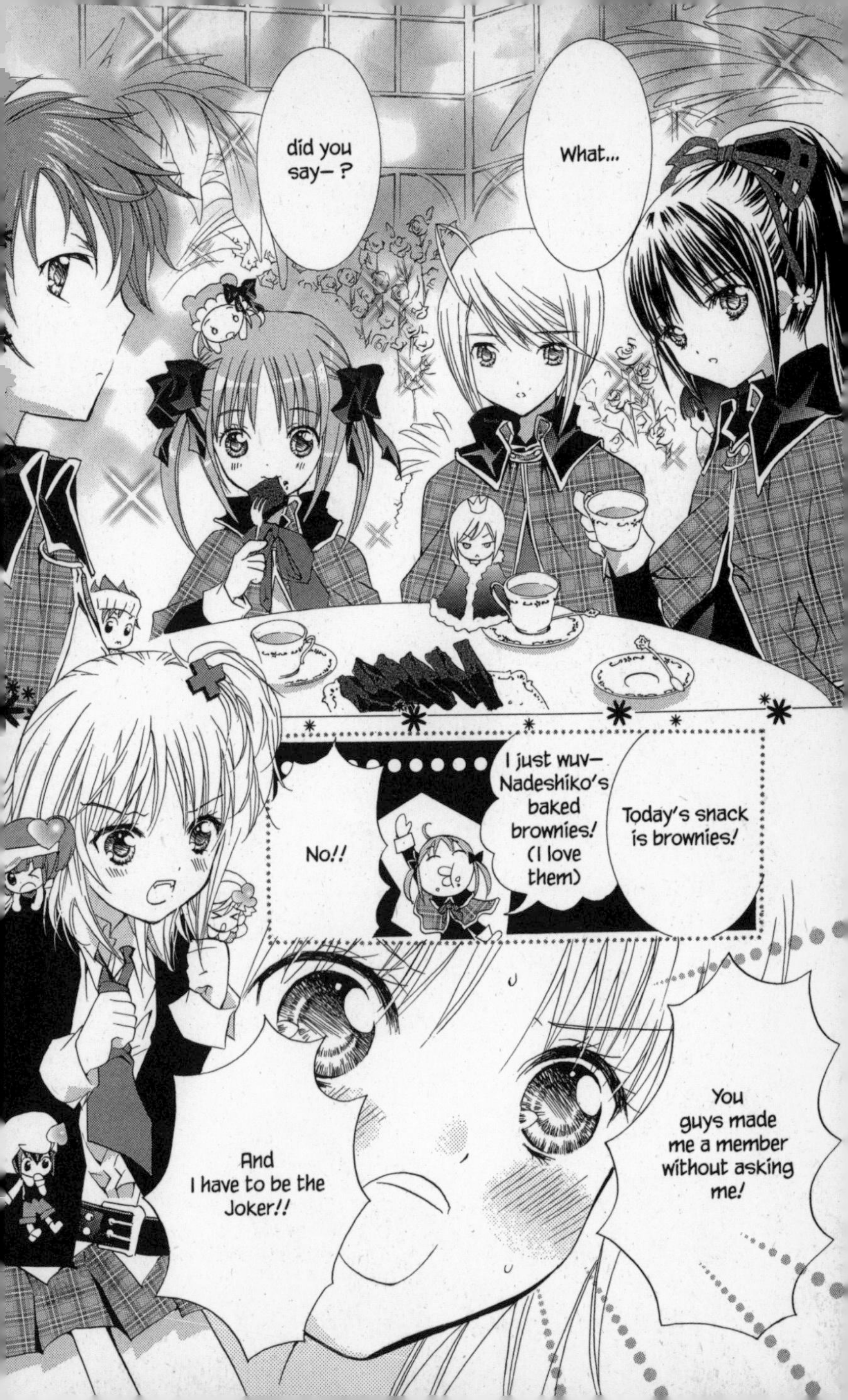
What...
did you say—?
Today's snack is brownies!
I just wuv— Nadeshiko's baked brownies! (I love them)
No!!
You guys made me a member without asking me!
And I have to be the Joker!!

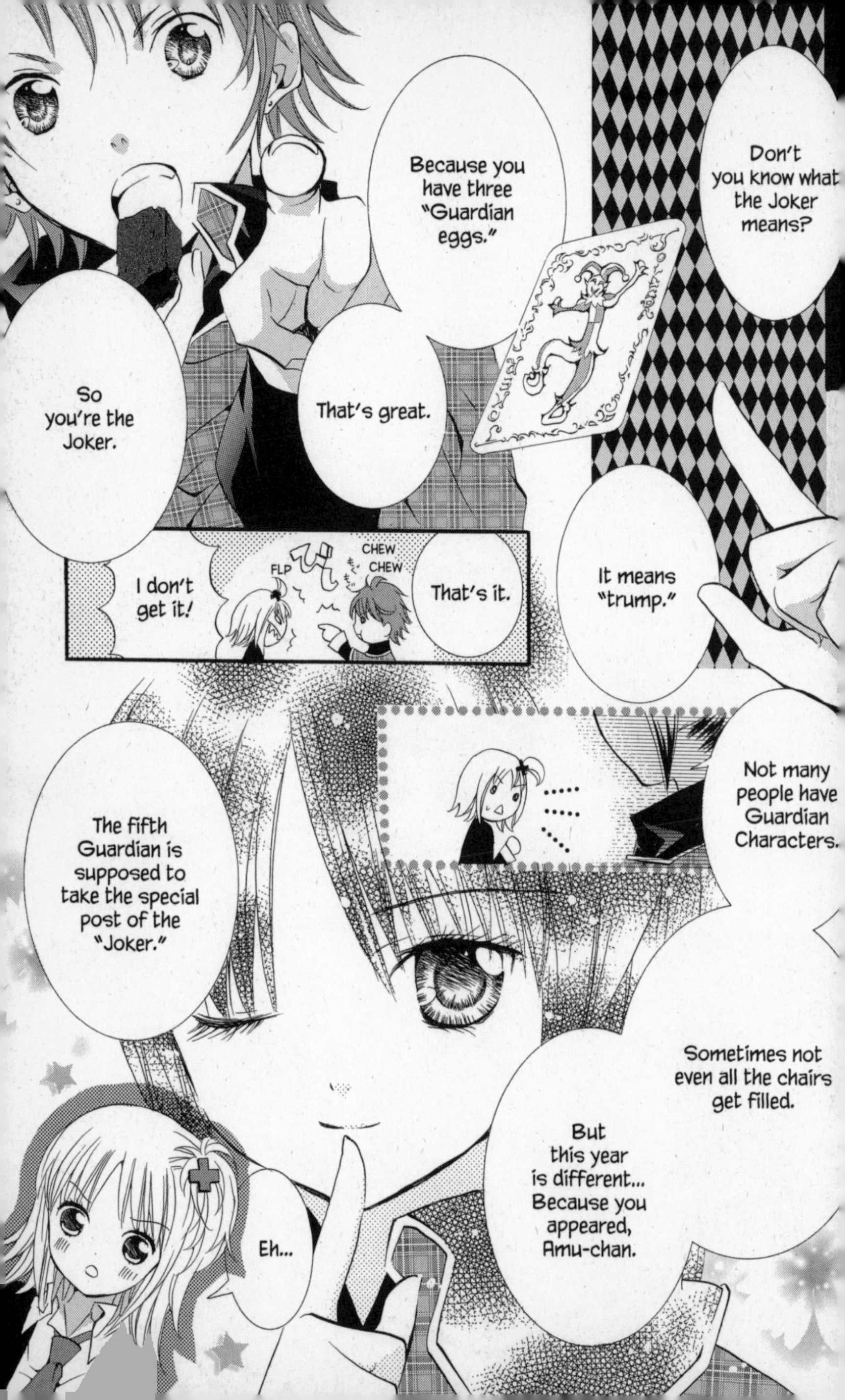
Don't you know what the Joker means?
It means "trump."
Because you have three "Guardian eggs."
That's great.
So you're the Joker.
That's it.
CHEW CHEW
FLP
I don't get it!
Not many people have Guardian Characters.
.....
.....
Sometimes not even all the chairs get filled.
But this year is different... Because you appeared, Amu-chan.
The fifth Guardian is supposed to take the special post of the "Joker."
Eh...

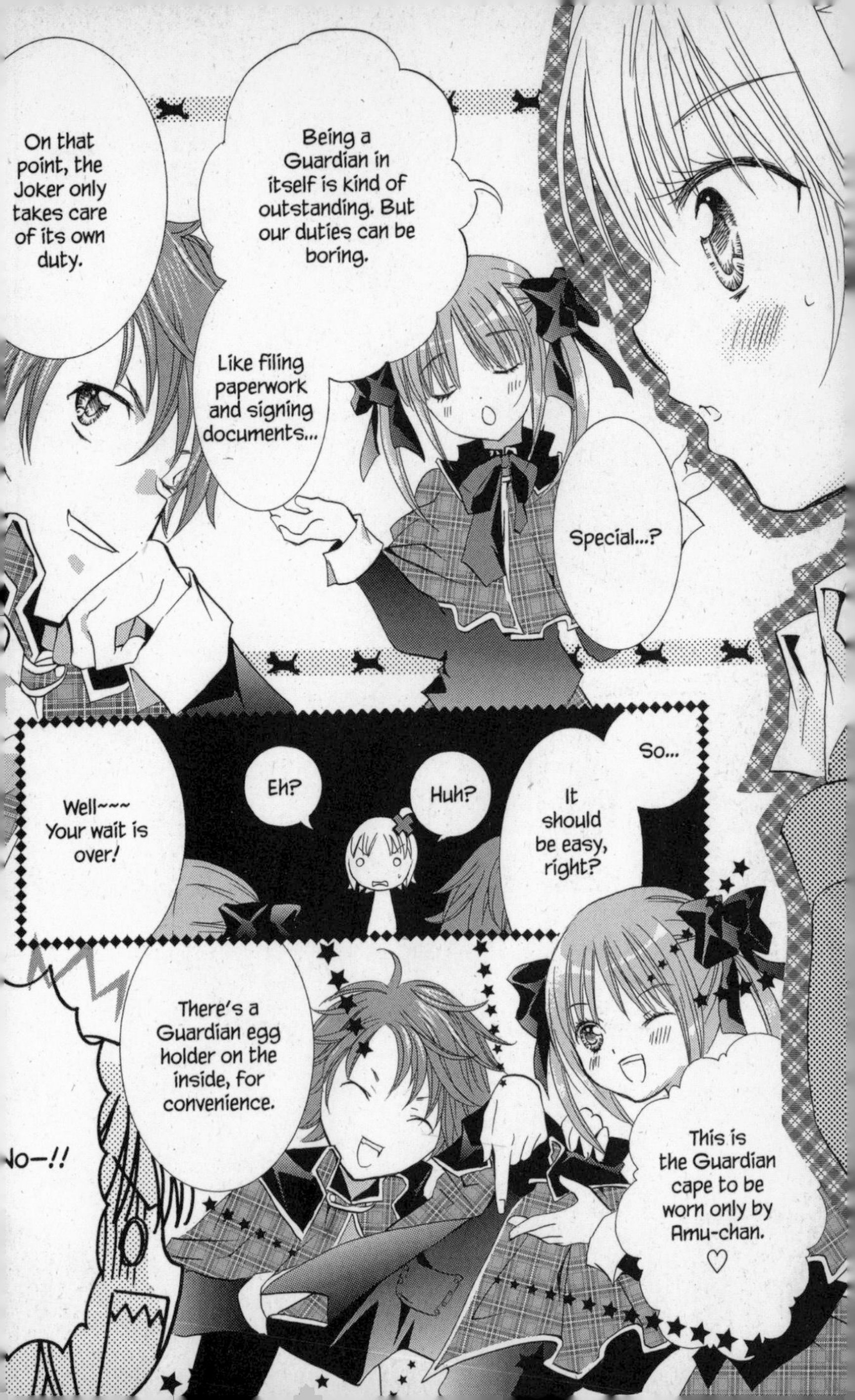

Special...?
Being a Guardian in itself is kind of outstanding. But our duties can be boring.
Like filing paperwork and signing documents...
On that point, the Joker only takes care of its own duty.
So...
It should be easy, right?
Huh?
Eh?
Well~~~ Your wait is over!
This is the Guardian cape to be worn only by Amu-chan. ♡
There's a Guardian egg holder on the inside, for convenience.
No—!!

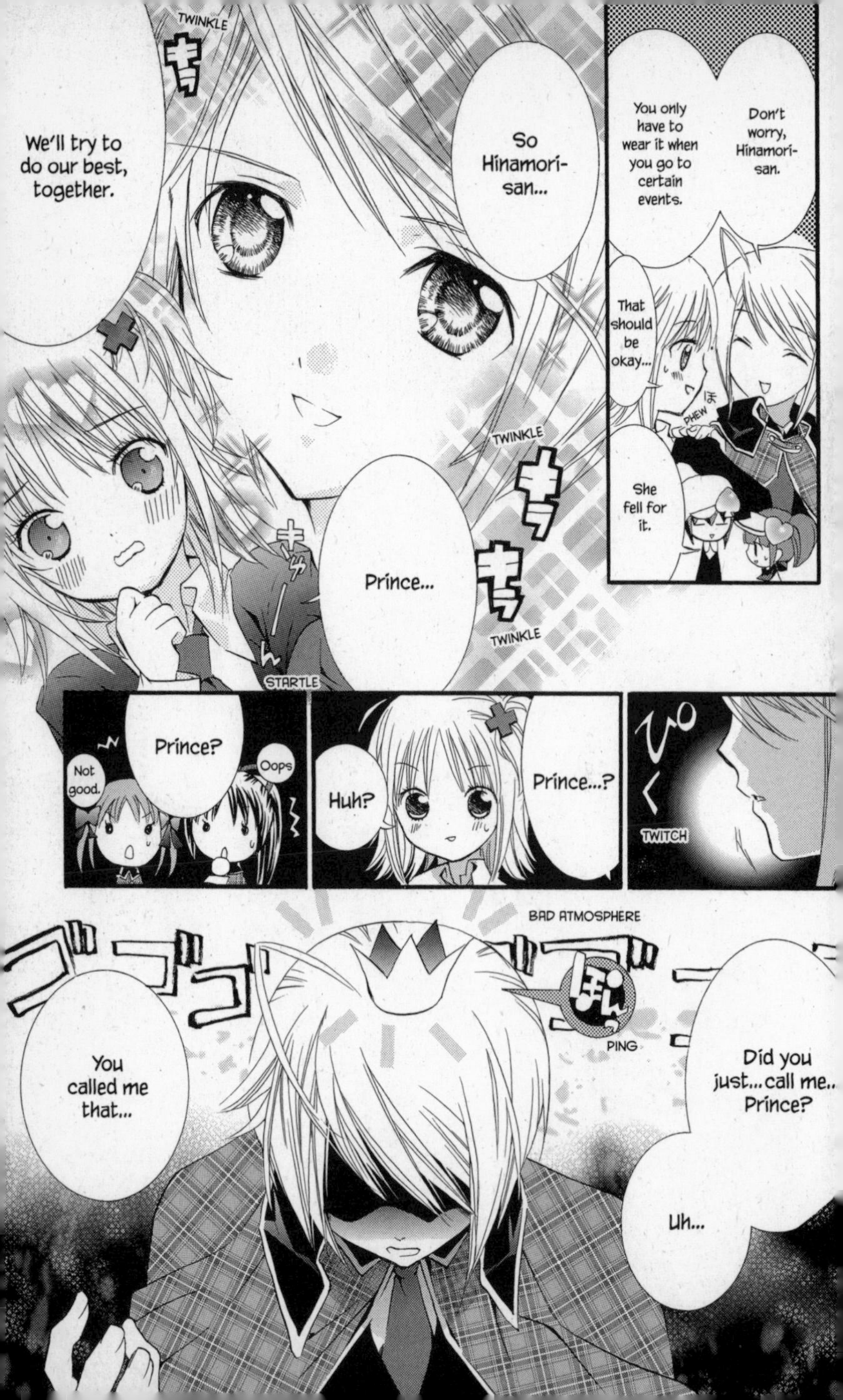
Don't worry, Hinamori-san.
You only have to wear it when you go to certain events.
That should be okay...
PHEW
She fell for it.
So Hinamori-san...
TWINKLE
We'll try to do our best, together.
TWINKLE
Prince...
TWINKLE
STARTLE
TWITCH
Prince...?
Huh?
Prince?
Oops
Not good.
BAD ATMOSPHERE
Did you just...call me.. Prince?
Uh...
PING
You called me that...

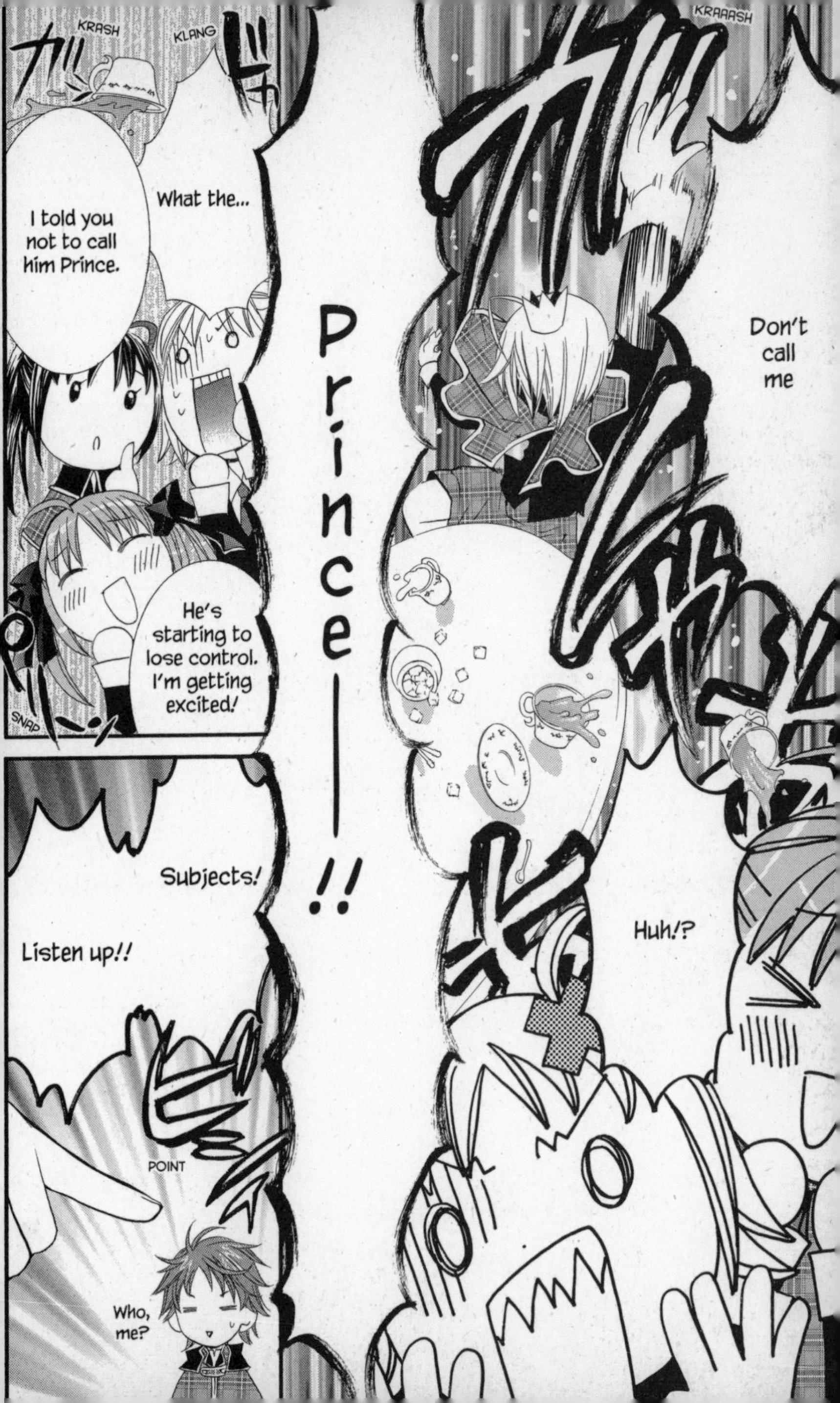
KRAAASH
Don't call me
Prince—!!
Huh!?
KRASH
KLANG
What the...
I told you not to call him Prince.
He's starting to lose control. I'm getting excited!
SNAP
Subjects!
Listen up!!
POINT
Who, me?

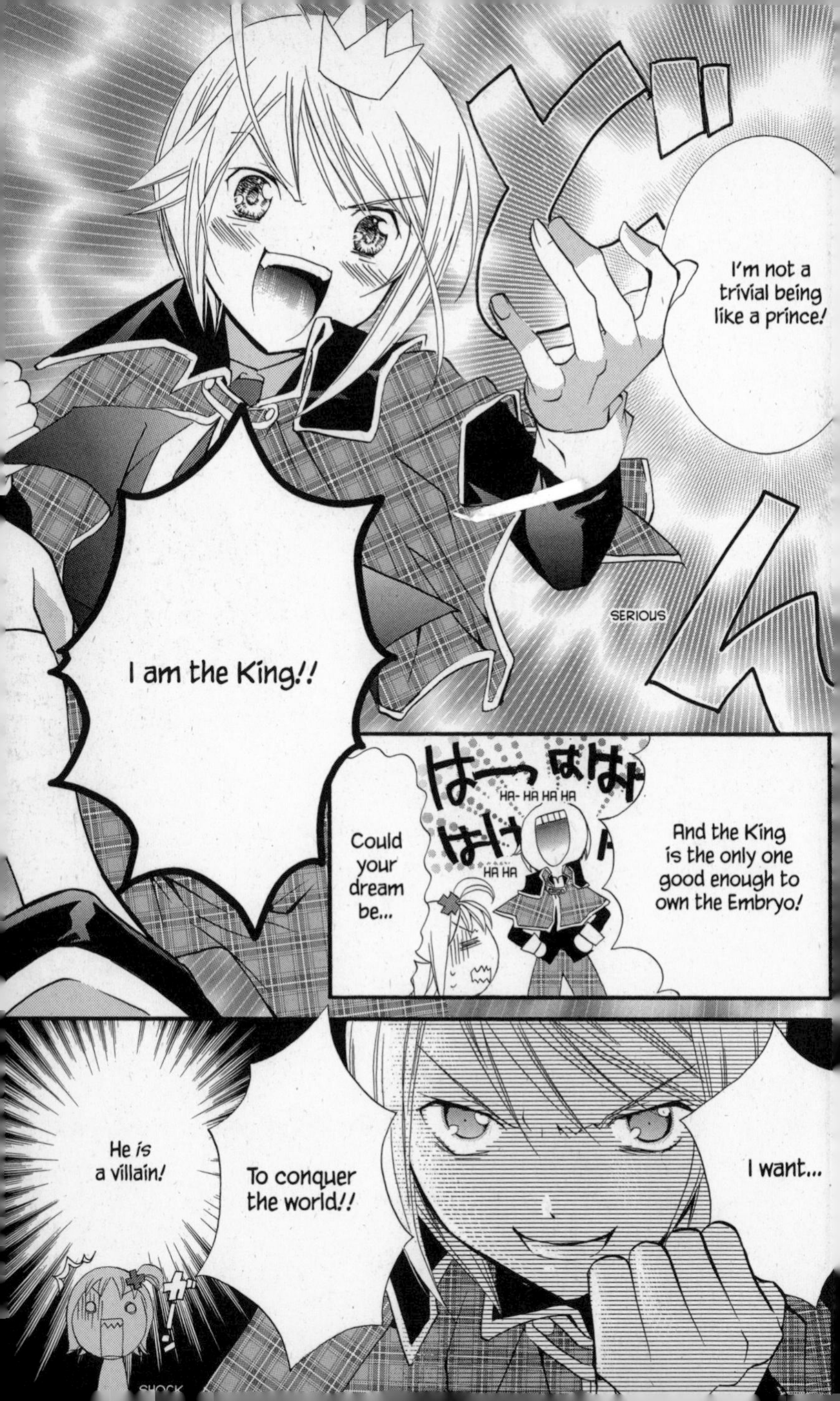

I'm not a trivial being like a prince!
SERIOUS
I am the King!!
And the King is the only one good enough to own the Embryo!
HA- HA HA HA
HA HA
Could your dream be...
I want...
To conquer the world!!
He *is* a villain!

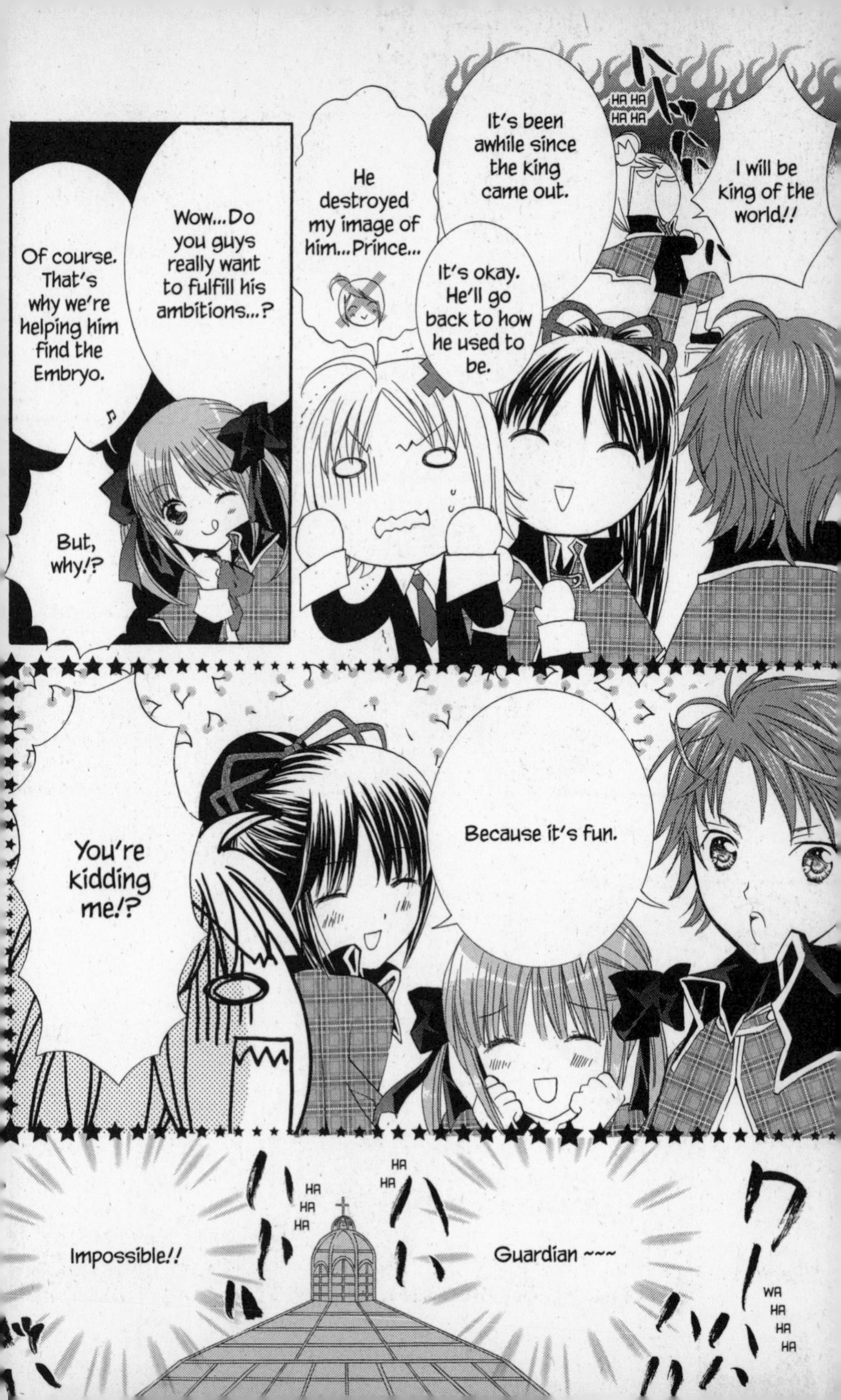
I will be king of the world!!
HA HA HA HA
It's been awhile since the king came out.
He destroyed my image of him...Prince...
It's okay. He'll go back to how he used to be.
Wow...Do you guys really want to fulfill his ambitions...?
Of course. That's why we're helping him find the Embryo.
But, why!?
Because it's fun.
You're kidding me!?
WA HA HA HA
Guardian ~~~
HA HA
HA HA HA
Impossible!!

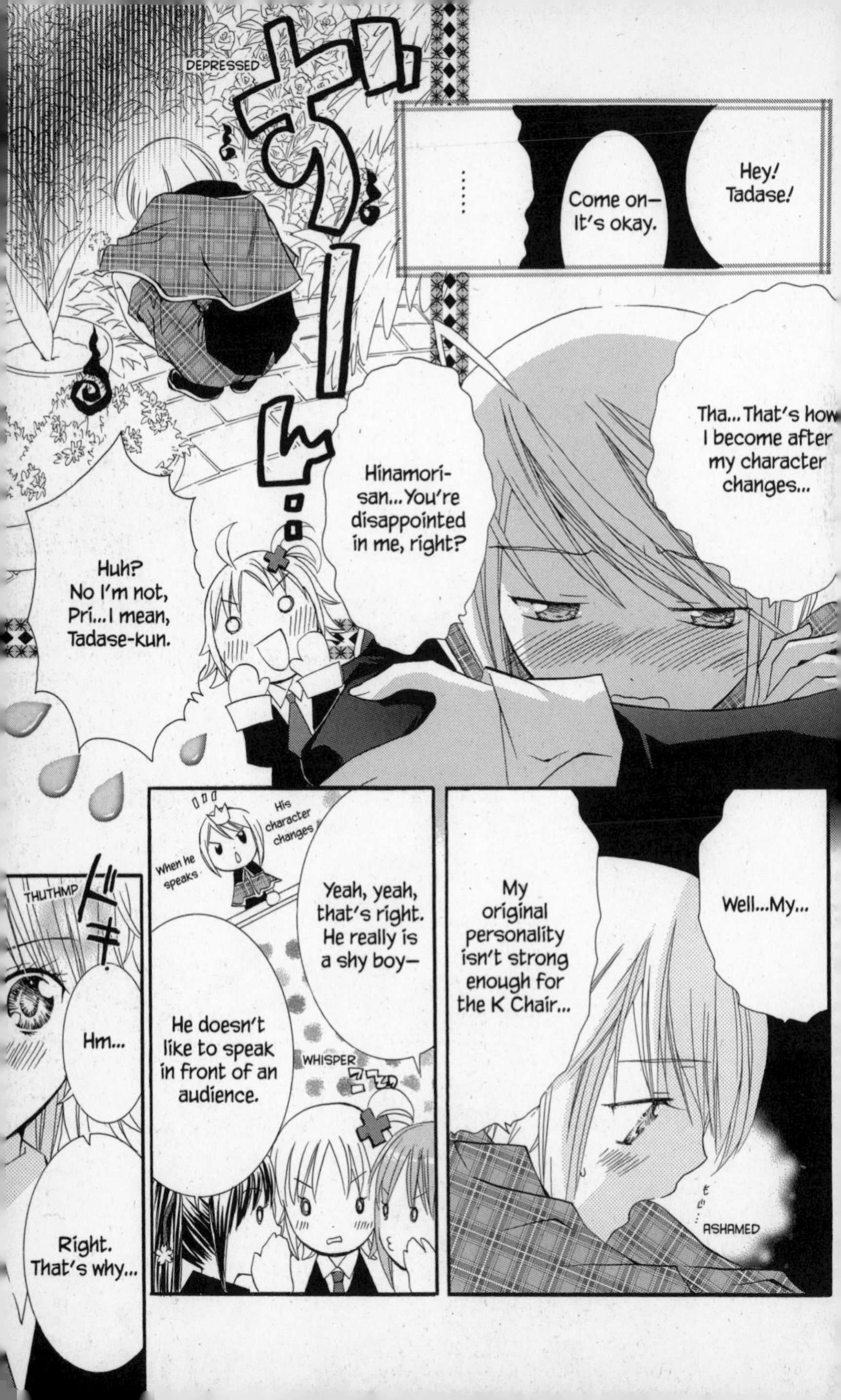

Hey! Tadase!
Come on— It's okay.
......
Tha... That's how I become after my character changes...
Hinamori-san... You're disappointed in me, right?
DEPRESSED
Huh? No I'm not, Pri... I mean, Tadase-kun.
Well...My...
My original personality isn't strong enough for the K Chair...
ASHAMED
His character changes
When he speaks
Yeah, yeah, that's right. He really is a shy boy—
WHISPER
He doesn't like to speak in front of an audience.
THUTHMP
Hm...
Right. That's why...

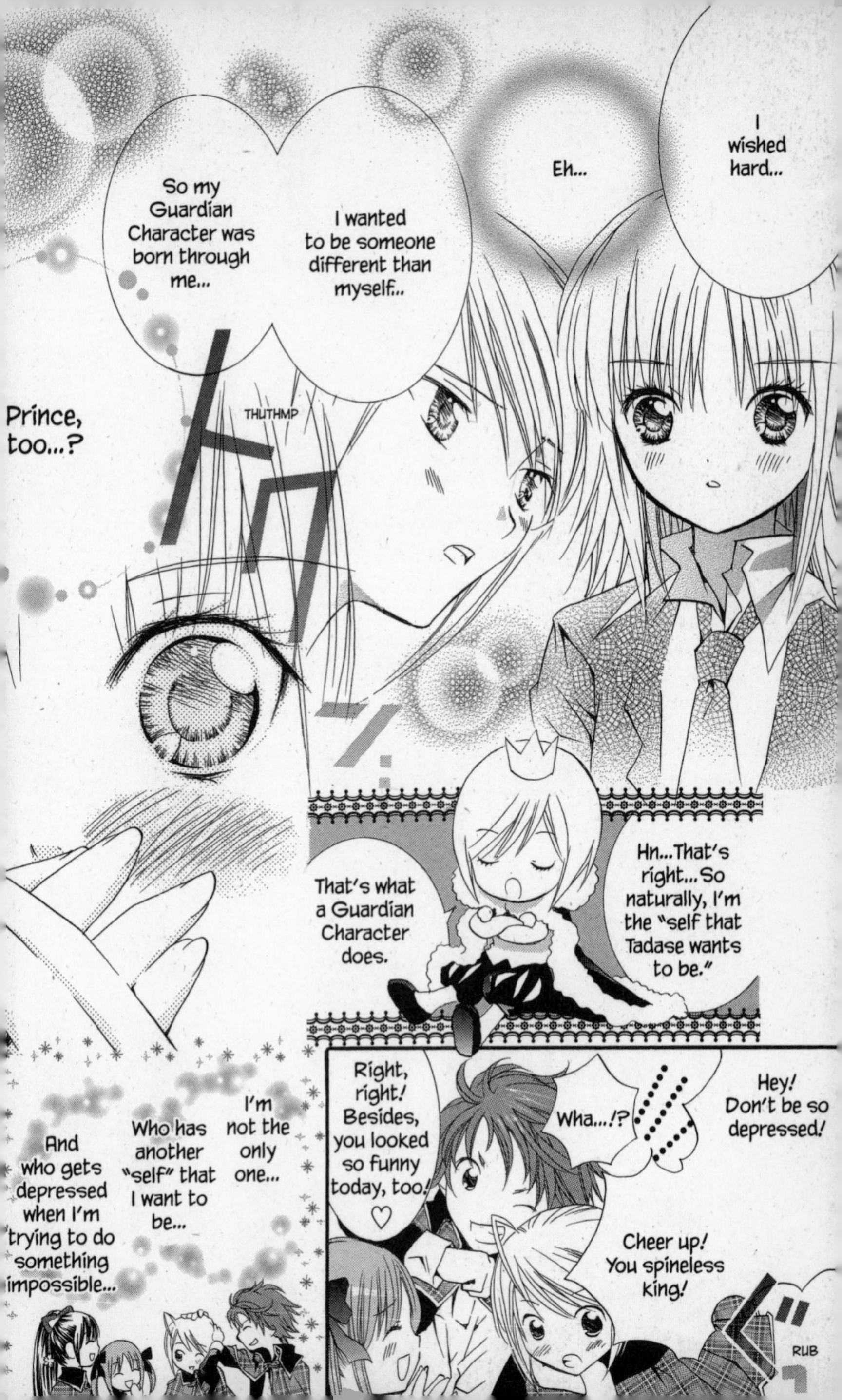
I wished hard...
Eh...
I wanted to be someone different than myself...
So my Guardian Character was born through me...
THUTHMP
Prince, too...?
Hn...That's right... So naturally, I'm the "self that Tadase wants to be."
That's what a Guardian Character does.
Hey! Don't be so depressed!
Wha...!?
Right, right! Besides, you looked so funny today, too! ♡
Cheer up! You spineless king!
RUB
I'm not the only one...
Who has another "self" that I want to be...
And who gets depressed when I'm trying to do something impossible...

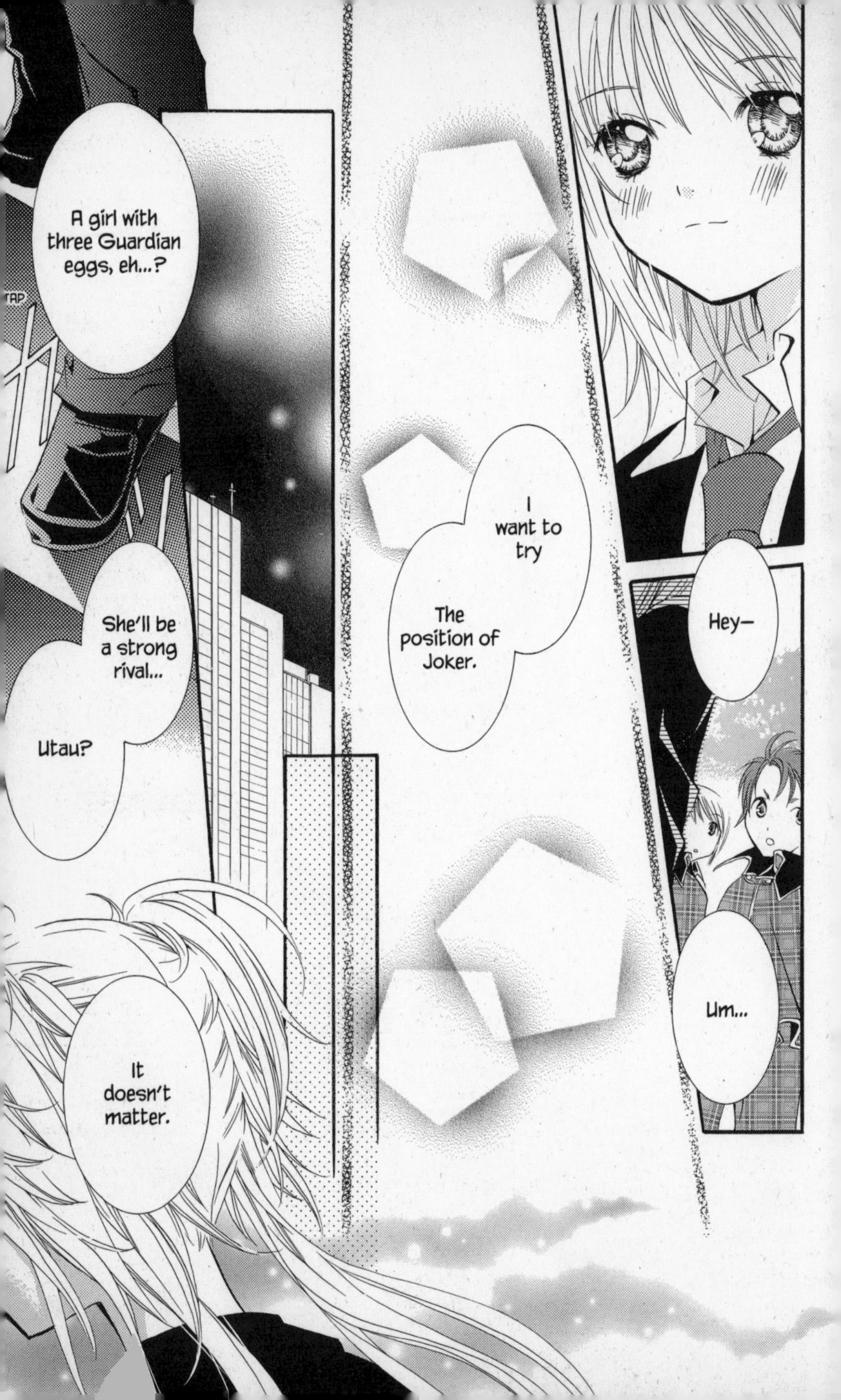
Hey—
Um...
I want to try
The position of Joker.
A girl with three Guardian eggs, eh...?
TAP
She'll be a strong rival...
Utau?
It doesn't matter.

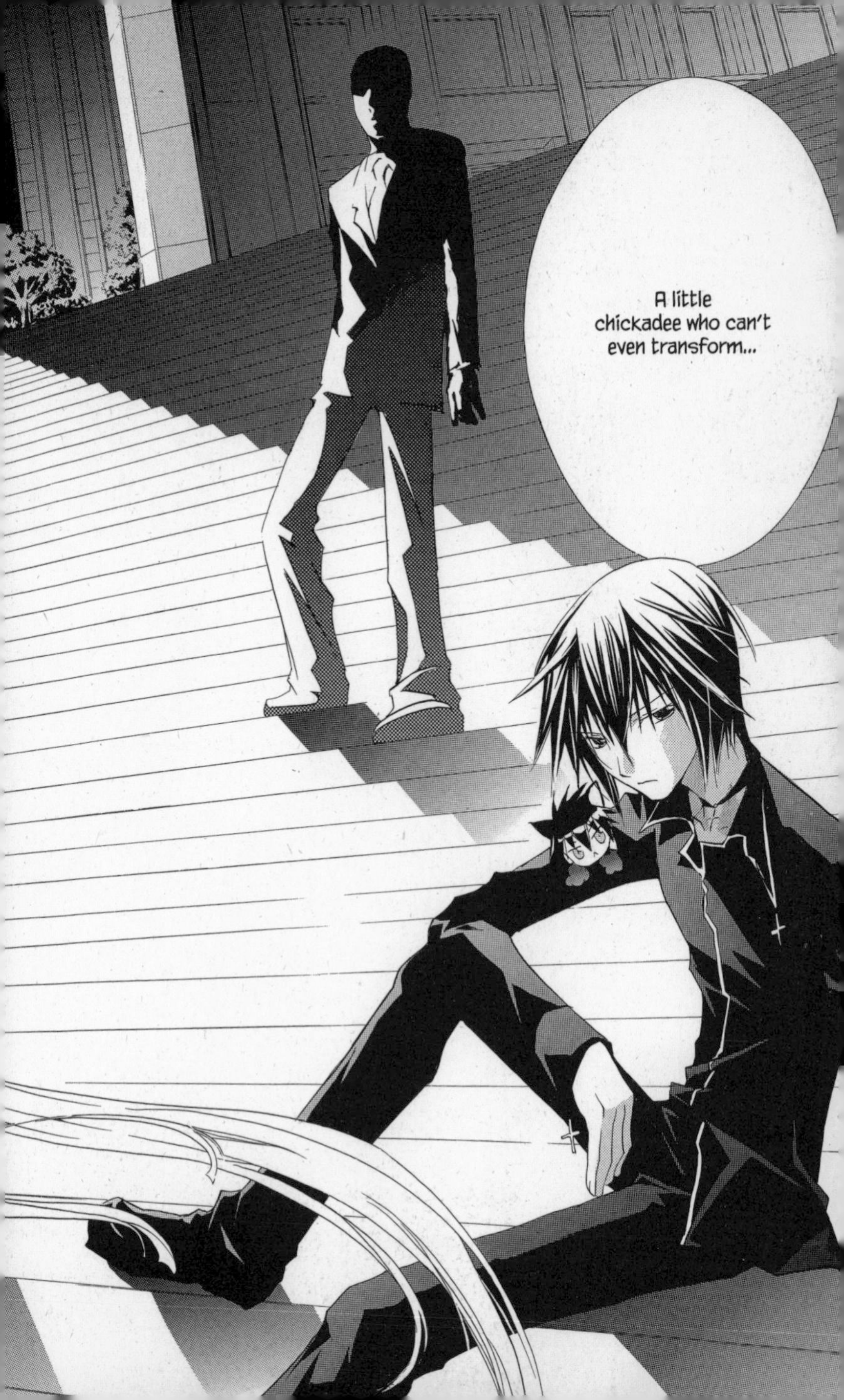
A little chickadee who can't even transform...

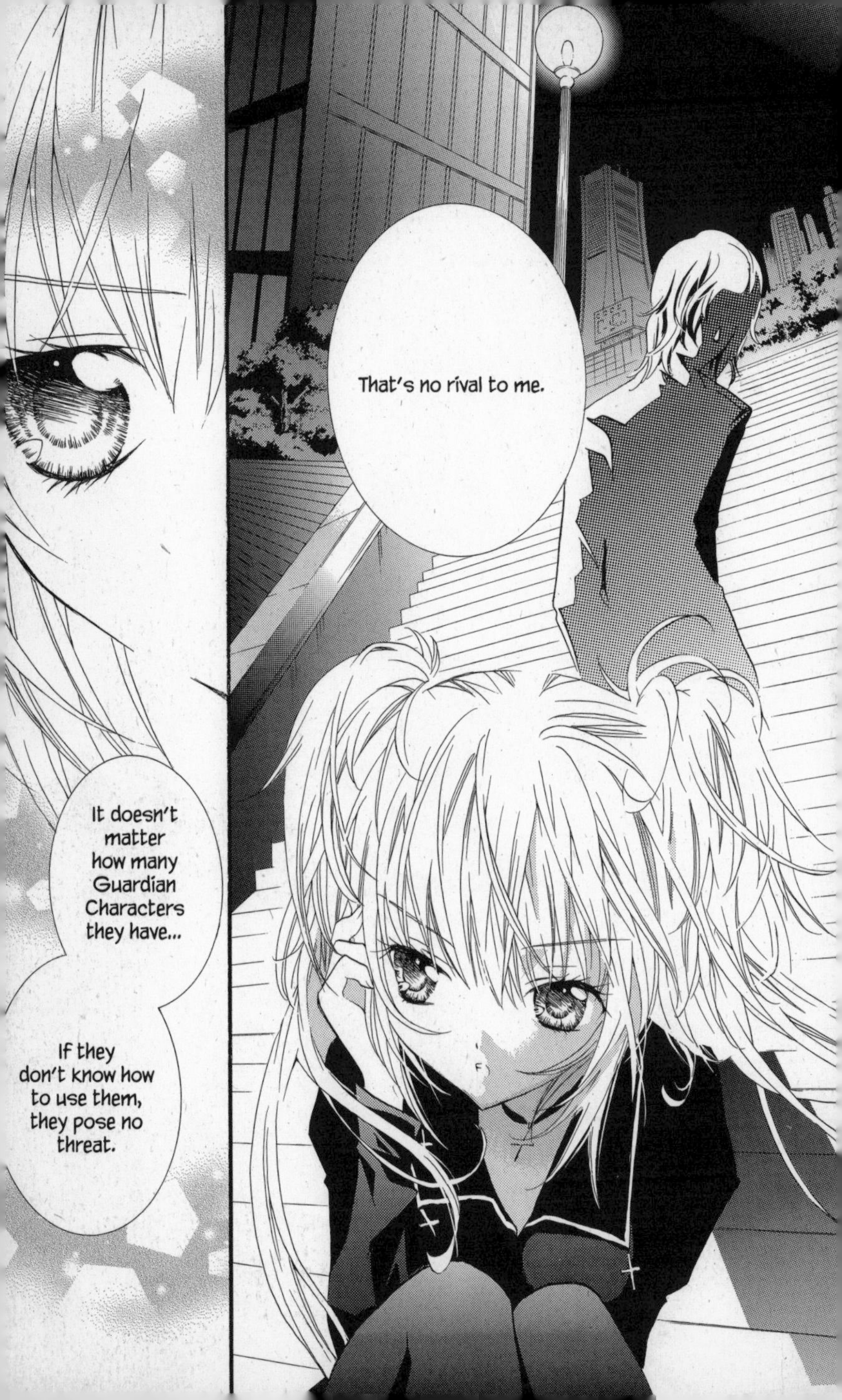
That's no rival to me.
It doesn't matter how many Guardian Characters they have...
If they don't know how to use them, they pose no threat.

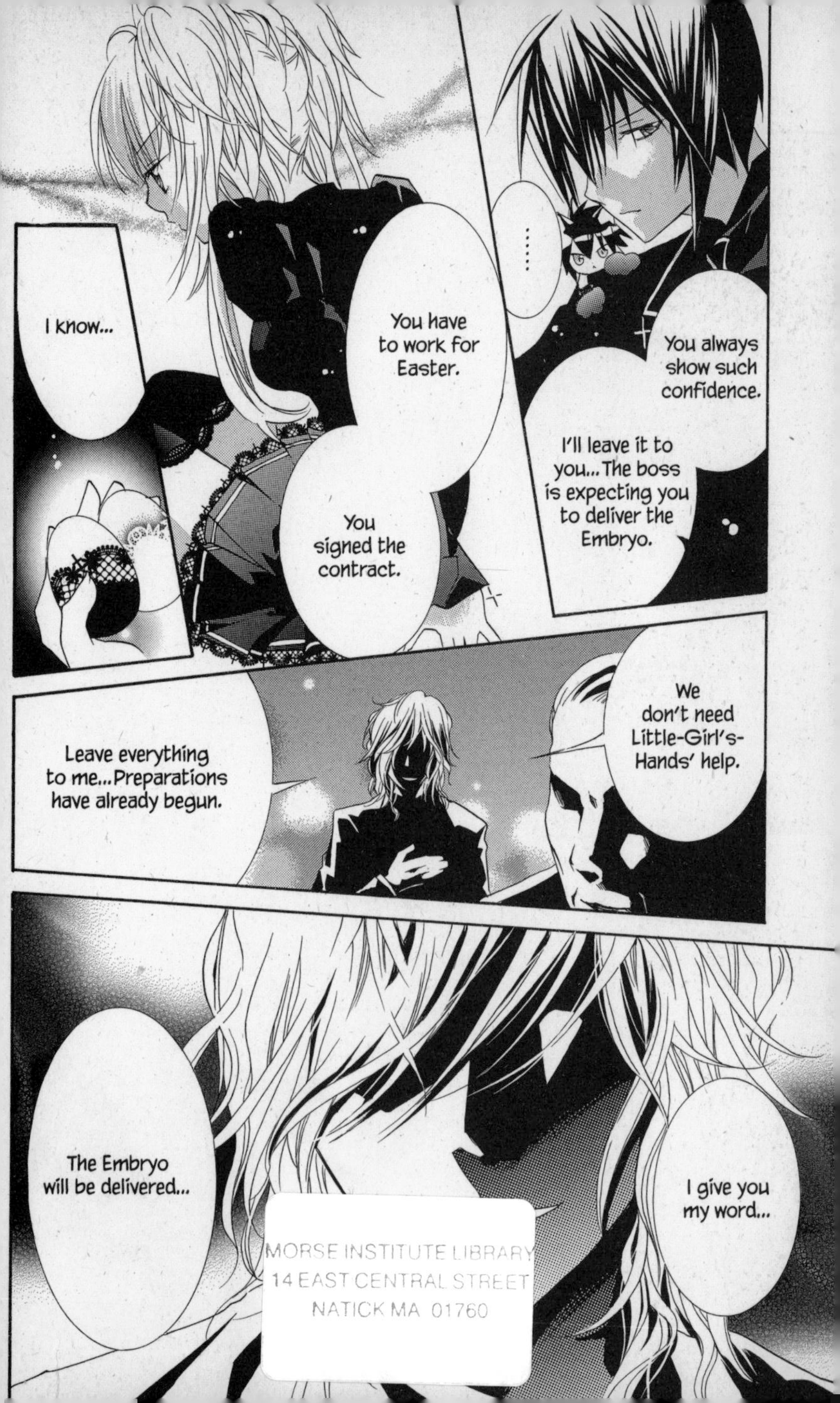
……
You always show such confidence.
I'll leave it to you...The boss is expecting you to deliver the Embryo.
You have to work for Easter.
You signed the contract.
I know...
We don't need Little-Girl's-Hands' help.
Leave everything to me...Preparations have already begun.
I give you my word...
The Embryo will be delivered...

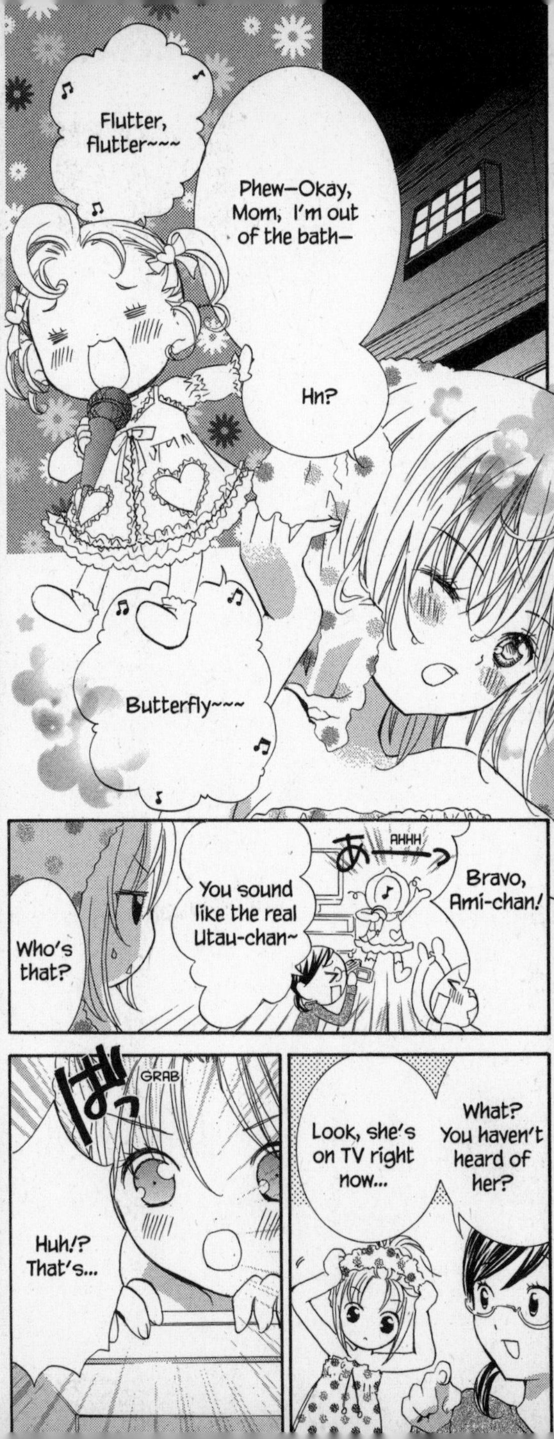
Phew—Okay, Mom, I'm out of the bath—
Flutter, flutter~~~
Hn?
Butterfly~~~
Bravo, Ami-chan!
あー
AHHH
You sound like the real Utau-chan~
Who's that?
What? You haven't heard of her?
Look, she's on TV right now...
ぱっ
GRAB
Huh!? That's...

character profile

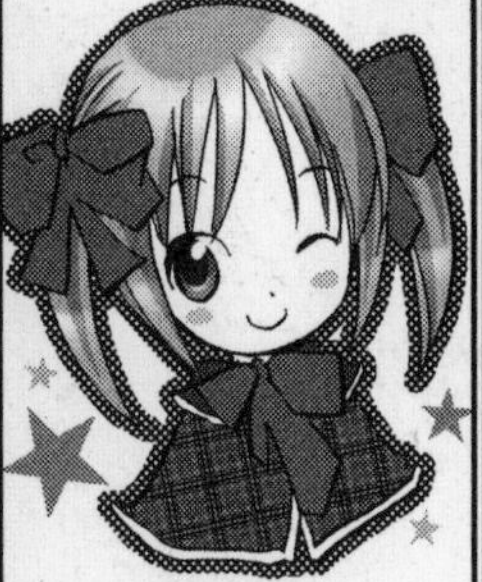

結木 やや

Yaya Yuiki

Birthday : 5/25
BloodType : O
Sign : Gemini
Shugo-Chara : Pepe

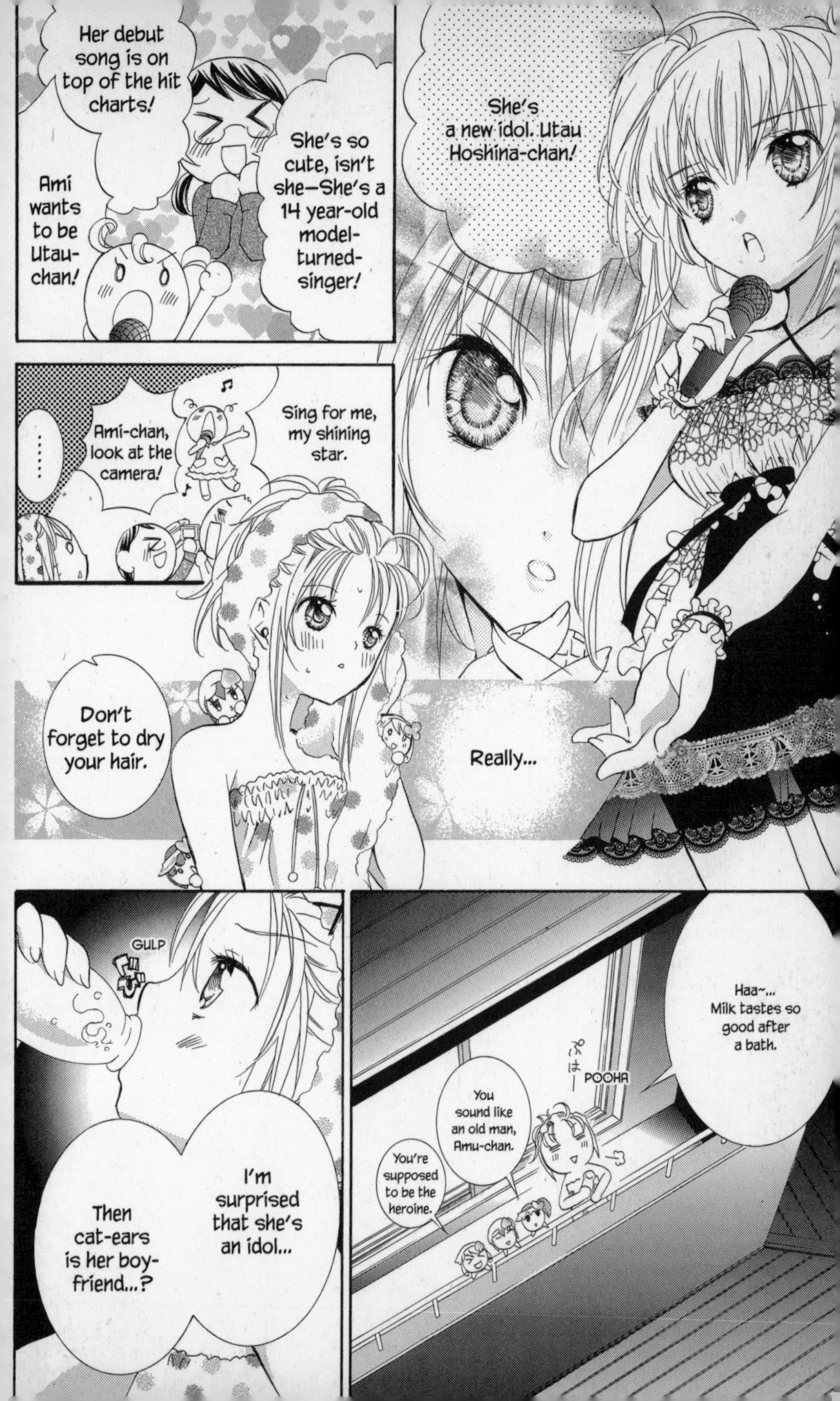
She's a new idol. Utau Hoshina-chan!
Her debut song is on top of the hit charts!
She's so cute, isn't she—She's a 14 year-old model-turned-singer!
Ami wants to be Utau-chan!
Sing for me, my shining star.
Ami-chan, look at the camera!
......
Really...
Don't forget to dry your hair.
Haa~... Milk tastes so good after a bath.
ぷはー POOHA
You sound like an old man, Amu-chan.
You're supposed to be the heroine.
GULP
I'm surprised that she's an idol...
Then cat-ears is her boy-friend...?

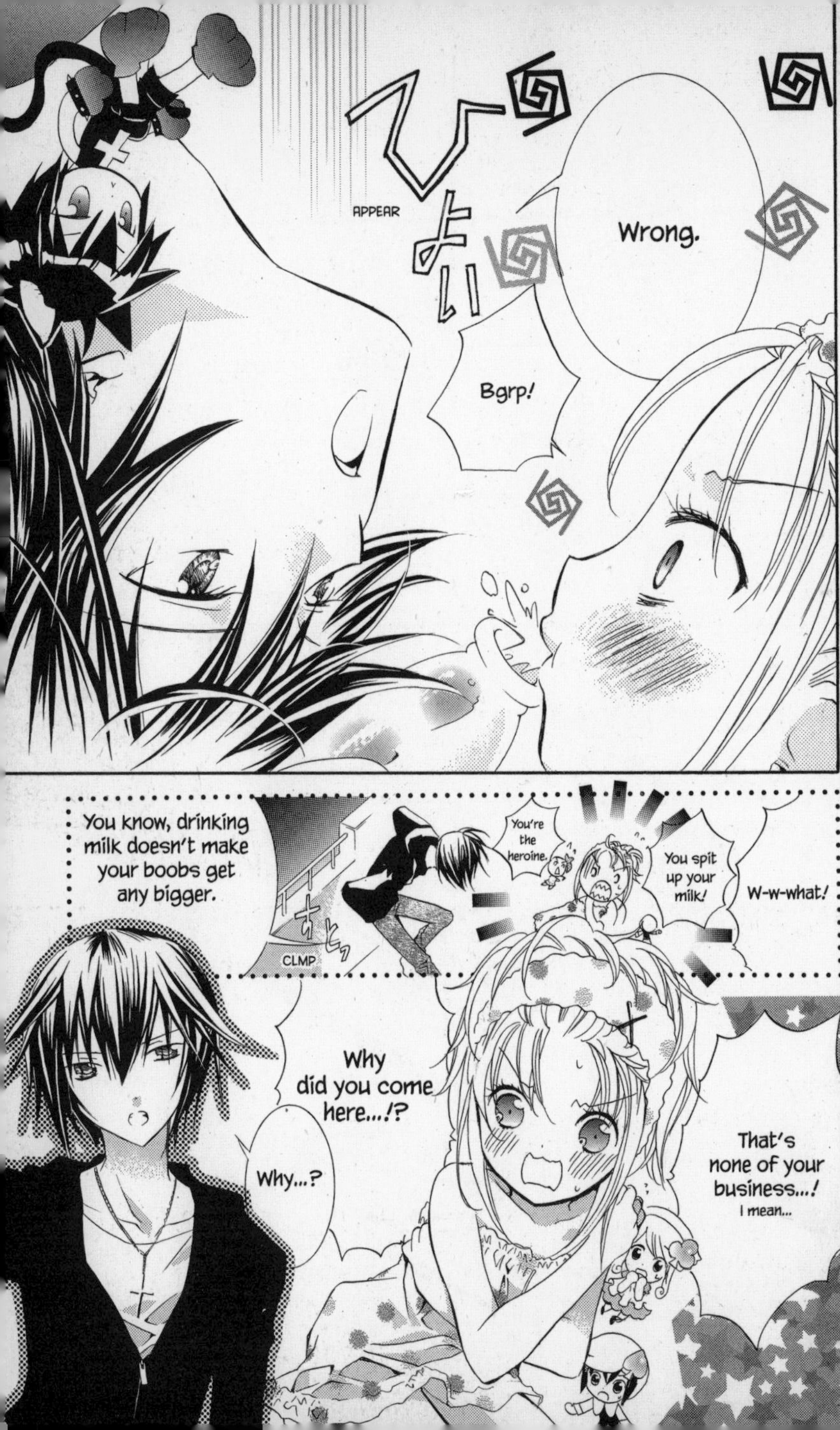

Wrong.
ひょい
APPEAR
Bgrp!
W-w-what!
You spit up your milk!
You're the heroine.
CLMP
You know, drinking milk doesn't make your boobs get any bigger.
That's none of your business...! I mean...
Why did you come here...!?
Why...?

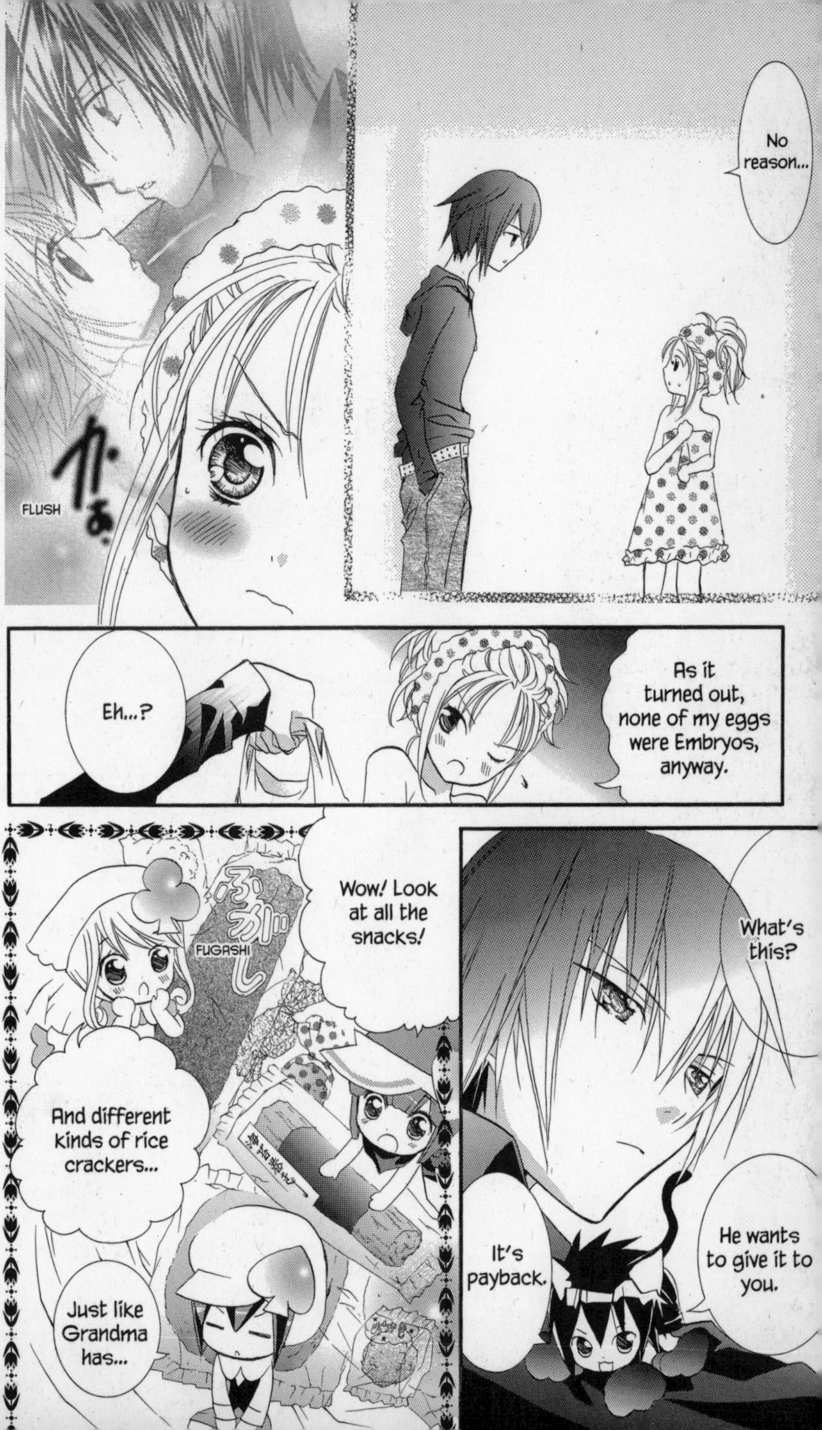
No reason...
FLUSH
As it turned out, none of my eggs were Embryos, anyway.
Eh...?
What's this?
He wants to give it to you.
It's payback.
Wow! Look at all the snacks!
FUGASHI
ふがし
And different kinds of rice crackers...
Just like Grandma has...

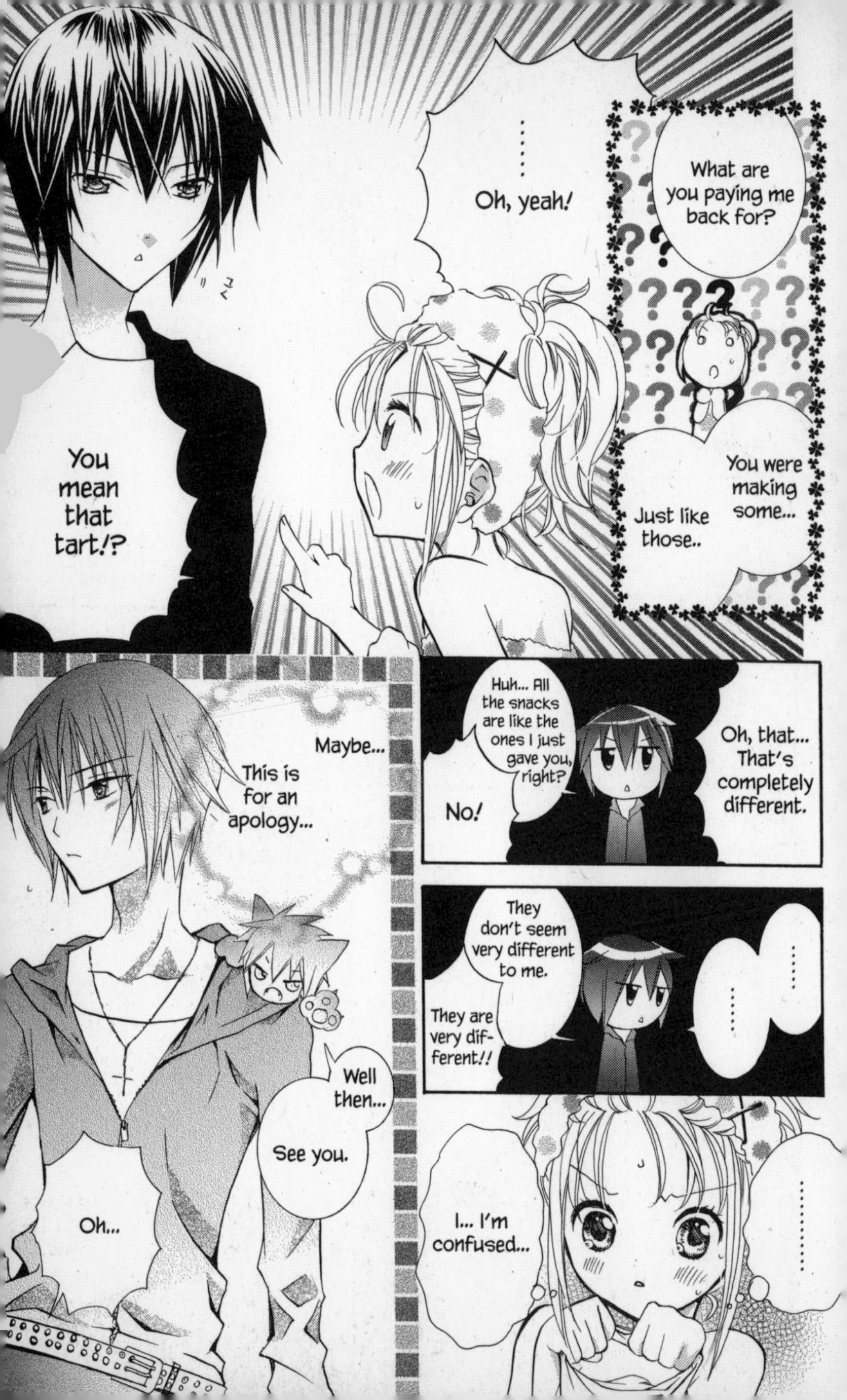
What are you paying me back for?
You were making some...
Just like those..
......
Oh, yeah!
You mean that tart!?
Oh, that... That's completely different.
Huh... All the snacks are like the ones I just gave you, right?
No!
......
......
They don't seem very different to me.
They are very different!!
......
I... I'm confused...
Maybe...
This is for an apology...
Well then...
See you.
Oh...

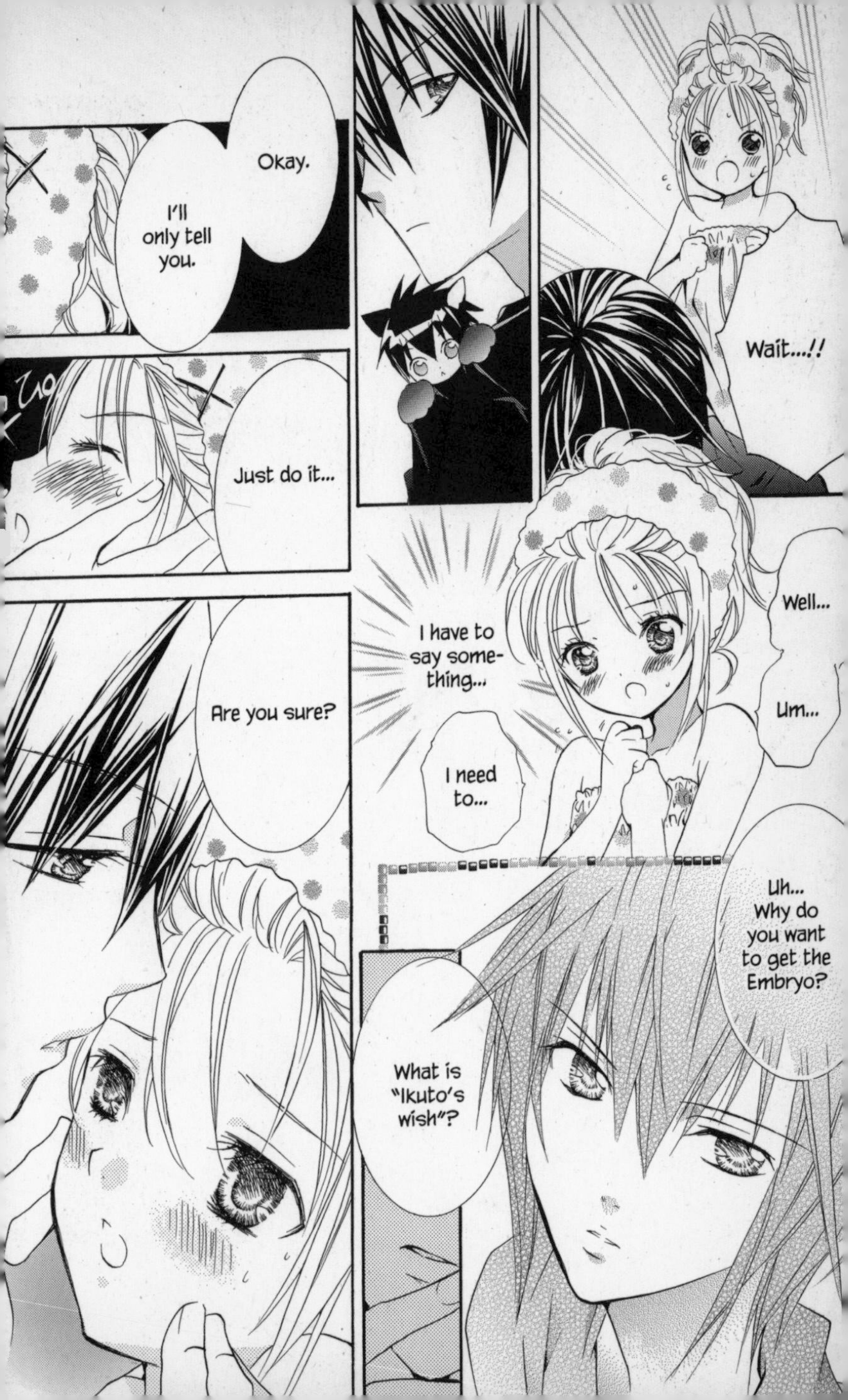

Wait...!!
Okay.
I'll only tell you.
Just do it...
Well...
Um...
I have to say some-thing...
I need to...
Uh... Why do you want to get the Embryo?
What is "Ikuto's wish"?
Are you sure?

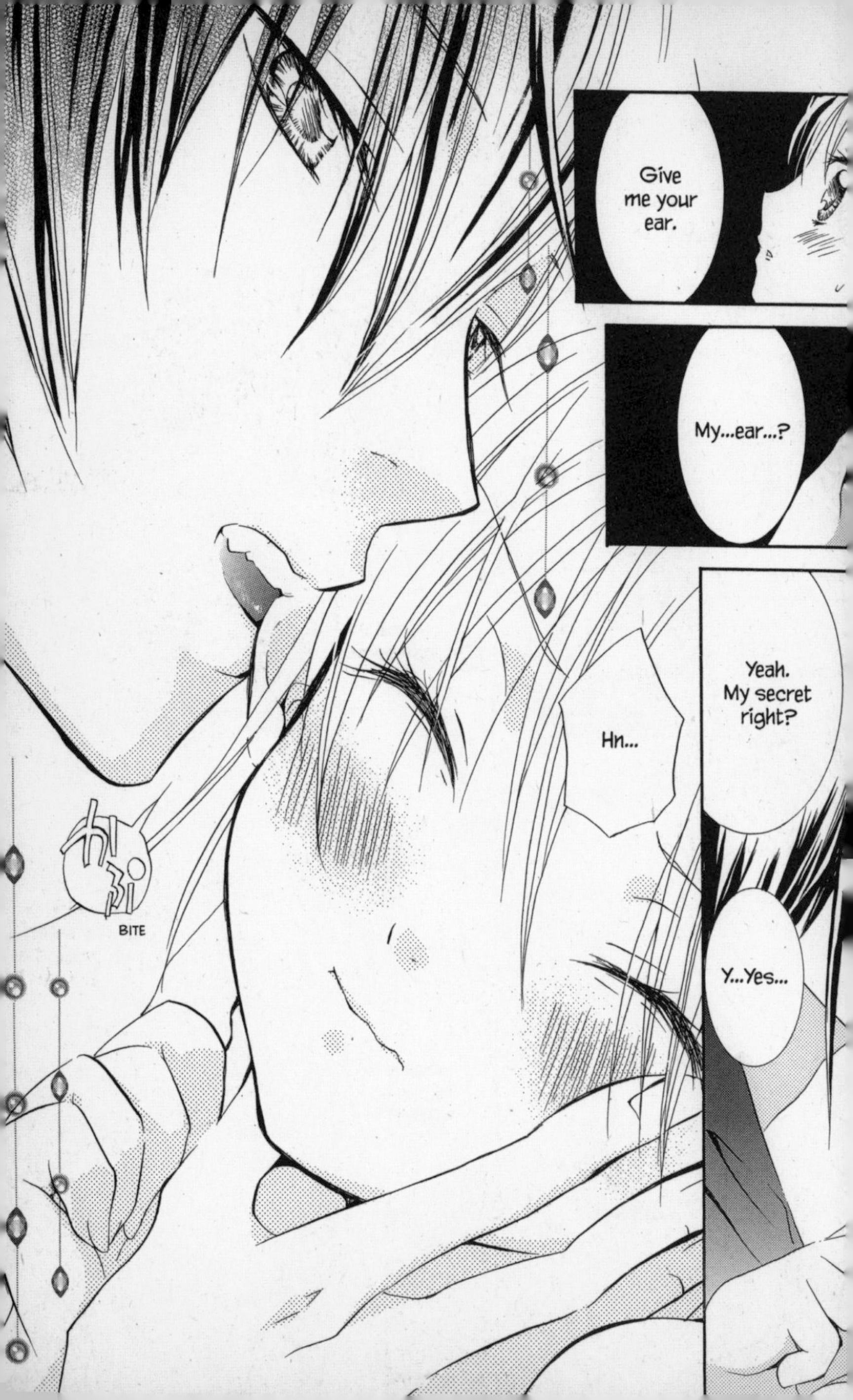
Give me your ear.
My...ear...?
Yeah. My secret right?
Y...Yes...
Hn...
BITE

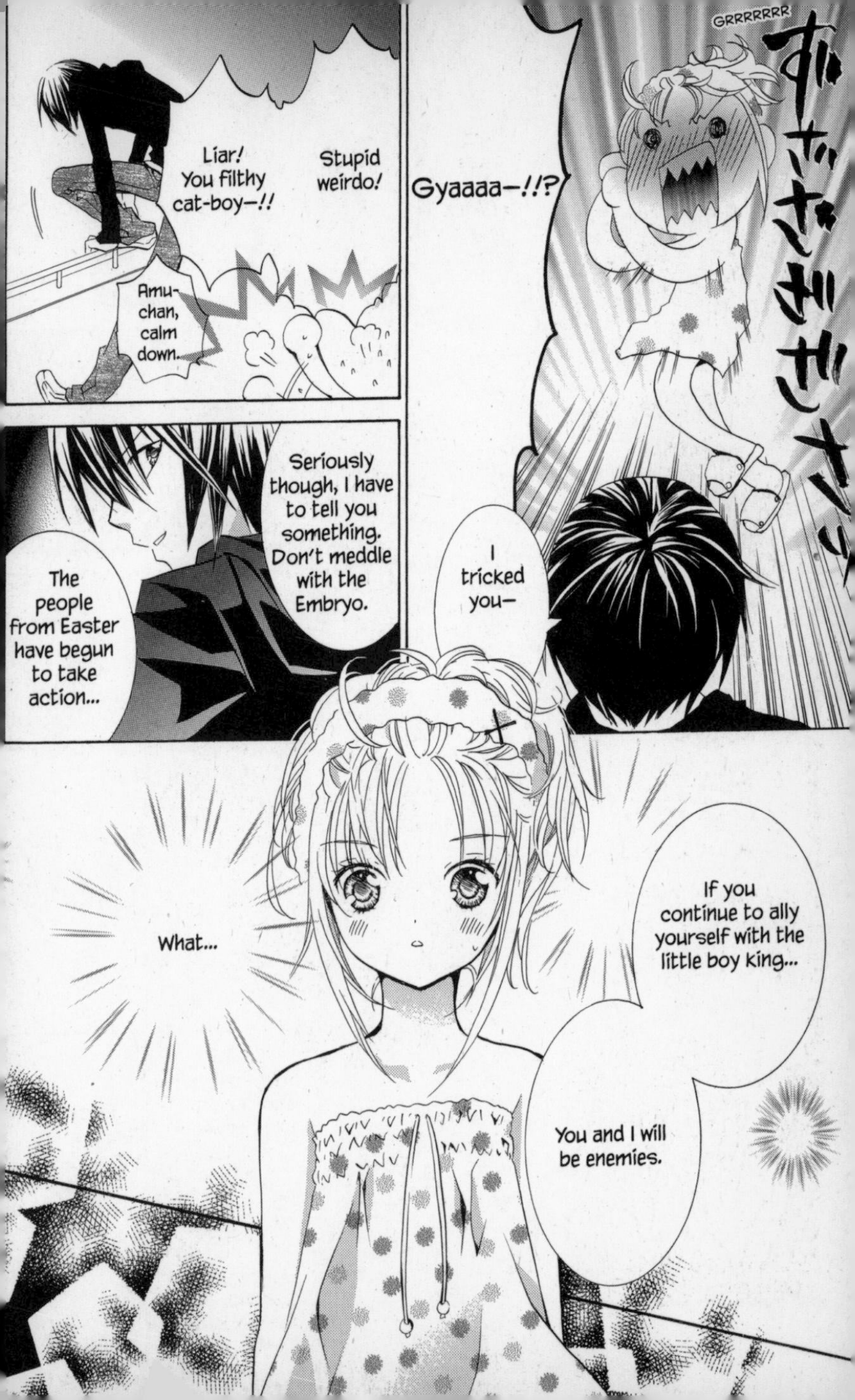
GRRRRRRR
Gyaaaa-!!?
I tricked you-
Stupid weirdo!
Liar! You filthy cat-boy-!!
Amu-chan, calm down.
Seriously though, I have to tell you something. Don't meddle with the Embryo.
The people from Easter have begun to take action...
If you continue to ally yourself with the little boy king...
You and I will be enemies.
What...

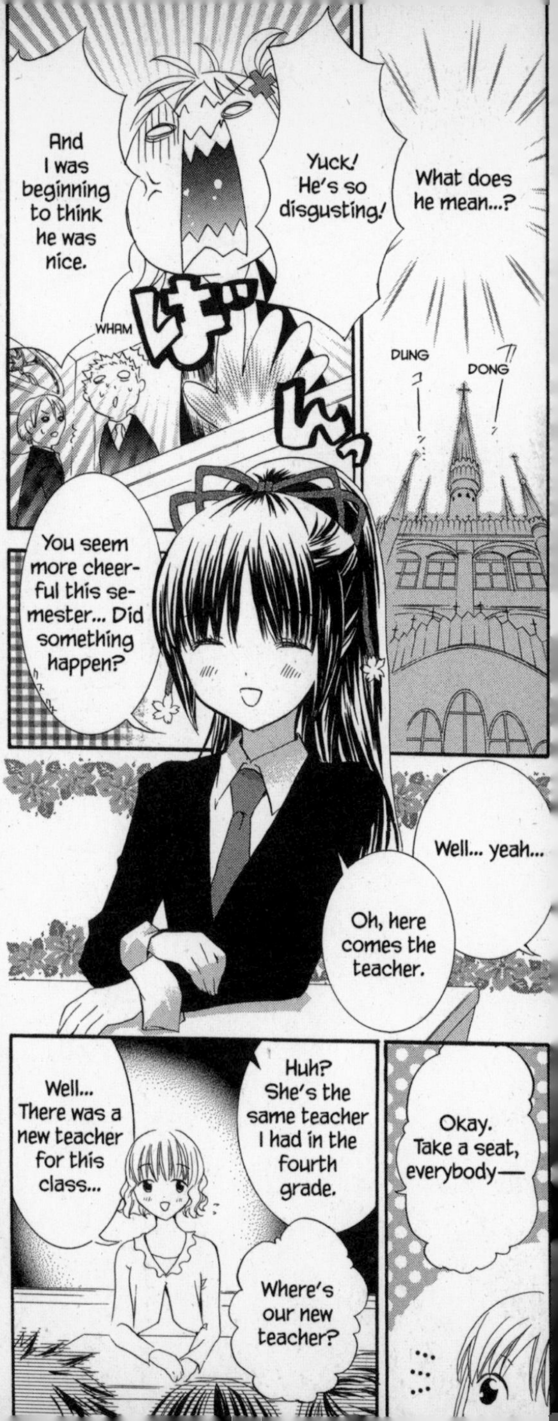
What does he mean...?
Yuck! He's so disgusting!
And I was beginning to think he was nice.
WHAM
DING
DONG
You seem more cheerful this semester... Did something happen?
Well... yeah...
Oh, here comes the teacher.
Okay. Take a seat, everybody—
...
...
Huh? She's the same teacher I had in the fourth grade.
Well... There was a new teacher for this class...
Where's our new teacher?
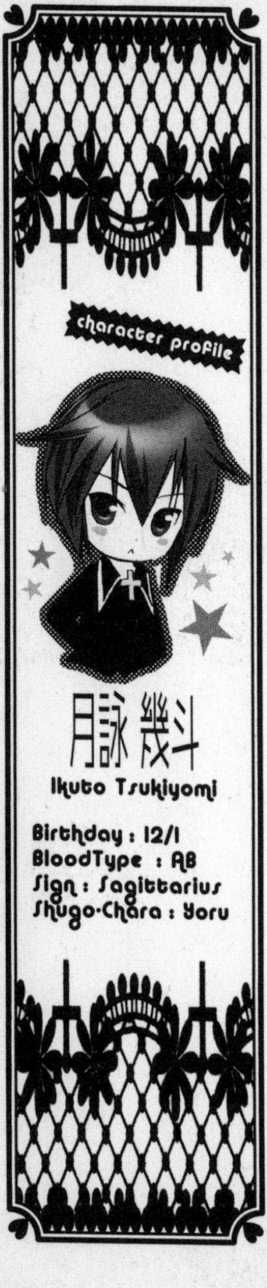
character profile
月詠 幾斗
Ikuto Tsukiyomi
Birthday : 12/1
BloodType : AB
Sign : Sagittarius
Shugo-Chara : Yoru

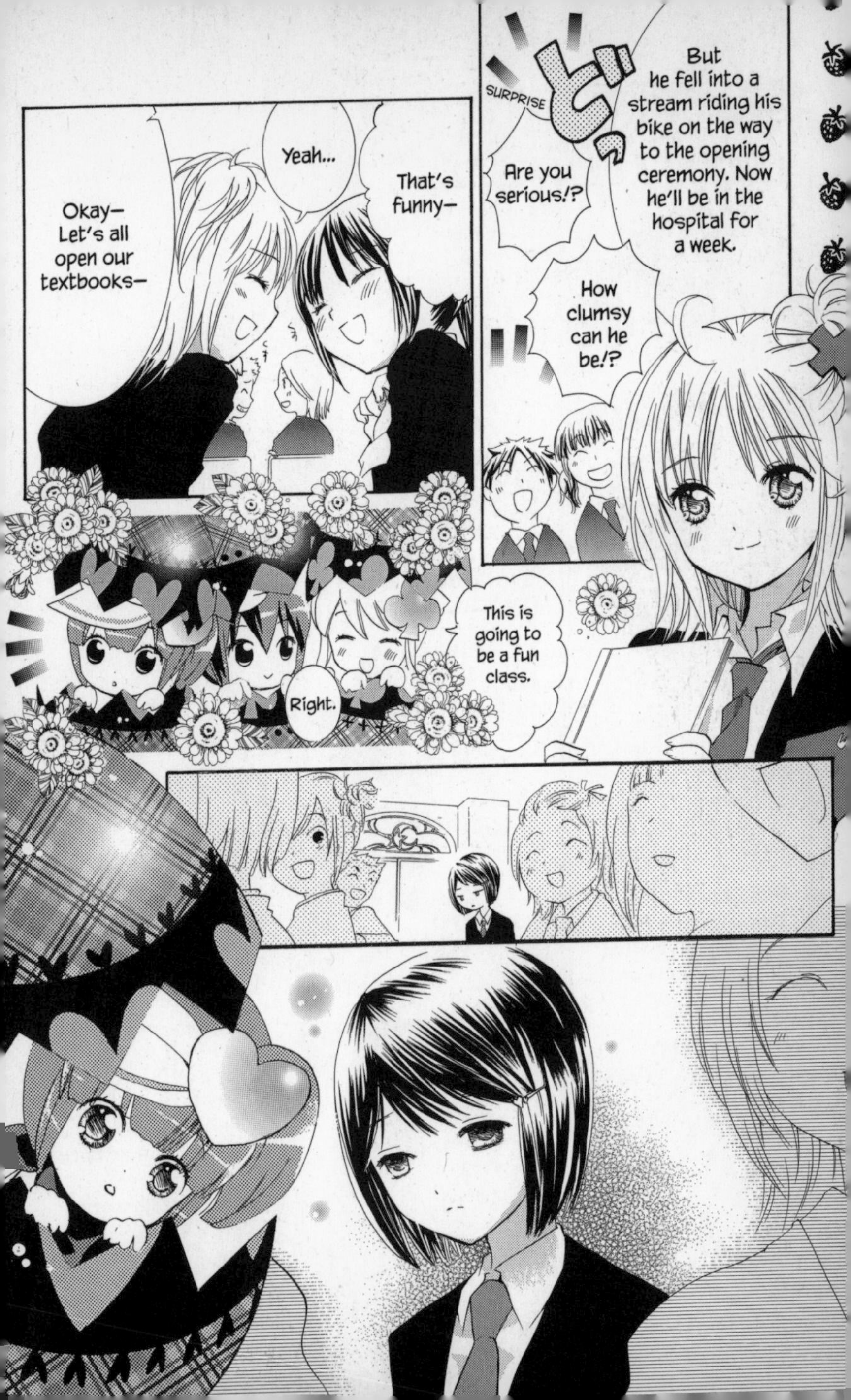
But he fell into a stream riding his bike on the way to the opening ceremony. Now he'll be in the hospital for a week.
SURPRISE
Are you serious!?
How clumsy can he be!?
That's funny—
Yeah...
Okay— Let's all open our textbooks—
This is going to be a fun class.
Right.

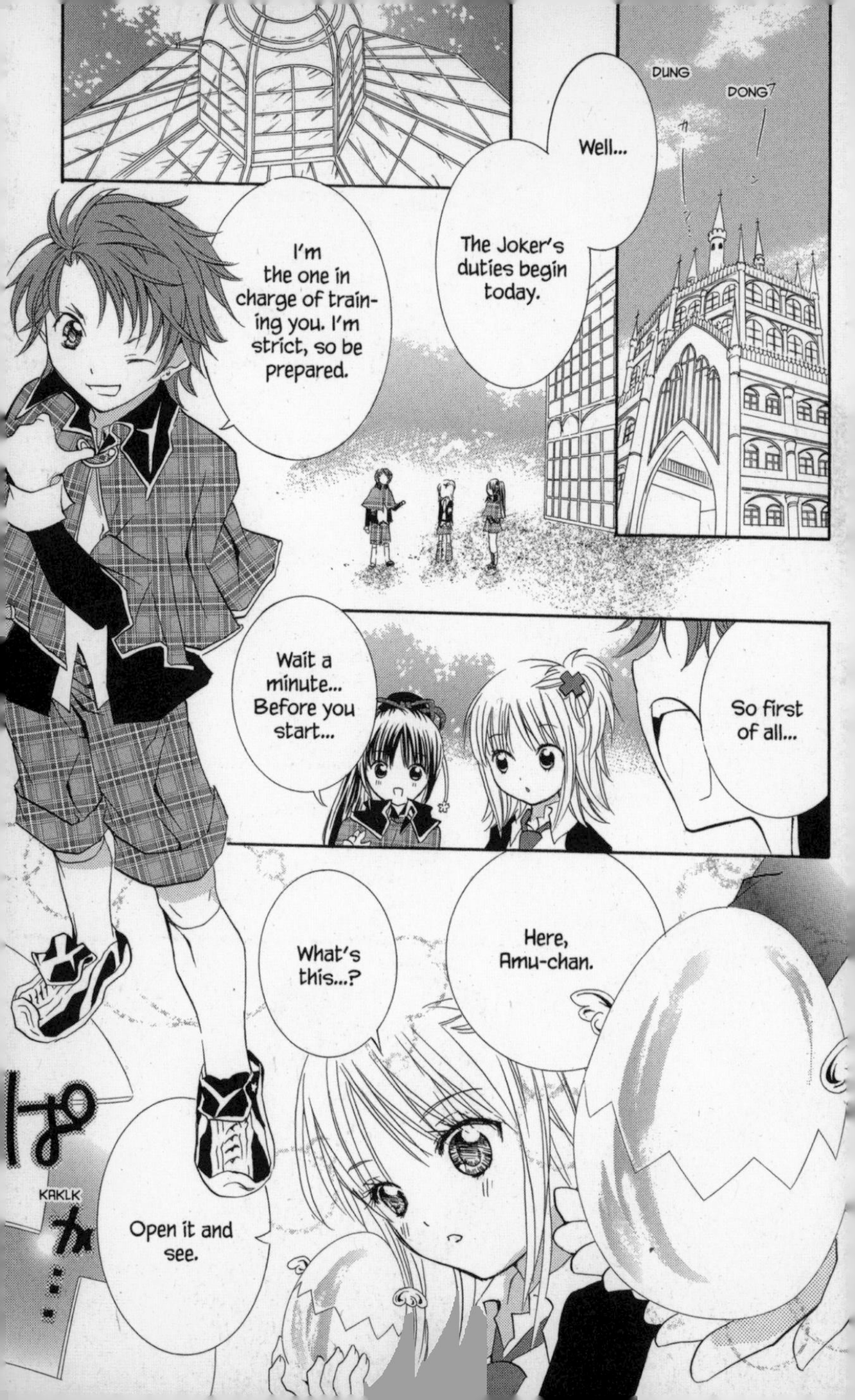

DUNG
DONG
Well...
The Joker's duties begin today.
I'm the one in charge of training you. I'm strict, so be prepared.
So first of all...
Wait a minute... Before you start...
Here, Amu-chan.
What's this...?
Open it and see.
ぱか…
KAKLK

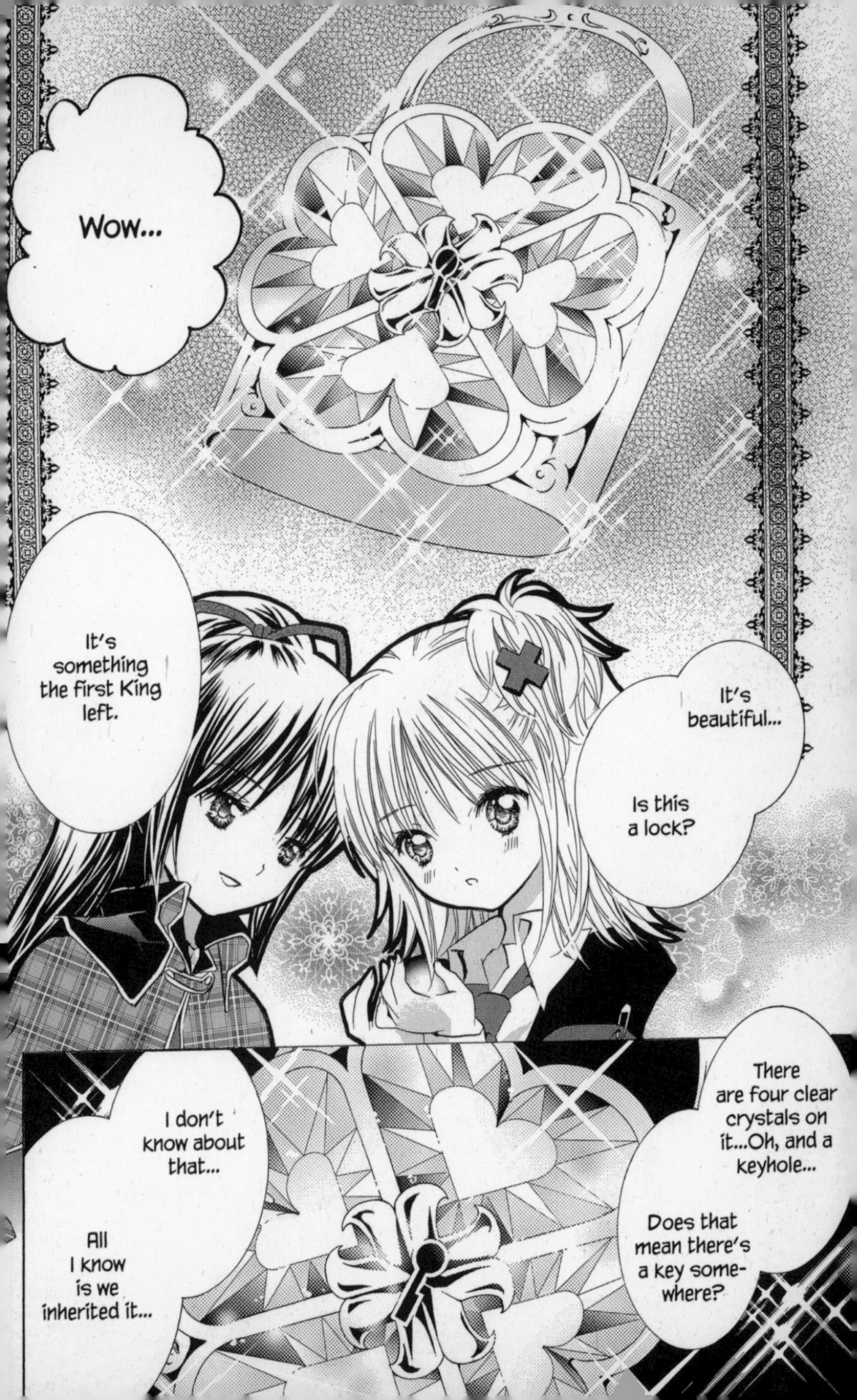
Wow...
It's beautiful...
Is this a lock?
It's something the first King left.
There are four clear crystals on it...Oh, and a keyhole...
Does that mean there's a key somewhere?
I don't know about that...
All I know is we inherited it...

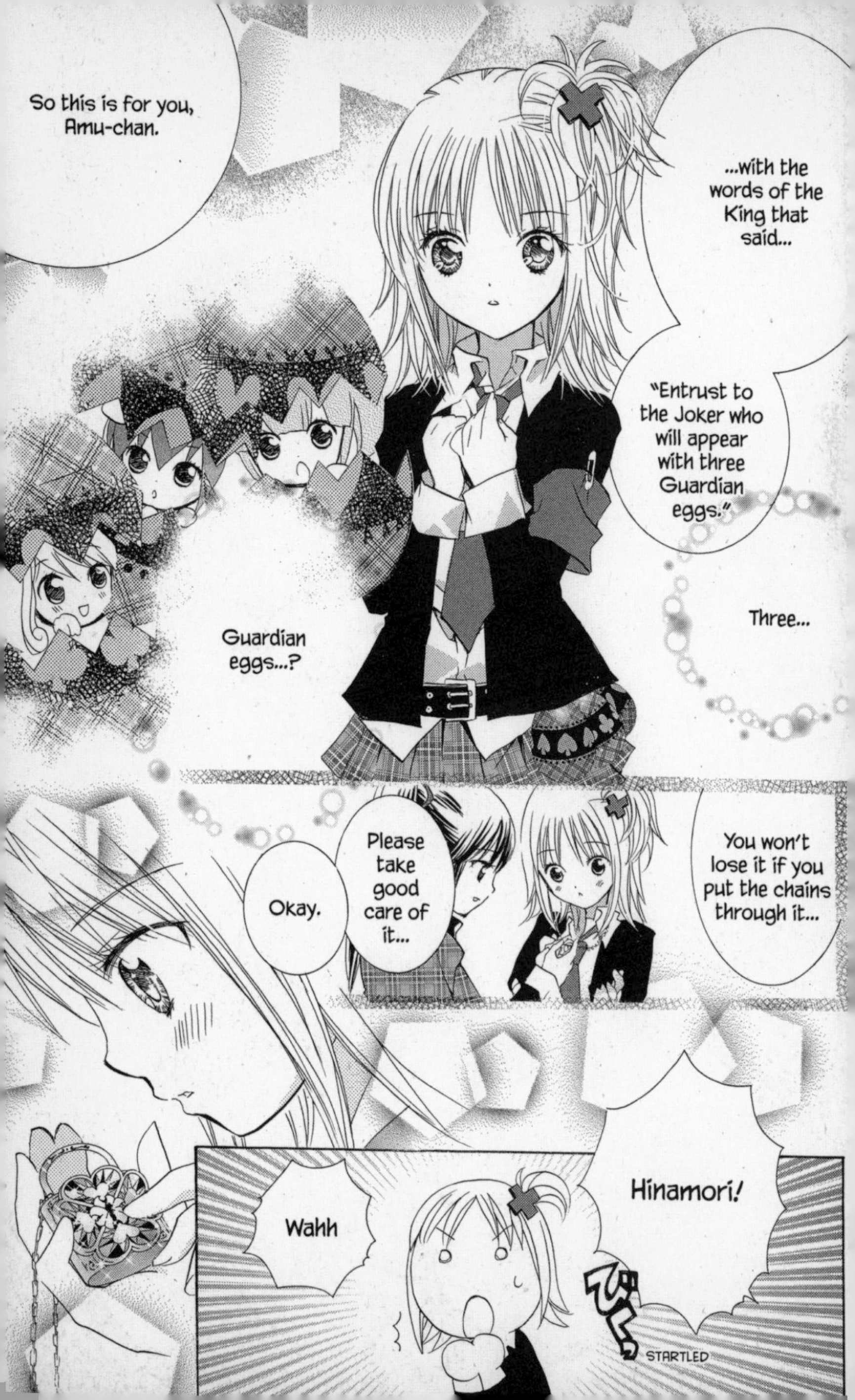
...with the words of the King that said...
"Entrust to the Joker who will appear with three Guardian eggs."
So this is for you, Amu-chan.
Three...
Guardian eggs...?
You won't lose it if you put the chains through it...
Please take good care of it...
Okay.
Hinamori!
Wahh
STARTLED

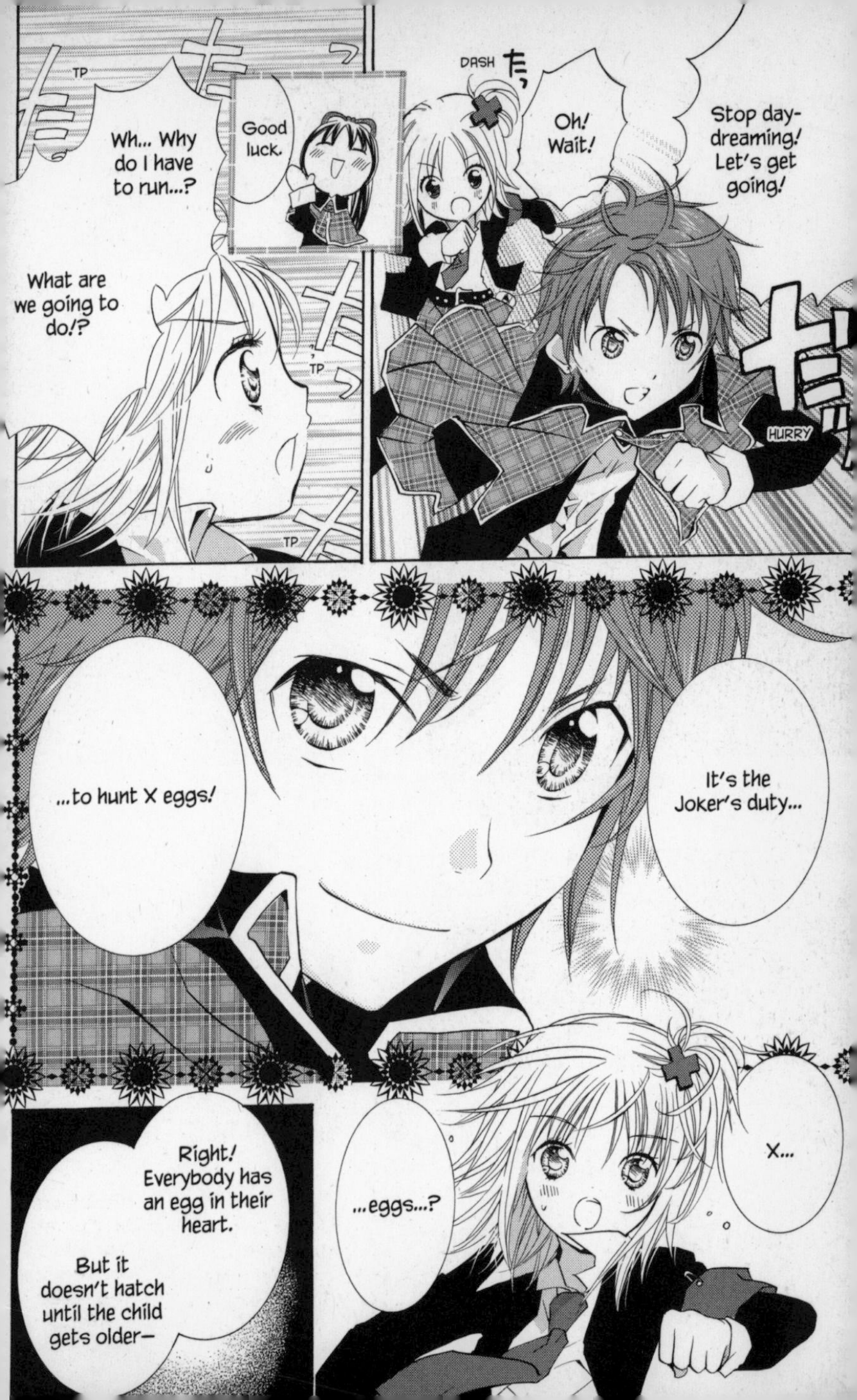
Stop day-dreaming! Let's get going!
DASH
Oh! Wait!
HURRY
Good luck.
TP
Wh... Why do I have to run...?
What are we going to do!?
TP
TP
It's the Joker's duty...
...to hunt X eggs!
X...
...eggs...?
Right! Everybody has an egg in their heart.
But it doesn't hatch until the child gets older—

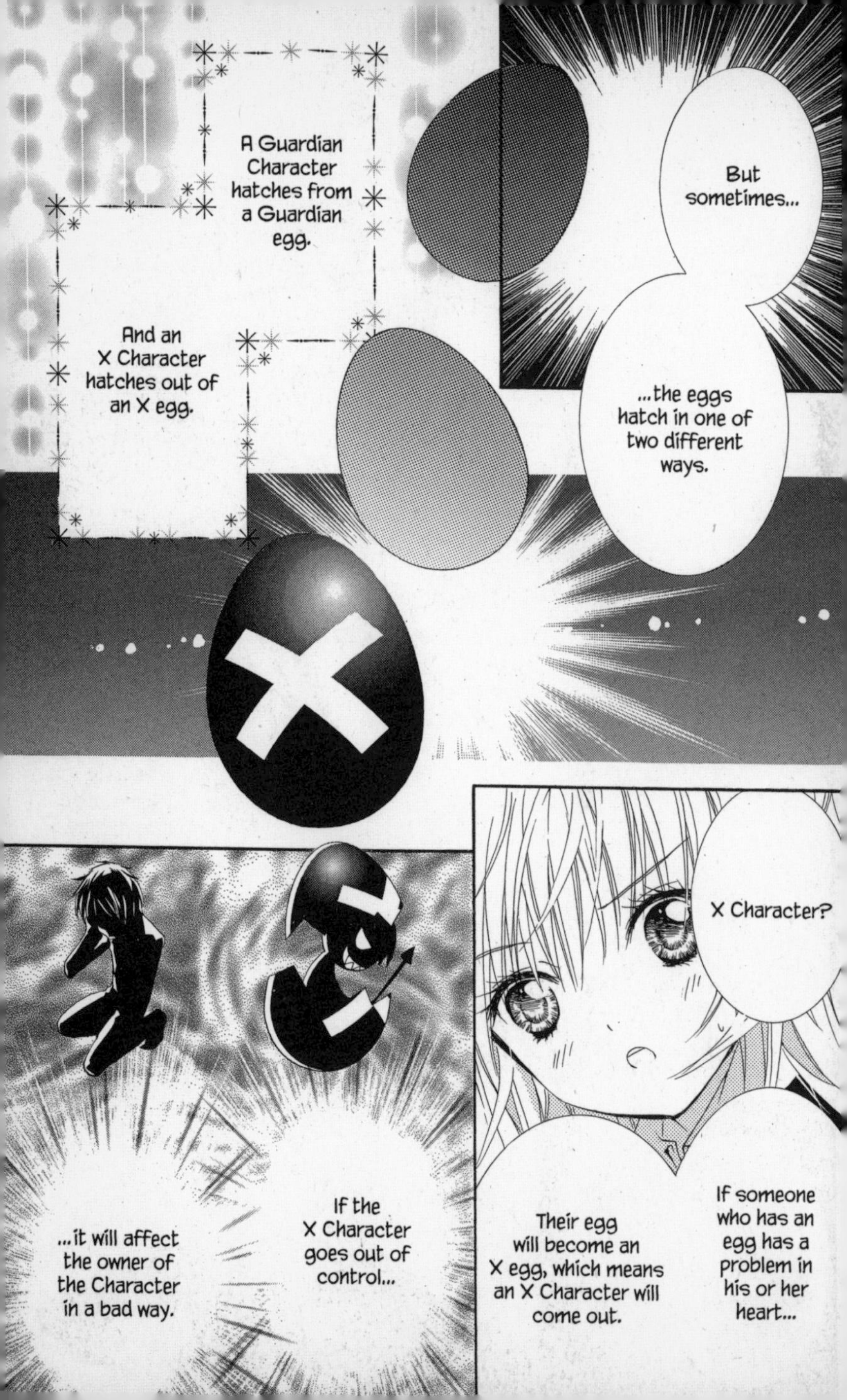
But sometimes...
...the eggs hatch in one of two different ways.
A Guardian Character hatches from a Guardian egg.
And an X Character hatches out of an X egg.
X Character?
If someone who has an egg has a problem in his or her heart...
Their egg will become an X egg, which means an X Character will come out.
If the X Character goes out of control...
...it will affect the owner of the Character in a bad way.

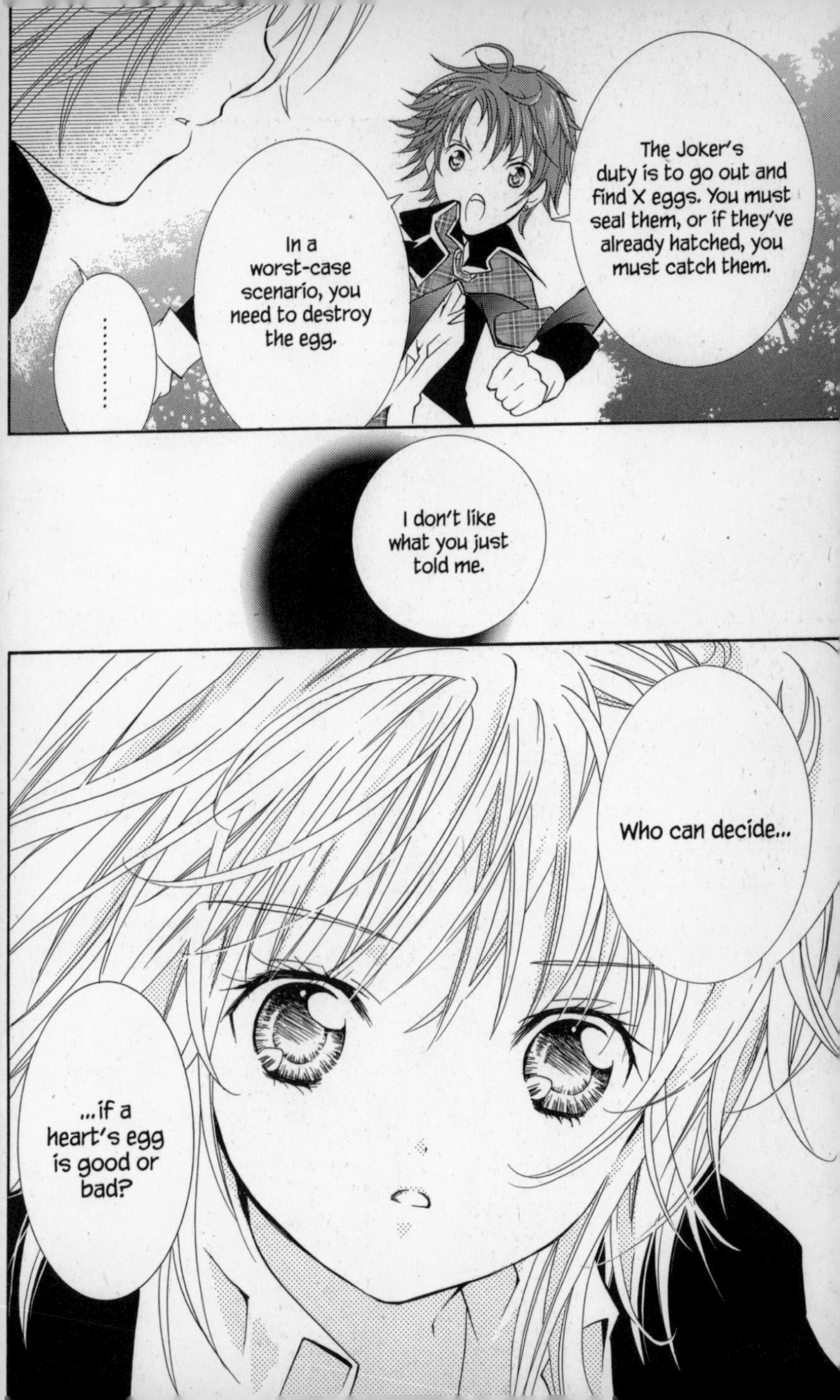
The Joker's duty is to go out and find X eggs. You must seal them, or if they've already hatched, you must catch them.
In a worst-case scenario, you need to destroy the egg.
......
I don't like what you just told me.
Who can decide...
...if a heart's egg is good or bad?

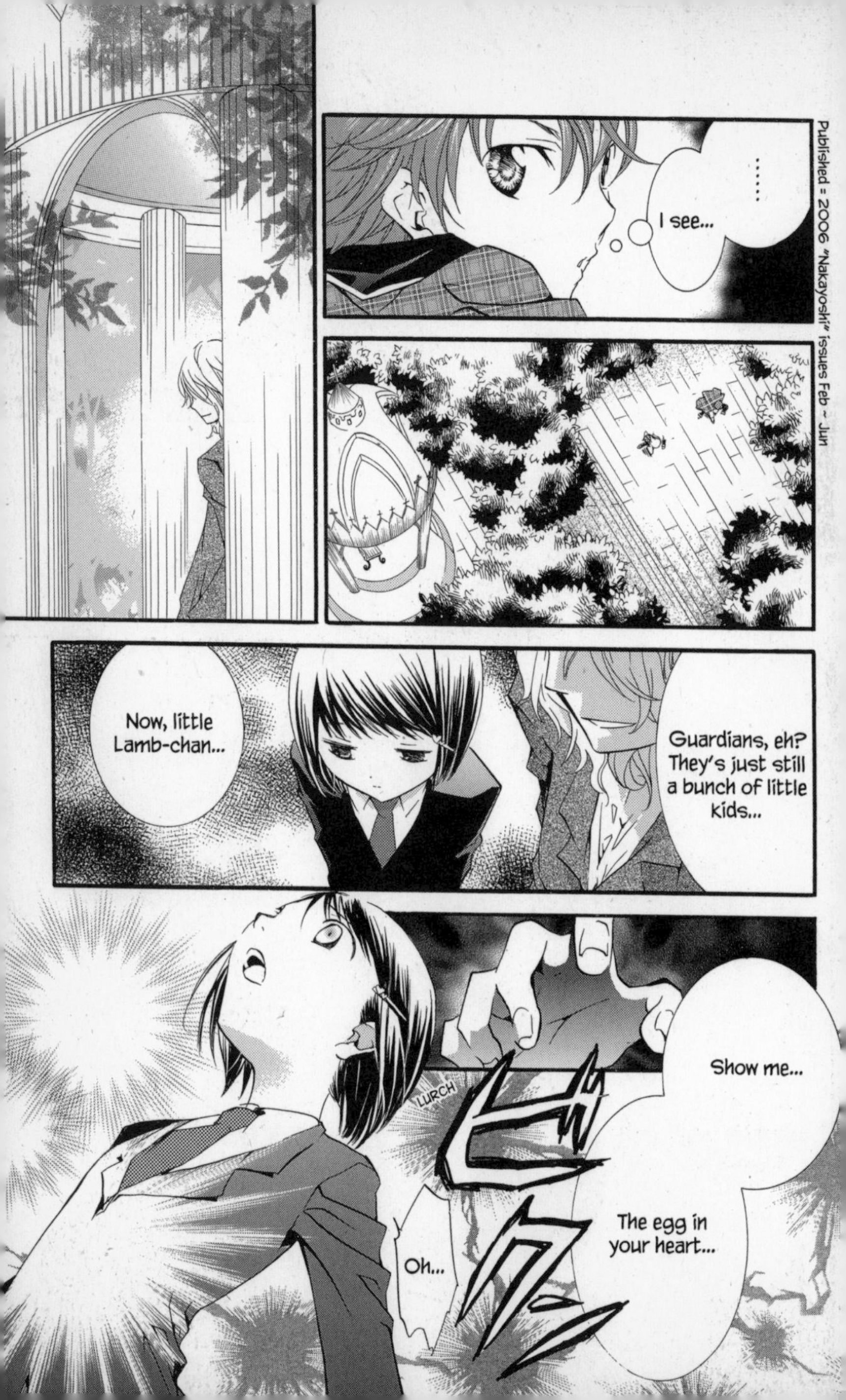
......
I see...
Guardians, eh? They's just still a bunch of little kids...
Now, little Lamb-chan...
Show me...
The egg in your heart...
LURCH
Oh...

Published = 2006 "Nakayoshi" issues Feb ~ Jun

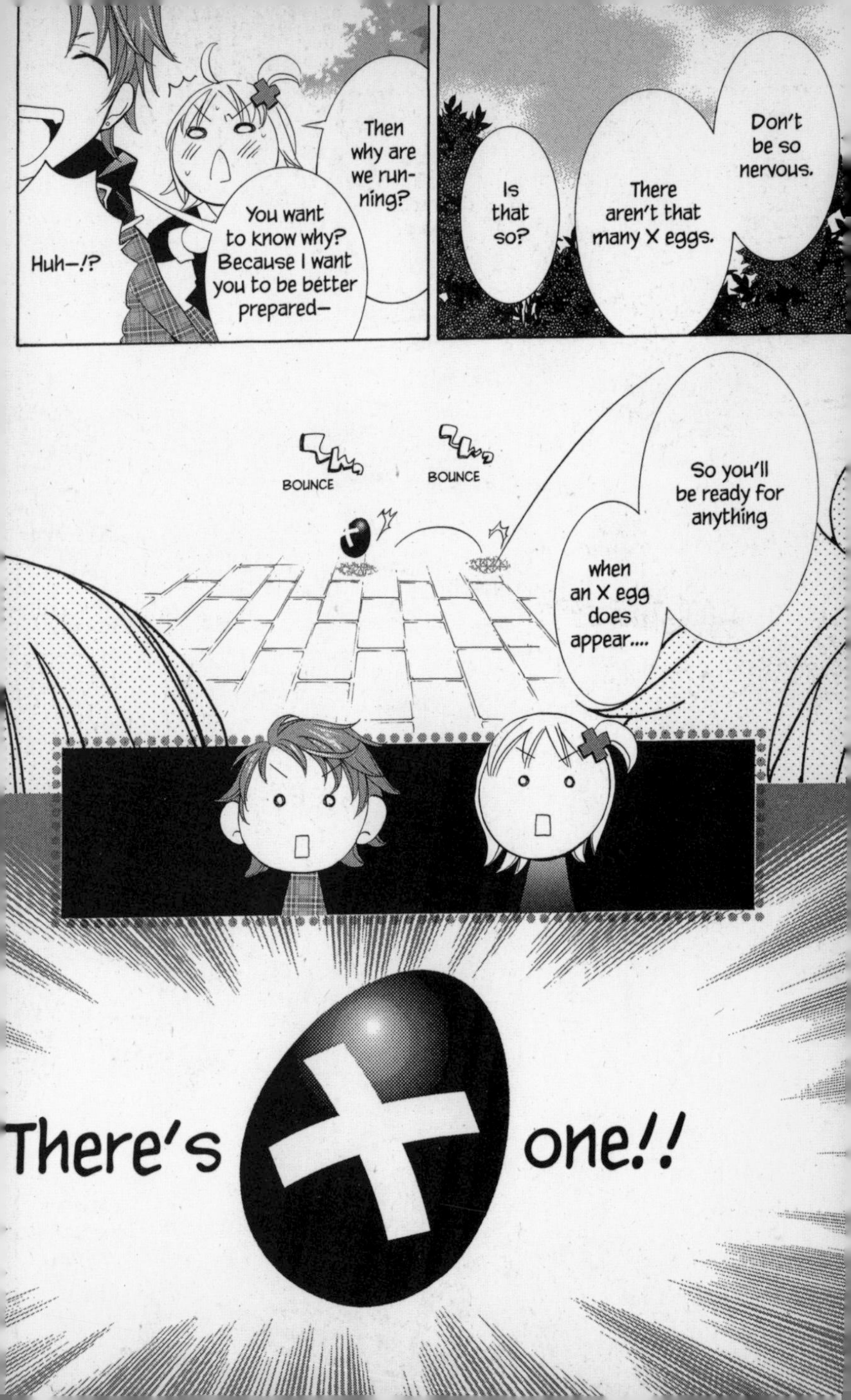
Don't be so nervous.
There aren't that many X eggs.
Is that so?
Then why are we running?
You want to know why? Because I want you to be better prepared—
Huh—!?
So you'll be ready for anything
when an X egg does appear....
BOUNCE
BOUNCE
There's one!!

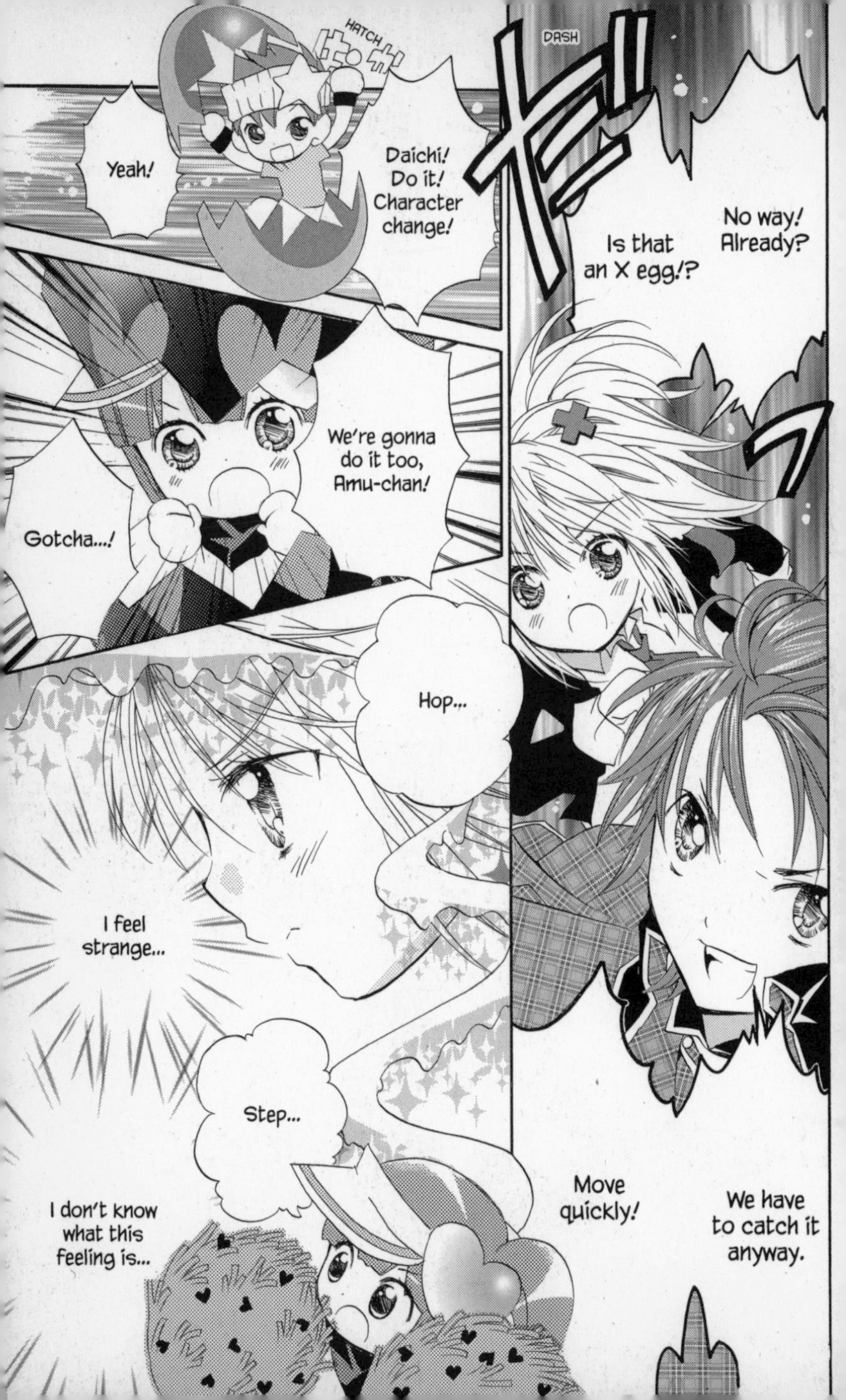
DASH
No way! Already?
Is that an X egg!?
We have to catch it anyway.
Move quickly!
HATCH
Daichi! Do it! Character change!
Yeah!
We're gonna do it too, Amu-chan!
Gotcha...!
Hop...
I feel strange...
Step...
I don't know what this feeling is...

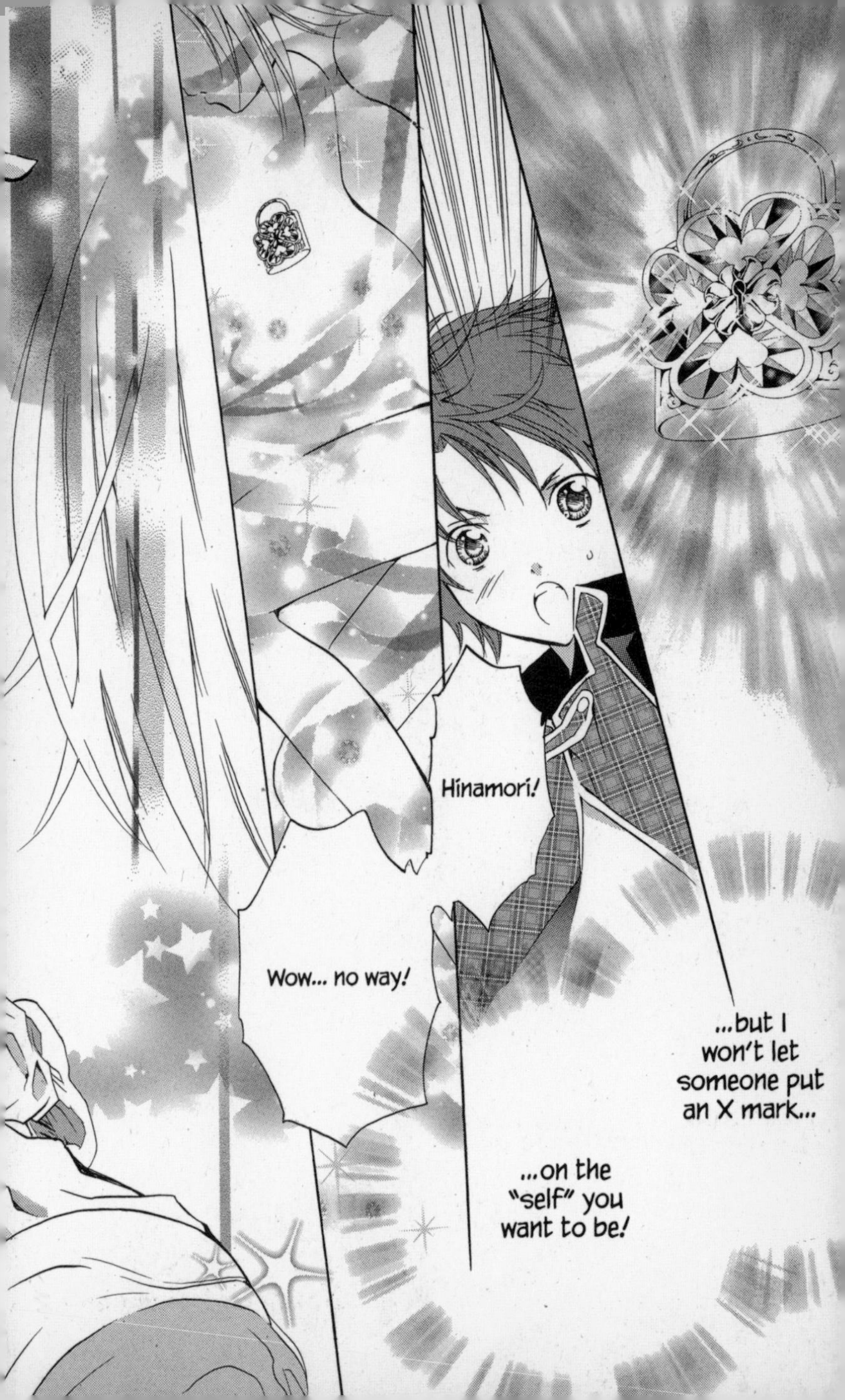
Hinamori!
Wow... no way!
...but I won't let someone put an X mark...
..."self" you want to be!

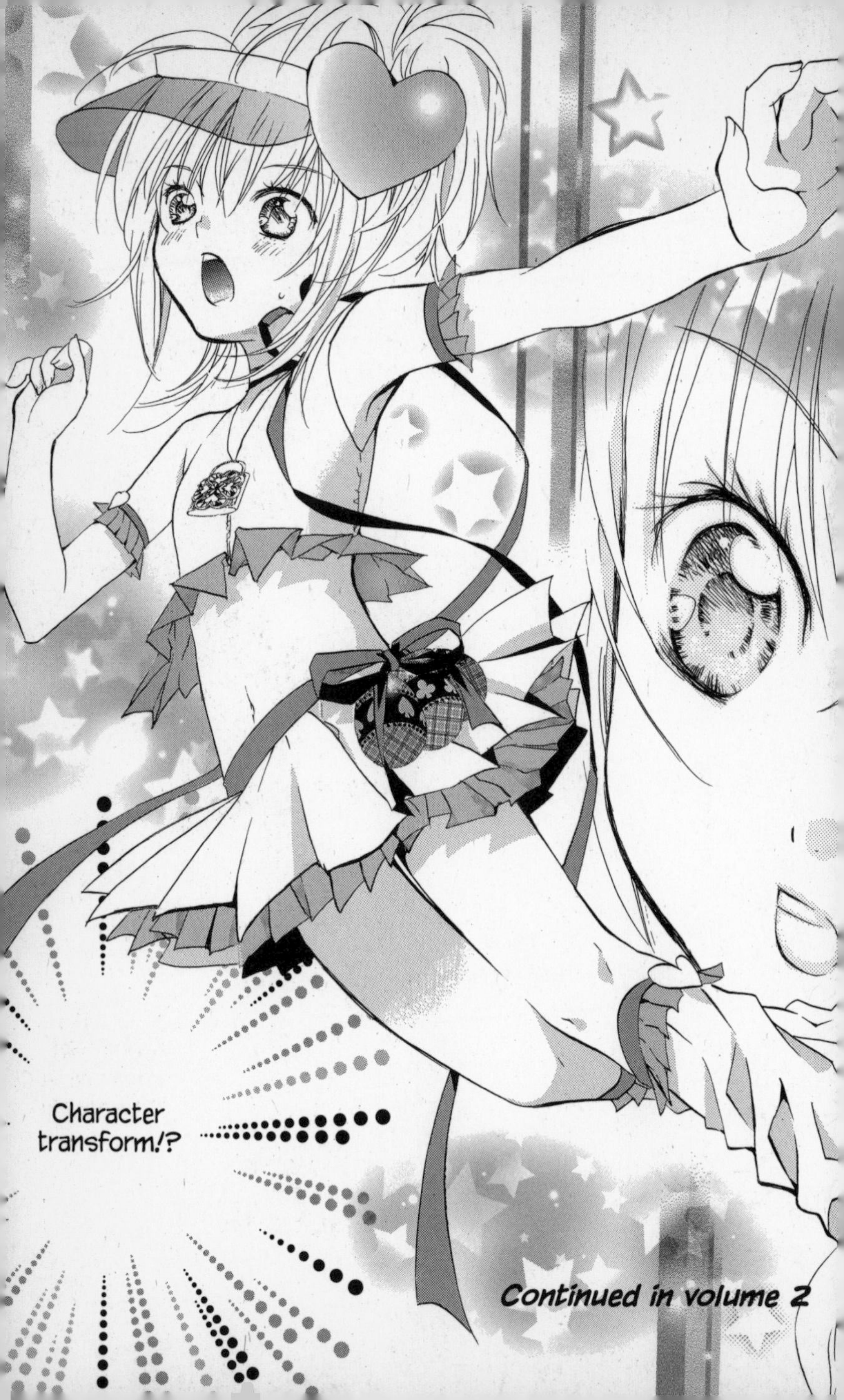
Character transform!?
Continued in volume 2

About the Creators

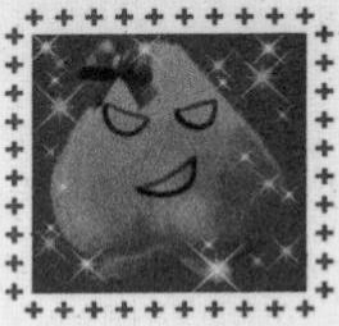

PEACH-PIT is:

Banri Sendo, born on June 7th

Shibuko Ebara, born on June 21st

We both are Gemini. We're a pair of manga artists.
Sendo enjoys sweets, but Ebara prefers spicy food. Our favorite animals are cats and rabbits, and our recent hobbies are making the ultimate *ajitama* and doing fingernail art.

Translation Notes

Japanese is a tricky language for most Westerners, and translation is often more art than science. For your edification and reading pleasure, here are notes on some of the places where we could have gone in a different direction with our translation of the work, or where a Japanese cultural reference is used.

Mushi Champ, page 3

This name is a play on *Mushi King*, a game by Sega that combines trading card and video gameplay. It's very popular among young boys in Japan, because the game features *mushi*, or bugs such as beetles and stag beetles.

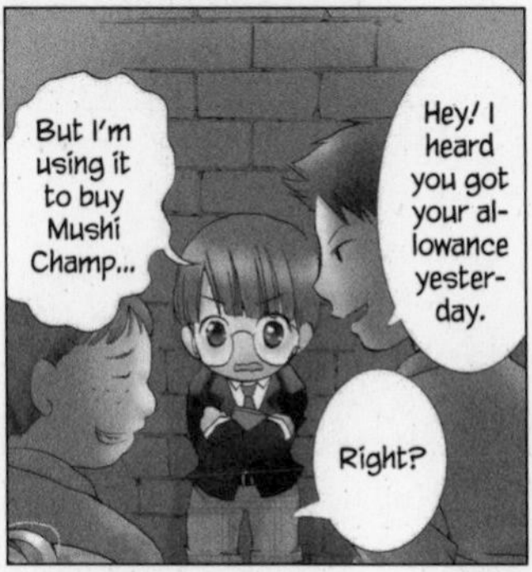
Hey! I heard you got your al-lowance yester-day.
But I'm using it to buy Mushi Champ...
Right?

Kanto-area schools, page 7

The boy is referring to schools in the area surrounding and including Tokyo, which is known as the "Kanto area."

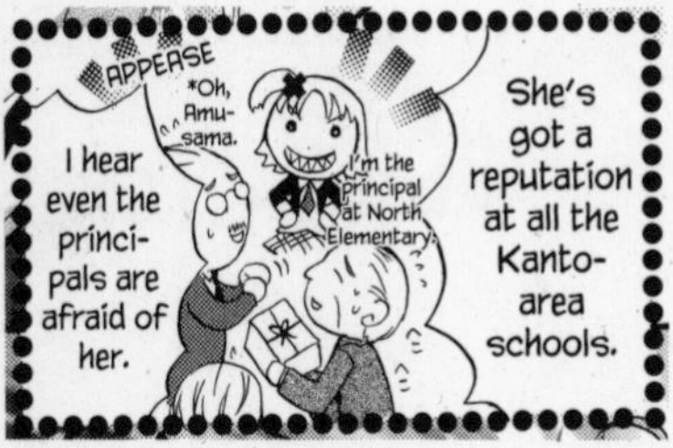
She's got a reputation at all the Kanto-area schools.
APPEASE
*Oh, Amu-sama.
I'm the principal at North Elementary.
I hear even the princi-pals are afraid of her.

Bonjour and *Je t'aime*, page 10

Amu's classmates are imagining that Amu probably has a super-cool French boyfriend. It is typical of Japanese girls (and women) to think another girl is awesome if she's dating a foreigner. *Bonjour* means "hello," and *je t'aime* means "I love you" in French.

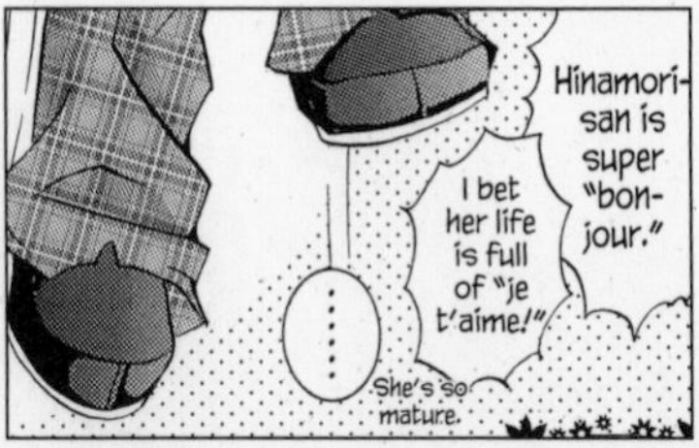
Hinamori-san is super "bon-jour."
I bet her life is full of "je t'aime!"
......
She's so mature.

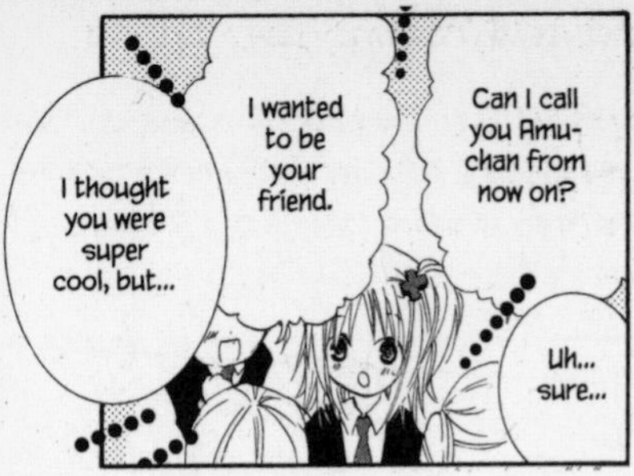
Can I call you Amu-chan from now on?
Uh... sure...
I wanted to be your friend.
I thought you were super cool, but...

"Can I call you Amu-chan?" page 63

In Japan, before you get to know someone a little better, it is most acceptable to call a person by their family name, such as Hinamori-san. This girl wants to feel closer to Amu so she is asking permission to call her by her first name.

Burglar Alarm, page 113

Amu is holding a little plastic burglar alarm that young children and women commonly carry when going out. These alarms are usually round devices on a strap, with a string hanging out from the other side. When you pull out the string, a loud alarm sounds. There are also some kinds of burglar alarms that are shaped like cartoon characters.

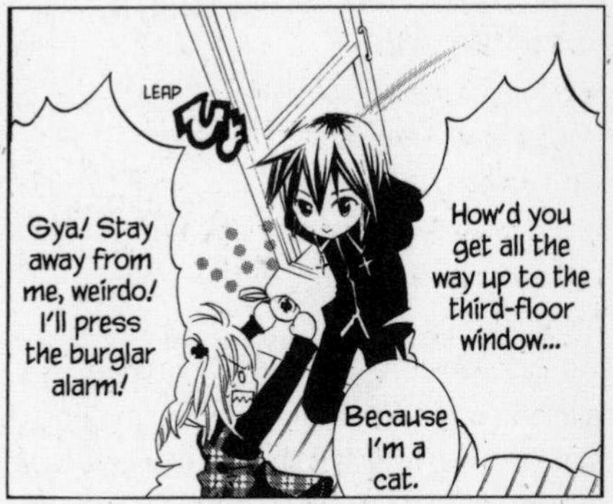
LEAP
How'd you get all the way up to the third-floor window...
Gya! Stay away from me, weirdo! I'll press the burglar alarm!
Because I'm a cat.

Chin, ton, chan, page 116

Chin, ton, and *chan* are three sounds the Japanese use to augment moves in a dance. It's nothing specific to any dance; it's just a way of singing a rhythm.

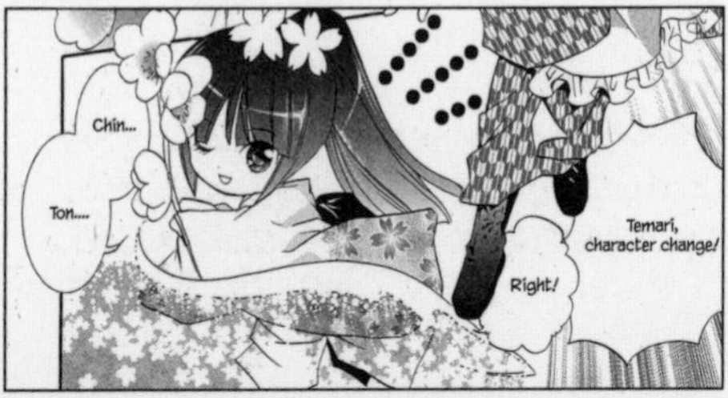
Temari, character change!
Right!
Chin...
Ton....

Kamenashi-kun, Akanishi-kun, and Yamapi, page 121

These are all names of popular idol singers in Japan. Kamenashi-kun and Akanishi-kun are from the same group of six known as KAT-TUN. They are known for looking alike, so that it would be tough for a non-fan to tell them apart. Tomohisa Yamashita, also known as Yamapi, is another pop idol.

Dollies, page 132

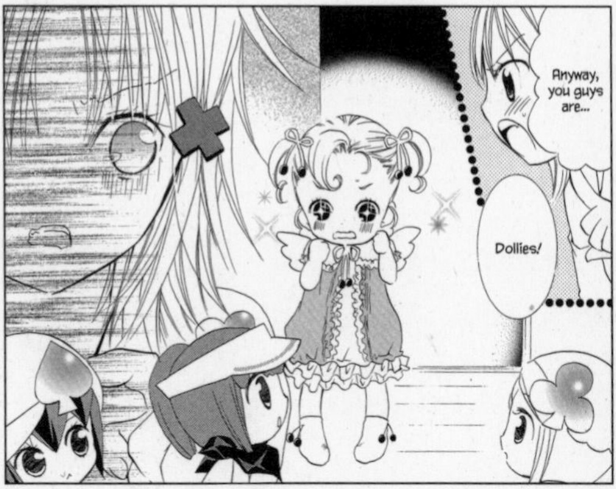
Anyway, you guys are...
Dollies!

In the Japanese version, when Ami first sees the Guardian Characters she yells "Sugoi!" which in this case is similar to yelling "Wow!" In the original Japanese, it's written in a "baby talk" style, making it "Shugoi!" Since the Japanese name of the series is *Shugo Chara!*, which means "Guardian Characters," the characters think Ami is mispronouncing their name. It was difficult to find an equivalent for this pun in English, so we went with "dollies," which is something a 3-year old would say, but also something the Guardian Characters most certainly are not.

Fugashi, page 174

Fugashi is an old-fashioned Japanese snack made with gluten and flour and then baked and covered with black sugar. It was popular before the 1980s in Japan.

Ajitama, page 192

Ajitama can be translated to "flavored eggs," which are boiled eggs made when boiled in flavored soup. They sell them at certain markets, but since they are easy to make, it seems PEACH-PIT is trying to make the "ultimate flavored one."

TOMARE!

[STOP!]

You're going the wrong way!

Manga is a completely
different type of reading
experience.

T͟o   ͟ng,

That's right! Authentic manga is read the traditional Japanese
way—from right to left. Exactly the opposite of how American
books are read. It's easy to follow: Just go to the other end of the
book, and read each page—and each panel—from right side to left
side, starting at the top right. Now you're experiencing manga as it
was meant to be!